THE ROCK

WHENCE WE
ARE HEWN

GOD, GRACE, AND COVENANT

THE ROCK
WHENCE WE
ARE HEWN

HENRY DANHOF
HERMAN HOEKSEMA

EDITED BY DAVID J. ENGELSMA

REFORMED
FREE PUBLISHING
ASSOCIATION

Jenison, Michigan

Scripture cited is taken from the King James (Authorized) Version

Reformed Free Publishing Association
1894 Georgetown Center Drive
Jenison, Michigan 49428
www.rfpa.org
mail@rfpa.org

Cover design by Christopher Tobias/www.tobiasdesign.com
Interior design by Katherine Lloyd, the DESK

ISBN 978-1-936054-95-4
Ebook ISBN 978-936054-96-1
LCCN 2015954896

Hearken to me, ye that follow after righteousness,
ye that seek the LORD: look unto the rock whence ye are hewn,
and to the hole of the pit whence ye are digged.

—ISAIAH 51:1

CONTENTS

T he various writings included in *The Rock Whence We Are Hewn* are all pamphlets or booklets written very early in the history of the Protestant Reformed Churches—between 1919 and 1940. The authors are two men whom God used in forming these churches—Herman Hoeksema and Henry Danhof. All the writings explain and defend the great doctrines of the Reformed faith that were fundamental to the founding of the Protestant Reformed Churches—covenant, predestination, particular grace, and antithesis. These writings therefore were used to establish these churches in the very beginning of their history. The contents of the book are their foundational writings.

The title of the book is taken from Isaiah 51:1: "Hearken to me, ye that follow after righteousness, ye that seek the LORD: look unto the rock whence ye are hewn, and to the hole of the pit whence ye are digged." In this figurative way the prophet called the people of Israel to look to their origins. This title calls the members of the Protestant Reformed Churches, including the ministers and other officebearers, and especially the younger generation, to find in the book the doctrinal truths that are of fundamental importance to the Protestant Reformed Churches still today. By the work of the Spirit these doctrines, confessed, defended, and explained in the writings in this book, are the source of the churches—the rock whence they were hewn.

Many of these writings are polemical. They defend the truths of the Reformed faith against the false doctrine of the Christian Reformed Church's three points of common grace. The renewing of this old, but continuing, controversy with the Christian Reformed Church by the publication of the book is not unfortunate or unwise. The members of the Protestant Reformed Churches are reminded why they are not, and may not be, members of the Christian Reformed Church or of any church that shares the common grace theology of the Christian

Reformed Church, and why they are and are called by God to be Protestant Reformed.

In addition, although it is now late in the day for this, the Christian Reformed Church ought to be confronted with its doctrinal and
church-political sins in the controversy over common grace in the early
1920s and in the ruthless discipline of Herman Hoeksema and many
others. Members of the Christian Reformed Church who yet have the
(saving) grace to wonder what has happened and is happening to their
church, and why, will find the answer in this book. Other Reformed
churches and their members who share the Christian Reformed theology of covenant, well-meant offer, common grace, and friendship with
the world of the ungodly might profitably reexamine their theology in
light of the biblical, creedal, and church-traditional arguments in the
book. They too might well look to the rock whence they were hewn:
John Calvin, the Canons of Dordt, and Romans 9.

All those in other churches who have any interest in what it means
to be Protestant Reformed, and in the reason for the existence of the
Protestant Reformed Churches, do well to allow this book to answer
their questions, rather than to listen to the biased explanations of the
enemies of these churches.

A number of the pamphlets in this book were originally written
in Dutch. The translators are identified. All footnotes are those of the
authors, unless otherwise indicated.

Because of the frequent reference throughout the book to the three
points of common grace, adopted as official, binding dogma by the Christian Reformed Church and forced upon Danhof, Hoeksema, George M.
Ophoff, and their consistories on pain of deposition from office and
exclusion from the Christian Reformed Church, I note that the three
points are included in the book in the appendix to *A Triple Breach*.

Many of the ministers, theologians, and other persons who had
some significant part in the controversy over common grace in the
Christian Reformed Church and who are mentioned in the writings
that make up *The Rock* are identified in an appendix.

—David J. Engelsma, editor

THE IDEA OF THE COVENANT OF GRACE

HENRY DANHOF

TRANSLATED BY DAVID J. ENGELSMA

And the scripture was fulfilled which saith,
Abraham believed God, and it was imputed
unto him for righteousness:
and he was called the Friend of God.
—JAMES 2:23

Introduction to *The Idea of the Covenant of Grace*

This booklet is the translation of the text of a lecture on the covenant of grace by Henry Danhof.[1] At the time a minister in the Christian Reformed Church, he gave the lecture at a conference of Christian Reformed ministers in Grand Rapids, Michigan, on June 4, 1919. Evidently the conference was held in connection with a meeting of a Grand Rapids classis of the Christian Reformed Church.[2]

The lecture was given at the special request of the ministers' conference. The arrangement was that Danhof's address would be followed the next evening by a speech presenting the opposite view. As Danhof urged the antithesis, Johannes Groen[3] was to argue for synthesis, that is, communion and cooperation of church and world. The purpose of the two lectures was that the ministers might come to clearer insights concerning the relation of church and world. Due to the illness of Groen, the second lecture was not given.

---

1 Henry Danhof, *De Idee van het Genadeverbond* [The idea of the covenant of grace] (Grand Rapids, MI: Van Noord Book and Publishing Company, 1920). The booklet is forty-two pages. The translation of this booklet, which first appeared as several articles in the April 1997 and November 1998 issues of the *Protestant Reformed Theological Journal*, is the first translation of the Dutch original into English.

2 Referring to the discussion that followed Danhof's lecture, Jan Karel van Baalen speaks of a statement made by Danhof at "a classical gathering." See Jan Karel van Baalen, *De Loochening der Gemeene Gratie: Gereformeerd of Doopersch?* [The denial of common grace: Reformed or Anabaptist?] (Grand Rapids, MI: Eerdmans-Sevensma Co., 1922), 47. (All translations in *The Idea of the Covenant* of Van Baalen's booklet are mine.) James Bratt says that Danhof made the remark to which Van Baalen refers "in the question-and-answer session at the classical meeting after delivering '*De Idee van het Genadeverbond.*'" See James D. Bratt, *Dutch Calvinism in Modern America: A History of a Conservative Subculture* (Grand Rapids, MI: Eerdmans, 1984), 265.

3 Johannes Groen was the minister in Eastern Avenue Christian Reformed Church just prior to Herman Hoeksema.

Controversial Lecture

As the title indicates, Danhof's address was a penetrating study of the fundamental idea of the Reformed doctrine of the covenant of grace. At the same time and as an aspect of the idea of the covenant, the lecture investigated the relationship between the church and the world. This led the speaker to consider and to pass judgment on the apparent good done by the ungodly.

The speech was controversial.

In response to Danhof's rejection of the popular notion that the life of unregenerated mankind is "full of all kinds of virtues," a Christian Reformed minister put the question to Danhof how we then must view the marriage of two unbelievers. Danhof's response is reported to have been that "the marriage between two non-Christians can be nothing other than bestiality and the kind of love which devils have for each other."[4]

This response with its condemnation of all the apparently noble deeds of the pagans infuriated Rev. Jan Karel van Baalen and, undoubtedly, the other Christian Reformed ministers who shared his esteem for the "good" in the unholy world. Three years later, in a polemical work against Danhof and Hoeksema concerning the doctrine of common grace, Van Baalen recalled Danhof's statement with not one but two exclamation marks and called it "nonsense."

At the end of his polemical work, *The Denial of Common Grace: Reformed or Anabaptist?* Van Baalen put several questions to Danhof and Hoeksema. He intended these questions to expose their false doctrine. The first was how Danhof viewed the marriage of Hector and Andromache: "May we ask Rev. Danhof whether he will be so good as to make clear to us what there is in the love between Hector and his wife, as sung by Homer, that is devilish or bestial?"[5]

Danhof's "bestial" and "devilish" was strong language. But Van

---

4   Van Baalen, *Denial of Common Grace*, 47; see Bratt, *Dutch Calvinism*, 111, 265.
5   Van Baalen, *Denial of Common Grace*, 87. Van Baalen quoted the touching conversation between Hector and Andromache from book 6 of Homer's *The Iliad*. See Homer, *The Iliad*, trans. W. H. D. Rouse (New York: The New American Library, 1950), 74–83.

Baalen's indignation at that strong language should not obscure the fact that the issue was whether the love between Hector and Andromache was sinful. If it was sinful—*only* sinful—it was devilish, for sin originates in the devil. If it was sinful—*only* sinful—it was worse than bestial, for beasts cannot sin in their mating. That the love of Hector and Andromache was sinful the passage from which Van Baalen took his quotation makes plain. The immediate context of Hector's and Andromache's expressions of love for each other was Hector's advice to the women of Troy to worship the goddess Athena ("Queen Athena, goddess divine, savior of our city!"); Hector's affirmation that his burning desire was his own glory ("to win credit for my father and myself"); and Hector's prayer to all the gods that his son would bring glory to himself and to his father ("O Zeus and all ye heavenly gods!").

Everything that issues from such an idolatrous, self-seeking heart is sin, including marital and family life. The Heidelberg Catechism passes judgment on the love of Hector and Andromache that it was sin: "But what are good works? Those only which are done from true faith, according to the law of God, for his glory."[6] Romans 1:18–23 condemns the life of such pagans as Hector and Andromache: "The wrath of God is revealed from heaven against all ungodliness and unrighteousness of men, who hold the truth in unrighteousness" (v. 18).

For all the vigor of his terminology, therefore, Danhof was only pronouncing the biblical, Reformed judgment on Hector and Andromache.

Why was this offensive to Van Baalen? Why could he be fulsome in his praise of Zeus-worshiping Hector and violent in his condemnation of Henry Danhof, who worshiped the true God? How, two years later, could Van Baalen and the entire Christian Reformed synod expel Danhof from their fellowship as a deposed minister, while keeping Hector and Andromache in good repute within the church? Already in the early 1920s there was a diseased love of pagan culture in the Christian Reformed Church. This did not bode well for its future.

---

6 Heidelberg Catechism Q&A 91, in Philip Schaff, ed., *The Creeds of Christendom with a History and Critical Notes*, 6th ed., 3 vols. (New York: Harper and Row, 1931; repr., Grand Rapids, MI: Baker Books, 2007), 3:339–40.

Historically Significant Address

Danhof's speech, delivered to an influential group of Christian Reformed ministers, was significant in the history of the Christian Reformed Church. Danhof gave the speech in 1919 during the throes of a struggle that would fundamentally determine the future of that Reformed denomination. The issue in that struggle was the relationship between the Christian Reformed Church and the world of the ungodly. Danhof and Hoeksema contended for the spiritual separation of the church from the world. The theological term they used to express this separation and warfare was *antithesis.*

Another group, among whom was Jan Karel van Baalen, fought as vehemently for the church's openness to the world—accommodation, cooperation, and reception—within limits. The deceptive watchword of that party was *Americanization.* The word was deceptive because what that party sought was not conformity to the innocent ways of America—language and clothes—but conformity to the corrupt ways of the world: the higher critical doctrines of European unbelief regarding the holy scriptures as well as other distinctly un-Reformed teachings; the principles and practices of the ungodly labor unions; and fellowship with the works of darkness in worldly amusements.[7]

---

7   For a helpful and highly readable analysis of this critically important struggle in the 1920s for the soul and future of the Christian Reformed Church, see Bratt, *Dutch Calvinism,* 93–119. The two chapters on these pages are titled "Forming the Battle Lines, 1919–1920" and "The Resolution, 1921–1928." Bratt characterizes Danhof and Hoeksema as the "Antitheticals." The party of friendly relations with the world he describes as "positive Calvinists," a description that may tip Bratt's hand. Hoeksema called this party "a latitudinarian party in the churches, a group of men...who opposed the antithesis, stood for a 'broader' view of the Christian's life and calling in the world, and strove to bridge the gap between the world and the Church" (Herman Hoeksema, *The Protestant Reformed Churches in America: Their Origin, Early History and Doctrine* [Grand Rapids, MI: n.p., 1936], 15–16). According to Bratt, the positive Calvinists attacked "otherworldliness...and a disregard for God's general grace and revelation" and advocated the church's fulfillment of its "cultural mandate." Such positive Calvinists as J. G. van Andel supposed, no doubt sincerely, that the Christian Reformed Church was called to solve the world's problems. As though that were a real possibility! But that, he said, cannot be done "if men think only like the Reformed."

One may disagree with Bratt's conclusion that although the "Antitheticals" went down to defeat in the common grace decision of 1924, the "progressive Calvinists"

The doctrine by which the church would relate positively to the world was Abraham Kuyper's, and especially Herman Bavinck's, doctrine of common grace.

The first ecclesiastical skirmish in this war was in 1922 when the Christian Reformed synod condemned seminary professor Ralph Janssen's views on the Bible as modernism.[8] The apparent triumph of the antithetical position was misleading and short-lived, for a scant two years later the decisive battle was fought at the Christian Reformed synod of Kalamazoo, Michigan. By its adoption of the three points of common grace, the Christian Reformed Church destroyed the antithesis in that church and established openness to the world as its official policy. In this decision, the synod was reacting in part against the well-remembered address by Henry Danhof, "The Idea of the Covenant of Grace."[9]

Danhof's lecture has also been significant for the history of the Protestant Reformed Churches. These churches came into existence as a separate denomination as the result of the Christian Reformed

---

also "came to grief." The decision of the Christian Reformed Church on common grace spelled the victory of the progressive Calvinists. In time Hoeksema's prophecy that common grace, nothing other than the theory for conformity to the world, would bring a real tidal wave of worldliness over the churches was sure to be fulfilled. The compromising "Confessionalist / Pietist" party (to use Bratt's label), who gave the victory to the progressive Calvinists and who exercised church power for the next twenty-five years, merely delayed the full manifestation of the victory of the progressive Calvinists in 1924. In terms of Hoeksema's figure of the tidal wave, the Louis Berkhofs and H. J. Kuipers spent the next twenty-five years sticking their fingers in various holes that the adoption of common grace had opened in the Christian Reformed dike. In the early 1950s the dike itself began to collapse.

Hoeksema's analysis of the leading figures in Bratt's Confessionalist/Pietist party—L. Berkhof, S. Volbeda, Y. P. de Jong, and H. J. Kuiper—is found in Hoeksema, *Protestant Reformed Churches*, 16–26. About this treatment Bratt remarks that Hoeksema "has especially good insight into the instincts and vacillations of the Confessionalist party" (*Dutch Calvinism*, 266).

8 On the history of the Janssen case in the Christian Reformed Church and its relation to the assault on Hoeksema by the advocates of common grace, see Hoeksema, *Protestant Reformed Churches*, 17–26. For an in-depth study of the relationship between the views of Ralph Janssen and the doctrine of common grace, see Herman Hanko, "A Study of the Relation between the Views of Prof. R. Janssen and Common Grace" (master's thesis, Calvin Theological Seminary, 1988).

9 For the history of this common grace controversy, see Hoeksema, *Protestant Reformed Churches*, 11–282; on the doctrinal issues of the controversy, see ibid., 285–402.

Church's rejection of the antithesis in 1924 and discipline in 1925 of officebearers who opposed the doctrine of common grace. In his lecture, Danhof developed the reality of the covenant of grace as fellowship that has become central to the theology and practice of the Protestant Reformed Churches. Some have suggested that Danhof's conception of the covenant was formative of Protestant Reformed covenant theology.

Profound Statement of the Covenant

Apart from its historical significance, Danhof's treatise on the covenant is important in its own right as a unique, profound, and thorough statement of the Reformed doctrine of the covenant. For Danhof the covenant of grace is central in the life of the believer: "The idea of the covenant of grace concerns the deepest and most intimate relation between God and man. The real covenantal relation governs every other relation."

The relationship with God that is the covenant consists of friendship: "The covenant causes God and man to live together as friends. In this the covenant-idea is completely realized."

The ultimate origin of the covenant as a relationship of friendship is the triune life of God.

> The covenant rests in the holy Trinity. God is the God of the covenant. He is such not only according to the counsel of his will in his relation to the creature, but first in himself by virtue of his nature. The divine life in itself is a covenant of friendship among Father, Son, and Holy Ghost...The absolute covenantal conception is hidden in the family life of the holy Trinity.

At its core the history of revelation is the development of the covenant of grace. "The beginning of the realization of the covenantal conception was evident already in the earthly paradise. In the state of rectitude, the relation between God and man was friendship." Man's fall did not annul the covenant of God:

> God wills the covenant. Therefore, according to God's good pleasure, behind Adam when he fell away stood Christ, God's companion, and in him the Lord's covenant of friendship with

man was firm. Out of grace in Christ, God realizes his covenant of friendship with man...so that man becomes God's covenantal companion and friend eternally.

The history of the world centers in the covenant of God with his people in Christ. "According to God's counsel, all things work together for the realization of this idea of the covenant of grace...The history of all things is the development of the covenant of friendship of our God."

In connection with the development of the covenant in history, Danhof proposes and expands on what he calls the "organic connection of our race." This organic connection of the race is "God's means to realize his covenant. That realization everywhere follows the organic lines...God created man as an organic creature and in organic relation to the world around him."

The conceptions of an "organic connection" of all people and of "organic development" were of great importance to Danhof and Hoeksema in the common grace struggle of the early 1920s. In their book *Van Zonde en Genade* Danhof and Hoeksema explained the development of sin in terms of the organic connection of the human race: "All human individuals, in their organic solidarity, have communion in the root sin of their organic head."[10]

This emphasis on the "organic" so exasperated their antagonist Van Baalen that he angrily charged that all Danhof and Hoeksema did was to chant "organic, ORGANIC, ORGANIC": "Yes indeed. But calling out 'organic, ORGANIC, ORGANIC'!! is not the same as explaining how we must conceive the organic development [of sin]."[11]

---

10 Henry Danhof and Herman Hoeksema, *Van Zonde en Genade* [Of sin and grace] (Kalamazoo, MI: Dalm Printing Co., n.d.), 202. The translation is mine.

11 Jan Karel van Baalen, *Nieuwigheid en Dwaling: De Loochening der Gemeene Gratie* [Novelty and error: the denial of common grace] (Grand Rapids, MI: Eerdmans-Sevensma Co., 1923), 63–64; cf. Bratt, *Dutch Calvinism*, 111. Bratt too has difficulty with the antitheticals' use of "organic": "It is difficult to interpret their obsession with the point because they put it to so many different uses." Perhaps, but one thing is certainly clear from this "obsession": long before it was theologically fashionable to do so, the fathers of the Reformed theology held in the Protestant Reformed Churches insisted on the natural solidarity of the human race, specifically of the elect people of God with the reprobate ungodly. They stressed that the church lives in natural solidarity with the entire created world. At the very

Within the organic, natural solidarity of the elect church and the reprobate world, God's regenerating Spirit creates and maintains the "absolute antithesis" between them. This is an essential element in Danhof's treatise on the covenant. "The idea of the 'absolute antithesis' must be placed emphatically on the foreground in our world view." Antithesis is an aspect of the covenant inasmuch as "also in practice the covenantal idea must always determine our relation to everything about us, especially in relation to the world in a moral sense." As God's friends, elect believers are of the party of the living God. As such, they cannot be friends of God's enemies, the unregenerated, ungodly world.

A few years after giving the lecture, Danhof reflected on it in a brochure he coauthored with Hoeksema, *For the Sake of Justice and Truth*. Danhof viewed the lecture, which by that time had been published, as a development of the basic covenantal conception in its most fundamental idea. He described this conception thus:

> Our entire life—inclination, imagination, desire, thought, word, and deed—must arise from the root of regeneration, the principle of true love. One who wills to be a friend of the world is an enemy of God. The believer is a friend of God, and by virtue of this, an enemy of the whole kingdom of darkness. As such he must take his place in this present world, with heartfelt trust in God and looking to his word alone. The promotion of the cause of the Son of God is his life's task. He is of the party of the living God. God's child is God's friend.

According to Danhof, his lecture emphasized the implication of this covenantal conception for the right relation of God's people to the ungodly world.

> We have put the idea of the "absolute antithesis" in our world view on the foreground. We did so especially to combat the continual zeal of some for a view of the relation of God's

---

foundation of this theology, therefore, is rejection of Anabaptist world flight. The antithesis does not, indeed cannot, mean physical separation from unbelievers or ascetic withdrawal from the creation and its ordinances.

people and the world that is hostile to God that, in our judgment, may not be ours.

The view of the relation of the church and the world that Danhof's lecture opposed was that of common grace: "the fellowship of believers and unbelievers."[12]

Danhof's study includes a knowledgeable survey of the history of the dogma of the covenant. His conclusion is that "in a dogma-historical sense the doctrine of the covenant dates from the time of the Reformation. It is almost exclusively a plant out of Reformed soil." Nevertheless, "the covenantal conception is no Reformed fancy or subtlety, but the most beautiful fruit of the theology of the whole Christian church."

Appropriately, Danhof concludes his masterpiece on the covenant with its eschatological implications. The antithesis will climax in the future in the persecution of the friends of Christ by the antichrist. The greatest of all spiritual conflicts is impending. It will concern the covenant:

> The enemy will know how to turn the temporal might of the emperor over the bodies and possessions of men against the friends of Christ...For this we must prepare ourselves beforehand. Also the fainthearted among us have to get ready. The issue will be the covenant of our God. There is no escape from the steel sword of our enemies.

But the covenantal friend of God has hope:

> However, because we fight on behalf of the cause of God, we are able to trust in the Lord who is truly Lord. He will accomplish it. His cause will triumph. Strengthened by his grace, we will not lose the crown. Redeemed from all the might of the enemy and more than conquerors, we enter into the joy of our Lord and into the everlasting covenant of the friendship of our God.

---

12 Henry Danhof and Herman Hoeksema, *Om Recht en Waarheid: Een Woord van Toelichting en Leiding* [For the sake of justice and truth: a word of clarification and direction] (Kalamazoo, MI: Dalm Printing Co., n.d.), 7–8. The translation is mine.

Stormy Ministry of the Author

The subsequent ministry of Danhof was stormy. He and his consistory, the First Christian Reformed Church of Kalamazoo, Michigan, were deposed and thus put out of the Christian Reformed Church by Classis Grand Rapids West of that church in January 1925. In 1926 Danhof and his congregation separated from those who were organizing as the Protestant Reformed Churches. For the rest of his active ministry, Danhof was pastor of the independent Protesting First Christian Reformed Church of Kalamazoo.[13]

By his ecclesiastical independency Danhof very definitely sinned against the covenant of friendship in its important manifestation as a federation of churches.

In 1945 Danhof and his congregation returned to the Christian Reformed Church.[14] Already in 1946 Danhof came again to the attention of synod. With seventeen other members of the Grace Christian Reformed Church of Kalamazoo, Danhof protested against a decision of the consistory of the Grace church. The decision of the consistory was that Danhof and the others cease the practice of convening in one of their private homes and entertaining one another socially by asking and answering questions about biblical, religious, and spiritual matters.

Synod upheld the consistory, judging that

the consistory was justified in its decision to condemn this practice in view of the following considerations: 1) The social character of these gatherings was obviously a camouflage for a Bible Study group, comprised of dissident members, many of whom were openly critical of the doctrinal position of the Christian Reformed Church. 2) The leader of the group, the Rev. H. Danhof, had made himself guilty, by means of his

---

13 This sad history is related in Hoeksema, *Protestant Reformed Churches*, 261–79.
14 Article 88, in *Acts of Synod 1946 of the Christian Reformed Church* (Grand Rapids, MI: Christian Reformed Publishing House), 63: "A statement of the Stated Clerk of Classis Kalamazoo informing Synod 'that the union between the Protesting First Christian Reformed Church and the Christian Reformed denomination had been accomplished on November 1, 1945, on the basis approved by Classis at its February 21, 1945, meeting in agreement with the advice of the Synodical examiners of Classes Zeeland, Holland and Grand Rapids South.'"

public utterances, of resisting the adjustment of the Grace
Church to the Christian Reformed denomination, and also of
undermining the teaching of its pastor.

Synod added that if Danhof and the others would not stop this
practice, the consistory should "declare the membership of the protestants in the Grace Christian Reformed Church terminated."[15]

Evidently, Danhof's membership was thus "terminated," for the
database of Christian Reformed ministers lists Henry Danhof as a
"released" minister of the Christian Reformed Church.[16]

This personal history may be the reason Danhof never fulfilled the
promise he showed in *The Idea of the Covenant of Grace*. With the
exception of several booklets and one book that he coauthored with
Hoeksema during the common grace controversy, Danhof did not publish after his *Idea of the Covenant of Grace*.[17] What writing he did seems
to have taken the form of filling the Sunday bulletins of the Protesting
First Christian Reformed Church of Kalamazoo with his thoughts on
various theological, philosophical, and ecclesiastical subjects.[18]

---

15 Article 14, in *Acts of Synod 1948 of the Christian Reformed Church* (Grand Rap-
    ids, MI: Christian Reformed Publishing House), 71–74.
16 http://www.calvin.edu/cgi-bin/lib/crcmd/search.pl.
17 The three booklets are *Niet Doopersch maar Gereformeerd: Voorloopig Bescheid
    aan Ds. Jan Karel van Baalen betreffende de Loochening der Gemeene Gratie* [Not
    Anabaptist but Reformed: provisional response to Rev. J. K. van Baalen concerning
    the denial of common grace] (Grand Rapids, MI: Grand Rapids Printing Co., n.d.);
    Langs Zuivere Banen: een Wederwoord aan Bezwaarde Broederen [Along pure
    paths: a reply to aggrieved brothers] (Kalamazoo, MI: Dalm Printing Co., n.d.);
    and *For the Sake of Justice and Truth*. The book is *Sin and Grace*.
18 These must rank as the strangest church bulletins in the history of the Reformed
    churches, perhaps in the history of Protestantism. There is almost nothing in them
    of congregational events and church news. Front and back, the four pages of the
    typical bulletin are crammed with Danhof's expositions and comments on all kinds
    of topics. Take the bulletin of Sunday, March 8, 1931, as an example. Page 1 (the
    front cover of the bulletin) is devoted to "Some Unsolved Problems of Philosophy";
    page 2 is full of a treatment of *Het Overblijfsel Behouden* [The remnant preserved];
    page 3, from top to bottom, explains *De Proloog van Johannes* [The prologue of
    John]; and more than two-thirds of page 4, the back of the bulletin, sets forth a
    "Brief Exposition of Our Doctrine." Less than one-third of the back cover is permit-
    ted to contain all of the church news for the week under the heading "Meetings." In
    the midst of the listing of meetings, and under that heading, appears the line, lost in
    the welter of philosophy, theology, and meetings, "Born to Mr. and Mrs. P. van den
    Berg, Jr., a son." Let a pastor try this with the church bulletin today!

Danhof failed to carry out what he proposed in his lecture on the covenant. Having noted the breadth of his subject, he declared, "The Lord willing, I hope to devote my powers to related subjects in the future. We must preserve what we possess by adding to what has been obtained."

This duty has fallen to the ministers in the Protestant Reformed Churches.

All footnotes in this chapter, as in the introduction to the chapter, are the translator's.

—David J. Engelsma

A complete set of these bulletins is held in the library of the Theological School of the Protestant Reformed Churches. One who would learn something of Danhof's theological development after 1926 must peruse these bulletins, although occasionally a printed sermon or set of sermons would appear as an "appendix" to certain bulletins. Some of these printed sermons are available.

PREFACE

I t was not my original intention to publish the following address, which was given for a general (Christian Reformed) ministers' conference in Grand Rapids, Michigan. Repeated and friendly requests from more than one quarter that I would publish it caused me to change my mind. Although rather late, the address is now published without change.

I have hesitated for a long time. I thought that I should wait until someone else would have explained the relation of church and world from another viewpoint than Groen's, who was prevented from making his contribution because of sickness. At the same time, I judged the circumstances unfavorable to a treatment of profound questions of principle. Our age seems to call to us, "Hold fast what you have, so that no one takes your crown; one should not in these times think of any development of doctrine."

Finally, I felt that this contribution calls for thorough study of many related subjects, such as common grace, the incarnation of the Word, the idea of central humanity, and so on. Indeed, the idea of the covenant of grace concerns the deepest and most intimate relation between God and man. The real covenantal relation governs every other relation. For reasons everyone will understand, I did not dare to think even of attempting to demonstrate and develop all this in a short speech. First, the time for this was too limited. But also the logical train of thought demanded that I limit myself to my subject. For this reason, I held back.

Nevertheless, there was also another side to this matter. The ministers' conference insisted on publication. There is in my opinion great need for more doctrinal truth. We must develop the truth. Something is better than nothing. The study of related subjects can, if need be, wait until later. Besides, about some of the matters that I have just mentioned I have already spoken repeatedly in public. I could not even suggest a hiding of my own conviction. In addition, the gathering of the general ministers' conference of last year was announced in the church papers.

Finally, it ought not be concealed that in the meantime a certain group is always zealously promoting a view of the relation of church and world that in my opinion may not be ours. The idea of the "absolute antithesis" must be placed emphatically on the foreground in our world view. We must be of the party of the living God. Also in practice the covenantal idea must always determine our relation to everything about us, especially in relation to the world in a moral sense.

This covenantal idea I have tried to present in its most fundamental sense. Let the sympathetic reader judge in how far I have succeeded.

The address appears unchanged. After careful deliberation, this seemed to me the most desirable.

The Lord willing, I hope to devote my powers to related subjects in the future. We must preserve what we possess by adding to what has been obtained.

May the Lord confirm the covenant of his friendship with us in the Beloved.

—H. Danhof
Kalamazoo, Michigan
May 1920

CHAPTER I

UNIVERSALITY
OF THE IDEA OF COVENANT

*Danhof asserts that the covenantal idea in a formal sense is embedded in the life of men and nations. It structures the entire life of humanity. Although this results in seeming virtues in the behavior of the ungodly, these virtues are merely apparent. The reason is that the ungodly lack the reality and genuine essence of the covenant, which Danhof will later define as fellowship with the triune God through Jesus Christ in the Spirit. There is therefore division and struggle between the ungodly and the godly—the antithesis. All footnotes in Danhof's essay are mine, as are the chapter divisions.—*Trans.

The idea of the covenant of grace is not strange to our race. On the contrary, our society is almost entirely permeated with that idea. Regardless of change, man continues formally to arrange his life according to the covenantal conception. Circumstances of minor importance, such as those of war and peace, monarchical and democratic government, revolution and development, do not change this at all. By origin, disposition, and destination, man is a child of the covenant, and he shows this by his way of life.

Precisely at the present time this comes out strongly in international politics. Hardly is the balance of the European great powers broken than many strive for a covenant of the nations. To be sure, that ideal does not enchant all, but the opposition does not concern the idea as such. Besides, the covenantal conception expresses no less strongly the desire for sovereignty in one's own sphere than the longing of the nations for unity. Indeed, the covenant rests on the physical and juridical unity of our race and the responsibility of the individuals. Therefore, the ideal is the right connection of sovereignty in one's own sphere with a worldwide covenant of the nations.

In the social sphere the idea of the covenant is basic [*schering en inslag*, warp and woof]. The absolute individualist cannot exist there. There the hallmark of everything is organization, combination, alliance, cooperation, and system. Associations and unions of every sort stand in the way of the forceful expression of character. The power of public opinion is enormous. The minority is always wrong and therefore powerless. The slanted and biased press binds together state and society, church and club, religion and morality.[19]

By this means the recent war was the common property of church and state, as well in the lands of the Central Powers as in those of the Allies. Not all were silent, but there was little mention of an independent opinion of the churches. Church and state went arm in arm; Christendom and world were friendly; revelation and reason lay lovingly intermingled and intertwined. Although impotent to fill up the terrible abyss between the warring powers, the covenantal conception still governed human life on both sides of the chasm.

Even the heart joined in. Almost everywhere the intercession of the churches took the form of a prayer for victory. Church and state were of one mind. Even though both allied groups of nations had objections against each other's pretentions of communion with God, each continued to mention such on its own behalf. This was the case also when W. H. Kerr of Great Bend, Kansas, urged America to break with the idea of God, so that she could more effectively stigmatize as hypocrisy the profession of the German kaiser to rule by the grace of God.

Obviously the covenantal conception, as it lives in men's consciousness, also includes faith in God and in a spiritual world—emphatically faith concerning a spiritual world. It is indeed the case that the sorcerers, astrologers, and magicians, as well as the theophanies and appearances of angels of the old world, have disappeared from our

---

19 Today, television must be added to the powerful "*tendentieuze pers*" (biased press) mentioned by Danhof.

society. It is also true that the belief in witches, ghosts, and exorcists is perhaps less strong than in former times.[20] Nevertheless, superstition still confidently seeks knowledge of and communion with the world of unseen things. Witness our modern theosophists, spiritists, fortune tellers, Christian Scientists, and preachers of heathen religions. Modern man feels the tug of the tie that unites and joins God and man, spirit and matter, the individual and the community.

There is still more. It is a fact that not only men such as Enoch, Noah, Abraham, David, Daniel, Constantine the Great, William the Silent, Gustavus Adolphus, Martin Luther, John Knox, and others knew themselves to be servants of the Lord, but the same is true of people like Balaam, Saul, Sennacherib, Nebuchadnezzar, Korah, Socrates, Titus, and even Napoleon. All truly great spirits seem to realize somewhat that in their special positions and with their work they stand in service of the God of the covenant. History notes different cases of extraordinary covenantal communion with God.

Besides, human life is otherwise so full of all kinds of virtues, such as receptivity to the good, thankfulness, sympathy, assistance, devotion (to duty), self-denial, tender love, and faithful friendship, that the question involuntarily arises whether man, obviously acting according to the nature of the covenant in a formal sense, does not also live according to the nature of the covenant in the material sense, insofar as he displays these virtues.

Indeed, the husband is faithful to his wife; the mother devotes herself sacrificially to her little child without complaint; the child honors his parents; the young man is ready to sacrifice his life for the fatherland; the merciful nurse bends sympathetically over the sickbed of the pitiable sufferer; and the friend is not disloyal. Do not science and art serve the true and the beautiful? Do not hospitals and sanitariums, asylums and homes, courts, prisons, and judicial system prove that man strives for righteousness and virtue? Even the pet animal shows the goodness of man in its dependency and trust toward its master.

---

20 This could be said in 1919. It cannot be said in 2015. The intriguing thing is that Danhof saw this superstition as evidence of the ineradicable reality of the idea of the covenant in man. The reference here and in what immediately follows is to the formal aspect of the idea of the covenant: relationship with God.

What is the ethical quality of these virtues?

The prevailing opinion is that man can choose the good. He commands his own destiny and, as a result, governs the future. Concerning his actual practice of the good, the spirit of the age proclaims the excellency of humanity with increasingly louder voice. However much history may testify against him and certain weaknesses may yet cling to him, man will eventually develop right self-knowledge, self-esteem, and self-control. He will banish what is evil and fittingly subject the entire realm of nature to himself.

Expectantly therefore the eye of hope is fixed on him, for regardless of everything that hinders him, he must rule as king. Both evolution and revolution will pave the way to the throne for him. Everything cooperates to this end. The bond of concord must be felt. State and society, capital and labor, religion and morality need to come together on the exalted level of the common brotherhood of humanity. Then the entire, spontaneous development of our race according to the demands of each one's individual virtues and talents will be possible. With this, man's absolute rule over the kingdoms of the world will be confirmed. Criminal behavior, war, sickness, and probably also death will disappear. The prosperity [*zaligheid*, salvation as it lives in the mind of the ungodly world] of man will be great, and there will be no end to the peace of his kingdom. Something like this is man's testimony concerning himself and his future.

Nevertheless, God judges differently. Scripture says that men are by nature haters of God. All have departed. There is no one who does good, who seeks God, not even one [Rom. 3:9–11]. In other words, the entire life of our race, apart from regeneration, in its relation to God is covenant breaking [*bondsbreuk*, breaking or rupturing a union] despite that it is permeated with the covenantal conception and even though it may be made serviceable to the coming of his kingdom by God himself. Only in the renewed kernel is a beginning of God's covenant again found.[21]

---

21 To distinguish the elect, regenerated church from the reprobate, ungodly world, Danhof uses a figure that was a favorite of himself and Hoeksema: the kernel of grain as distinguished from the surrounding husk or the wheat and the chaff. The figure is biblical.

According to the testimony of God, humanity is divided into grain and chaff, church and world, bride and whore, children of light and those of darkness. Only in the first does God realize his covenant in a positive sense, out of grace. This takes place, according to the lesson of scripture, history, and experience, in the way of a dreadful struggle in the world and in the life of humanity. Despite their natural solidarity and although their life on earth is in various ways strikingly inter-related, the children of Adam separate on account of their different spiritual relation to God and form an antithesis along the whole line of human activity. In principle this happens always and everywhere. This separation takes place according to the nature of each dispensation and the differing circumstances of time, place, domain, sphere of life, and relationship.

All of this serves to keep our subject constantly and clearly in mind in my treatment of it and must as much as possible be explained. Therefore, I do not restrict myself to a theological exposition of the idea of the covenant per se. After the theological exposition, I consider also the realizing of this covenantal conception. Finally, I point out the struggle caused by this.

CHAPTER 2

THE DOCTRINE OF THE COVENANT IN THE REFORMED TRADITION

In this second section of his treatise on the covenant of grace, Henry Danhof gives a brief but helpful account of the history of the doctrine of the covenant, especially in the Reformed tradition. I have retained in the text Danhof's references to sources, which appear in parentheses. The translation of the Dutch titles into English can be found in the bibliography at the end of this book. Nevertheless, many of the Dutch works to which Danhof refers have not been translated into English.—Trans.

In a dogma-historical sense the doctrine of the covenant dates from the time of the Reformation. It is almost exclusively a plant out of Reformed soil. As an integral part of dogmatics, it does not appear in the church fathers, the Roman Catholics, the Socinians, or the Lutherans, nor is it found in the Anabaptists and the Baptists.[22] The real covenantal conception has been developed only in the Reformed churches.

Especially in Switzerland the reformers came into conflict with the Anabaptists. This external circumstance served as a goad to a deeper examination of the covenantal conception. Anabaptism did away with almost the entire scripture, especially the Old Testament. Having no eye for our natural solidarity, Anabaptism held fast to an existence of isolationism and individualism [*zandkorrel bestaan*, grain-of-sand existence] and fled the sphere of natural life as much as possible. It wanted a congregation of the truly regenerated and an immediate,

---

22 Danhof distinguishes a third, related group: *de Doopsgezinden* (a distinct sect of Baptists who were disciples of Menno Simons).

perfectly holy life in the Spirit. The Anabaptist had no eye for the truth of the means of grace. Baptism is only a sign of one's own personal faith and may therefore be administered only to those who obviously have been regenerated. As a result, there is no place for infant baptism. The Old Testament therefore must be shoved far into the background in relation to the New Testament, as well as the covenantal relation in regard to the reality of being a child of God.[23]

With the maintenance of infant baptism, the reformers asked concerning the connection between the Old and New Testaments, as well as the significance of the means of grace. Thus they took issue not only with Rome and Anabaptism, but also with various movements of their time that were spiritually related to the earlier Gnosticism and the different Jewish sects. The church of the Reformation saw itself called to explain the Christian religion both in connection with and in distinction from the religion of Israel. This it did in the doctrine of the covenant. This makes plain that the covenantal conception is no Reformed fancy or subtlety, but the most beautiful fruit of the theology of the whole Christian church.

The focus in this controversy was undoubtedly infant baptism. The Reformation had unanimously rejected Rome's doctrine that the sacraments communicate grace and righteousness and had proclaimed the word as the chief means of grace. Exactly for this reason, however, the reformers had to look for another ground for infant baptism, especially in the controversy with the Anabaptists. All of the reformers found this in their conception of the sacraments as signs and seals of God's grace. In this way all preserved the baptism of infants.

Concerning the question about the cause of God's grace in infants, however, there was sharp divergence of thought, notably between Luther and Calvin, especially after the controversy with the Anabaptists.

---

23 That Danhof subjects Anabaptism to penetrating, severe criticism is ironic. In the conflict over common grace that would soon follow, the Christian Reformed foes of Danhof and Hoeksema would charge them with the error of Anabaptism. In 1922 Van Baalen would publish against them the booklet *The Denial of Common Grace: Reformed or Anabaptist?* Van Baalen's answer to his question was emphatically, "Anabaptist." Danhof and Hoeksema would respond with *Not Anabaptist but Reformed.*

Luther and his followers really fell back into the sacramentalism of Rome. According to Luther the sacrament must also work what the word works, although not without that word. Therefore, the ecclesiastical administration of baptism again had regeneration as the effect, and baptism again was absolutely necessary. With this teaching the door of the authentic Lutheran system was closed to the development of the real covenantal conception.

In contrast Calvin maintained the existence of the church from the beginning and the essential oneness of the testaments, in opposition to the Anabaptists.[24] In connection with this, he maintained the essential oneness of Israel and the Christian church. According to Calvin there is in reality only one testament, although regarding administration one must distinguish between shadow and fulfillment. In a twofold administration, the Messiah is really one, and faith is one, as well as the way of salvation. The continuity of the congregation finds its origin in the fact that grace continuously works in the line of generations. Against Rome and Luther, Calvin put the covenant of God behind word and sacraments. That covenant is also the ground of infant baptism.

Thus Calvin's view of the covenant, which does not govern his system but comes up merely in an appendix, received the form of a doctrine of the testaments. Many, both before and after the Synod of Dordt, have followed him in this. The real covenantal idea then is less developed. Probably it is also because of Calvin's example that the doctrine of the covenant receives such scanty treatment in the Belgic Confession and in the Canons of Dordt.

The covenantal conception is much more prominent in the Zurich theologians. Dr. G. Vos calls the Zurichers the predecessors of the federal theologians in the narrower sense, inasmuch as the covenant became for them the governing idea for the practice of the Christian life (*De Verbondsleer in de Geref. Theologie*). According to Vos the well-known authors of the Heidelberg Catechism, Olevianus and Ursinus, stood in the closest relationship to the Zurich theologians. This

---

24 John Calvin, *Institutes of the Christian Religion*, ed. John T. McNeill, trans. Ford Lewis Battles, The Library of Christian Classics (Philadelphia: Westminster Press, 1960), 2.10–11, 20:436–59.

has certainly influenced the composition of the Heidelberg Catechism. Although the Catechism does not devote much attention to the concept of the covenant formally, still in a practical way the idea of the covenant permeates the Catechism.

We find the covenantal conception more beautifully developed in the Form for the Administration of Baptism. According to this Reformed liturgical form, believers with their children, although conceived and born in sin and therefore children of wrath, have an eternal covenant of grace with God. Therefore, they must also be baptized. Thus they also have fellowship with the triune God, are called to a new obedience, may fight and overcome sin, the devil, and his entire kingdom, and extol and praise the God of the covenant forever.

Indeed, these are precious thoughts!

What they mean for us concerning the real covenantal idea depends on our own understanding of the concept *covenant*. Is the covenant, referred to here, essential or merely incidental? Do we have an eternal covenant of grace with God, or does grace come to us by means of the covenant? The expression "whereas in all covenants, there are contained two parts," appears to allude to the latter. In this case, we would have to say with Maccovius that the covenant between God and man is not a real covenant but an arrangement similar to other covenants: a treaty in which God promises something to man, for example life, and in turn requires something from him as a condition, for example obedience (*Godgel Ondersch.*, chap. 12). After the fall, God has repeated that same covenant (which he supposedly established with Adam) in order to teach us our duty, admonish us to obedience, and so on. In this case, although in my struggle against Satan and sin I may rejoice, "God has confirmed a covenant with me in the spiritual strife! The triune God is at my side!" I still do not have a real covenant with God.

But such is indeed the case if I say, with Dr. B. Wielenga, that this covenant is no appearance but adorable reality; no pale imitation of a human covenant but the real and original covenant rooted in God's eternal decree;[25] the highest reality and truth, which is the perfect pattern

---

25 Danhof is here denying that the biblical covenant of grace owes its origin to, is fashioned after, and is to be understood in light of earthly covenants among men.

for all human activity (*Ons Doopsformulier*, 64). By that conception, the baptism formula says to me that according to its essence, the covenant is friendship between God and man. In this case the believer bears in baptism the sign and banner of King Jesus. He fights on behalf of the cause of the Son of God. In the arena of this life, he is of God's party. He is such, above all, because he is God's friend. The choice between these two opinions depends, in my view, on the meaning that we ourselves attach to the term *covenant* in our baptism formula.

The Westminster Confession of Faith goes farther into the covenant idea per se.

> The distance between God and the creature is so great that although reasonable creatures do owe obedience unto him as their Creator, yet they could never have any fruition of him as their blessedness and reward but by some voluntary condescension on God's part, which he hath been pleased to express by way of covenant.[26]

The importance of this denial cannot be emphasized too strongly. Many today assume that the covenant revealed in scripture, especially between Jehovah and Old Testament Israel, originates in and must be explained according to various ancient, Near Eastern treaties and covenants. The Presbyterian theologian Meredith G. Kline has been influential in introducing this notion into conservative Presbyterian and Reformed churches. In his *By Oath Consigned: A Reinterpretation of the Covenant Signs of Circumcision and Baptism* (Grand Rapids, MI: Eerdmans, 1968), Kline has written, "Now since in certain notable instances, particularly but not exclusively in the Mosaic covenants, it pleased the Lord of Israel to describe his covenant relationship to his people according to the pattern of these vassal treaties, no other conclusion is warranted than that 'covenant' in these instances denoted at the formal level the same kind of relationship as did the vassal covenants on which they were modelled" (21). See also his *Treaty of the Great King: The Covenant Structure of Deuteronomy, Studies and Commentary*, with its discussion of "suzerainty treatises" (Grand Rapids, MI: Eerdmans, 1963).

Danhof repudiates the notion root and branch. Apart from its derivation of the holiest things of the people of God from idolatrous, profane nations, it puts us on the wrong track in understanding the nature of the covenant of God with his people. Not old records of treaties among or within ungodly nations but divine revelation in holy scripture must make known to us what the covenant of grace essentially is. The life of Jehovah with Israel, and of Israel with Jehovah, is patterned not after the life of the nations but after the life of God.

26 Westminster Confession of Faith 7.1, in Schaff, *Creeds of Christendom*, 3:616.

The first covenant made with man was a covenant of works, wherein life was promised to Adam, and in him to his posterity, upon condition of perfect and personal obedience.[27]

Man by his fall having made himself incapable of life by that covenant, the Lord was pleased to make a second, commonly called the covenant of grace: wherein he freely offereth unto sinners life and salvation by Jesus Christ, requiring of them faith in him that they may be saved, and promising to give unto all those that are ordained unto life his Holy Spirit, to make them willing and able to believe.[28]

This covenant of grace is frequently set forth in the Scripture by the name of a testament, in reference to the death of Jesus Christ the testator, and to the everlasting inheritance, with all things belonging to it, therein bequeathed.[29]

Concerning the real idea of the covenant, obviously two thoughts are here intertwined. The first sentence describes the covenant as means of fellowship between God and man. The covenantal idea is then identical with the idea of religion. The following sentences really present the covenant as means to the highest blessedness and salvation of men. The covenant of works serves for the reception of something that man in paradise did not yet possess, at least not yet unchangeably; the covenant of grace is a means for the redemption and salvation of men. In the latter case, the covenant is something incidental, something that conceivably might not have been. It is a kind of conditional promise.

Also the Westminster Shorter Catechism gives this representation. To question 12 the answer is given, "When God had created man, he entered into a covenant of life with him, upon condition of perfect obedience: forbidding him to eat of the tree of knowledge of good and evil, upon pain of death."[30]

---

27 Westminster Confession of Faith 7.2, in ibid, 3:616–17.
28 Westminster Confession of Faith 7.3, in ibid, 3:617.
29 Westminster Confession of Faith 7.4, in ibid.
30 Westminster Shorter Catechism A 12, in ibid., 3:678.

To question 20, treating of the covenant of grace, there is the answer, "God, having out of his mere good pleasure, from all eternity, elected some to everlasting life, did enter into a covenant of grace, to deliver them out of the estate of sin and misery, and to bring them into an estate of salvation by a Redeemer."[31] Here too the covenant is understood as means to the highest blessedness of men and to the realizing of election.

The Irish Articles of Religion (1615) likewise speak of the covenant of works as a conditional promise of God. The Walcheren Articles (1693) use the covenants for an explanation of our depravity in Adam and our redemption in Christ.

According to Abraham Kuyper, the covenant is essentially an alliance between God and man against every actual and possible hostile power (*Dict. Dogm., Loc. de foedere*). The making of a covenant, according to him, is an act of friendship (*Gem. Gratie*, 1:287). Whether the essential idea of the covenant must be sought in the friendship out of which the alliance arises, or in the alliance in which the friendship takes form against the mutual enemy, is less obvious.

According to this historical survey, the idea of the covenant has been understood as a means to men's highest blessedness, redemption, and salvation; the essence of religion; or an alliance arising from friendship. I cite yet a few quotations demonstrating each of these conceptions.

A. Hellenbroek gives this answer to the question what the covenant of grace is: "The covenant of grace is that way along which God through Christ becomes the possession [*het eigendom*] of the sinner, and he becomes the possession of God" (*Voorb. der Godd. Waarheden*, 44). T. Bos gives a similar definition (*Genadeverbond en Bondzegelen*).

M. J. Bosma expresses himself concerning the covenant thus:

What was the covenant of works?

A covenant is an agreement. The covenant of works was an agreement between God and Adam, wherein God promised eternal life to Adam and all his posterity upon condition of perfect obedience to the probationary command not to eat of

---

31 Westminster Shorter Catechism A 20, in ibid., 3:680.

the tree of knowledge of good and evil, God threatening that Adam would die in case he broke this command. The elements of this covenant, therefore, were:

1. A condition expressed: perfect obedience.
2. A promise implied: eternal life.
3. A penalty threatened: death.

What is the covenant of grace?

It is the gracious agreement between God and his people, whereby God promises them complete salvation in the way of faith, and they accept in faith. (*Exposition of Reformed Doctrine*, 91, 111)

These quotations express a view of the covenant as not really a covenant at all [*oneigenlijk*]; as a means to men's highest blessedness, redemption, and salvation; and as a conditional promise.

In the Westminster Confession and in men such as Vos, Bavinck (*Geref. Dogm.*, 2:611–14), Kuyper, Wielenga, and others, we find the conception that the covenant is the essence of religion. Kuyper is representative: "The covenant idea is not something that is added to religion, but it is identical with religion. It is the idea of religion itself" (*Dict. Dogm.*, *Loc. de foedere*).

Vos says, "Friendship is the essence of the covenant relation" (*Compendium van de Systematische Theologie*). One finds similar expressions in almost all well-known Reformed writers. Herman Hoeksema recently spoke in the same vein in his articles in the *Banner* of April 10 and 17. Also according to him, the covenant is essentially friendship.[32]

---

32 Hoeksema is the one Christian Reformed colleague Danhof mentions in this history of the doctrine of the covenant. As Danhof indicates, in 1919 (when Danhof gave the address on the covenant) both he and Hoeksema had rejected the view of the covenant that had become standard in the Christian Reformed Church and were developing the conception of the covenant as a bond of fellowship. Which of them might have been father to this conception is an intriguing question. Hoeksema related that upon graduating from Calvin seminary in 1915 he was certain that the doctrine of the covenant taught by Prof. William Heyns—the covenant as conditional contract—was erroneous, but Hoeksema was uncertain what the truth of the covenant might be. Within a few years of the publication of Danhof's treatise on the covenant, Danhof and Hoeksema were battling together in the

How has it come about that there are these three views of the covenant in the Reformed tradition? In my opinion this has happened as follows. After the break with Rome, especially Anabaptism occasioned the search for a biblical ground for infant baptism. This led to clearer insight into the connection of the generations of men. All men share in Adam's guilt. In the same manner, although in a more limited sphere, there is also communion in the righteousness and life of Christ. The tendency was to view Adam and Christ more as our representatives than as covenantal friends [*bondgenooten*] of God. The term *covenant head* was applied to both. In our relationship to the head of the covenant was seen the real covenantal relation. Thus one could explain the common depravity of the children of men, as well as the continuity of the working of the grace of God in the line of generations. One also had a ground for infant baptism.

However, that thinking almost inevitably resulted in confusing the covenant of works with the probationary command. Generally, the covenant of works was considered to be a conditional promise of life. But since Adam already possessed life and therefore did not have to obtain it for himself or for his descendants, the promise of God was made to refer to the unchangeable life of eternal glory. The covenant must serve for the obtaining of salvation in the highest degree. The promise, condition, and threat remained. To the question why Adam would in fact be guilty if he did not desire that higher life for himself, the answer was that such was Adam's obligation toward God. Because God willed that Adam should be partaker of the unchangeable life of salvation in the highest degree, Adam must, for God's sake, desire it for himself and his descendants. *Covenant* is figurative, a manner of speaking, no reality. It serves merely to indicate the obligation that men have toward God.

This left the special and frequent use of that term unexplained. Therefore, others sought something real in the term and concept

Christian Reformed Church for the truth of particular grace. Shortly thereafter, virtually simultaneously, both were cast out of the Christian Reformed Church for their united opposition to the doctrine of common grace that the church adopted as official dogma in 1924. The subsequent sad separation between the two is described in my introduction to this translation of Danhof's work on the covenant.

covenant. It is impossible for man to enjoy God in his infinite exaltation. The worship of God is possible only if God condescends to man and raises him up to himself. That explains the creation of man after the image of God. Religion is fellowship with God, and the covenant is the essence of true religion.

This also implies that the real covenantal relation is not our relationship to Adam or Christ. Rather, the covenantal relation is identical with the relationship in which, through Adam or Christ, we stand to God. The covenant points to our fellowship with God. Therefore, the question is not first what the head of the covenant, Adam or Christ, does for those who are included in him, but what he is and does in his relation to God. Rightly understood, it may be said that he does not have to earn life for us. Rather, he has to realize the covenant of God. He is the servant and covenantal friend of God. He must serve God, but unconstrained, according to his own free choice, as a friend. God's servant is God's child, and the child resembles his father; they are friends. Religion is fellowship, covenant fellowship, friendship.

CHAPTER 3

SOURCE AND NATURE
OF THE COVENANT OF GRACE

In this section of his booklet, Danhof sets forth his understanding of the doctrine of the covenant. Noteworthy is his derivation of the covenant from the triune being of God.—Trans.

The covenant rests in the holy Trinity. God is the God of the covenant. He is such not only according to the counsel of his will in his relation to the creature, but first in himself by virtue of his nature. The divine life in itself is a covenant of friendship among Father, Son, and Holy Ghost. That divine love-life is then the basis for every covenantal relation between Creator and creature and between the creatures mutually. The absolute covenantal conception is hidden in the family life of the holy Trinity.

No one therefore will ever succeed in fathoming the covenantal idea in all its depth. Yet one can see fairly easily that all relation, reciprocal action, and mutual fellowship among Father, Son, and Holy Ghost must be and take place according to the nature of the covenant, for God is one in being and three in persons. The three persons are all equally possessors of the same divine essence. In their personal substances they are equal with each other. But in their individual, personal properties they differ from each other.

Their oneness of essence gives harmony. The identical substance of the persons implies agreement. At the same time, in the differences of their individual, personal properties is found the possibility for the highest fellowship and cooperation. The oneness and differences of the persons give eternal, divine harmony. The love-life of God, welling up out of the unfathomable depths of the essence and decreed by Father, Son, and Holy Ghost, pours forth in the multiplicity of the forms of the individual, personal properties, manifesting in the most glorious hue the full riches of the eternal friendship of the Trinity.

In all the outgoing works of God, something of this covenant of friendship is necessarily revealed outside of God. Even though these outgoing works are free and decreed, they are nevertheless works of a self-revealing God. Because the absolute covenantal idea is grounded in God's nature and manner of life, all revelation must be revelation of the God of the covenant, since it can be nothing other than self-revelation of the Trinity. Although we may not suppose that God exhausts himself in his self-revelation, we will certainly have to assume that an impression of the absolute covenantal idea in the Trinity is found in the highest creature, since God created man according to his image.

In my opinion, this covenantal idea in man is not completely identical with the religious idea. Yet, as man was created according to God's image immediately at creation and by virtue of this could attain at once to active religious fellowship with his Creator, thus his religion finds its goal in the fellowship of the covenant. Through the band of the covenant, God lets his absolute covenantal life vibrate continuously in the creature, and by the vibrating of that band, man echoes the life of God in his life.[33] In his most sublime fellowship with the Eternal One, man is friend of God. The covenant causes God and man to live together as friends. In this the covenant-idea is completely realized. Accordingly, in his wonderful vision of the kingdom of glory John saw the tabernacle of God with men.

Man is friend of God. God has conceived him so. That is God's will concerning man. Toward the fellowship of friendship with God man has been directed. In this he finds his destiny. He can truly rest only in the fellowship of friendship with his God. To be sure, as a moral and

---

33 Danhof's figure is unusual and vivid. The covenant between the triune God and (elect) man is a kind of spiritual string, as of a musical instrument. Along it God's own covenantal life vibrates (*natrillen*) in man. God "plucks" the string so that his life may echo in man.

rational being he can turn into his very opposite and by this become a covenantal companion and friend of Satan. But even then, in his formal, covenantal life he still shows his origin, nature, and original destiny. The damned in hell is the complete opposite of the man of God in the kingdom of glory.

In that man of God, God's conception of the covenant has been fully realized in a positive sense. According to the measure of his comprehension, the life of the friendship of the Trinity continues to vibrate in him. The God of friendship is known, enjoyed, mirrored, and reflected by him. With his whole heart, soul, mind, and powers, he responds to the Eternal's act of friendship that penetrates, qualifies, arouses, and provokes him. God's friend is of God, through God, and to God.

In the covenant, God finds the most excellent form for the revelation and bestowal of his friendship. The covenant of friendship exalts the reciprocal relationship of life and fellowship between God and man to the highest order and greatest intimacy. In no other relation than as friend of God would man ever be able more perfectly to show forth the praises of him who called him out of darkness into his marvelous light.

God then has also willed the covenant first for his own sake. It serves him in his highest self-revelation and self-glorification. Since he reveals and glorifies himself by it as the God of love and friendship, and by it exalts man as his own covenantal companion and friend, therefore in my judgment this divine, sovereign will loses all the apparent lack of feeling and coldness that, according to the impression of some critics, adheres to the sovereignty of God (as that is understood by the Reformed faith), in contrast to the love of God. We may not say with James Orr (*Progress of Dogma*, Lect. IX, 292) that Calvin "errs in placing his root idea of God in sovereign will rather than in love. Love is subordinated to sovereignty, instead of sovereignty to love." With Calvin we must very really explain the entire creation from a free act of the will of God. Also the covenant therefore, although grounded in God's nature, is no less a fruit of his will. Strictly speaking the one presupposes the other. Nevertheless, the sovereign will of the God of the covenant is a willing to reveal and glorify the life of the friendship of the triune God. It is therefore entirely encircled in the glow of love.[34]

The will of God includes the forms of the covenant and all means and ways for the complete realizing of the covenantal conception. Also the forms of the covenant are of God. The covenant of works was not replaced by the covenant of grace, but according to God's ordinance the covenant of God changed from the form of the covenant of works into that of the covenant of grace.[35] For God's sake! It was he, first of all, who willed the deeper way through the fall and rising again of man for the most perfect development of his covenantal conception. His purpose was that the life of the friendship of the Trinity would shine the more gloriously. From the counsel of peace—the agreement among the three persons in the divine being for the redemption of man[36] (Ten Hoor, *Korte Schets der Geref. Dogmatiek*, 45–46)—

---

34 This is a remarkable insight. Obviously Danhof rejects the charge that the sovereignty of God as conceived by the Reformed faith is cold and unfeeling. His defense is that the sovereign decree (of creation and redemption) is centrally the decree of the covenant, which is essentially warm, intimate friendship between God and his people. Apart from this, Danhof suggests, sovereignty might well be cold and unfeeling. The covenant "saves" the sovereignty of God from the charge of such as James Orr. Is it perhaps the case today that Reformed people fail to proclaim and defend the sovereignty of God in predestination and providence, indeed cannot proclaim and defend the sovereignty of God, exactly because they do not see the sovereignty of God as freely ordaining and realizing the covenant of grace as fellowship with God? They do not conceive the divine sovereignty as "entirely encircled in the glow of love" (*geheel gehuld in den gloed der liefde*).

35 Here is a different view from what is traditional with many Reformed theologians regarding the relation between the covenant with Adam in paradise and the covenant of grace with Christ and the elect church after the fall. The covenant with Adam was not a completely different covenant from the covenant of grace. Rather, it was a form of God's one covenant with man. Clearly implied is the sovereignty of God in the fall of Adam, governing also this aspect of history in the interests of his covenant. At the writing of this booklet in 1920, Danhof still accepted the traditional name of the covenant with Adam, although he differed radically with the tradition as to the nature of this covenant. Later Hoeksema would reject the name as well.

36 The reference is to the source of the covenant of grace in God, what in Reformed theology has been called "the covenant of redemption." Regarding Zechariah 6:13 as a biblical basis for the origin of the covenant in God, Reformed theologians also spoke mistakenly of the counsel of peace. Traditionally, this was presented as an agreement either between the Father and the Son or among all three persons of the Trinity. Danhof still accepted the tradition's view of the source of the covenant as an "agreement."

radiates to us, first, God's love-life. Exactly therein seems to be found the explanation for God's will in this. Further, in this rests also God's covenant of grace with man in Christ. That covenant cannot fail, since it is grounded in the agreement of Father, Son, and Holy Ghost, which in turn roots in the love-life of God and has as its purpose the revelation and glorifying of the same.

From this viewpoint, Christ and the Holy Ghost must also be explained from the will of the God of the covenant. The same holds for the regeneration, faith, struggle, and victory of the people of God. Even though ultimately the will of God in reprobation is somewhat different from what it is in election, nevertheless he wills reprobation no less than election. God realizes his covenantal conception according to his eternal counsel of election and reprobation.

Hoeksema would radically rework the doctrine of the source of the covenant. The covenant of grace has its origin in God, but this origin is the decree of the triune God appointing Jesus Christ as head and mediator of the covenant, in whom God will establish his covenant with the elect church. Hoeksema called this eternal source of the covenant—this reworked "covenant of redemption"—the "decree of the covenant" (Herman Hoeksema, *Reformed Dogmatics* [Grand Rapids: Reformed Free Publishing Association, 1966], 401–80).

CHAPTER 4

ORGANIC DEVELOPMENT
OF THE COVENANT IN HISTORY

*The subject of this section is the organic development
of the covenant in history as the central part of the
organic development of all things. The importance of
this aspect of the truth of the covenant is, first, that it
repudiates the teaching of a positive development of
the ungodly world alongside the church by virtue of
common grace; second, that it establishes the reality of
a (spiritual) antithesis between the covenantal friends
of God and the enemies of God, who live in closest
physical proximity; and third, that it wards off all Anabaptist world flight.—Trans.*

Especially the organic connection of the human race must also be
involved in the will of God. All the connections of head and members, of parents and children, and of church and world are God's
means to realize his covenant. That realization everywhere follows the
organic lines: in the individual and in the generations, positively in the
church and negatively in the world. God created man as an organic
creature and in organic relation to the world around him. For this
reason he lives organically. Therefore, humanity reaches its completion
in and through all the different individuals of the human race, and the
realization of the covenantal conception keeps pace with the progression of the organic development of the life of our race.

We must emphasize this strongly. Adam was not merely the moral
representative of all persons so that the guilt of his first sin is imputed
to them. In Adam we find also the principle of humanity: our organic

head. Therefore, as persons, we are not only born with guilt and subject to condemnation, but also, according to Psalm 51:5, all humans are conceived and born in unrighteousness and sin. The result of the latter is that all humans actually sin and bring the sin of the race to development according to their participation in the root sin of their organic head. Our daily sins cannot be explained from inherited corruption, as is commonly done, since corruption and actual sin are wholly dissimilar ideas. But daily sins spring up in the individual children of men from the root sin of our race on account of their organic connection with the head of the race, Adam.

The human race is not to be compared to a tree, of which the trunk is preserved and the branches go lost, as if God would save a damaged humanity. Rather, it is to be compared to a forest that has sprung from one tree. The individual trees of such a forest are then not only independent trees, but also individuals that in different ways continue and develop the life of the tree from which they all sprouted. If the life in the root of that tree from which all the others sprouted is wild, so will it be also in all the trees of the forest, since each individual tree will bring out a particular aspect of the wildness of the parent tree. In this way the wild life of the forest comes to full development. Then you can afterward also introduce new life by inoculation in such a manner that the forest is transformed, although very many trees that remain wild must be condemned to the fire.

This figure is applicable to the human race. Humanity is an organism. The different members of it are both independent persons who share in Adam's guilt and individuals differing from each other in thousands of ways, who have organic communion in the root sin of the head of their race, Adam. The sin of the race bears an organic character. As a result, the same holds also for our lives in sin; for the operations of curse, death, and perdition; for the temptations of the devil and the inspiration of the Spirit; for the life of grace and spiritual development, and so on. With the development of the various connections and relationships, the principles of sin and grace are unfolded and practiced by the individual children of God and children of the world agreeably to the nature of each age and according to the demands of time, place, and circumstance.

Therefore, the manner of the operation of God in realizing his covenantal conception in the organic whole of his creatures must be further explained on the basis of this organic character of humanity. In this connection, the mutual relation of church and world during this earthly age especially demands our attention.

We consider then the development of the covenant of God. The beginning of the realization of the covenantal conception was evident already in the earthly paradise. In the state of rectitude, the relation between God and man was friendship. According to Genesis 2:15, the Lord God took the man and set him in the garden of Eden to cultivate and to guard it. Those words unfold to us the conception of the covenant of works. Adam is servant, covenantal companion, and friend of God. What he does in that relation yields results for all included in him. But his task is the practice of God's covenant.[37] He must cultivate and guard the garden of Eden in the service of the Lord. He represents the cause of God in opposition to the devil. Especially in opposition to Satan, man must reveal himself as God's friend. However, in keeping with the nature of friendship this may not be coerced but must be a free choice. In this way the relation of friendship between God and man, which as yet was not fixed, would have been unchangeably established.

The probationary command of verses 16–17 presented man with the opportunity for this. The probationary command did not promise life to man but threatened God's servant and covenantal companion with death. It put his friendship with the Lord to the test. Such appears plainly from the wording of the command, as well as from Satan's words to the woman; Eve's evaluation of the tree; God's judgment on the serpent; and the result of the sin of man (Gen. 2:16–17; 3:4–6, 15, 22).

God's friend failed the test. Under the influence of the temptation, he treacherously defected to the enemy, as far as he was concerned. In the heart of man, in the choice of his will, the covenant of friendship between God and him was broken.

However, it now became evident that the covenant was God's.

---

37 *Zijne taak is de betrachting van Gods verbond.* Danhof's thought is that Adam's work in paradise was his active carrying out of his part in the covenant; it was covenantal work.

Man could break it in his own will, that is, by a free choice refuse to will it. But this did not nullify the covenant. God is greater than man's heart. His cause is not dependent on man's choice. On the contrary, the choice of man is dependent on God's will. God wills the covenant. Therefore, according to God's good pleasure, behind Adam when he fell away stood Christ, God's companion, and in him the Lord's covenant of friendship with man was firm. Out of grace in Christ, God realizes his covenant of friendship with man, contrary to his sinful will and unto his sanctified will, so that man becomes God's covenantal companion and friend eternally.

Behold, the idea of the covenant of grace!

According to God's counsel, all things work together for the realization of this idea of the covenant of grace. For a time the earth bears the burden of the curse of the Lord, and for a while the creation resigns itself to the bondage of corruption. The angels, as ministering spirits, go out from before the presence of God on behalf of those who will inherit salvation. The world that perishes serves the church that is saved as chaff serves the grain. It bears the grain and causes it to ripen for the heavenly granary, namely, the communion of friendship. At the same time the chaff is being prepared by the grain for the fire that is not quenched.

Meanwhile the devil, having no light of himself, nor being capable of producing a single independent thought concerning the kingdom that he supposes himself to be establishing through man, is in all his rampaging dependent on the light that God causes to shine forth from the people of his choice. Therefore, with his kingdom of darkness, he only serves the reality of God's covenant and the loveliness of the heritage of God's friends, although against his will. The devil also manifests ever more plainly, through all ages and indeed unto eternity, the lying, deceitful, and abominable character of himself and of his society.[38]

The history of all things is the development of the covenant of friendship of our God.

God realizes his covenantal conception by the power with which he acts upon the organic whole of his creatures according to his

---

38 "Society" is *gemeenschap*, the word that with reference to the covenant means fellowship.

counsel of providence. Each creature, in its organic participation in the totality, receives God's preserving, cooperating, and governing power by which it attains to the perfect realization of the original creation conception of God. With this the creature receives its eternal salvation, provided it is standing in the right spiritual relation to God, the creator. In the regenerated person, the spiritual relation to God is in principle again restored and therefore is good, so that he by that internal, powerful operation of his Creator can fulfill his calling and reach his blessed destiny.

However, this positively good power of God works death and destruction for the unregenerated world, since it reverses that operation into its opposite by sin. Certainly God does good to all creatures. He causes his sun to rise upon evil and good and causes the rain to fall upon just and unjust. It should be understood, however, that the evil do not become better by this but even worse, and that the unrighteous do not become righteous by this but still more godless.

According to Hebrews 6:7–8 the world of plants teaches us that if ground and field are moistened with a gentle rain and nurtured by the sun, the good wheat soon sprouts and grows luxuriously. However (and let this be noted!), then and only then do the weeds also develop. God's good rain and sunshine cause also the thistles to grow. By means of the positively good powers of God the thistles and thorns develop. However, apart from re-creation they do not develop into myrtles and fir trees but into still larger thistles and thorns, in order presently to kindle a great fire. Also the unregenerated person develops by means of the good gifts and power of God, but as unregenerated, according to his own nature, out of his own principle of life, and unto his own complete development in evil.

Since the regenerated and the unregenerated are inseparable and exist organically intertwined during this earthly dispensation, it must be maintained that the whole creation develops in organic oneness by the power that comes to it from the Creator, but from the twofold principle of sin and grace. The life of regeneration then is not supported by the life that originates from creation, and the covenant of special grace is not surrounded on all sides by a broader covenant of common grace [*gemeene gratie*]. Rather, the elect kernel of Adam's race and its reprobate husk are organically bound together during this earthly dispensation. God's grace is not common but is directed to the kernel. As the result, there is only one organic development of the whole creation, especially of humanity, out of the principles of grace and sin, along the lines of election and reprobation, and by means of the positively good power of the Creator that comes to it according to the counsel of God's providence.

In this way, by the almighty operation of the good power of God in the kingdom of light and also in the kingdom of darkness, the creation reaches its complete development in the way of a fearful struggle and along the lines of the Lord's original plan for the life of his covenantal people. An independent development by each kingdom individually is impossible. Indeed, limiting ourselves to the world of the children of men, the children of both these kingdoms are of one blood; owe their origin concerning the flesh to each other; live simultaneously and under similar circumstances; possess a similar disposition and a common kind of life; and therefore can develop only in mutual communion and according to the same laws of life. Their life on earth is in all kinds of ways marvelously intermingled. They also realize their solidarity and therefore feel a need for cooperation toward a common goal of life.

The children of Adam then would desire no division in their ranks, nor permit any tearing of the bands of their communion, were it not that they differ radically in one point, namely, in their spiritual relation to God. That different relation to their Creator, the fount of their lives, is the wedge that causes them, with their opposing world and life views, to separate to the right and to the left in every sphere, even to the smallest details, and with compelling consequence. Thus at the end of this earthly dispensation they, as children of light and of darkness, respectively attain to the perfected kingdom of the light and that of the darkness. No matter how they formally resemble each other in all respects, they will form as absolute and eternal a contrast as that of pole and antipole, of plus and minus, of life and death, because of their different spiritual relations to God.

CHAPTER 5

PROGRESSIVE REVELATION
OF THE (ONE) COVENANT OF GRACE

In this section Danhof explains the development of the covenant of grace in Bible history, beginning with its revelation by God immediately after the fall. In what immediately precedes, Danhof proposes the organic development of the covenant of grace in history in connection with the development of all things under the providential government of God. The human race of elect and reprobate is "marvelously intermingled" in all kinds of close earthly relations. But the radically different relation in which they stand to God—love and fellowship on the part of the regenerated elect and hatred and enmity on the part of the unregenerated reprobate—is "the wedge that causes them, with their opposing world and life views, to separate to the right and to the left in every sphere, even to the smallest details, and with compelling consequence." Thus world history is at its core the story of the fearful struggle between the covenantal people of God and God's enemies.—Trans.

This enables us to understand the course of history. The covenant in its entirety was essentially present immediately after the fall. All that follows is development of this seed. However, the progress of the revelation of the covenantal conception is bound up with the development of creation and humanity and of conscious life. Therefore, even the mention of the covenant is lacking here, and the spiritual difference between church and world fades completely into the background. God's grace seems to concern not only the organic kernel, but also the entire human race.

Genesis 3:15 mentions the ruin of Satan and his kingdom. The seed of the woman will triumph. However, the expression "thy seed" points to the coming struggle between the sons of God and the children of men. The contrast between the elect and forgiven kernel of the human race and the reprobate husk that surrounds the kernel during the present time is manifested in the different relations of hate and love in which they stand to Satan, to God, and to each other. Only with the ripening of the fruit does the everlasting kernel more and more break through the husk.

The different periods of this development therefore do not present any gradation in grace, as Cocceius wanted.[39] This notion would lead to the absolute destruction of the covenantal idea. Rather, the different periods of development present the formal phases of development of the life of the covenant in our race. With this they present the working out of the principles of sin and grace: the concentration of spiritually similar elements and the progressive dissolving of the natural fellowship of spiritually dissimilar elements [people].

Each preceding phase is type and shadow of the following, more developed form of the covenant. The covenant of grace is never the kernel of a more common covenant, but although essentially ever the same, it always comes to manifestation in higher forms. The forms develop. The form of revelation in paradise is type of the form of the covenant with Noah, as this is shadow of the Abrahamic covenant, and as the form of the covenant with Israel is shadow of the New Testament form of the covenant. In like manner the entire earthly dispensation is image of the everlasting form of the covenant.

The covenant with Noah therefore is the covenant of grace in its second phase of historical development. The new creation, the kernel

---

39 Cocceius (1603–69) was a Reformed theologian who taught for many years in the Netherlands. He made the covenant central in Reformed theology. He has been charged with having so sharply distinguished the various phases of the covenant in the Old Testament as to lose the oneness of the covenant and thus fall into the error of dispensationalism. Danhof insists on and explains the unity of the covenant of grace in all the phases of its revelation.

of the first world, stripped of the old wrapping that perished in the flood, arises out of the water of baptism and beholds in the clouds of heaven the sign of God's covenantal faithfulness.[40]

In a very short time, however, it turned the somewhat altered and richer expression of God's good gifts and powers into an all-consuming curse, according to the operation of the principle of sin. The intertwining of church and state and the society of church and world in one and the same organization made possible the moral degeneration of the human race and the establishment of the principle of the kingdom of Babel: the world power inspired by Satan that is opposed to God. That apparently absolutely universal world federation, which was hostile to God, seemed to leave God's covenant of friendship in our race neither root nor branch. The second world had come to the beginning of the end. The final end, however, was put off for ages by the confusion of speech and the separating of Abraham.

In Abraham the holy line continues. God made Abraham to be a pattern of his grace and realization of the covenant before the face of the peoples. Abraham's separation is only temporal and typical. The people that sprouts from Abraham is spiritually one with Adam, Seth, Enos, Enoch, Noah, Shem, Arphaxad, Heber, Terah, and the congregation of the new covenant. According to its spiritual kernel, it represents the elect humanity. In its separate existence as a people, it forms an antithesis with the heathen. Over against the whole world, it is of God's party.

Here, however, we do not yet have the everlasting and absolute antithesis between the kingdom of light and that of darkness. Israel in its historical existence is shadow, picture, prophecy, and preformation of what comes in higher form in Christ and his congregation and in the kingdom of glory. Presently, God first returns to the peoples in his only begotten Son, who according to the flesh is from Israel, in order to take to himself a congregation from every race, language, people, and nation. Therefore, God returns to the peoples through Israel. Thus Abraham becomes a father of all those who believe, from both the

---

40 This view of the covenant with Noah differs radically from the popular view that the covenant with Noah was a covenant of common grace with all men involving merely temporal existence and earthly gifts.

uncircumcised and the circumcised, and an heir of the world. With this, the middle wall of partition is broken, and in principle the separate existence as a people of Israel and of the heathen is abolished [Eph. 2:14]. From now on, neither Jew nor heathen can maintain itself in its separate existence.

The congregation is the spiritual kernel of our race. On Pentecost humanity according to its spiritual kernel repeals the tower of Babel and Adam's breaking of the covenant; abolishes the confusion of language and with this the dividing of peoples by its speaking in tongues; and grants us a glimpse into the kingdom of glory. This entire earthly dispensation has come to the beginning of the end. It is the last time and day and hour. The entire creation is in travail [Matt. 24:8; Rom. 8:22], and in the birth pangs the ripe fruit breaks through the husk. Out of the temporal wrapping the everlasting kernel makes its appearance.

Two observations still need to be made. Historical Israel according to its typical aspect was not only an image of the congregation of the new day, but also pointed more directly to the kingdom of glory beyond the entire new dispensation. The outward appearance of Israel's existence as a people was shadow of the eternal dispensation. The church lacks that outward, typical feature. Although richer in spiritual goods than old Israel, since the shadows relating to those goods were fulfilled, she is nevertheless poorer in typical possession of physical and temporal treasures.

The New Testament believer is temporally subjected to the emperor, not to David. In that sense he lives and dies in the world, not in the holy land. To be sure, he has a king, a citizenship, a treasure of salvation, but as yet only spiritually. The shadow of the natural possession of everything in which old Israel could rejoice, sometimes to the point of dancing, has perished in the Babylonian captivity, not only for the Jew, but also for the believer. Although Christ is in the believer and consequently the spirit is life on account of righteousness, even so the body is as yet dead on account of sin [Rom. 8:10]. During this dispensation, the kingdom of God does not come with observation [Luke 17:20]. God's children are in dispersion. They are strangers here below [Heb. 11:13]. They have no earthly fatherland, no "home rule," like the Jews at the time of Christ. Their captivity lasts until Christ's return.

We do indeed live in the last times. It is the last day, indeed the last hour. But still it is the last hour of this earthly dispensation; the everlasting day has not yet risen upon us. We certainly may not revert to the old dispensation in order with the chiliast to expect during this dispensation the fulfillment of the shadows that are as yet unfulfilled.

Even less may we conceive that fulfillment after the manner of the postmillennialists. During this spiritual dispensation there is no gradual progression in the fulfilling of the shadows. We never reach the eternal reality by our own efforts. The transition from one stage of development into a higher comes about by a special intervention of God. Although there is progression in revelation, consciousness, application, and expectation according to the nature of each dispensation, nevertheless the dispensations do not thus gradually merge with each other. The church does not produce heaven nor the world, hell. Presently, the everlasting dispensation is fruit of the final catastrophe.[41]

Thus the relationship of the elect kernel of the human race to the reprobate husk that temporarily surrounds it during the New Testament dispensation is spiritual and organic in nature. Along those lines proceeds the realizing of the covenantal conception. What at first lies hidden and intertwined in one and the same root comes to revelation, development, and separation by the word of God that is "quick, and powerful, and sharper than any two-edged sword, piercing even to the dividing asunder of soul and spirit, and of the joints and marrow, and is a discerner of the thoughts and intents of the heart" [Heb. 4:12]. Because no creature is hidden from the God of the covenant, but all things are naked and open before him, with the full realizing of his covenantal conception he will also complete the separation of spiritually dissimilar elements, both in the individual and in the community, as one separates chaff from the grain, no matter how these may share in the society of natural life and may formally agree.

---

41 This penetrating objection to the dream of postmillennialism is characteristically Reformed. The church does not bring about the glorious victory of the messianic covenant and kingdom in history. She does not bring about this victory even with the help of the Messiah. The final victory comes by a wonder of grace, that is, the coming of the Head of the covenant on the clouds.

CHAPTER 6

COVENANT AND ANTITHESIS

*The aspect of the covenant that comes to the fore in this chapter is the antithesis. The antithesis is the separation of the covenantal friends of God from his enemies and the warfare between the two parties throughout history. Historically, it was this confession of the antithesis that brought down on Danhof and his colleague at that time, Herman Hoeksema, the rage of those who embraced common grace. Danhof and Hoeksema criticized the theory of common grace as the denial of the antithesis. In the treatment of the antithesis that follows, Danhof sets forth the antithesis as an aspect of the life of the covenant, if (as he has earlier demonstrated) the covenant is viewed as fellowship with God. Antithesis is a covenantal truth. The reason that antithesis becomes a foreign, even detested, word in Reformed circles and the reason that the reality of the antithesis disappears from the life of the churches and of the individuals is that there is little covenantal consciousness in the churches. Nominally Reformed people do not know themselves as God's friends and their life as friendship with God. For this reason they are able to cultivate friendships with the ungodly and enjoy fellowship with the unfruitful works of darkness.—*Trans.

This spiritual-organic separating from each other of what naturally belongs together occasions strife. This operation is carried out not in a soulless body but in a living organism. Moreover, this living organism resists this special work. Natural humanity is no stock or block but an enemy of God. Passivity is an utter impossibility. Inspired by Satan, humanity resists and opposes God.

According to its kernel that human race must be changed into God's friend. Such happens in regeneration. As a result the original organism of the human race lives, according to kernel and husk, out of two antithetically opposed and mutually exclusive principles. The principles of sin and grace work through. Adam's race becomes increasingly like a house divided against itself. The one people rises up against the other. Men hate each other and deliver each other up to prisons: the brother, his brother; the father, his child; the daughter-in-law, her mother-in-law. Indeed, the individual human is divided against himself. There is strife in one's own heart, in one's own house, in state and society, in the spheres of business and industry, of science and art, in each sphere of influence, along the whole line of all human deliberation, inclination, and practice, in ever-increasing measure.

Strictly speaking, this entire fearful struggle is warfare between God and Satan. As the covenantal conception is from God and its realization is through God, so also is the warfare of the covenant God's. The tightening of the band of the covenant, which for the elect kernel is life, salvation, and communion of friendship and for the reprobate husk is death, destruction, and communion of wrath, takes place through God. In that absolute sense, man has no warfare on earth. But where the devil, tempting man, attacks God in his kingdom in and for and through man, there God for the maintenance of his covenant also attacks Satan in the kingdom that Satan supposed himself to have established. In other words, God attacks Satan in and through man. The battle line in this warfare runs through the world of the children of men, dividing it into children of light and children of darkness. In the final analysis, God and Satan fight each other through man. In this warfare, regenerated humanity fights for God against the entire kingdom of darkness, and unregenerated humanity, under the spell of Satan's enchantment, fights against the kingdom of light.

According to its regenerated kernel humanity again guards the Lord's inheritance. As covenantal companion of God it fights the Lord's battle. It is very willing in the day of the Lord's power [Ps. 110:3]. In the warfare for the cause of the Son of God it finds its purpose [*ideall*] during this dispensation. In keeping with the original covenantal conception, it maintains God's sovereignty over every creature, claims the entire life of creation in principle for Christ, and opposes everything that withstands. That is God's triumph over Satan.

In that warring people of the Lord, God's creation conception concerning man according to the principle of the covenant of grace is initially realized.[42] By warring, that people reveals that it stands in active covenantal fellowship with God. It shows subjectively the enmity established by God against Satan and his kingdom. The covenant of works is fulfilled in the covenant of grace, and the rupture of sin is healed. God's thought that man would build and guard a garden of the Lord is realized in principle in the people whom he sanctified in Jesus Christ.

Out of this practical covenantal view, the most outstanding children of God have lived in their best moments. Abraham's prayer for Sodom and the prayers of Moses and Daniel for Israel can be explained only out of their love to God. They did not pray for themselves and, strictly speaking, not even for the people of Sodom and the children of Israel. According to Genesis 18:25; Exodus 32:11–13; Exodus 33:12, 16; Exodus 34:8–9; Numbers 14:13–19; and Daniel 9:17, 19 these prayers were for God himself. They purposed the maintenance of God's holiness, righteousness, covenantal faithfulness, and honor.

Were not these men accepted of God exactly in this way? Daniel was a man who was very pleasing to God. With Moses the Lord spoke face to face, as a man speaks with his friend. Abraham was called a friend of God. Undoubtedly, especially in their intercession, these men were types of him whose seeking of God's honor can only be explained from his friendship to the Father.

Granted, neither regarding the children of God nor regarding Christ does the idea of friendship always stand on the foreground.

---

42 Danhof speaks of God's "creation conception concerning man." The Creator's purpose with Adam on day six of creation week was not an unfallen race living peacefully and developing "culture" in and around paradise. Rather, God's purpose was the people of the covenant of grace in Jesus Christ, who are now battling, against huge odds, on behalf of the Godhead of the triune God.

Nevertheless, their life in fellowship with God reaches its zenith in this friendship. Certainly Christ came to seek and to save the lost, and at the same time he has endured the cross and despised the shame for the joy that was set before him [Heb. 12:2], while his work also aimed at the disturbance of Satan's kingdom. Yet in and through all of that he still purposed the honor of his Father above all. His love to the Father was friendship.

Similarly God's child flees perdition, according to the very nature of spiritual life keeps the Lord's commands, and strives after his own crown of glory. But even more, he fights against the powers of darkness and for the coming of Christ's kingdom out of love for the God of the covenant. For him the friendship of his God exceeds everything else. God is his creator, lord, and father, but especially and above all his friend. As far as he is concerned, all other communion is subjected to the fellowship of the friendship of God. Therefore, as formerly Enoch and Noah walked with God (Gen. 5:22; 6:9), so also in his best moments does the believer walk with the God of the covenant. In this he finds his life's goal and final destiny.

Even though the life of God's child does not always attain the heights of conscious fellowship with God, still his way of life often cannot be explained other than from love to the Lord. Why would Enoch otherwise have continued prophesying of the Lord's coming for judgment until men sought his life [Jude 14–15; Heb. 11:5]? Noah condemned the world by the ark that he built [Heb. 11:7]. David conducted the wars of the Lord [vv. 32–34]. Elijah desired the Lord to answer him by fire so that Israel would recognize the Lord as God; in this connection, he slew all the prophets of Baal [1 Kings 18]. Even though he might have gotten away with simply not praying, Daniel kneeled three times a day before his God, exactly as always before, despite the firm command of the king [Dan. 6].

Believers of every age, place, and people "had trial of cruel mockings and scourgings, yea, moreover of bonds and imprisonment: they were stoned, they were sawn asunder, were tempted, were slain with the sword: they wandered about in sheepskins and goatskins; being destitute, afflicted, tormented" [Heb. 11:36–37]. Why all of this, if not on account of their friendship with God? How else can persecution of the faithful and martyrdom be explained than from the principles of hate and love with regard to God? The gathering together of Herod and Pilate with the Gentiles and the people of Israel against God's holy child Jesus, whom God had anointed, permits no other explanation [Acts 4:27]. The same holds for the roaring rage of Satan against the elect of God. Especially the prayer of the souls under the altar demands this explanation (Rev. 6:9–11).

Indeed, another reason for the existence of God's people on earth cannot even be conceived. If that people has been created to proclaim God's praise, as scripture teaches, and by grace has been made worthy and fit for this, how could it ever have for its task "to make this world better," "to create a social uplift," or the like? Also, how would such a thing harmonize with the doctrines of predestination, man's inability for good, and the organic development of the sinful life of our race?

Strictly speaking, it must then also be decisively denied that "in Christianizing social life the church finds its duty and opportunity." No! Rather, in the struggle of all the ages the issue is the name of the Lord. That was the issue in paradise. That was the issue between Cain and Abel, Lamech and Enoch, Abraham and the king of Sodom, Moses and Pharaoh, Samuel and Agag, David and Goliath, Nebuchadnezzar and the three friends of Daniel, Antiochus Epiphanes and Mattathias the priest, Stephen and the blinded Jews, Polycarp and the Roman emperor, and John Hus with many thousands of martyrs and the false church of Rome. That will be the issue between the Lord's faithful witnesses and the antichrist.

That humanity, or even the more civilized peoples, has known how to develop unto a higher ethical life before God by the influence of the regenerated congregation cannot possibly be maintained by one who knows history. Rather, it appears from every page of history that the different spiritual relations to God have divided the members of the children of men throughout all ages.

According to that dividing line the believer is of the party of the living God. Being of the Lord, he lives to the Lord, and he dies to the Lord [Rom. 14:8]. His relation to God determines for him every other relation. He knows no duties or rights that do not proceed from the principle of the worship and service of God. He lives from that principle always, everywhere, in every sphere, and in every relation. Since his God is the God of the whole earth, nowhere is he neutral in relation to God. He serves God with wife and child; with ability and energy; by means of family, school, state, and society; and in relation to every creature. In this service of God he opposes whatever resists God. He serves God according to the demand of the circumstances and the nature of this dispensation.

There is for him no isolated life of world flight.[43] Even less are there any spheres to which the antithesis of good and evil during this dispensation would not have to be applied. There is no culture independent of man and consequently neutral. This holds also for science and art and for all work of man. Therefore, the believer never seeks anything in itself, that is, apart from its relation to God, but in everything he seeks God.

Regarding the absolute difference of the deepest principles from which the unregenerated and the regenerated live in their relation to God, the believer does not seek any unnatural, premature division. Believing, he waits upon the Lord without impatience.[44]

Nevertheless, he recognizes no essential wisdom for life that originates from creation, including a system of science on which all the spiritually dissimilar children of Adam might together build. He maintains that the regenerated kernel of man, and they only, again in principle know all things by the anointing of the Holy Ghost. Therefore, as a Christian he mentions in the hearing of the children of men man's relation to God; redemption in Christ; regeneration of the Spirit; godly principles for his personal, family, social, and political life; true wisdom, science, and art; right and justice; morality and religion; and man's past, present, and future. He demands acceptance and application of his preaching, prophesying of Christ's return to judgment.

---

43 *Een afzonderlijk leven uit de schepping.*
44 Danhof warns against all rash, radical application of the antithesis. One thinks of the parable of the tares of the field in Matthew 13:24–30, 36–43.

With this the believer does not run ahead of the time.[45] He expects no salvation in the future from the moral improvements of humanity. He does not try to renew the earth. He desires true separation of church and state. He does not aim at any regeneration of family, school, society, magistrate, science, and art. The natural is indeed very really first for him, and only then the spiritual.

However, he will allow no false separation between nature and grace, no fictitious dividing of life into creation and regeneration. Humanity, as well as the entire cosmos, is for him an organism that on account of man's sin and God's grace lives from a twofold principle of life, according to the lines of election and reprobation. Since his own life is rooted in regeneration, as much as in him lies he tries to direct the entire life of the organic whole of the creatures, according to the nature of this earthly dispensation, to the Creator of all things, who is worthy of this. In this way his life becomes a serving of God out of love.

We who are called Christians because we are members of Christ by faith and thus are partakers of his anointing ought to do this, so that we confess his name, present ourselves a living thank offering to him, and fight against sin and the devil with a free and good conscience in this life, and hereafter in eternity reign with him over all creatures.[46] This is a demand now more than ever, because of the seriousness of the time, our own weaknesses, the ever-growing might of the enemy, and most of all, for the cause of the Son of God.

No matter how many centuries still separate us from the final end of this dispensation, concerning the development of all sorts of connections and relations we undoubtedly stand at the beginning of the very end. According to its social aspect, human life in church and world is beginning to be permeated with the Spirit of Christ and with the spirit of the antichrist. A further positive development of mutual earthly relationships is inconceivable. Indeed, the period of thorough decay can last for a considerable time, and many positive institutions,

---

45 In this paragraph Danhof exposes the error of millennialism, that is, Christian reconstructionism and other forms of postmillennialism, which expect in history what God has destined for the end of history.

46 Heidelberg Catechism A 32, in Schaff, *Creeds of Christendom*, 3:318.

such as family, state, and society, could be replaced by more negative human institutions and organizations. However, scripture does not seem to recognize such a radical development in the sphere of family and society.

Although I grant the possibility of such a development, it seems that according to biblical testimony the institution of family life, the organization of society, and the relation of civil authority and citizen and of master and servant [heer en knecht, employer and employee] during the reign of the antichrist will not essentially differ from our present conditions and relationships. Regarding this question, recall the conditions at the time of the flood, in the days of Antiochus Epiphanes, and at the destruction of Jerusalem. Recall also the outlining of the time of the final end by Jesus and in Revelation 13. Of course, there will be a difference of degree. For the rest, however, the types of the final battle seem to outline also the conditions of that time.

Then the possibility must be conceded of an extremely fast development of unregenerated, nominally Christian peoples unto the measure and intensity of hate and hostility against God and his witnesses that have been appointed for them. This speedy development is a very real possibility in light of the powerful concentration of all sorts of forces and powers, especially in the social sphere.

Our battle will then increase in severity and be fought on every side. The opposition between flesh and Spirit grows as the life of divided humanity on earth develops itself. Principles work through. History proves this. If the difference between Cain and Abel had been a merely personal quarrel, rising out of different viewpoints in the matter of sacrificing, soon thereafter the children of Adam would have gone their own ways in choosing their calling, dwelling place, and manner of life. However, already before the flood Lamech had distinct features of a materialistic-humanistic world and life view, and Enoch had distinct features of a spiritual-theological world and life view. Therein lay the beginning of the end of the first world. This must be understood.

The tower of Babel and the confusion of speech attendant on it cause us to see the very first end of the second world. Already then the concentration of the powers of wickedness seemed complete, but the perfection of this concentration is yet delayed. This is due to the interventions of God and the radical changes he brought about.

On account of the separation of Israel, the antithesis between church and world during the old dispensation displayed a national color. During the captivity there was a brief, violent concentration of hostile powers under Antiochus Epiphanes, which enables us to view the final battle of the spirits in a sharply outlined, typical picture.[47]

After Pentecost and prior to Constantine, the nature of this battle was emphatically spiritual. It had to do exclusively with the nature of the authority of the emperor: whether the emperor ruled by the grace of God, yes or no. One should take note of this.

The dark Middle Ages brought about some abatement of the battle but little essential change. The conversion of Emperor Constantine did not in reality introduce a period of power and rule for the true disciples of Christ. It was not the emperor but Constantine who was converted.[48] The false rest of the historical church of those days was not a victory seized too soon, but a victory that was wrongly conceived.[49] People did not understand that the emperor per se does not fall into the category of regeneration.

Later on, people understood that even less. With the Reformation came unique development on this point. The battle was begun against the false church. Christendom now saw itself positioned over against the open enemy, heathendom, just as before, and over against a secret enemy, the false church in the church of Rome. From now on the church must develop itself in the way of that twofold battle. Help from the state, however, was by no means despised. To be sure, people sang, "We desire no earthly might," but they depended on the sword just the same.

---

47 Danhof refers to Antiochus Epiphanes more than once as significant for the hostility between the elect, believing church and the reprobate, ungodly world. Antiochus (d. 163 BC) was the king of Syria who persecuted Judah and attempted to destroy the worship of Jehovah God in the period between the testaments. This history is recorded in the two apocryphal books of the Maccabees. Antiochus is prophesied in the latter part of the book of Daniel.

48 Danhof distinguishes between the office ("emperor") and the man ("Constantine").—Ed.

49 Danhof employs an effective play on words: *"niet een te vroeg gegrepen, maar eene verkeerd begrepen triumf."*

Especially in German lands, princes decided the worship of the country. Also in the Netherlands church and state were wrongly united in more than one respect, and many among us still find nothing strange in this. We are still so accustomed to living in the seventeenth century in these matters. We live as though it were still the time when Gustavus Adolphus with thousands of brave soldiers rushed to the aid of the desperate congregation of the Lord,[50] and when men, assembled in synod, decided on doctrinal differences under the protective custody of Prince Maurice.[51] Nevertheless, we must carefully guard against every mistaken notion.[52]

The French Revolution changed the historical nature of the battle. The sphere of the conflict was greatly expanded. Over against the comprehensive world and life view of Calvinism, the most beautiful fruit of the Reformation, the French Revolution posited its atheistic-humanistic program for the life of the entire human race. According to that program, the lights of heaven must be extinguished, and the church doors closed. The civil magistrate must rule by the grace of the people, and life in society is established according to social contracts. The battle then encompassed every sphere of life, and it affected the practice and experience of all. The program begun by the French Revolution did not contain idle fantasies of this or that philosopher, but ideas that were applied practically and forced upon the world by a mighty people with the sword in its fist. The steel sword passed from the hands of those who promised to defend the truths of the gospel into the hands of those who placed themselves at the head of the enemies of Christ.

Obviously this movement could not immediately succeed in all its efforts, because initially an extremely negative nature of the movement was necessary. Nevertheless, the principles worked through, right up to our own time, in every sphere, among all ranks and stations,

---

50 Gustavus II Adolphus (1594–1632) was king of Sweden. He is popularly regarded as the savior of Protestantism in Germany by military interventions and victories.

51 The reference is to the Synod of Dordt in 1618–19, which was called and supervised by Prince Maurice of the ruling House of Orange in the Netherlands.

52 That is, regarding the relationship of church and state. Danhof obviously was no friend of the idea that the state is called to defend the true church and punish heretics and other spiritual enemies of the church with what he calls "the steel sword."

until the movement will culminate in the coming and completion of the kingdom of man. From now on the people of the Lord, especially Calvinists, have to fight not only against heathendom and the false church, but particularly against the ever-increasing might of man who has "come of age" under the inspiration of hell. This conflict extends to every sphere of life.

The development of the life of the human race is now powerfully directed by liberation [emancipatie], specialization, and union. The need for cooperation is felt everywhere. Salvation is expected from organization, management, and system. Men work for union especially in the social and industrial sphere. One is permitted to maintain worship, provided the worship is subjected to the judgment of man. Dividing lines, however, must be done away with. As a result, like-minded people more and more unite to work out their own fundamental principles, systematically and effectively, in the highly varied and complicated life of our age. Naturally in this way the mingling of spiritually dissimilar elements ceases, and there is a grouping of powers according to the spiritual principles from which one lives. One should not expect anything other than this in the near future. The battle will concern the covenant of our God.

The typical picture of that coming battle was the fearful struggle of the Maccabees against Antiochus Epiphanes. Then the battle concerned the holy covenant still in its theocratic form.

The church's battle becomes more spiritual, although not in the sense that our enemy will make no use of the steel sword. He will indeed make use of the sword. Already today all kinds of social reforms are introduced with the help of the state. Everything is decided by the voting of the people. Presently, perhaps, such will be the case with the Christian school. Evidently even the family does not remain entirely unassailable.

All of this occurs while we—exactly because the issue has to do with principles about which men in the nature of the case may not vote—are unable to use even the few votes we might have at our disposal in other instances. To place our confidence in the outcome of the ballot box is very foolish. Counting votes is not only impractical but also unspiritual—impractical because it is a foregone conclusion that every cause of a somewhat Reformed nature will be defeated at the ballot box; unspiritual because the issue in our battle in a special sense consists of eternal, divine principles that are not to be decided by voting.

Those principles must be presented to all peoples plainly and clearly, so that the conflict exactly for this reason may grow worse. Then we are the most at home in our spiritual element. Then we are able to fight the most purely with spiritual weapons. Then as a result we stand the strongest.

Pressure from the side of the enemy is bound to come. The enemy will know how to turn the temporal might of the emperor over the bodies and possessions of men against the friends of Christ. All the types and preformations of the antichrist and his kingdom and the experiences of individual Christians, who powerfully come to the fore in critical times, prove that such will indeed take place in the future. For this we must prepare ourselves beforehand. Also the fainthearted among us have to get ready. The issue will be the covenant of our God. There is no escape from the steel sword of our enemies.

However, because we fight on behalf of the cause of God, we are able to trust in the Lord who is truly Lord. He will accomplish it. His cause will triumph. Strengthened by his grace, we will not lose the crown. Redeemed from all the might of the enemy and more than conquerors, we enter into the joy of our Lord and into the everlasting covenant of the friendship of our God.

ON THE THEORY
OF COMMON GRACE

HERMAN HOEKSEMA

INTRODUCTION

Introduction to *On the Theory of Common Grace*

On the Theory of Common Grace was discovered in the personal papers of Herman Hoeksema after his death. The content indicates that it was a paper presented for discussion to a gathering of Christian Reformed ministers. The meeting was held when Hoeksema was yet a minister in good standing in the Christian Reformed Church, but already the theory of common grace had become a controversial topic in that church. This was due to Professor Ralph Janssen's[1] appeal to the theory in his defense against the charge of holding and teaching a higher critical view of scripture. Hoeksema wrote the essay, therefore, shortly before his expulsion from the Christian Reformed Church in 1925.

The essay is an exegetical exposure of the theory that God's grace is common to all humans, reprobate and elect alike, and an exegetical defense of the Reformed doctrine that God's grace is particular—only toward, for, and in those humans who belong to Jesus Christ according to eternal election.

Evident toward the end of the essay are Hoeksema's practical concerns in his opposition to the common grace theory of Abraham Kuyper and the Christian Reformed Church. The doctrine of a common grace of God "obliterates the antithesis." In Hoeksema's judgment, the loss

---

1 Ralph Janssen was professor of Old Testament in Calvin Theological Seminary in 1902 to 1906 and in 1914 to 1922. He was removed from office by the synod of 1922 due to his errant views on scripture. Both Hoeksema and Danhof were members of the committee appointed to investigate Janssen's views. For more information see Herman Hanko, *For Thy Truth's Sake* (Grandville, MI: Reformed Free Publishing Association, 2000), 37–53.

of the antithesis was clear both in the Netherlands and in the Christian Reformed Church already at that time.

Highly as Hoeksema esteemed Kuyper, he put the great man's theory of common grace to the test of scripture and found it wanting. In Hoeksema's words, there were two Kuypers: the Kuyper of the antithesis and the Kuyper of common grace. The latter negated the former.

The essay was first published in the *Protestant Reformed Theological Journal* (2, no. 1 [December, 1968]:19–45).

—David J. Engelsma

Among the personal papers of the late Rev. Herman Hoeksema, I discovered two essays on common grace. The essay here presented is the second. As far as I know, neither paper has been published previously. The first paper would also have made interesting reading, but it was not feasible to publish because the last couple of pages were missing, and it was impossible to fill in the missing section editorially except by guesswork. Besides, the second essay is in more than one way the more valuable, especially because of the exegetical material contained in it.

Perhaps the reader wonders why an essay on this subject is published, especially since the author's views on the subject have been thoroughly and frequently expounded in various other publications. The answer to this question is twofold.

The first reason is historical. The contents of both essays make clear that they were written before 1924, probably during the very early period of the common grace controversy in the Christian Reformed Church. I do not know the exact time and occasion when they were delivered. Since the author works with the Hebrew and Greek, the occasion was almost certainly some kind of ministers' gathering, either an area ministers' conference or possibly a meeting of the group of ministers who wrote in the *Witness*. Obviously the subject of common grace had already been discussed. Yet the time was such that supporters and opponents of the theory of common grace were still meeting and engaging in face-to-face discussions. It seems therefore that these essays were delivered in the early 1920s, before the controversy had reached the stage of ecclesiastical polemics.

The second reason for publishing is that this essay demonstrates that from the outset Hoeksema dealt with this subject in a thoroughly exegetical manner and that over the years, apart from some refinements and clarifications, he did not deviate from his original exegetical approach and position. The question he insisted on asking and to which he gave answer throughout the years was, in the light of scripture, what grace do the wicked receive?

This is interesting, because it explains the author's approach at that time. His approach is found in the introductory section of the first essay:

For more than one reason I have looked forward to this occasion with eager anticipation, and I am glad that it has come. First, it gives me pleasure to think that the interest in matters of such a purely doctrinal nature as common grace is still alive in our circles. It cannot be called a characteristic of our age in general that it is deeply interested in doctrinal and theological questions. It rather busies itself with the practical problems of this world. It is, however, a sad delusion that the practical side of life can be divorced from its doctrinal foundation. For that reason I am glad to notice, in the midst of much unrest in our churches these days, that there still is a lively interest in questions pertaining to our Reformed doctrine and Calvinistic life view.

Second, I like nothing better than a public and open discussion. When I say this, I mean on subjects extra-confessional, concerning which there is room for difference of opinion. I consider common grace to be such a subject. If it were otherwise, I would not speak to you tonight. If I intend to make propaganda for any ideas that run contrary to our Reformed standards, my place would not be here tonight. But this I do not intend to do. From beginning to end I will remain four-square on the basis of the Reformed standards. The subject on which I speak to you this evening is plainly extra-confessional, as I will show presently. On such subjects I like public discussions. That is why I am here this evening. I invite discussion. If you wish, I invite debate and contradiction. I have only one condition: tackle the subject, not the person. Not because I am so over-anxious about my person, but I am about my subject.

Third, I think the subject we will discuss tonight is of grave importance. Not, of course, as long as it remains a mere question of rain and sunshine. A person asked me the other day whether I could not see that the Lord sent his rain also upon the wicked. I told him in my opinion there would be very few umbrellas and raincoats sold if he didn't. That is not the question tonight. But if the question is asked, not whether the wicked receive rain and sunshine and whether they develop, but whether they receive grace—grace they have in common with the righteous—I think it is a significant one. To my mind, as you answer this question, you will answer the question of the antithesis. The reporter on the speech of Volbeda in *Onze Toekomst* [Our future] saw this clearly, I think.

But—and after this "but" I will plunge headlong into my subject—I realize that I have a difficult task before me tonight, and I kindly beg you to realize this with me. My view, which I will propose, differs from the general opinion among our people on this subject. The general opinion has been trained to believe in common grace. If this were all, my position tonight would not be so precarious. But it is not all. Great theologians for whom I too have the highest esteem, men like Abraham Kuyper, have taken a stand for this view and developed it. Over against such a giant I am but a small man. Yet I do not agree with him. It is almost inconceivable that such a little man as I could possibly be right on any subject on which Kuyper differs with him. It even makes some people smile piteously to think of the very idea. Therefore, I will ask you to grant at least the possibility—let us say, it's a very small, a faint one— that my view is after all correct, and Kuyper's is misleading in this case.

The body of the first essay was then devoted to the demonstration that the doctrine of common grace is not confessionally Reformed, that is, not a truth that has been expressed or developed in the three forms of unity; a brief exposition of Kuyper's theory of common grace;

an exposition of the scriptural concept *grace*; and a refutation of the idea that both the righteous and the wicked, the elect and the reprobate, receive grace from God in this present life.

In the last section of the first paper (the incomplete section), the threefold conclusion mentioned in the introductory part of the second essay was set forth. That second essay I now present in its entirety.

—Homer C. Hoeksema

Introduction

The conclusion reached in my last paper was threefold. First, I maintained that there is only one grace operating through Jesus Christ as the mediator of redemption, and that grace is based only on his atoning blood. Second, I explained that although in this world the wicked are organically connected with the righteous, live under the same external influences, both evil and good, and develop in the same world, they receive no grace. All things are to them a curse. Third, I developed the idea that there is no such thing as a check upon sin. Sin, finding its root in the principal sin Adam committed in paradise, develops as fast as possible along the organic line of the development of the human race.

The criticism passed on my paper was varied. Most of the brethren did not agree with me, which was no more than I had expected. But I wish to state also that there was not unanimity of thought among the brethren with regard to the subject we are discussing. More than one expressed the opinion that the view of the late Abraham Kuyper cannot be maintained as correct. I received the impression that some of the brethren agreed that there is only one grace. Also in regard to the idea of grace there were different opinions. I think there is room after this essay for one more paper in which the brethren meet the difficulties I raised and clearly set forth their views of this theory.

Some of the difficulties connected with the theory of common grace were simply passed by in silence. Especially I call attention to the very serious question, how is it possible that the righteous and holy God can in any way assume an attitude of loving-kindness to the wicked, whether you consider them as reprobate, as unregenerate, or as actively wicked? The question is of great importance, because it deals with our relation to the world, and is worthy of our most serious consideration. Although I do not expect the brethren to agree with me over against a man like Kuyper, I humbly submit my presentation of this truth once more to you, begging at least to be heard with a certain measure of sympathy.

If I am not seriously mistaken, the question is an actual one even in the Netherlands. It cannot escape our attention that Dr. Valentijn Hepp, of Watergraafsmeer, one of the keenest minds in the Netherlands, who has disagreed with Kuyper regarding the doctrine of common grace in his dissertation *Testimonium Spiritus Sancti* [Testimony of the Holy Spirit], employs quotation marks whenever he writes common grace.[2] Dr. F. W. Grosheide,[3] in a speech recently given in Leeuwarden, called attention to the worldly mindedness especially among the youth and then mentioned as one of the causes of this transformation to the likeness of the world a false conception of the doctrine of common grace [*een verkeerd opvatten van het leerstuk der algemeene genade*]. The problem therefore is worth our most serious consideration.

The chief criticism—or at least what I consider the chief element in the brethrens' criticism—was that I had not based my paper on scripture. This was hardly correct. I reasoned throughout my paper from such fundamental scriptural truths as the covenant, the image of God, total depravity, God's righteousness, and the organic development of

---

2   Valentijn Hepp (1879–1950) was a prominent minister and theologian in the Reformed Churches in the Netherlands. In 1922 Hepp succeeded Herman Bavinck as professor of theology, in the field of dogmatics, at the Free University in Amsterdam. Although Hoeksema here speaks favorably of Dr. Hepp and even supposes that he—Hoeksema—can find support for his denial of common grace in a certain doubtfulness in Hepp concerning the doctrine, later Hoeksema chides Hepp for intruding into the controversy over common grace in the United States. Hoeksema took it ill of Hepp that Hepp superciliously—as Hoeksema saw it—offered advice to the combatants in the Christian Reformed Church in America without entering into the issue of common grace itself. Hoeksema was reacting to a series of editorials in the Dutch periodical *De Reformatie*. These articles were published and distributed in a booklet titled *Het Misverstand in zake de Leer der Algemeene Genade* [The misunderstanding in the matter of the doctrine of common grace], 2nd ed. (Grand Rapids, MI: Eerdmans–Sevensma, 1923). In his booklet Hepp sided with the Christian Reformed proponents of common grace and accused Danhof and Hoeksema of misunderstanding the doctrine of common grace as it was held by Kuyper and Bavinck and as it was being promoted by Christian Reformed theologians such as Van Baalen. The work in which Hoeksema and Danhof express their disgust for Hepp's meddling in the controversy over common grace is *Along Pure Paths*. They consider their refutation of the American advocates of common grace in this booklet to be the refutation also of Hepp (84–85).—Ed.

3   Frederik Willem Grosheide (1881–1972) was a Dutch New Testament scholar who served as professor of New Testament at the Free University in Amsterdam.—Ed.

the human race. I regard as a scriptural basis not only the exegesis of a few or even of many passages, but also the employment of and deduction from those fundamental conceptions that are commonly accepted among us. Besides, I called attention to three passages from scripture that, according to Kuyper, constitute the classical passages for the doctrine of common grace. Naturally, time was lacking for more detailed work. Nevertheless, I welcome the opportunity the brethren offered me to present some of the passages from the word of God that may be quoted in favor of my view, as well as to offer a more or less exegetical study of the conception *grace* as revealed in Holy Writ. This I propose to do in this paper, to which I ask that you give your kind attention.

First, I will speak on the scriptural idea of *grace*. Second, I will refute the passages offered for discussion by some of the brethren in support of common grace. Third, I will call attention to a few passages in support of my view of the matter.

The Scriptural Idea of *Grace*

The difference regarding the scriptural use of the term *grace* is that the Old Testament uses several words to express approximately the same idea, while the New Testament constantly uses one term, which for that very reason is broad and elastic in meaning. The three words from the Old Testament that must be considered are *hesed*, *rason*, and *chen*. Of these, *chen* is the word the Septuagint renders almost invariably by the New Testament *charis* (grace). It is derived from the root *chanan*, which signifies "to incline toward anyone or something," denoting an attitude of the body. Clearly the word could further denote an inclining of the mind and heart toward anyone, being favorably disposed. Hence etymologically *chen* signifies "favor, good will, kindness, grace." It is used often in the most general sense, as in Genesis 18:3: "My Lord, if now I have found favor in thy sight, pass not away, I pray thee, from thy servant."

This expression occurs frequently. Especially the verb is used in cases where the opposite of God's favor might be expected, as in Psalm 6:2, where the poet, after having implored Jehovah that he might not rebuke him in anger nor chasten him in sore displeasure, says, "Have mercy upon me, O LORD." Thus it is also in Psalm 51:1, where the poet, having fallen deeply into sin, comes to Jehovah with the well-known prayer, "Have mercy upon me, O God." Thus *chen* also denotes what God in his favor bestows on his people, in contrast with his dealings with the wicked and scoffers. We read in Proverbs 3:34, "Surely he scorneth the scorners: but he giveth grace unto the lowly." *Chen* thus signifies "favor, good will, loving-kindness." It may denote an attitude of God, an attitude of his favor, perhaps revealed to those who are unworthy. It is employed to express what Jehovah in loving-kindness bestows on the objects of his grace.

Rason comes from the root *rasah*, which means "to delight in any person or object, to be pleased with one's presence, to be on good terms with anyone," and hence, "to have friendly association with someone." Thus the substantive derivation also means "good will, delight, favor, grace." In this way the word is used in Isaiah 49:8: "In the time of goodwill, delight, the time of grace, have I answered thee." This word is also used to denote concretely the benefits bestowed in good pleasure and grace—gracious gifts or gifts of grace.

Hesed, often translated by *eleos* (mercy) in the Septuagint, comes from the root *hasad*. Its fundamental meaning also seems to be that of loving-kindness and favor, but with the connotation of zeal and fervor. When used with regard to Jehovah, it expresses that he burns with zeal and eagerness to show his grace and favor to those who fear him. In the King James *hesed* is frequently translated as "mercy." Yet *hesed* is very closely akin to *chen* and *charis* and is used sometimes in the most general sense. Thus it is used in Daniel 1:9: "Now God had brought Daniel into favour and tender love with the prince of the eunuchs," a passage where the translation "mercy" would hardly fit. The same word is used by Isaiah in chapter 55:3 when he speaks of the gracious gifts of God's covenant bestowed on David as "the sure [or faithful] mercies of David." *Hesed* is used to denote both an attitude of God toward men and a relation of man to God. As an attitude of God it denotes zealous love, ardent favor, and mercy. As a relation of man to God it expresses love, gratitude, and piety.

In the New Testament there is only one word (*charis*) for *grace* that has a variety of meanings, yet with one fundamental thought beneath it. That fundamental significance is always favor, loving-kindness, friendship.

First, *charis* is used with a connotation closely akin to that of *rason*; then it means that which is delightful, charming, lovely, attractive. In this way it is used in Luke 4:22, where the word clearly has the sense of pleasing and charming: "And all bare him witness, and wondered at the gracious words which proceeded out of his mouth." The genitive, literally meaning "words of grace," is used here to denote the impression the words of Jesus made on his audience. His words were charming and pleasing in their effect on the people's minds. He spoke gracefully.

Second, *charis* is used to denote favor and goodwill in the most general sense, with respect to God and man. Thus it is used in Luke 2:52: "Jesus increased in wisdom and stature, and in favour with God and man." In Acts 7:46 we read of David "who found favour before God," where the word is evidently used in the same sense as the Hebrew employs it, and it signifies favor in the most general sense.

Third, *charis* is used with the same fundamental meaning of favor and loving-kindness, but directed toward those who are unworthy in themselves but worthy in Christ. The definition given last month by some of the brethren, that grace is love to the wicked or guilty, is a very imperfect one. It does not consider the fundamental significance of the word with its variety of uses, and it forgets that God does not and cannot show his favor to those who are absolutely unworthy in every sense.

The cross of Christ is the plainest testimony of this truth in history. If God could have shown his favor to the wicked, the atonement would become a mystery. But his grace is revealed to those who have not merited it themselves, but who are worthy because they belong to Christ Jesus and are considered in him. In this sense according to grace becomes the opposite of according to debt and according to works. So it is in Romans 11:6: "And if by grace, then is it no more of works: otherwise grace is no more grace." Thus it is also in Romans 5:20:

"But where sin abounded, grace did much more abound." This grace is called the grace of Jesus Christ for the evident reason that it reaches us only from Christ Jesus as its source and meritorious basis. It is the grace of God as received through faith.

Fourth, *charis* is used to denote the operation, or action, of God's favor, or loving-kindness, on the minds and hearts of his people. God's grace becomes an active power through Jesus Christ: it regenerates, brings to faith, justifies, sanctifies, and perfects. In this sense the word is used in Ephesians 2:8: "For by grace are ye saved through faith" and in Acts 18:27: "Who, when he was come, helped them much which had believed through grace."

Fifth, *charis* is used to denote the result, the effect, the fruit of the operation of God's grace. Then it is used in a twofold sense. Sometimes the word is employed to denote the entire subjective spiritual condition of one governed by the power of grace operative in his heart. Thus scripture says in Romans 5:2, "By whom also we have access by faith into this grace wherein we stand." In 2 Peter 3:18 the apostle admonishes, "But grow in grace, and in the knowledge of our Lord and Saviour Jesus Christ." The word is also used to denote all the gifts of grace as we receive them, as mentioned most fully and beautifully in John 1:16: "And of his fulness have all we received, and grace for grace."

Finally, *charis* is used to signify thanks, or gratitude; that is, the acknowledgment of God's loving-kindness and favors as they are received by his people. In this way Paul uses the word frequently, as in Romans 7:25: "I thank [grace] God through Jesus Christ our Lord."

From this brief review of the uses of the word *grace* in the scriptures it becomes evident that the term is used with a great variety of meanings. It may mean an attitude of God toward his people, the operation of that attitude, or the result of God's attitude upon and for the objects of the same. In both testaments it is used to express man's attitude of piety, love, and gratitude to God.

Underneath all the uses of the word *grace* lies the always present and fundamental meaning of favor and loving-kindness. This fundamental thought must always constitute the chief element in the definition of *grace*. The objects, the manifestations, and the operations of this favor may vary, but grace is always favor of God.

If this fundamental significance of grace is connected with man's creation in the image of God and, on the basis of God's image in man, is further connected with the idea of the covenant, you conclude that the grace of God—his favor or loving-kindness—assumes the character of friendship. Favor can be shown to an inferior, to one who stands far below us and is by that favor not lifted from his inferior position. I can show favor to a slave or a servant. But that servant never becomes my friend because of the favor shown to him. I do not live on a level with him. I do not take him into my counsels. I do not confide to him my secrets. I do not live with him in friendly association.

Such is not the nature of God's relation to man. He willed that man would be the creature he could receive into his most intimate communion. Although always remaining creature and servant of the Most High, he would be a friend-servant. To that end God created man in his own image. There is a creaturely likeness of God in man. In a creaturely way man lives on a level with his God. If God reveals to that creature his favor, his grace, this favor actually assumes the nature of friendship that results in friendly association.

Thus we find that the saints are called the friends of God. They walk with God and talk with God. God receives them into his counsels and treats them as his friends. He has no secrets from them. Thus we read in Psalm 25:14: "The secret of the LORD is with them that fear him; and he will shew them his covenant." The original for "secret" (also translated as "friendship") makes us think of a symposium where God exercises friendly association with his people, the people of his covenant. The passage is most beautifully rendered in this versification: "The friendship of the Lord / Is ever with his own / And unto those that fear his name / His faithfulness is shown."[4]

The same idea of confidential association, of a dwelling in most intimate communion, is symbolically expressed in tabernacle and temple;

---

4   No. 62:2, in *The Psalter with Doctrinal Standards, Liturgy, Church Order, and added Chorale Section*, reprinted and revised edition of the 1912 United Presbyterian *Psalter* (Grand Rapids, MI: Eerdmans, 1927; rev. ed. 1995).—Ed.

is tangibly realized in the incarnation of the Word, God's dwelling with man, Immanuel; is often expressed in the New Testament under the symbol of supping together with God or dwelling under one roof with him; and will be realized fully in the New Jerusalem when the temple will be no more and God will spread his tabernacle over all his people. God's loving-kindness, grace, and favor, as shown and imparted to his people, created after his image and received into his covenant, assumes the character of friendship. In grace God is our friend; through grace he makes us his friends.

This relation of friendship, or grace, God assumes and establishes only with those who are righteous before him. As long as man stood in his original righteousness, grace flowed toward him directly. But he sinned, and as a sinner he is cursed, condemned to bear the wrath of God eternally, unless his state is changed. Not to the unworthy but to the worthy God's favor is shown. God's incomprehensible grace is not that he reveals his loving-kindness regardless of their sin and guilt and with the surrender and abandonment of his righteousness, but he gave his only begotten Son—himself—to the depths of death and hell in order to establish his covenant and to make his people the objects of his grace.

The objects of God's grace are unworthy in themselves. It is not of works that they are the objects of God's favor. Nevertheless, they are worthy in Christ, through whom they are justified by faith before God. Faith is reckoned to them for righteousness, and as righteous in Christ Jesus they enter into God's covenantal communion and are the objects of his grace.

Therefore, I maintain that God's grace is his loving-kindness, or favor, assuming the character of friendship toward his covenantal people who receive his favor on the basis of the merits of Christ Jesus alone. Outside of Christ Jesus and his atonement there is no grace. The wrath of God abides on those who do not believe in Jesus. It does not come on them at some future time, but it abides on them forever. For this reason we must preach a God of wrath and anger to all who refuse to believe in Christ Jesus and who trample underfoot the blood of the covenant. For this same reason we must preach to every man that all things are a curse to him as long as he will not flee to the God of grace and salvation in Christ Jesus.

Refutation of the Passages Quoted in Favor of Common Grace

How in the light of this clear and current scriptural doctrine of grace one can speak of common grace, I confess is a mystery to me. Never is the word employed with respect to the wicked, whether they are designated as wicked, reprobate, unregenerate, or unbelievers. You may take your starting point in God's eternal counsel of peace, if you please; or you may begin at the total depravity of the sinner, whose mind is always enmity against God and the imaginations of whose heart are always evil. Or you may take your ground in the covenantal idea. Never will you arrive at any other conclusion than that grace is only for those who are in Christ Jesus.

I will turn to scripture and maintain that the word of God never uses the word *grace* as imparted in any sense to the wicked outside of Christ. They may live under the outward manifestation of grace. They may receive the good things of God's grace together with the righteous. They may receive the same sunshine and rain, the same food and drink and shelter and protection; they may sit under the influence of the same word of God, be baptized with the same baptism, and partake of the same Lord's supper. But the wicked, the unregenerate, the totally depraved, receive no grace. The passages quoted in support of this theory prove nothing else.

The one passage quoted where the word *grace* is used is Isaiah 26:10: "Let favour be shewed to the wicked, yet will he not learn righteousness: in the land of uprightness will he deal unjustly, and will not behold the majesty of the LORD." Apart from the context the future clause means "favor is shown." But even a superficial reading of the entire text reveals very plainly that the clause may not be translated in this manner. It is a hypothetical clause, the protasis of a conditional sentence, the apodosis of which is "yet will he not learn righteousness." The meaning is that even if favor is shown to the wicked, it will do him no good; he will not learn righteousness. The same construction appears in Nehemiah 1:8, where the original reads literally, "Ye shall trespass, and I will scatter you abroad among the peoples," but where the meaning is plainly that of a conditional sentence. Hence the text does not present it as a fact that grace is shown to the wicked.

What is the meaning of Isaiah 26:10? Does Isaiah mean to grant the possibility that the wicked man receives grace? The opposite is true. He means to assert that the wicked man is not at all receptive to grace. Even though he lives right in the midst of the manifestations of God's grace, yet he does not receive them. This is plain from what follows: "yet will he not learn righteousness." This is still more evident from the last part of the text: "in the land of uprightness will he deal unjustly, and will not behold the majesty of the LORD." The meaning is clear. The wicked man lives in the land of uprightness. In that land God reveals the tokens of his grace, in this instance the punishments of Jehovah. In verse 9 the prophet had said, "When thy judgments are in the earth, the inhabitants of the world will learn righteousness." But in verse 10 he singles out the wicked as an exception to this rule. He does not learn righteousness, even though he lives under Jehovah's punishments and judgments. Although Jehovah's majesty through these judgments becomes very evident, he will not behold it.

The passage expresses that even though you place the wicked in the midst of the outward manifestation of God's grace, yet he receives no grace—exactly what I contended in my last paper. I do not deny that the wicked live in the land of uprightness. But I deny that they receive grace. By not heeding the manifestations of grace in the land of uprightness, he is cursed by these very manifestations.

A second illustration of common grace referred to is Ahab. To all his wickedness Ahab had added the crime of shedding Naboth's innocent blood and depriving him of the inheritance of his fathers. Elijah is sent to Ahab to announce God's punishment upon him. What is the punishment announced? Complete destruction, the extermination of Ahab and his house. Jehovah threatens to make the house of Ahab like that of Jeroboam and Baasha. The punishment threatened is final and therefore presupposes that the measure of iniquity is full.

When this final punishment is announced, Ahab humbles himself and wears sackcloth and ashes. He does not come to repentance; it is not his sin that troubles him. No, the hard blow of Jehovah, as announced in Elijah's prophecy, simply crushes him. He is broken. This reveals that the wickedness of Ahab and his house has not reached its culmination. It is not fully ripe. He still fears Jehovah's judgments. The sin of Ahab's house would become ripe in his son. For that reason the threatened extermination, the final punishment of Ahab and his house, is postponed until the next generation. Then the measure of iniquity will be full, and the time for final punishment will have arrived.

In other words, the passage teaches what is taught in all scripture—that final punishment will be inflicted when the measure of iniquity is full. Thus it was with the flood. Thus it was with Sodom and Gomorrah. Thus it will be at the end of the world. The sign of the fullness of this measure of iniquity will be that the world will not be frightened and humbled anymore, even under the threats of severest punishment. Thus it was with the prediluvian world. Thus it was with Sodom. Thus, according to the Lord Jesus, it will be at the end of the world. People will continue to live unconcernedly, marrying and giving in marriage, even though a thousand Noahs are preachers of repentance and righteousness. Sin develops gradually and ripens along the historical, organic line of the development of the human race, and when it is fully ripe final punishment will be inflicted.

Another illustration of the same truth is the example of Nineveh. We must consider the incident of Nineveh as historical fact. The chief significance of the book of Jonah is its prophetic character. Nineveh is typical of the world to whom the gospel will be preached after Christ has risen from the dead. Even as Jonah goes forth after his three days in the fish's belly to preach the word of God to a people outside of Israel, so the risen Christ will go forth after a three days' stay in the heart of the earth to preach the glad evangel to every nation. But that is not our consideration at present. We must view the matter as historical reality.

The wickedness of Nineveh is great, and because of this Jonah is sent to preach its destruction. Also here final punishment is preached:

Jonah must announce extermination of Nineveh as a city. The question also in this case is whether Nineveh, as Sodom of old, is ripe for destruction. Jonah preaches, and Nineveh humbles itself. The announcement of punishment still terrifies its inhabitants. As in Ahab's case, this is a sign that the time for final punishment is not yet ripe.

The destruction of the city is postponed for a while. Surely, not long afterward Nineveh is destroyed. But when Jonah preached against the city, the wickedness of its inhabitants had not reached its culmination. Hence the Lord's final sentence is not executed. Nineveh's example, like that of Ahab, assures us that final punishment will be inflicted only when the measure of iniquity is full. This filling of the measure of iniquity takes place only along the organic line of the development of the race, and even of individual tribes and families.

Other Supporting Passages

The significance of other passages of the word of God can hardly be disputed. It would overturn the entire structure of theology to maintain that God assumes an attitude of grace toward the wicked outside of Christ Jesus. The word of God assures us in strong, indubitably clear language that God hates the wicked, that his wrath is on them continually, and that his curse dwells in their habitations.

We read in Psalm 11:5, "The LORD trieth the righteous: but the wicked and him that loveth violence his soul hateth." Notice the contrast in the text: "the righteous" is contrasted with "the wicked." Over against "his soul hateth" stands "trieth." The idea is that Jehovah may send afflictions to the righteous, but he does so in his grace, to prove, to try, to sanctify them. Even apparently evil things are a manifestation of his grace to the righteous.

It is different with the wicked. God's constant attitude toward them is hatred. His soul hates them. He is filled with enmity against them. Whatever they may have in this life, the fact remains that Jehovah's soul hates them. How the idea of grace in any sense can be forced into this text is a mystery to me.

The same idea is expressed in Proverbs 3:33: "The curse of the LORD is in the house of the wicked: but he blesseth the habitation of the just." Again "the just" and "the wicked" are contrasted. Corre-sponding to this contrast is "to bless" and "to curse." The idea of the text is that Jehovah's curse, his damning power, dwells in the house of the wicked. No matter how that house may appear, the curse of Jehovah dwells in it. But the dwelling place of the righteous is the home of God's blessing.

There is no exception to this text. Wherever you have the house of the wicked, however right and abundant it may appear, there you have the curse of Jehovah; and wherever the righteous dwell, in whatever circumstances you may meet them, there is Jehovah's blessing. Again I ask, where is common grace?

The same antithesis is expressed in verse 34: "Surely he scorneth the scorners: but he giveth grace unto the lowly." Here one who derides is a scoffer, a profane person, who mocks at sacred things and tramples underfoot the things of God. God assumes precisely the same atti-tude toward him that he assumes toward God and sacred things. God mocks him, derides him, laughs at him, and makes him the object of his scorn. In contrast the text speaks of the lowly, the meek, the righteous, as they suffer affliction and bear it with the patience of faith. They receive grace. The implication is that the scoffers receive no grace. God assumes an attitude of grace and bestows his grace on the lowly, not on the wicked. There is no common grace. There is always-present and ever-recurring antithesis.

This same contrast is not foreign to the New Testament. In 1 Peter 5:5 we read, "For God resisteth the proud, and giveth grace to the humble." God opposes, assumes an attitude of opposition toward, sets himself against the high-minded, the haughty; but to the lowly he gives grace. The contrast of the text is self-evident. Over against the high-minded stand the lowly. Only the lowly receive grace. The high-minded always meet with God's opposition. The implication is naturally that they receive no grace.

The same thought occurs in 1 Peter 3:12, where the apostle quotes from Psalm 34:15–16: "The eyes of the LORD are upon the righteous, and his ears are open unto to their cry. The face of the LORD is against them that do evil." These passages are sufficient to prove my contention that scripture teaches that the wicked receive no grace. Jehovah's soul hates the wicked; he mocks at them; he assumes an attitude of opposition against them; he sets his countenance against them; he makes his curse dwell in their houses. It would not be difficult to multiply the passages of the word of God expressing this truth.

I wish, however, to substantiate one more thought by passages from Holy Writ. I claimed that the outwardly good things the wicked receive in common with the righteous in this world become a curse to the wicked, and that through the good things sin and evil flourish and develop. In proof of this contention I refer to Psalm 92:5–7. Here the poet sings of the glory of God's works and the depths of his thoughts. "O LORD, how great are thy works! and thy thoughts are very deep. A brutish man knoweth not; neither doth a fool understand this." What is that glory of the works of God? Of what is the poet thinking as a manifestation of the depth of God's thoughts? This is expressed in verse 7: "When the wicked spring as the grass, and when all the workers of iniquity do flourish; it is that they shall be destroyed for ever." The *niphal* infinitive used here denotes the purpose of their blossoming forth. This is God's purpose, for the poet has said in the preceding verses that in their blossoming forth he beheld a work of God and the depth of his thoughts. Through those things by which the wicked flourish as the green herb, God brings them to everlasting destruction. Their prosperity is their curse from God!

The same truth is expressed in Psalm 73:18–19. We are all acquainted with the general content and thought of this beautiful psalm. The poet, considering things from a merely human viewpoint, is grieved because the wicked prosper and the righteous suffer. He cannot understand this. Of this "common grace" the wicked receive much more than the righteous. This is painful to the poet, and he sometimes wonders when he looks at everything whether there is knowledge in the Most High of this state of affairs. But when the poet enters into God's sanctuary, when he changes his viewpoint, when he looks at the same phenomenon in the light of God's doings, all becomes plain to him. He exclaims, "Surely thou didst set them in slippery places: thou castedst them down into destruction" (v. 18). The meaning is that prosperity to the wicked becomes slippery places on which they slide and stumble and hasten to final destruction. They prosper as wicked, develop in wickedness in the midst of these good things, and with and through all this prosperity hasten to utter ruin.

Notice that the poet beholds all this as the work of God. God sets them on those slippery places. God causes them (the causative *hiphil* form of the verb is used) to hasten to utter desolation. The means God employs to this end is the prosperity they enjoy. They flourish, yes, but as wicked, and as wicked they develop only for desolation and woe. If you prefer to call this grace, I do not understand the meaning and power of grace.

In this light I would also explain Hebrews 6:4–8, where the author speaks of "those who were once enlightened, and have tasted of the heavenly gift, and were made partakers of the Holy Ghost, and have tasted of the good word of God, and the powers of the world to come." We would almost think they were people who had actually received the grace of God in their hearts, for here it is not a matter of food and raiment, of rain and sunshine, but of the blessings of grace on the church. They have been enlightened, they have tasted of the heavenly gift, they have become partakers of the Holy Spirit, and they have tasted the good word of God and the powers of the age to come. Yet they received no grace, for they are described as those who have fallen away. They have fallen so deeply that it is impossible to renew them again to repentance.

They are therefore people who live very near the central current of God's grace. They live in the church. They are under the influence of the good word of God. They understand it; they even see its beauty. They live in the sphere where the Spirit of grace operates, and they partake of the sacraments. They even taste some of these things. They are sometimes enraptured by the view of the age to come. They are very near the central stream of God's grace. Yet the result for them is hardening. They become worse than heathen. They cannot come to repentance. They evidently commit the sin against the Holy Spirit, doing despite to him, trampling underfoot the blood of the New Testament, and crucifying Christ afresh.

The author of the epistle explains this phenomenon by the illustration of a field: "For the earth which drinketh in the rain that cometh oft upon it, and bringeth forth herbs meet for them by whom it is dressed, receiveth blessing from God: but that which beareth thorns and briars is rejected, and is nigh unto cursing; whose end is to be burned" (vv. 7–8). Notice the significance of this illustration. There is a field, and rain descends often on that field. There is no question as to the quality of the rain; it is good. If under the influence of rain the field brings forth good herbs, it receives blessings from God in that rain. But if it bears thorns and thistles, the field is unable to stand the test and is disapproved and rejected. It received the rain, but it brought forth only thorns and thistles.

Through the rain that came often upon it, the evil nature of the field was brought to light and developed. Therefore, the rain is nigh unto a curse. Thus the author explains that there are some upon whom the rain of God's grace falls often, who live under the continued influence of that rain, and who yet receive no blessing.[5] The accursed nature of their wickedness is brought out and developed, and they fall so deeply that they cannot be brought to repentance.

I have fulfilled my task. In my estimation it is not the best method to call attention to individual texts. But it is very easy to do so regarding the subject under discussion. Besides, most of the objections brought against my former paper are answered at the same time.

Response to Criticism

I confess that some of the criticism impressed me rather strangely. More than once the remark was made that the unregenerate do good, that they subjectively receive grace; otherwise they could not do despite to the Spirit of grace. I confess that I do not understand this. How grace can do despite to the Spirit of grace is to me incomprehensible.

---

5 As the preceding context makes abundantly clear, Hoeksema is not affirming that the grace of God is actually bestowed on the reprobate ungodly. Rather, in keeping with the figure in Hebrews 6 of rain falling on a field, Hoeksema acknowledges the close contact that some reprobate unbelievers in the church institute have with the grace of God. They live in the sphere of grace—under the preaching of the gospel, using the sacraments, reading the Bible, and formally participating in the fellowship of the saints. But by their own unbelief and according to God's predestination, gospel, sacraments, the Bible, and Christian fellowship are not grace and blessing to them personally.—Ed.

It was also said that the seeds of the doctrine of common grace are present in the confessions, and reference was made to the Heidelberg Catechism where it says that we are *prone* to evil. The argument was that total depravity merely means an inclination to all evil, while still the sinner may do good. This then is considered to be a seed of common grace.

Perhaps I understand neither the doctrine of total depravity nor the Heidelberg Catechism, but I nevertheless call attention to the fact that the Catechism is very explicit on this point. In Lord's Day 3, the passage referred to by the critic, the Catechism asks the question, "Are we then so corrupt that we are wholly incapable of doing any good, and inclined to all wickedness?" The answer is explicit: "Indeed we are, except we are regenerated by the Spirit of God."[6] It seems to me that if there are seeds of the doctrine of common grace in the confessions, they must be sought elsewhere.

Someone asked the question, do the unregenerate do nothing but evil? I answer with the word of the apostle Paul, "Whatsoever is not of faith is sin" (Rom. 14:23) and with the word of the author of Hebrews: "Without faith it is impossible to please [God]" (11:6). One of the brethren asked, can we say to the unregenerate, to the wicked, "All things are a curse to you"? I answer, most assuredly. I always preach that all things are a curse to them if they do not repent.

Neither can I understand the view expressed by someone that the proper receptivity for grace is special grace, and all the rest is common grace. Perhaps some of those remarks must be attributed to their being spur-of-the-moment questions. What must we make of the counsel of election, of the sending of God's Son, of his humiliation and exaltation—in short, of the entire work of God's salvation, if the sphere of special grace were limited to the subjective?

There is one question about which a special paper might well be written: do the elect ever occur as sinners? My brief answer would be that they do. Nevertheless, from eternity they occur as sinners in Christ Jesus, as the objects of God's free grace. This brings us to the

---

6 Heidelberg Catechism Q&A 8, in *The Confessions and the Church Order of the Protestant Reformed Churches* (Grandville, MI: Protestant Reformed Churches in America, 2005), 86.—Ed.

entire subjects of supralapsarianism and infralapsarianism, which I cannot be expected to discuss now.

Finally, regarding the rich young ruler, Edersheim thinks that he was one of Jesus' sheep according to election, that Jesus loved him as one of his own, and that the young ruler, although turning away for the moment and thereby proving that the rich enter the kingdom with difficulty, later returned and became one of Jesus' disciples. I admit that this is a conjecture. But if you read the entire narrative carefully, there is much in favor of this supposition.

The Practical Significance of the Antithesis

The practical significance of my view is evident. If you consistently develop the line of common grace, particularly as indicated by Kuyper, you are bound to lose the antithesis between the people of God and the world, between light and darkness. Everywhere there is an intermediate sphere where the church and the world meet on common ground and live from a common principle. The doctrine of common grace obliterates the antithesis. For this reason it is easy to prove that there are two Kuypers. The one is the man of the antithesis; the other of common grace. The latter will lead us right into the world, as is already evident in the Netherlands and in our church.

Therefore, I will maintain the antithesis of light and darkness, of sin and grace, of God and the devil, and of Christ and antichrist. Christ and Belial have nothing in common, least of all grace. I will continue to fight the battle against the forces of opposition. The antithesis compels. It is an antithesis between God and the devil, Christ and antichrist, and God's people and the world; but it is an antithesis also found within my being. The law of grace opposes the law in my members and wars against the flesh. Fighting that battle, we live on earth as strangers and pilgrims, like the saints throughout history, the witnesses and heroes of faith.

In principle we have the victory now. We look for the city that has foundations, whose builder and maker is God. For the glory that is set before us we are willing to suffer with Christ. For the crown that is ours in Christ we gladly bear the cross behind him.

NOT ANABAPTIST
BUT REFORMED

Provisional Response to Rev. J. K. van Baalen
Concerning the Denial of Common Grace

HENRY DANHOF

AND

HERMAN HOEKSEMA

TRANSLATED BY DANIEL HOLSTEGE

Introduction to *Not Anabaptist but Reformed*

The pamphlet *Not Anabaptist but Reformed*, by Henry Danhof and Herman Hoeksema, was written soon after the Christian Reformed synod of 1922 and before the Christian Reformed Church's adoption of the doctrine of common grace at its synod of 1924. At the time of the writing of the pamphlet, both men were ministers in good standing in the Christian Reformed Church.

The pamphlet is a response to an attack on Danhof and Hoeksema and their theology by another Christian Reformed minister, Jan Karel van Baalen. His attack took the form of the pamphlet *The Denial of Common Grace: Reformed or Anabaptist?*

Van Baalen's attack, which was praised highly by leading ministers in the Christian Reformed Church when it appeared, was occasioned by the role of Danhof and Hoeksema in the condemnation of the teaching of Ralph Janssen and his removal from his position as professor of theology in the Christian Reformed seminary by the synod of 1922. Janssen was guilty of teaching especially the Old Testament according to the viewpoint of higher criticism of the Bible. Van Baalen and other supporters and friends of Janssen turned on Danhof and Hoeksema in unholy anger and with the evil purpose of avenging their hero. In Van Baalen's attack, as in other attacks on the two ministers by Christian Reformed ministers at the time, lust for the blood of Danhof and Hoeksema is palpable.

Danhof and Hoeksema shared the conviction that the doctrine that gave birth to Janssen's heretical, unbelieving view of scripture is erroneous: the doctrine of a common grace of God. Therefore, Van Baalen assailed Danhof and Hoeksema regarding their denial of common grace. He charged that their rejection of this theory rendered them guilty of Anabaptism. By this charge Van Baalen especially intended the error of world flight.

The lasting worth of their response to this charge, for the Protestant Reformed Churches as for all others who are interested in the controversy, is that *Not Anabaptist but Reformed* conclusively denies the charge. The charge of Anabaptism against those who deny common grace was then, and remains today, mere mud-slinging by the advocates of common grace. To make the charge is scurrilous. If the Christian Reformed Church never repents of its ecclesiastical murder of Danhof and Hoeksema, simple honesty and mere scholarly integrity should compel it to admit that the charge that the denial of common grace is inherently Anabaptist is false witness.

The pamphlet confesses and demonstrates that the Reformed rejection of common grace regards the creation as good; acknowledges the gifts that God bestows on the reprobate ungodly as good (although not good for them in any grace of God toward them); and calls Reformed Christians actively to live in all spheres of earthly life.

Very early in the controversy over common grace between the Christian Reformed Church and the Protestant Reformed Churches it had become evident to the members of both denominations, as to the watching Reformed world, that common grace would spawn the most grievous heresies in the Christian Reformed Church—higher criticism of holy scripture!—and that the rejection of common grace by the Protestant Reformed Churches is soundly Reformed, not Anabaptist.

Regarding the text of the pamphlet, all footnotes not otherwise identified are those of the authors of the pamphlet. Also, apparently the collaboration in producing the pamphlet took the form of each of the two men writing certain sections. Hence the use of the pronoun "my" in chapter 4 evidently is a reference to Hoeksema.

—David J. Engelsma

A WORD TO OUR CHURCHES

The conflict in our churches is gradually focusing on the subject of grace and especially on what bears the name *common grace* among us.[1] This has been expected for a long time.

The controversy in our midst has actually focused on this point for quite some time, and we do not hesitate to add that in principle the struggle of the last few years has always concerned this matter. There was one group that more and more emphasized the importance of the doctrine of common grace. They were very enthusiastic about it. They called it one of the most important doctrines of the Reformed faith. For them this doctrine was a Boaz [pillar] in God's temple. For them the discussion of common grace is the order of the day and has become quite common.

The history of this struggle spans a few years. Johannes Groen emphatically wanted to place this doctrine on the foreground for the defense of unionism and the right of women to vote. In the name of common grace our men were advised to join the labor unions. In the name of the same doctrine our women were urged to go to the polls and to help improve the world. The group that wrote in the former *Christian Journal* under the leadership of Henry J. van Andel emphasized common grace to maintain a broad world view, to give entrance into the world and allow freer movement in it.[2] Whoever questioned that was quickly branded an Anabaptist. Thus a way of thinking has gradually crept into our circles that is enthusiastic about common grace and that either forgets or denies the antithesis, the opposition between God's people and the world. That way of thinking is really bent, although perhaps unconsciously, on making us identify ourselves with the world and go into the world.

---

1 "Our churches" and "us" refer to the Christian Reformed Church.—Trans.
2 Henry J. van Andel was a professor in Calvin College who taught Dutch and literature.—Trans.

We have warned against this from the beginning. We have protested against this application of common grace with word and pen. We have also examined this doctrine, especially as it was developed by Abraham Kuyper. We have concluded that not only is conformity with the world due to a wrong application of the doctrine, but also that the doctrine itself is contrary to the Reformed confessions and scripture and therefore must be rejected. We have spoken out with all boldness concerning this. It is then no wonder that the conflict among us broke out over this point.

This disagreement over common grace, however, did not immediately show itself when the battle over the instruction of Ralph Janssen started.[3] When the doctor was attacked because of his instruction, he insisted that his attackers had to contend with the matter of common grace. He accused everyone who opposed him of not standing correctly on the subject of common grace. He vowed also to show the connection that according to him existed between his instruction and common grace, but until now he has failed to show this. We have gradually become convinced that this connection certainly exists. At first we thought that Janssen's shifting of the main point was merely an attempt to distract attention from the real issue and to fix it on something else. But we changed our minds and concluded that Janssen's view of scripture can in principle be defended from the viewpoint of common grace. We therefore agree with the contention of the brethren who attack us and defend Janssen that the controversy among us concerns the doctrine of common grace.

Therefore, we also want to fight this to the very end. The Janssen affair itself has been settled. The fact that his teaching was not in agreement with the view of the churches, with the confessions, or with scripture became sufficiently clear at synod. The synod came to a unanimous verdict. Not easily will one persuade our churches again to give a place at our school to Janssen, who did not even once take the opportunity to defend his view.

But concerning the principle, we are still not certain [that it will

---

3   See Hanko, "A Study of the Relation between the Views of Prof. R. Janssen and Common Grace."—Trans.

not cause trouble]. It is our firm conviction that if our churches do not examine the subject of common grace as developed by Kuyper, and if they remain under the impression that this view is at bottom Reformed and in agreement with the confessions, then the few have won. The teaching that has now been condemned in Janssen and that is most certainly connected with the view of common grace will yet again lift up its head and assert itself.

Principles work through.

That is how the doctrine of common grace worked through [in the Netherlands]. At first a strong maintenance of the antithesis kept the balance more or less in equilibrium. But as soon as Kuyper died and the younger generation in the Netherlands lifted up their heads and cried for something new, something different, something that could allow them to live more freely in the world and to adapt themselves to the existing forms of society, the antithesis was forgotten, and they embraced the notion of common grace in order to build an entire world-view on it. The result is world conformity in almost every respect.

They want culture! They want art! They want cooperation with the world. They want to go to the dance, opera, and theater. They no longer desire anything sound. Doctrinal preaching must make way for topical preaching. In a word, they have gone out into the world.

As it is in the Netherlands, so also in the United States.

Some in the Netherlands and also in America say that this conformity to the world comes from a wrong view of common grace. F. W. Grosheide spoke that way a couple of years ago in Leeuwarden. There are more like him in the Netherlands; there are also those like him among us. Some among us say that they do not agree with Kuyper's view of common grace, but they do believe in general grace. These brethren are still obligated to tell us what their view of general grace actually is.

There are also those among us who, in spite of the troublesome fruits that this doctrine is already beginning to produce, still promote common grace to the utmost of their power. These include Groen, who for several years has been pushing God's people into the world so they can identify themselves with that world, for example, in the labor unions; the editors of *Religion and Culture*, with Van Andel leading, who calls this doctrine a Boaz of the Reformed view; and Janssen, who defends his modern view of scripture with this doctrine and labels all those who attack him Anabaptists, even in his latest pamphlet. These include our "cultured people," which really means only that they bathe themselves as they should, look after their teeth, and start the day decently clothed.

It is noteworthy that those in this corner must not expect much encouragement from the Reformed confessions. These people do not speak readily about principles, unless it is the principle of common grace. It is also noteworthy that the doctrine of free election is pushed into the background and that of free will into the foreground. The actual point of the Reformed confessions is forgotten and disregarded, weakened to such an extent that one can scarcely find it. But this common grace, about which the confessions do not actually speak, and which our fathers certainly did not take into account, is exalted to a fundamental doctrine of the confessions.

Our conviction is not that a wrong view of common grace underlies all this, but that the doctrine of common grace itself is at root false and un-Reformed.

We believe we must fight for this conviction, and we feel obliged before God and our churches to do so unto the end. In this regard we want to point out that neither Janssen nor Van Baalen started this fight. Long before these brethren wrote, we had warned against the danger of the viewpoint that seeks its justification in general grace.

One of us wrote about this matter almost four years ago. At that time no one had a problem with our articles. When Janssen was confronted, and the doctor thought he had to attack us on the matter of common grace, we promised to present a series of articles. However, the publication committee [of the *Banner*] prevented this from happening. Nevertheless, we still intended to do this in a pamphlet, as soon as our busy labors would permit and the proper time should come.

We were busy writing when the critique of Van Baalen appeared.[4]

---

4 The "critique of Van Baalen" to which Danhof and Hoeksema responded in *Not Anabaptist but Reformed* was the brochure *The Denial of Common Grace: Reformed or Anabaptist?*—Ed.

The brother attacks us regarding something we wrote long ago. His pamphlet has met with much approval. Our church papers have recommended it, even though it clearly is, in effect, a defense of Janssen. Henry Beets has nothing but praise for it.[5] Rev. H. Keegstra is captivated by it.[6] Rev. K. W. Fortuin again issued a call to action, although he himself does not appear inclined to take action.[7] Dr. John H. Kuizenga of Holland laughs up his sleeve.[8] Indeed we may congratulate Van Baalen for writing a pamphlet that is received so favorably. Concerning both form and content, it is praised, and no criticism has been leveled against it.

We did not plan immediately to disrupt this flow of praise. We thought to quietly continue work on our own pamphlet, which eventually would see the light of day. We intended to devote a few pages in it to Van Baalen's work. However, when we examined his pamphlet a little more closely, we found much that in our opinion could not sustain a thorough critique. Thus we thought it best to devote a separate pamphlet to a review of his writing.

Moreover, we thought it was also time to put an end to the often unfair and hollow criticism leveled at us by word and pen. The mud of Anabaptism must not be hurled any longer. In the last few years people have been much too eager to fling this mud. Just how eagerly Van Baalen does this is evident from the almost desperate attempt he makes in his pamphlet to prove his contention. If one needs to twist and turn that much to prove that two brethren are Anabaptists, when they themselves say that they are disgusted with Anabaptism, it almost becomes absurd. But the matter is getting serious. It is time to put an end to this superficial criticism.

---

5   Henry Beets was editor of the *Banner* from 1903 to 1928.—Trans.

6   Henry Keegstra (1871–1955) was minister from 1919 to 1928 in Sixteenth Street Christian Reformed Church in Holland, Michigan.—Ed.

7   Karel W. Fortuin was a minister in Borculo Christian Reformed Church. He praised Van Baalen's booklet defending Janssen's teaching. Fortuin called for immediate action by the Christian Reformed Church, evidently against Danhof and Hoeksema, who had been instrumental in the condemnation of Janssen's modernist teaching regarding the Old Testament. —Ed.

8   John H. Kuizenga was a professor in Western Theological Seminary from 1915 to 1930.—Ed.

Finally, we also thought it irresponsible to let his pamphlet enter the churches unchallenged. Our church papers have recommended the pamphlet. They have not leveled any criticism. The pamphlet is indeed a defense of Janssen and Harry Bultema.[9] It is a slap in the face of our whole church. We just get back from synod, where Janssen was condemned, and behold, our church papers recommend a work that effectively defends him. We do not understand this attitude. Beets and Keegstra should have known better. That was another reason we were pressed to publish this part of our work first.

Therefore, the reader must be aware that the positive development of our view is yet to come. This pamphlet does not intend to do anything but reply to Van Baalen's criticism. The brother has done bad work. He has evidently imagined the matter to be a bit simpler than it is. This is our judgment, and in the following pages we hope to show the grounds for this judgment.

—Henry Danhof
—Herman Hoeksema

---

9 Harry Bultema was a Christian Reformed minister who was condemned by the synod of 1918 and subsequently deposed for his premillennial views.—Trans.

CHAPTER I

THE COVENANT
WITH NOAH

The first subject Van Baalen treats in his pamphlet is the covenant with Noah. Rather, the subject of the brother's treatment is not that covenant per se, but the differing views with respect to that covenant held by Kuyper and by Danhof and Hoeksema. These last two brothers had denied that the covenant established with Noah was a covenant of general grace, in the common sense of the term, and had written that there must be seen in that covenant a phase of the development of the covenant of grace. According to us, then, God reveals the covenant of grace with Noah as inclusive of all generations of the earth, upholding all that exists in time, so that God's creation might soon be delivered from the curse and be glorified.

Hoeksema had criticized Kuyper's reasoning with respect to this covenant with Noah. The first argument raised, which has been cut to pieces by Van Baalen, is that nothing can be built on the different uses of the names God and Jehovah in this connection. Kuyper's argument in his *De Gemeene Gratie* (Common grace) was that in Genesis 9, which speaks of the covenant with Noah, not the name Jehovah but the name God is used. Jehovah is the covenant name, and God is the name that describes the Most High as the God of all flesh. Where the covenant of particular grace is spoken of in Genesis 3 and in Genesis 9:25–27, Jehovah is used. Genesis 9:9–17 uses not the name Jehovah but the name God.

This is one of Kuyper's grounds for concluding that the last passage speaks not of the covenant of particular grace, but of a general grace covenant, a covenant of general grace. We respond that nothing can be built on this use of names with respect to that covenantal idea, because the names God and Jehovah are used interchangeably in this regard. Van Baalen thinks he must criticize that. Let us see to what extent his criticism is correct.

First, our critic writes that we have not done justice to Kuyper's position. He did not write that this distinction always occurs, but only in the places mentioned, namely, in Genesis 3 and Genesis 9:9–17 and 25–27. We agree with that, but we do not agree that this concludes or settles anything in the matter under discussion. It is not true that only the name Jehovah is used in Genesis 3. Both names appear there, often together (Jehovah-God). This does not take away from our argument in any way.

What underlies Kuyper's argument is the idea that the name Jehovah indicates the covenant of particular grace and the name God indicates the relation of the Most High to all flesh. The first name expresses the covenantal relationship to his people, the second his relationship as creator to every creature. If this is not true, nothing can be built on the use of names in Genesis 9 either. Our argument is simply this: if the names God and Jehovah are used interchangeably in Genesis, and no attention is given to any particular or universal relation of God to his people or to his creatures, no one has the right to make an argument for the institution of a covenant of common grace in the use of those names in Genesis 9. Then we pointed out that in Genesis 17, certainly a classic chapter (if we may use such an expression) for the establishment of the covenant of particular grace, the name God and not Jehovah is used repeatedly. No one concludes from the use of that name in Genesis 17 that there too a covenant of common grace is spoken of. Therefore, the argument also fails when it is applied to Genesis 9.

Van Baalen now supposedly refutes this last argument by a proposition that simply astonishes us. The proposition is that we never read that God "*introduced himself* as Jehovah" to Abraham, so he did not know the name Jehovah and therefore cannot be presented as employing that name. Moses knew that name well, and consequently he also made that distinction. But before Moses there was no one who knew that name.

It appears nowhere that the Supreme Being *introduced himself* as Jehovah to Noah or Shem or Adam or Eve or the snake, for he would do that first to Moses. But it is noteworthy that Moses, who certainly knew the name Jehovah, made that distinction when he wrote the book of Genesis. Moses wrote under the inspiration of the Spirit that Jehovah spoke to Shem and Noah when it pertained to the covenant of particular grace. But Moses wrote that God spoke when it pertained to common grace.[10]

So strongly is the writer convinced of the validity of this argument that he considers it crazy to think of it differently.

No, Dr. Kuyper was not so crazy that he did not know that the Lord would not have used the name Jehovah with Abraham. The Lord God could not have done that, not even if he spoke of the covenant of grace. And why not? For the simple reason that it was his plan to make known that covenant name first to Moses. See Exodus 6:3: "And I appeared unto Abraham, unto Isaac, and unto Jacob by the name of God Almighty, but by my name JEHOVAH was I not known to them."[11]

Understood, reader? Supposedly Abraham knew nothing of the name Jehovah. Moses was the first to be aware of that name. Therefore, Moses never presents the matter in such a way that anyone before his time took that name on his lips or that God would have revealed himself as Jehovah to anyone before Moses' time. Hence the name God is used in Genesis 17. The author even thinks it would be crazy for someone to claim anything else!

There is not one letter of truth in this entire argument. We were actually shocked that a man like Van Baalen would write something like this. If he had done a little bit of study on this matter, he would not have written such a thing. This certainly does not fit with scripture. It is not true that Moses wrote Jehovah when the covenant of particular

---

10 Van Baalen, *Denial of Common Grace*, 17.
11 Ibid., 16.

grace was spoken of and God if it had to do with the covenant of common grace. Moses absolutely does not make such a distinction. We will quote a few passages to prove this.

When scripture relates the conversation between God and Cain, the name LORD is continuously used. For the sake of clarity, we will write Jehovah every time that name appears in scripture.[12]

In the following passages the name Jehovah is used for God when he speaks with Cain: "Jehovah said unto Cain, Why art thou wroth? and why is thy countenance fallen? And Jehovah said unto Cain, Where is Abel thy brother? And Cain said unto Jehovah, My punishment is greater than I can bear" (Gen. 4:6, 9, 13). "Jehovah said unto him, Therefore whosoever slayeth Cain, vengeance shall be taken on him sevenfold. And Jehovah set a mark upon Cain, lest any finding him should kill him" (verse 15 is sometimes quoted to prove common grace.)

In the following verses that deal with God's relationship to man in general, and especially to ungodly humanity, the name Jehovah is used: "Jehovah said, My spirit shall not always strive with man, for that he also is flesh" And Jehovah saw that the wickedness of man was great in the earth, and that every imagination of the thoughts of his heart was only evil continually. And it repented Jehovah that he had made man on the earth, and it grieved him at his heart" (Gen. 6:3, 5–6).

Furthermore, the names are sometimes used interchangeably.

"Noah found grace in the eyes of Jehovah" (Gen. 6:8). (Van Baalen, was that common grace? By that grace Noah did not perish with the world. Read this verse in connection with verse 7. Yet it was really particular grace, wasn't it? You will certainly agree with that.)

"Jehovah said unto Noah, Come thou and all thy house into the ark...And Noah did according unto all that Jehovah commanded him. There went in two and two unto Noah into the ark, the male and the female, as God had commanded Noah. And they that went in, went in

---

12 The Dutch version (*Staten Vertaling*) used by the authors translates the Hebrew name *Yahweh* as HEERE (Lord). Here the authors change HEERE to Jehovah wherever *Yahweh* appears. Similarly, the King James Version translates *Yahweh* as Lord. I have taken the citations from the King James and changed Lord to Jehovah.—Trans.

male and female of all flesh, as God had commanded him: and Jehovah shut him in" (Gen. 7:1, 5, 9, 16).

"And God remembered Noah, and every living thing, and all the cattle that was with him in the ark: and God made a wind to pass over the earth, and the waters assuaged; and Noah builded an altar unto Jehovah; and took of every clean beast, and of every clean fowl, and offered burnt offerings on the altar. And Jehovah smelled a sweet savour; and Jehovah said in his heart, I will not again curse the ground any more for man's sake" (Gen. 8:1, 20–21).

Furthermore, the name God is used when it has to do with the relationship of the covenant in the particular sense.

"And Enoch walked with God: and he was not; for God took him" (Gen. 5:24). This walking with God is certainly particular grace and has its eye on the inner covenantal relationship between God and his people, does it not?

"Noah walked with God" (Gen. 6:9).

"And Abram fell on his face: and God talked with him, saying, As for me, behold, my covenant is with thee." "And God said unto Abraham, Thou shalt keep my covenant therefore, thou, and thy seed after thee in their generations" (Gen. 17:3–4, 9).

In light of these passages of scripture, what remains of Van Baalen's contention that Moses wrote *Jehovah* where it had to do with the covenant of particular grace and wrote *God* when it pertained to a covenant of common grace? This entire argument is no good. Not for a moment does it hold any water in the light of scripture, and therefore it cannot be applied to Genesis 9:9–17. Moses does not make that distinction.

Even stranger is Van Baalen's exegesis of Exodus 6:3. According to him, no one before Moses would have known the name Jehovah! God could not call himself by the name Jehovah before Moses. Kuyper was not so crazy that he did not know this. This is what Van Baalen writes.

But what does scripture say?

"Abram said to the king of Sodom, I have lift up mine hand unto Jehovah, the most high God, the possessor of heaven and earth" (Gen. 14:22).

"Abram said, Lord Jehovah, what wilt thou give me, seeing I go childless…? And he said unto him, I am Jehovah that brought thee out of Ur of the Chaldees to give thee this land to inherit it. And he said, Lord Jehovah, whereby shall I know that I shall inherit it" (Gen. 15:2, 7–8)?

"Abraham called the name of that place Jehovah-jireh [Jehovah shall foresee it]" (Gen. 22:14).

"Abraham said unto his eldest servant of his house, that ruled over all that he had, Put, I pray thee, thy hand under my thigh: and I will make thee swear by Jehovah, the God of heaven, and the God of the earth." A little later we read that Abraham's servant called out to God, "O Jehovah God of my master Abraham, I pray thee, send me good speed this day, and shew kindness unto my master Abraham. And he said, Blessed be Jehovah God of my master Abraham" (Gen. 24:2–3, 12, 27).

These examples could be multiplied, but we trust that Van Baalen will look them up and conclude that he is making a colossal mistake. The entire argument on pages 16–17 [of his pamphlet] rests on this error. This is the result, brother, if one reasons from a single text of scripture and simply ignores all the rest. This weakness is revealed more often in your pamphlet, as we will later demonstrate.

Nothing can be concluded from the use of the name God in Genesis 9:9–17 with respect to a universal covenant of common grace. The names God and Jehovah are used interchangeably in the holy scriptures with respect to this point. The remark "No, Dr. Kuyper was not so crazy that he should not have known"[13] is erroneous, and the entire argument following the remark is also a misunderstanding. Moses again and again presents the saints from before his time as knowing the name Jehovah. God also introduced himself to them as Jehovah.

Once again, Van Baalen, acknowledge that you have erred!

The second argument we raise against the idea that the covenant with Noah was a covenant of common grace established with all men without distinction is that the expression "thee and thy seed" in scripture is always understood organically and never pertains to every person among that seed.[14] Scripture speaks not only in Genesis 9 but

---

13 Van Baalen, *Denial of Common Grace*, 16.
14 The first argument was "that nothing can be built on the different use of the names God and Jehovah in this connection" (paragraph 2).—Trans.

also throughout about an establishing of the covenant with "thee and thy seed." However, this seed does not refer to every individual of that seed head for head. Thus in Genesis 3:15 there is a general designation of the seed of the woman, yet clearly not every seed of the woman according to the flesh is meant. The same is true in Genesis 17:7. God says to Abraham, "And I will establish my covenant between me and thee and thy seed after thee in their generations for an everlasting covenant, to be a God unto thee, and to thy seed after thee." In the case of Abraham it goes so far that all those born in his house and all bought with money must receive the sign of the covenant.

"Thee and thy seed" may never be explained in any other way than organically. The organic line of the covenant in history does not do away with the lines of election and reprobation. See especially Romans 9. Hence the expression "thee and thy seed" never refers to all descendants without distinction having the essential part in the blessings of the covenant. Ishmael and Esau fell away. Entire multitudes fell away from Israel, so many that it seems justified to ask, has God disowned his people? But all of this is explained by the fact that within the sphere of the historic-organic development of the covenant, always the remnant according to the election of grace is meant.

We have applied this entirely scriptural idea to Genesis 9:9 as well. When we read there, "And I, behold, I establish my covenant with you, and with your seed after you," we cannot immediately conclude that this will soon pertain to all men head for head. This idea does include the entire human race, for God is speaking to Noah and his sons, but the organic meaning of "you and your seed" must not be lost sight of here either.

Van Baalen thinks he has to criticize this too. However, his criticism is quite deficient. He first says, "But it does not now follow from that fact that this idea [the organic meaning of 'thee and thy seed'] must come into play in the covenant with Noah as well." From this he concludes that we knock down our own position. How? We had shown that God first establishes his covenant of grace with Abraham in the line of Abraham's seed in general, but that this covenant is subsequently limited to the line of Isaac and Jacob, so that Ishmael and

Esau immediately fall away from this "seed." Van Baalen says, "That is exactly the point." With Abraham the Lord limited the seed. "But in the covenant with Noah there is no mention of such limitation. This indicates that it is a completely different covenant."

It offends us that one of our ministers appears in public with such an argument. On top of that, he writes in a tone that clearly shows his firm conviction that he has refuted someone's positions, so that there can no longer be any doubt that the striving brethren have grossly erred and that a call for repentance is in order! For what does this argument mean? Even if it were true that we read of a limitation in relation to the covenant with Noah this would neither add to nor detract from the prevailing thought of scripture. Do we read anywhere of the limitation that runs through all history? Does not Israel soon fall in the wilderness? Yet we do not read of such a limitation in the establishment of the covenant?[15] When the ten tribes and even a great part of Judah soon fall away, so that there remains only a small remnant according to the election of grace, was that announced beforehand in the establishment of the covenant? No, Van Baalen, this whole way of reasoning is unbecoming of you. "Thee and thy seed" in scripture never means every person head for head. That is certain. We have never knocked that down, and you still less.

Moreover, is there truth in the assertion that in the establishment of the covenant with Noah we do not immediately read of a limitation? No. In fact, in Genesis 9:25–27 we read of such further limitation. There one of the sons of Ham is cursed, while it is remarked that the Lord is the God of Shem, and Japheth is given the blessing that he will soon dwell in the tents of Shem. Thus only by removing Genesis 9:9–17 from its context and explaining it by itself, without paying attention to what precedes and follows it, can we come to Van Baalen's conclusion.

This applies also to Genesis 6:18: "But with thee will I establish my covenant." Again we read in Genesis 9:9, "And I, behold, I establish my covenant with you, and with your seed after you." Our argument was

---

15 This falling away from Israel is so strong that Paul says concerning Israel in the wilderness that God was not well pleased with many of them. Yet they all belonged to "thy seed" (1 Cor. 10:5).—Trans

that the expression "establish my covenant" in scripture has its eye on the one covenant of grace. Van Baalen described this expression as follows: "that [God] would go on to conclude a certain kind of covenant with him [Noah] as soon as the great flood was past."[16] But Van Baalen fails to supply proof that this description is correct. "Establish my covenant" is a recurring expression in the scriptures that never gives rise to "a certain kind of covenant," but to the one covenant of grace that repeatedly takes on a different form throughout history and comes to a fuller revelation.

The covenant in paradise, and with Noah, Abraham, and Israel, and soon also in the new dispensation, remains essentially the same. That is what Danhof meant when he wrote that the covenant with Noah is the covenant of grace in its second phase of development. That is what Hoeksema meant as well. But Van Baalen does not reply to that. He simply says that things are as he writes. Until now, he fails to prove it.

When Van Baalen writes, "The idea...that the covenant of particular grace, that is, of saving grace, should be established with all men, yea with all flesh, as we heard Hoeksema say, is truly something new to the Reformed tradition!"[17] our answer is, first, that Van Baalen has never heard us say that. The brother surely knows that we have never taught that the covenant of grace should be established with all men. How could he then attack us later for pushing the doctrine of election too strongly, if that were our view? We do contend, though, that the covenant of grace includes all races of the earth and that this is actually promised already in the covenant with Noah.

Second, we answer that Van Baalen does not need to write with an indignant exclamation mark that something new has been introduced into the Reformed tradition. As a progressive Reformed man he should have been thankful for that.

Third, we answer that it is a thoroughly Reformed idea that God's covenant of grace blesses all the generations of the earth that proceed from Noah and includes the whole creation, although not in the sense

---

16 Van Baalen, *Denial of Common Grace*, 20.
17 Ibid., 21.

that the dumb creation is a conscious party in this covenant. Not even Van Baalen will want to make that claim with regard to his universal covenant of common grace. But it is true that in and through that covenant of God all flesh is upheld in time, and soon every creature will take part in the glorious liberty of the children of God (Rom. 8:19–22).

Also, we pointed out that in every passage of scripture outside of Genesis 9 which mentions the rainbow, this everlasting sign concerns the covenant of grace as it embraces the whole creation. Now Van Baalen makes little of this point, and then he treats it as such. He readily admits that in Ezekiel 1 and Revelation 4 and 10, where the rainbow is mentioned, the reference is to the covenant of grace.[18] But he sees therein the symbolic description of the unity of the mediator of creation and the mediator of redemption. We eagerly looked for Van Baalen to develop this notion of unity somewhere, but nowhere does he develop the idea. He simply criticizes with ideas taken from others. Apart from this, we may certainly still expect the brother to provide proof for his contention that in the passages mentioned, the rainbow is a sign of the idea of unity or a symbolic description of it.

In the scriptures the rainbow is a sign of the covenant. We know of no passage where it is also a symbolic description of the unity between the mediator of creation and the mediator of redemption. The brother does not give proof either, but simply says this is the way he explains it. He forgets that this is not an explanation but simply a contention. We have demonstrated that in every passage outside of Genesis 9 where the rainbow is mentioned, the rainbow is given as a sign of the covenant of grace. The bow is a sign of the covenant. As it bends through the clouds and stretches over every creature, so also God's covenant encompasses and upholds all things, in order shortly to glorify all things. Therefore, let Van Baalen provide exegesis and demonstrate why our contention is incorrect. Then we will believe him.

That is the extent of Van Baalen's criticism in his second chapter. The brother will undoubtedly realize that his criticism nowhere holds good. We have demonstrated that nothing can be built on the use of the names God and Jehovah regarding a universal covenant of

---

18 Ibid., 22.

common grace in Genesis 9:9–17, and that Van Baalen's view that the name Jehovah would never have been used before the days of Moses and that God would never have called himself by that name is in glaring contradiction with the scriptures. God reveals himself as Jehovah. The saints of those days called to him as Jehovah. They even named places with his name.

We have also demonstrated that the organic conception of "thee and thy seed" is thoroughly scriptural. Van Baalen does not refute this. He also does not refute the idea that the expression "establish my covenant" appears in scripture again and again in connection with different forms of the covenant, but it is always essentially the same covenant of grace. We have demonstrated that the rainbow appears in Ezekiel 1 and Revelation 4 and 10 as a sign of the covenant of grace in its all-inclusive meaning. Van Baalen must still explain and prove his view of these facts.

Once again, Van Baalen, acknowledge that you have erred!

We want to go a step further and show that our view of the covenant with Noah is actually scriptural and that the Reformed fathers described it thus when the confessional writings were drawn up. We point you to the biblical idea that the flood is a type of baptism, according to 1 Peter 3:21: "The like figure whereunto even baptism doth also now save us (not the putting away of the filth of the flesh, but the answer of a good conscience toward God,) by the resurrection of Jesus Christ." The idea is clear, insofar as the text relates to our subject. The context speaks of the flood, of which baptism is the antitype. Baptism is a picture of our going under in the blood of Christ in order to rise out of that blood with him, purified to be a people unto the Lord, free from sin and guilt. Through baptism we enter into covenantal fellowship with God. The flood is a type, a picture, of it.

Noah and his family typically go into the flood in order to come out of the flood as a covenantal people unto the Lord, cleansed of the wicked husk of the ungodly world. In the flood God causes the human race to perish to preserve the new core in Christ. How could you have a type of baptism in the flood, and a type of God's church as it passes through baptism and arises with Christ in the ark, if you

NOT ANABAPTIST BUT REFORMED   105

make all of this universal? Or what gives you the right to agree with all this but to insist that we must dissociate Genesis 9:9–17 from its entire context? In any case, scripture is on our side if we maintain that in the covenant with Noah God establishes his covenant of grace with his people—Noah and his seed taken organically. What God saves out of and through the flood are his covenantal people. The people with whom he establishes his covenant after the flood are his covenantal people, always taken organically.

Our fathers also understood it this way, as may be seen in the prayer before baptism. Nowhere do our confessions mention the all-important doctrine of a covenant of common grace. But in the prayer before baptism, the flood and the passage through the Red Sea are on a par. According to the baptism form both are types of baptism. What passed through the sea were the covenantal people of the Lord. What pass through baptism are also the covenantal people of the Lord. What passed through the flood were that same covenantal people, and unto that covenantal people, always taken in the organic-historic sense, the Lord says, "And I, behold, I establish my covenant with you, and with your seed after you."[19]

In this way one can also understand Hebrews 11:7: "By faith Noah, being warned of God of things not seen as yet, moved with fear, prepared an ark to the saving of his house; by the which he condemned the world, and became heir of the righteousness which is by faith." By faith he built the ark. By faith he condemned the world. By faith he was saved. By faith he became heir of the righteousness that is by faith.

You must focus your attention especially on this last point. This cannot mean that Noah inherited righteousness, for this would not fit. He was already righteous by the faith with which he built the ark. But the meaning is evidently that he inherited as a man who was righteous by faith. He received the inheritance by faith, and that inheritance was the second world that came out of the flood. The ungodly lost that world through unbelief. Noah, who lived by faith, received it as

---

19 The close connection between type and antitype with respect to baptism, the passage through the sea, and the flood may be derived from 1 Corinthians 10:2, where the apostle literally says that the children of Israel were baptized in the sea.—Trans.

his inheritance. Thus that entire history is also a picture of the end. Just as God once caused the first world to perish, so will he also cause this second world to pass through the fire and cause the form of it to vanish. Then too the people of God will be heirs of the new world in which righteousness dwells.

Therefore, brother, our thinking is entirely in line with scripture and the confessions. However, you find no sign of a universal human covenant in the confessions. What right do you have, then, to attack us and declare us unscriptural, un-Reformed, and Anabaptist in this respect and publicly to call us to repentance? Had you given a thorough treatment of the subject, or produced anything new, and then demonstrated that our view does not hold up, there may have been a basis for bold language that no other view could possibly be allowed. But your arguments are much too weak. We fully agree, although perhaps in a somewhat modified sense, with what you write on page 22: "And thus our investigation into the criticism of Hoeksema concerning Kuyper's conception of the covenant with Noah has ended in disappointment." Certainly, brother, your investigation ended in disappointment. We were bitterly disappointed by this investigation.

With that we should be able to conclude our criticism, for the idea that the covenant with Noah is not the covenant of grace but a covenant of common grace must form its foundation from what follows. If the foundation is not good, what is built on it will not stand firm. We will demonstrate this in the following chapters.

CHAPTER 2

SUPERFICIAL JUDGMENT
AND RASH ACCUSATION

We can pass by Van Baalen's third chapter in silence except for one observation: he surely could have gathered his facts and material a bit better and studied more thoroughly. That is the first requirement, and that the brother has not done. He constructs his view of the theology of these brethren out of a single paragraph from the hand of Danhof and a few fragments from the pen of Hoeksema. The weakness of this method comes to light even more in chapter 4, where Van Baalen makes his accusation and presents his objections to our view.

We now turn to chapter 4 of Van Baalen's pamphlet and will briefly follow him and demonstrate how hastily and superficially the brother has written. He begins this chapter by devoting a few pages to Hoeksema's dispute with Janssen in the *Banner*. We will not get into that, but not because we cannot. Van Baalen, who so loosely accuses us of transgressing Christian morals, is guilty of the same by penning this and other accusations without really knowing the issue or having thoroughly examined it. But getting into that would divert us too far from our subject. If Van Baalen wants to defend Janssen, let him try; but a few sidelong remarks are of no use to us here.

Not until page 36 of his pamphlet does Van Baalen finally arrive at his subject and present his objections concerning our view.

The first criticism is that we have taken the dangerous path of rationalism and are guilty of this dreadful error. Certainly, according to Van Baalen, there is no evil intent involved here—we do this in our ignorance—nevertheless the sad fact is that our pamphlet fosters that error: "We do not say that Hoeksema intentionally makes himself guilty of this dreadful error. Rather, we believe just the opposite. Therefore, we endeavor to show him the dangerous path on which he finds himself."

Brother Van Baalen has good intentions. He is concerned about us and wants to correct erring brethren, as becomes evident in his repeated call to repentance and confession of guilt. We appreciate these good intentions in the brother. However, if one wants to correct erring brethren by way of a pamphlet instead of speaking and corresponding with those brethren; if one would take the very public way of loudly voicing the call to repentance to two erring brethren, then he should be doubly certain of his objection. The brother was not. He has viewed us wrongly. He has judged superficially. He has accused rashly.

So it is with the accusation of rationalism. If the brother had just thought about it, he would never have written that severe accusation. Let the reader judge.

Rationalism is the school of thought that places the principle of reason above the holy scriptures. If anything in scripture is not in line with or comprehended by reason, rationalism either rejects or distorts that portion of holy scripture. What had we written? This: "Now it must be said that such an attitude of God is simply inconceivable in the light of scripture and Reformed doctrine." Van Baalen responds, "Right there you have it. Pure rationalism."[20]

But let the reader judge. Do we place reason above the scriptures there? Or do we distort the scriptures in one way or another? For us, "in the light of scripture" means "if you let your thinking be controlled by the light of scripture." This is the exact opposite of rationalism, which says, "In the light of reason this or that in scripture is inconceivable." We maintained that "in the light of scripture this or that position is inconceivable." No further argument is necessary here. Even Van Baalen will realize this. He called for repentance unnecessarily.

We have also maintained that God cannot show any grace outside of Christ. Is this rationalism? Absolutely not. In fact, this too means exactly the same as "in the light of scripture." It simply means that something is

---

20 Van Baalen, *Denial of Common Grace*, 37.

not in agreement with the scriptural understanding of God and must be rejected. The scriptures maintain that God is absolutely righteous and holy. Because he is absolutely righteous, grace, mercy, goodness, and so on always reside with God as an inviolable right. Therefore, it can certainly be said that something is inconceivable because it conflicts with our understanding of God without thereby falling into rationalism, as long as our understanding of God is derived from scripture. This explanation will suffice. Van Baalen will certainly understand and realize that he has publicly and rashly written dreadful accusations.

We do not understand the argument that now follows (concerning our conception of the decrees of God that starts on page 37). We think we understand what the brother writes there, but it is beyond our comprehension why he writes it. What stands out the most is that Van Baalen's perception of us has been much too simple. To be sure, we were not surprised when he felt obliged to write that we could still profitably study Bosma's work on the Reformed faith.[21] Anyone who holds to such a view as Van Baalen thinks we would perhaps do better to begin with Borstius.[22] The brother writes without any warrant that we know of only one decree of God, and that is the decree of election. He does not give any proof for this, and yet he states:

> And unfortunately we must now go further and express our firm conviction that the theology of Hoeksema runs along "the single track" of election and reprobation. And it is not any better with Danhof. He also knows of only one decree of God, as appears in his pamphlet, *The Idea of the Covenant of Grace*. And that is the decree of election.[23]

We repeat that it is beyond us how anyone writing a pamphlet could present such things in the light of day. Do you truly think, brother, that

---

21 M. J. Bosma, *Onderwijzing in De Gereformeerde Geloofsleer* (Exposition of Reformed doctrine).—Trans.

22 Jacob Borstius wrote simple catechism books for little children widely used in the Netherlands, such as *Eenige korte Vragen Voor de kleyne Kinderen* (Simple short questions for the little children) and *Catechismus, Voorgestelt in Korte Vragen en Antwoorden* (Catechism, set forth in short questions and answers).—Trans.

23 Van Baalen, *Denial of Common Grace*, 37–38.

we are as foolish as you present it here? Then demonstrate once that we ever wrote anything resembling this. As for us, we will demonstrate to you that we have written just the opposite.

> First, there is the most general notion of God's counsel with respect to all things in its all-encompassing sense. You can call this counsel of God his decree, purpose, will, plan, counsel, hidden will, or will of decree as long as you keep in mind that in the general sense the counsel of God is all-encompassing. In this counsel of God, however, we distinguish between the counsel of God's providence and the counsel of predestination. It is not true that these are two different counsels or decrees of God. On the contrary, they are one, and they stand in close connection with each other. But we distinguish them as elements in the one counsel of God.[24]

Also here it may be said that Van Baalen has cried "fire" too soon, accused of rationalism too carelessly, and worried about his brethren needlessly. He could have left much in the pen if he had but read our articles, or if he had at least fully gathered his material prior to setting himself to writing against two brethren. Therefore, we also believe, brother Van Baalen, that you can once again profitably read what these brethren have written in the past.

It gets even worse. The "single track" gets narrower and narrower. Earlier Van Baalen was afraid that Hoeksema's "mind" went along a "single track." He is now decidedly convinced of it. Not only do the brothers Hoeksema and Danhof believe in only one decree of God, the decree of election, but they believe in nothing else. They deny man's responsibility. Just read it on page 38, which solemnly concludes, "But you who build your theology on merely one of the two truths of holy scripture, what principle enables you to rouse the impenitent sinner to repentance?"

You see, our brother Van Baalen teaches that there is yet another line running through scripture: the line of man's responsibility! He

---

24 Herman Hoeksema, *Banner* (April 8, 1920).

maintains that we fail to appreciate that line. We have no eye for it. We move along one little line.

We wish to point out our genuine fear that brother Van Baalen's two lines deviate from the Reformed faith. We doubt that he stands correctly on this point concerning election. His entire reasoning does not make a very favorable impression on us, at least not from a Reformed viewpoint. We especially fear the worst about Van Baalen when we see him quote, "Who will have all men to be saved" (1 Tim. 2:4). This, writes Van Baalen, is God's revealed will. Thus, according to him, God's hidden will is that not all men are saved, but according to God's revealed will we say, "Who will have all men to be saved." Look, brother, this is how we draw the two lines [of your theology], which you certainly have not done.

Your explanation, as seen from the quotation, is certainly not Reformed. Brother, already in Calvin's day people quoted this text as an objection to election. Although you do not do that, you still explain the text as do all Arminians, namely, that "all men" must be understood as everyone head for head. Calvin pointed out, however, that this cannot be the idea, because the context clearly shows that the apostle has his eye on "classes of men, not men as individuals. Because in that case this text would conflict with the clear doctrine of election, and that cannot be.[25] Therefore, it is definitely incorrect to declare that on the one hand God desires that some be saved and others go lost, and on the other that God also desires that all men be saved. In this way you obscure the pure doctrine of election in a manner that causes the simple believer to become very confused.

We do believe in two lines, brother, but we are also convinced that you do not draw them correctly. The accusation that we do not believe in man's responsibility or do not do it justice is simply pulled out of the sky, as will become evident from the following, which was written by our hand:

> Thus far we have strictly maintained the all-encompassing character of God's decrees on the one hand and the moral freedom and responsibility of man on the other hand.

---

25 Calvin, *Institutes*, 3.24.16, 21:983–84.—Ed.

We have firmly refused to diminish the power and sovereignty of God or to grant that man is in any way able to destroy the counsel of God. To do this would deal the death-blow to our Reformed doctrine. God is and remains absolutely sovereign. His counsel has never been destroyed, nor changed, nor led aside by any deed of men or devils. All of history, evil included, is an unfolding of the counsel of the Almighty.

On the other hand, we have just as emphatically maintained the responsibility of man. The accusation of determinism, sometimes brought against the Reformed confessions, we have cast far from us. Man is a creature who acts freely. What he does, he does consciously and willingly. He is and remains free in the formal sense.

Although these two lines of God's counsel and man's moral freedom and responsibility might run parallel insofar as our eye can see, and as McCosh expresses it in his *The Divine Government*,[26] we will still hold fast to both of these truths on the basis of scripture without compromise or surrender.

It may be freely granted that we are dealing with a mystery here. The question how God maintains his irresistible counsel over against his moral creatures; how it is possible for God to cooperate with these moral-rational beings so that his counsel is worked out and their responsibility still maintained, may ultimately put us in a dilemma. But this does not mean that we simply abandon one of the two horns of the dilemma and delude ourselves into believing that we have the truth in only one of the horns. We must emphatically hold fast to both.[27]

We could quote more, but this language is clear enough. Van Baalen could also have read this language, and he should have read it before writing a brochure in which he ascribed to us all kinds of errors

---

26 James McCosh (1811–94) was a Presbyterian preacher from Scotland who was appointed the eleventh president of Princeton. He wrote *The Method of Divine Government, Physical and Moral* (Edinburgh, 1850) over against rationalism's rejection of God's control of all.—Trans.

27 Herman Hoeksema, *Banner* (June 17, 1920).

that are not ours. The brother will certainly want to rejoice that he has worried about us needlessly. He will certainly also feel the need to be ashamed for his superficial piece of work, which is not at all grounded on the necessary study of the sources. As an honorable man he will certainly want to take back publicly what he wrote and admit that he has been grievously mistaken regarding us.

On pages 40–42 follows a discussion about the attributes of God, which seeks to prove that we eliminate some of God's attributes that cannot be brought into agreement with others. Thus we supposedly deny the love of God because in God there is also punishing righteousness! Van Baalen could easily have kept this entire argument in his pen. Nowhere have we ever written what Van Baalen presents as our view. However, if Van Baalen wants to show a "double track" here too and thinks that before our consciousness God's love cannot be in harmony with his punishing righteousness, we differ with him.

Certainly, God is love. But since he greatly cherishes himself as the Most High, as the absolute good, that same love reveals itself as punishing righteousness on all who turn themselves against him. There is no conflict or contradiction here. When in connection with this Van Baalen attributes to us an exegesis of Luke 6:35 that basically says the goodness of the Lord is no goodness at all, we ask him where he ever read such an explanation by us. The brother really thinks we would thus explain the text, but that is simply because he has never tried to think through our view.

Van Baalen remarks that Hebrews 6:4–8 does not apply to our subject. That text speaks about spiritual blessings, about men who have lived very close to grace, about very specific gifts given to some men. The writer explains this by using the figure of a field on which rain frequently falls and that produces thorns and thistles under the influence of the rain. According to Van Baalen, that is not to be applied to the general gifts of nature, but only to those specific blessings named there. But Van Baalen does not tell us why this should not apply to all gifts. The point of agreement is that the natural man in himself does not have access to the blessings of God. In himself he is unclean. Because he is unclean, all gifts become unclean to him as well.

This applies to those who live closest to grace and receive the most generous rain, but also to those who live farther from the center. It is a good Reformed notion, expressed repeatedly by Calvin and implied in the Reformed confessions, that all things are unclean to the unclean. The natural man certainly receives gifts, many gifts, gifts that in themselves are even good, for they come from God. But for the wicked sinner these never become blessings in the proper sense. God is good. Certainly he is gracious and merciful and kind. Everything that comes from God is always good. There is absolutely no darkness in him. But that good God with his good gifts is wrath and punishment to the wicked sinner.

Therefore, Van Baalen's next argument, which is simply borrowed from Kuyper, does not hold good either. In short, it comes down to this: whoever denies general grace denies one of two things, the total depravity of man or that man by nature is still capable of "some civic righteousness." Thus says Kuyper, and thus says Van Baalen after him. Neither of these is true, and Van Baalen cannot think of any other possibility. This does not prove there is not a third possibility that is truly in harmony with scripture and the confessions. We present that possibility.

We certainly deny that the unregenerate does any good before God. You certainly cannot say it more strongly than the Heidelberg Catechism: "But are we so far depraved that we are wholly unapt to any good, and prone to all evil? Yes; unless we are born again by the Spirit of God."[28]

I know Van Baalen thinks ill of us that we maintain this position. He says we must come to one of two evils. The one evil is that we "maintain the position that natural man can perform absolutely no good whatever."[29] He thinks that Pharaoh's daughter performed a good deed (good in the sense that she did something good before God, so that her deed could be reckoned to her as good) when she drew a beautiful child out of the water, even though she surely did not care about the many other children who perished in the Nile. Well then,

28 Heidelberg Catechism Q&A 8, in Schaff, *Creeds of Christendom*, 3:310.—Ed.
29 Van Baalen, *Denial of Common Grace*, 47.

Van Baalen, we indeed maintain the Catechism's position that natural man can do absolutely no good whatever unless he is regenerated by the Spirit of God. You are accountable for your departure from this.

The Catechism is not alone in expressing it this way. The rest of the confessions are in complete agreement. Thus we read in article 24 of the Belgic Confession, "Therefore it is so far from being true, that this justifying faith makes men remiss in a pious and holy life, that on the contrary without it they would never do anything out of love to God, but only out of self-love or fear of damnation."[30]

Now if you want to say that this self-love, which is also in Pharaoh's daughter, is good, you are accountable for that. We call it sin. In article 14 of the Belgic Confession we read, "And being thus become wicked, perverse, and corrupt in all his ways, he hath lost all his excellent gifts which he had received from God, and only retained a few remains thereof, which, however, are sufficient to leave man without excuse; for all the light which is in us is changed into darkness."[31]

That is according to scripture. It does not say that the few remains are sufficient to attain unto the good that is also good before God. Rather, the few remains leave him without excuse, as he consciously and willingly and at all times performs sin and wickedness with those remains. Likewise is it in the Canons:

> There remain, however, in man since the fall, the glimmerings of natural light, whereby he retains some knowledge of God, of natural things, and of the difference between good and evil, and discovers some regard for virtue, good order in society, and for maintaining an orderly external deportment. But so far is this light of nature from being sufficient to bring him to a saving knowledge of God, and to true conversion, that he is incapable of using it aright even in things natural and civil. Nay further, this light, such as it is, man in various ways renders wholly polluted, and holds it [back] in unrighteousness; by doing which he becomes inexcusable before God.[32]

---

30 Belgic Confession 24, in Schaff, *Creeds of Christendom*, 3:410–11.—Ed.
31 Belgic Confession 14, in ibid., 3:398–99.—Ed.
32 Canons of Dordt 3–4.4, in ibid., 3:588.—Ed.

You see, brother, this is Reformed language. And God's word has the same language.

5. For they that are after the flesh do mind the things of the flesh; but they that are after the Spirit the things of the Spirit.
6. For to be carnally minded is death; but to be spiritually minded is life and peace.
7. Because the carnal mind is enmity against God: for it is not subject to the law of God, neither indeed can be.
8. So then they that are in the flesh cannot please God. (Rom. 8:5–8)

10. As it is written, There is none righteous, no, not one:
11. There is none that understandeth, there is none that seeketh after God.
12. They are all gone out of the way, they are together become unprofitable; there is none that doeth good, no, not one. (Rom. 3:10–12)

23. For whatsoever is not of faith is sin. (Rom. 14:23)

Clearly, Van Baalen, you do not do justice to this view of scripture and the confessions. You may want to change that a bit. In your view, by nature man is so corrupt that he is wholly incapable of doing any good and inclined to all wickedness, but the corrupt nature by God's general grace once again becomes capable of doing positive good. We profess with all boldness that exactly this last part is neither according to the confessions nor according to scripture. This view closes its eyes to scripture—first looking around in the world and then allowing itself to be tempted by the apparent good of the world to say that natural man still indeed does good. You did not draw this out of God's word, since scripture and the confessions do not speak about man in the abstract, that is, about man who would be corrupt if God's general grace did not make him somewhat capable of doing good; rather, they describe man as he really is, as he lives and functions in this world. Therefore, our view is not opposed to scripture and the confessions, but yours is.

Do we say then that natural man has not retained any of his gifts? Absolutely not. We want to emphasize that. Without those natural gifts man would not be able to sin or even continue as a creature who is accountable before God. But we insist that with those gifts he cannot will anything other than wickedness before God and that in various ways he completely pollutes them and holds them under in unrighteousness, even in natural things. That is the language of the confessions.

Is it perhaps our view that sin already reveals itself in all its fullness in the world? That is not true either. We understand perfectly well that sin has not yet come to its full maturity. However, we do not explain this by a restraining work of God, of which there is never any mention in either scripture or the confessions, but simply from the organic development of things. That is our perfect right. Van Baalen may differ from us here and attempt to show that our view does not hold good, but he has no right to accuse us of being un-Reformed in any respect.

We conclude this chapter with the assertion that we have supported with all necessary proofs that Van Baalen has wrongly judged and has rashly accused us. He will surely want to acknowledge this himself.

CHAPTER 3

CALVIN AND KUYPER ON COMMON GRACE

As Van Baalen proceeds to judge our view in light of Reformed theology, he says, first, that he will limit himself to Reformed theologians of the last half-century. The reason he gives is that we are dealing "with an immense field." If this means that the field of Reformed theology per se is immense, we are relatively agreed, but we do not see the sense of these words in this connection. The author clearly wants to leave the impression that before half a century ago there was already so much written about common grace that it would be impossible to get through it if one would begin to draw this doctrine out of Reformed theology. This is all new to us. If it is truly Van Baalen's conviction that there are still a whole bunch of little flowers to be plucked in this immense field in support of the doctrine of common grace, he could really do a service to Reformed theology, which no one has yet done, and we would ask that he get to work. Kuyper laments that this doctrine was so poorly developed by Reformed theology, and he went all the way back to Calvin.

Therefore, what Van Baalen unearths from Reformed theology of the last half-century is almost not worth the trouble, except for Kuyper and Bavinck. Surely even brother Van Baalen does not concur with Hodge's view. The quotation from Gravemeyer is preposterous, and what Van Baalen cites from Van Andel does not even relate to the present question among us. We deny neither the long-suffering of God nor the glimmerings of natural light. That Van Baalen cites these passages demonstrates that although he has certainly searched diligently, he has been able to find very little on common grace outside of Kuyper and Bavinck.

Then Van Baalen again begins to attack us concerning what we wrote against Janssen. This continually recurring phenomenon is typical. *Ex ungue leonem* [From the claw one knows the lion]. Van Baalen is of the opinion that we have dragged Janssen's good name through the mud. We disagree with the brother on this point as well. We have done the churches a service by calling their attention to the dangerous instruction of Janssen. Van Baalen should be thankful for that.

He has, however, not one word of appreciation for us. He condemns everything we have done, and thereby he also condemns the church. It is simply absurd to assume that Hoeksema, who never served on the Janssen committee at synod, could alone have effected Janssen's deposition and our churches' condemnation of his teaching as un-Reformed. Van Baalen, who certainly has the right to protest a synodical decision, gives the whole church a slap in the face.

This aside, we ask on what basis he claims that we have dragged Janssen's good name through the mud. Is it simply because we wrote, "One cannot but be speechless at the audacity of the claim that the doctrine of general grace is one of the most prominent doctrines that Calvin distinguished"? We still hold to this position, and we will show the reason.

We are also speechless at the way brother Van Baalen argues in this connection: we drag Janssen's good name in the mud, and we should not write like that. Why not? Because in claiming that the doctrine of common grace is one of Calvin's most prominent doctrines, Janssen has simply followed Kuyper and quoted Bavinck. Therefore, we should not say that the claim was audacious and we were speechless! Well then, brother, here is our explanation. This time we have purposely scoured Calvin. We have read over his *Institutes*, and on that basis we have come to the conviction that Janssen's claim mentioned above was audacious. Now we want to demonstrate that.

It would be worth the trouble to produce a separate brochure on what Calvin actually taught about general grace. Determining what Calvin taught is not all that easy, especially since the meaning attached to a specific term at a certain time is sometimes entirely different from the meaning given to it later on. Still, we must attempt to state briefly what his view is. Our conviction is that with regard to the essential point, Calvin's view is fundamentally different from that of Kuyper.

The difference comes down to this: Calvin, Kuyper, and Bavinck all teach that God gives good gifts to all men in this life. We agree with this. Gifts of understanding and reason, artistic talent and sense, rain and sunshine, money and goods, houses and fields, love and merriment are all good gifts of God. God is good, and his gifts are always good. He always treats all his creatures well. But the great difference is that Calvin always holds the position that natural man with all his gifts can never will or do good before God but always remains wicked, whereas Kuyper supposes that natural man by the power of general grace is inclined unto good.

As we will soon see, Calvin also teaches that the fact that natural man does not always fall into the most dreadful sins is to be attributed to a restraint of sin by God. We believe that we have found another explanation for this phenomenon in the organic development of things. But Calvin never permits any good to come forth from that restraint; Kuyper does. Let us try to make this clear with quotations from both writers.

In his dedication to the king of France, Calvin writes,

> For what is more consonant with faith than to recognize that we are naked of all virtue, in order to be clothed by God? That we are empty of all good, to be filled by him? That we are slaves of sin, to be freed by him? Blind, to be illuminated by him? Lame, to be made straight by him? Weak, to be sustained by him? To take away from us all occasion for glorying, that he alone may stand forth gloriously and we glory in him...? When we say these and like things our adversaries *interrupt and complain that in this way we shall subvert some blind light of nature*, imaginary preparations, free will, and works that merit eternal salvation, even with their supererogations.[33]

Especially this last part is significant. One can hear the same complaint against the total depravity of natural man also in our day.

---

33 Calvin, *Institutes*, 20:13. The emphasis is that of Danhof and Hoeksema.—Ed.

Concerning the natural knowledge of God in the sinner, Calvin writes,

> Yet that seed remains which can in no wise be uprooted: that there is some sort of divinity; but *this seed is so corrupted that by itself it produces only the worst fruits.*
>
> From this, my present contention is brought out with greater certainty, that a sense of divinity is by nature engraven on human hearts. For necessity forces from the reprobate themselves a confession of it. In tranquil times they wittily joke about God, indeed are facetious and garrulous in belittling his power. If any occasion for despair presses upon them, it goads them to seek him and impels their perfunctory prayers. From this it is clear that they have not been utterly ignorant of God, but that what should have come forth sooner was held back by stubbornness.[34]

The summary of all this is that there is knowledge of God engraved in natural man, which, however, never produces anything in him but exceedingly wicked fruits. He is not thereby induced to honor God, but only to make use of him as an instrument in times of need and anguish. This is something entirely different from what Janssen wished to force upon us in the Reformed churches in wanting to put man above scripture with this natural knowledge of God.

Concerning this natural understanding over against the general revelation of God in nature and in history, Calvin writes,

> But although the Lord represents both himself and his everlasting Kingdom in the mirror of his works with very great clarity, such is our stupidity that we grow increasingly dull toward so manifest testimonies, and they flow away with profiting us.[35]

Concerning the philosophers of the heathen world, Calvin writes,

> As each was furnished with higher wit, graced with art and knowledge, so did he seem to camouflage his utterances; yet if

---

34 Ibid., 1.4.4, 20:51. The emphasis is that of Danhof and Hoeksema.—Ed.
35 Ibid., 1.5.11, 20:63.—Ed.

you look more closely upon all these, you will find them all to be fleeting unrealities.[36]

Concerning general revelation, he writes,

It is therefore in vain that so many burning lamps shine for us in the workmanship of the universe to show forth the glory of its Author. Although they bathe us wholly in their radiance, yet they can of themselves in no way lead us into the right path. Surely they strike some sparks, but before their fuller light shines forth these are smothered.[37]

This language is in agreement with the Reformed confessions. But we [the Christian Reformed Church] have not followed this route with our doctrine of common grace. On the contrary, we have so fanned those sparks that they are spreading a blaze of light in the enlightened world around them, in which even the believer may bathe himself! True, Kuyper has not dared to follow this through consistently. But those who apart from common grace do not need much of Kuyper, who abhor and hate the antithesis and want to build almost entirely on his common grace, surely do this. Thus we are led into the midst of the world. So also Janssen arrives at his notion that man naturally seeks after truth.

In *Institutes* 2.2.12–17, Calvin deals with the natural gifts that remain in man after the fall. It would require too much space to copy this entire passage here.[38] We will reproduce the thought and cite the sharpest sections. One must also understand that Calvin never speaks of natural gifts as one of his most prominent doctrines. He treats these gifts in connection with the depravity of man, and subordinately he dedicates a few paragraphs to the natural gifts.

Calvin begins by saying, "And, indeed, that common opinion which they have taken from Augustine pleases me: that the natural gifts were corrupted in man through sin, but that his supernatural gifts

---

36 Ibid., 1.5.12, 20:65.—Ed.
37 Ibid., 1.5.14, 20:68.—Ed.
38 Ibid., 2.2.12–17, 20:270–77.—Ed.

were stripped from him."[39] Among these last, supernatural gifts, Calvin names the love of God, the love of the neighbor, and the exercise of holiness and righteousness. He says that these were destroyed in man by sin. Nevertheless, there have remained in man a few natural gifts of the understanding and will. But even natural reason has been so corrupted that it seems to be in unsightly ruins.

Further, Calvin deals with a few things that are brought about by these natural gifts, such as civil justice, beautiful works of art, perception, and reasoning. He attributes all those gifts to the Holy Spirit, who distributes them to everyone as he wills. He even calls this something in which we have to recognize God's particular grace—particular not in the same sense that we now use that word, but in the sense of distinction. There are indeed men who are deprived of these gifts, such as those who are insane. He concludes this consideration by saying,

> For with the greatest truth Augustine teaches that as the free gifts were withdrawn from man after the Fall, so the natural ones remaining were corrupted...*Not that the gifts could become defiled by themselves, seeing that they came from God. But to defiled man these gifts were no longer pure, and from them he could derive no praise at all.*[40]

Take notice that here again is the same thought. Man does receive good gifts from God, but they are unclean to him. He pollutes them. This pertains to the natural gifts.

In *Institutes* 2.3.3, Calvin returns to this subject. Here also he does not speak of these gifts as one of his most important doctrines. Just the opposite is true. This chapter deals with the fact that natural man can never produce anything other than what is damnable before God. After Calvin has very sharply and powerfully developed this, he foresees a potential objection, and he goes into that objection. Some of the heathen have indeed been adorned with excellent gifts. Therefore, the opinion is untenable that man's nature is entirely corrupted. To that Calvin gives the reply, "Amid this corruption of nature there is some

---

39 Ibid., 2.2.12, 20:270.—Ed.
40 Ibid., 2.2.16, 20:275. The emphasis is that of Danhof and Hoeksema.—Ed.

place for God's grace: not such grace as to cleanse it, but to restrain it inwardly."[41]

To know what Calvin understands by this grace amidst the corruption of human nature and how he conceives God's restraint of sin, one must continue reading to the end of this paragraph. There Calvin writes,

> Hence some are restrained by shame from breaking out into many kinds of foulness, others by the fear of the law—even though they do not, for the most part, hide their impurity. Still others, because they consider an honest manner of life profitable, in some measure aspire to it. Others rise above the common lot, in order by their excellence to keep the rest obedient to them. Thus God by his providence bridles perversity of nature, that it may not break forth into action; but he does not purge it within.[42]

This too is clearly sufficient. Calvin does not speak of grace that works in the heart of natural man, by which in one way or another he feels impelled to do and will the good. But Calvin speaks of other influences, such as shame before others, fear before the law, and selfishness, which can serve as deterrents to sinful deeds. His mind always remains just as wicked and sinful, but he does not always break out into the act. Note that this is also completely different from the newer view that the process of sin is checked in history. Calvin never makes natural man even a little bit better by a working of general grace.

Calvin feels that an objection remains. How, by a restraining of sin in man, by a bridling whereby the sinful man does not break out into the act of sin, will the good yet be performed by that man? Even if the act of sin is held back in him out of fear or shame, he is still not performing the good. Yet it seems to be true that some heathens have led virtuous lives. Thus we have the example of Camillus. Calvin replies that this is no more than appearance. Even under the greatest appearance of purity, he says, human nature is impelled unto

---

41 Ibid., 2.3.3, 20:292.—Ed.
42 Ibid., 20:292–93.—Ed.

corruption because the mind of man is and remains wicked. What-ever appearance of virtue he may practice, he does this with a wicked mind. Apart from that, Calvin explains cases like Camillus in this way: "These [virtues] are not common gifts of nature, but special graces of God, which he bestows variously and in a certain measure upon men otherwise wicked."[43]

Note that graces (plural) here simply has the meaning of gifts, and that these are not common but peculiar. Then Calvin adds, "But because, however excellent anyone has been, his own ambition always pushes him on—a blemish with which all virtues are so sullied that before God they lose all favor—anything in profane men that appears praiseworthy must be considered worthless."[44]

So much for Calvin. We think all this can be briefly summarized as follows. First, he does not deal with any doctrine of general grace. What he does write in this respect is not treated as a prominent part of his instruction, but in reply to objections that men would bring against his exposition of the total depravity of man. Second, he views what has remained in man after the fall as gifts of God, and he calls those gifts "graces," for which man owes gratitude to God. Third, that natural man does not always break out into the act of sin Calvin attributes to a certain restraining of sin through shame, fear, selfishness, and so

---

43 Ibid., 2.3.4, 20:293. Note 5 on page 293 in the Mc Neill/Battles edition of Cal-vin's *Institutes* explains Calvin's reference to Camillus in Calvin's treatment of total depravity. Camillus was a "noble Roman," who behaved bravely in defense of his nation. Calvin recognized the difference, morally, between such an ungodly idolater and other heathens, who behaved shamefully. Calvin attributes the civil nobility of a Camillus to a "special grace" of God (not to a "common grace"). Advocates of common grace appeal to this analysis of the pagan Camillus by Calvin in support of their doctrine of common grace. What these advocates of common grace ignore is that Calvin goes on virtually to identify what he has called "special grace" with God's providence. Such gifts as Camillus exhibited are aspects of a "heroic nature" in ungodly persons. Devastating to the proponents of common grace is Calvin's concluding judgment upon Camillus and all such "noble" unbelievers: "all estranged from Christ lack 'the fear of God,' which is the beginning of wisdom [Ps. 111:10p]." Calvin continues, "As for the virtues that deceive us with their vain show, they shall have their praise in the political assembly and in common renown among men; but before the heavenly judgment seat they shall be no value to acquire righteousness" (Ibid., 20:294).—Ed.
44 Ibid., 20:294.—Ed.

on.[45] Fourth, he always very emphatically maintains that natural man, with all those gifts, can never will or do good, but that all those gifts are impure to him because he himself is impure.

Now compare this with the newer view of common grace. Kuyper writes,

> It follows from Romans 2:13–14 that this common grace not only left a notion in the fallen sinner of what is honorable and dishonorable, just and unjust, good and evil; it not only holds him in place and allows him to work, *but this common grace still also grants the sinner the power to do good.* He [Paul] indeed says that, "When the Gentiles, which have not the law (of Sinai), do by nature the things contained in the law..." They, therefore, not only *know* them, but they do them as well, and exactly from that fact that they do them Paul draws the conclusion that they have knowledge thereof. That doing is therefore a point of departure for the apologetic argument. Now if it is maintained that even a child of God professes "to be incapable of thinking, and much less of doing, any good of himself," then it follows from this that the heathen do not do this good of themselves either, nor of their own strength, but only through the fact that common grace drives and enables them to do it.[46]

In the explanation of this text from Romans 2, Kuyper deviates fundamentally from Calvin. To be sure, Calvin also explains the same text:

> There is nothing more common than for a man to be sufficiently instructed in a right standard of conduct by natural law (of which the apostle is here speaking). Let us consider, however, for what purpose men have been endowed with this

---

45 What Calvin means is not an internal improvement by a working of God's grace that yet enables natural man to do good within his consciousness, will, and inclinations. But he simply has his eye on the difference between the external act and the heart. The heart always is and remains just as wicked. It is even very possible that by sin not breaking out into the external act, it becomes even greater before God.

46 Abraham Kuyper, *De Gemeene Gratie* [Common grace] (Amsterdam: Höveker & Wormser, 1902–4), 2:17. The emphasis is that of Danhof and Hoeksema.—Trans.

knowledge of the law. How far it can lead them toward the goal of reason and truth.[47]

Calvin then demonstrates that this law can serve only to take away from natural man every cloak of innocence. Calvin argues that the apostle does not mean that the heathen actually obey the law, but that they formally walk according to a law and thus sin against a law that is written in their hearts.

Moreover, let us pay attention to the theorem expressed here by Kuyper. He speaks of good in the sense of practicing God's law, or even in the sense in which the Heidelberg Catechism speaks about it, when he says that we are by nature incapable of any good. No man does this good by nature. We are by nature so depraved that we are incapable of any good. The child of God does this good in principle by the power of regeneration. Not of himself but out of the life of regeneration he is once again capable of doing good. But the heathen man does this (even in the same measure) by the power of common grace that works in him.

You might hold it against us if we attack a great man like Kuyper, but the fact remains that Kuyper has herewith fundamentally strayed from the path of Calvin, who always maintained that natural man can never will or do good with his remaining gifts. Kuyper has also strayed from the clear pronouncements of the confessions. The proposition can be briefly restated thus: "Natural man is incapable of any good unless common grace grants him the power to do this good." We deny that anyone who professes this proposition is Reformed.

We are completely aware that Kuyper attempts to justify this idea in every possible way and to explain it in harmony with the confessions, which always maintain that man is by nature wholly incapable of doing any good. This endeavor is never successful. Kuyper first declares it to be true that good exists in unregenerate man only on the outside. God causes him to do good by his common grace without man's wanting or intending it himself. This is a strange theorem indeed![48]

Later Kuyper feels that this theorem cannot give any satisfaction

---

47 Calvin, *Institutes*, 2.22, 20:281.—Ed.
48 Kuyper, *Common Grace*, 2:300–1.—Trans.

either. After all, whatever man does he does consciously and willingly. Otherwise in the doctrine of general grace you get a sort of determinism by which God forces the sinner against his will to do some good that he does not mean to do. Therefore, Kuyper later declares that common grace improves natural man to some extent, even in his understanding, will, and inclinations, so that in reality he wants to do the good that he performs. The core of the ego (whatever this might mean) stays out of it, but "the unconverted man in his inclinations, in his consciousness, and in his will can be influenced by common grace."[49]

So then you get an operation of God's grace by which natural man is turned to the good in his understanding, will, and inclinations, by which he can think and will that good, and that finally differs from saving grace only in that it does not penetrate to the ego. Therefore, by common grace the nature is indeed improved (understanding, will, and inclinations certainly belong to the nature of man), but the ego stays out of it.[50] However great Kuyper may be, we cannot reconcile this with scripture and the confessions. Not even Kuyper is successful in this. We profess with all boldness before God and the church that we must fundamentally differ with this view. Outside of the regenerate, there is not such an operation of God's grace in natural man.

The main goal of our exposition was only to demonstrate that this doctrine of Kuyper is found nowhere in Calvin, and that therefore our claim stands that it is audacious to say the doctrine of common grace is one of the most prominent doctrines Calvin distinguished. Moreover, we can also take our leave of Van Baalen's chapter on this. He mainly points out that we differ with Kuyper and Bavinck on this point. We had written that ourselves for a long time already. In this chapter we have once again and emphatically asserted it.

---

49 Ibid., 2:306.—Trans.
50 Ibid., 2:309.—Trans.

CHAPTER 4

THE CONFESSIONS
AND COMMON GRACE

Next Van Baalen devotes a chapter to the confessional side of the matter. We will respond accordingly.

If the brother's attempt here should fail, certainly his entire booklet will be a failure. In fact, both this chapter and the entire pamphlet are a total failure. We cannot imagine that our church papers have recommended this work to our people just as it is, without any criticism. Especially we do not understand the high praises from Henry Beets in the *Banner* and from Karel Fortuin in *De Wachter*.[51] The brothers have nothing but praise. Language and form and content are considered praiseworthy. Fortuin even thinks that the matter is clear enough now to take action. We do not understand this. But let us take a look.

Van Baalen attempts to demonstrate that the confessions clearly teach common grace. The very term appears in the Canons! Well then, that must mean our fathers believed in common grace. The fact that our confessions speak of common grace only one time must prove all the more that the fathers believed in it. The brother strays here from the subject being discussed. Let us suppose once that what he says is true. Even then the question is not what our fathers believed, but what they set down in the confessions.

Van Baalen gets back on track. He attributes to us a reprehensible argumentation that we greatly resent,[52] because it leaves the impression that we are dishonest. According to him, we indeed recognize that the confessions teach common grace, but we rationalize it away

---

51 *De Wachter* was a Christian Reformed periodical written in Dutch.—Ed.
52 Van Baalen, *Denial of Common Grace*, 64–65.

as follows: the confessions name a certain doctrine only one time. But another doctrine, which Hoeksema cannot bring into agreement therewith, is expounded in the confessions much more at length. Van Baalen claims that our remedy to this is simply to eliminate what does not please us and preserve what seems good to us. Since the latter has been expounded much more at length, we still have the greatest part of the confessions on our side. Thus, says Van Baalen, we calmly proceed, all the while claiming that we are in agreement with the confessions.

Van Baalen adds that this comes from men who were convinced that Bultema had to be deposed because he taught something not stated anywhere in the confessions! In this last point the brother once again shows his ignorance regarding the confessions and the Bultema affair. He is obviously not very well informed on this matter, or else he is totally ignorant of Bultema's positions, which were condemned by synod. The kingship of Christ over his church—is it not stated in the confessions, brother Van Baalen? The unity of the Old and New Testament church—is it not stated in the confessions, brother? You might do well to investigate this matter first, before you bring such an idea any farther into the church.

Concerning the argument you want to attribute to us, we definitely take it evil of you. To argue like that would be low and dishonest. You know as well as we do that we never have argued like that. The whole argument is a figment of your imagination. That you think we would argue like that reveals more about yourself than about us. Such arguments do not arise in our brains, brother. You are once again quite wrong.

The confession puts the point we are dealing with like this:

> The true doctrine having been explained, the Synod *rejects* the errors of those...Who teach that the corrupt and natural man can so well use the common grace (by which they understand the light of nature), or the gifts still left him after the fall, that he can gradually gain by their good use a greater, namely, the evangelical or saving grace and salvation itself.[53]

---

53 Canons of Dordt 3–4, error 5, in *Confessions and Church Order*, 171.—Ed.

What was our argument? It is that the fathers who drew up the Canons placed the term *common grace* on the lips of the Remonstrants. The Remonstrants spoke of nothing other than common grace. The fathers, however, did not want to be accountable for this term. They preferred to speak of the "light of nature," as the Canons do in 3–4.4, or of the gifts still left to fallen man, as in Belgic Confession 14 and Canons 3–4, error 5. In my view the meaning and sense is that this is "the common grace by which they understand the same thing as we do when we speak of the light of nature." It was the Remonstrants who preferred to speak of common grace; the fathers avoided that term.

You will surely agree that this argument is entirely different from what you ascribed to us, will you not? As a brother, will you not also want to express publicly that you have wrongly ascribed to us this foolish argument, and that this truly grieves you?

We now go a step further. The explanation we gave above, which can in itself also be interpreted differently, is confirmed by the fact that the confessions speak nowhere of common grace, not even where one would expect to see it.[54] How do you explain this fact, brother Van Baalen? We explain it this way: they have intentionally avoided that term, for example, in Canons 3–4.4. "There remain, however, in man since the fall, the glimmerings of natural light, whereby he retains some knowledge of God, of natural things."[55] Why have our fathers not used *common grace* in this article? You admit that they were familiar with it. You will also agree that, if anywhere, they would have used it here. How do you explain that they did not? You cite the example of

---

54 It is indeed quite clear that in the drawing up of the confessions, especially of the Canons, our fathers were not thinking about the doctrine of common grace (*gemeene gratie*) as it is being developed among us now. The subject that they always defended tooth and nail was that of sovereign election and reprobation. Common grace for them belonged within the framework of universal reconciliation. According to the Arminian interpretation, man by common grace became capable of accepting saving grace. It is noteworthy that Van Baalen comes with the argument that whoever does not believe in universal grace cannot preach the gospel! *Ex ungue leonem* (From the claw one recognizes the lion)!

55 Canons of Dordt 3–4.4, in Schaff, *Creeds of Christendom*, 3:588.—Ed.

the deity of Christ. But if you are actually positive about the deity of Christ, would you avoid the term? Explain this, brother.[56]

The same thing is in the Belgic Confession:

> And being thus become wicked, perverse, and corrupt in all his ways, he hath lost all his excellent gifts which he had received from God, and only retained a few remains thereof, which, however, are sufficient to leave man without excuse; for all the light which is in us is changed into darkness.[57]

Here again is the same reality. You will agree with me that the confession is speaking about things that you would call common grace. Correct? You also agree that our fathers were familiar with that term. Why did they not use the term there?

In the rejection of errors, they lay this same term on the lips of the Remonstrants. It is indeed strange, brother, when you imagine that the term was a favorite with our fathers. Would you please give your explanation of that? If, for example, you would write the confession, would you also handle it this way? Would you omit the term from article 14 of the Belgic Confession and Canons 3–4.4 and then use it in the way our fathers did in the rejection of errors? No, you

---

56 Regarding the rejection of common grace by the Reformed creeds, Danhof and Hoeksema argued, in part, that the creeds never speak of common grace, except once, and in this single instance attribute the theory of common grace to the Arminians. Danhof and Hoeksema called attention to the fact that the creeds fail to speak of common grace particularly in those articles in which, if the Reformed fathers did believe common grace, the theory would surely be mentioned.

Van Baalen responded to this argument against common grace with a strained, strange, hypothetical counter-argument consisting of the contention that a defense of the doctrine of the Godhead of Jesus that fails explicitly to state that Jesus is God does not necessarily imply that the author of the defense denies the Godhead of Jesus. To this counter-argument Danhof and Hoeksema reply with the obvious question, "If you are actually positive about the deity of Christ, would you avoid the term?" (Van Baalen, *Denial of Common Grace*, 64–66).

At the very least, common grace is not a creedal, Reformed doctrine.

For the Christian Reformed Church to have made the theory binding on Danhof, Hoeksema, and many others in 1924–25, so that it exercised church discipline on those who denied common grace, was un-Reformed, unconscionable, and indefensible.—Ed.

57 Belgic Confession 14, in Schaff, *Creeds of Christendom*, 3:398–99.—Ed.

wouldn't, would you? You would put *common grace* everywhere you possibly could.

My explanation is that the fathers purposely avoided the term. It had a bad aura for them. They did not want it. Therefore, they spoke of natural light and of the gifts that remained and intentionally spoke nowhere of common grace. This explanation does not lack clarity, don't you agree? It is a completely different way of reasoning from what you attributed to us, brother!

But all this still pertains only to the term *common grace* [*algemeene genade*], and we do not like to quarrel over words. After all, Kuyper criticized the term as such and preferred to use the word *gratie*.[58] If the argument over common grace involves only a term, we would not have been so insistent that with our church's view of common grace, as it has been further developed in recent times and powerfully promoted among us, we have taken such a dangerous path. It has to do with principles, not terms.

We now return to the confessions. Where do they speak of the process of sin being restrained? Indeed nowhere. Certainly you will not claim that, according to the Reformed confessions, we must believe and preach that sin is restrained in its course, will you? Where do the confessions say that natural man is improved by an operation of common grace in the understanding, will, and inclinations, so that he can perform good? Nowhere. Where do the confessions identify the few remains and the natural light as grace, much less as common grace? Nowhere. Where do the confessions discuss a covenant of common grace that was concluded with Noah? Nowhere.

Van Baalen, you have exhausted yourself to show that the confessions speak clearly about this doctrine. But it is in vain, brother. Of all these main topics of the doctrine of general grace that we have summarized above, the confessions do not speak at all, and in some places they are decidedly opposed. In the strongest possible terms the confessions contradict the claim that natural man can still do good out of the power of general grace. Regarding natural light, the confessions teach that thereby natural man performs some civic justice and reveals

---

58 The Dutch word means "grace" and is a synonym of *genade*.—Trans.

some regard for virtue, but that he renders this light wholly polluted even in natural things and holds it under in unrighteousness.

Van Baalen, you claim that a confession is almost always born out of conflict, that the conflict in those days had little to do with this point, and that therefore general grace is not mentioned as we might wish it to be. But we ask once again, if that claim is true, why does the term appear only in the rejection of errors and never where you would certainly expect it—in the positive development of the doctrine?

My answer you know, and it is diametrically opposed to your assertion. Besides, why is not any trace of this "important doctrine" to be discovered in the Heidelberg Catechism? Why not in the Belgic Confession? Why, Van Baalen, must you resort to claims that you simply snatch out of the sky, as, for example, that we deny the doctrine of providence as developed in Lord's Day 10? You simply say that, but you do not prove it. You do not demonstrate how this necessarily follows from our view. We have never expressed this.

Why is the term *common grace*, which is supposed to be a fundamental doctrine of our faith, a Boaz of God's temple,[59] used only when placed on the lips of the Remonstrants? Why does this remarkable phenomenon occur, that you, and others who think they must do battle with us, raise the accusation that we push the doctrine of election too strongly? Why is it that you quote the text "God wills that all men be saved" in such an Arminian fashion?

You see, brother, all of this is characteristic. Our fathers avoided that term because it had the flavor of the Remonstrants. You fight so strongly against the denial of common grace with a pamphlet that here and there also exhibits a tone that makes us fear the worst.

This may also serve as the answer to the "excellent words" you quoted from Groen out of *Onze Toekomst*. The same basic reasoning for common grace is found in *Onze Toekomst* and in the pamphlet

---

59 In a work entitled *The Foe within the Gates*, Henry J. van Andel identified the two pillars of the temple of God's truth as the doctrines of particular grace (Jachin) and common grace (Boaz) (1 Kings 7:21). Hoeksema preferred to identify these two pillars of God's truth as the doctrines of God's sovereign grace and God's covenant (see *Believers and Their Seed: Children in the Covenant*, rev. ed. [Grandville, MI: Reformed Free Publishing Association, 1997], 1–2).—Trans.

B. K. Kuiper published in connection with the Janssen case. Both wanted to maintain and defend through common grace the "neutrality standpoint" of Janssen. It will not be unknown to you, brother, that G. Doekes, well-known in the Netherlands, in *De Wachter* has condemned this use of common grace as definitely un-Reformed. There he condemned Kuiper's pamphlet and made known in terms even less mild that no good concerning form or content could be found in that booklet. Perhaps without even knowing it, he condemned at the same time the writing of Groen in *Onze Toekomst*.

Let the following suffice for this point: We have never denied natural light as the confessions interpret it. We do deny that many in our day, including especially Janssen, follow and maintain this point of the confessions. Under the positive development of natural light, what Groen quotes is only part of what is said.[60] The Canons teach that natural man is incapable of using this light rightly even in natural things, but he holds it in unrighteousness and in various ways renders it polluted. Without any reservation we fully endorse articles 13 and 14 of the Belgic Confession and Lord's Day 10. If Groen claims that this is inconceivable without our believing in common grace, and you quote this with such approval, the burden of proof is still on you, is it not? We have never denied that God is an overflowing fountain of all good gifts.

Finally, this entire chapter makes a poor impression on us. All kinds of things are dragged in that have absolutely no connection to the doctrine of common grace. In exactly this way the brother has left the impression that it is well-nigh impossible to demonstrate that this doctrine was ever included in the confessions. Truly, this chapter is a complete failure!

---

60 Van Baalen, *Denial of Common Grace*, 66. Van Baalen is quoting Groen's quotation of the Canons of Dordt.—Trans.

CHAPTER 5

VAN BAALEN'S METHOD OF SCRIPTURAL INTERPRETATION

T
he chapter in which Van Baalen thinks he can prove that our view is against holy scripture is concluded with the profoundly grave statement, "Once again, acknowledge that you have erred." The author is quite convinced that his line of argument is conclusive and his proof is binding. After Van Baalen has written this, there is only one way still open to us, and that is the way of remorse, repentance, and reform from our erring way.

We have already expressed our appreciation for the brother's grave concern for us. In his call to return [to the right path] you can feel his heart burning with brotherly love toward us, and that is moving. But it must also be said that possibly Van Baalen has been a bit carried away by his brotherly love, calling for repentance too quickly. One can be so driven by love and concern for someone that at the slightest sign of danger he cries out, "Repent!" It also happens once in a while that one receives a sharp and serious application in a less-than-sharp sermon. This latter is the case in the chapter of Van Baalen's pamphlet titled "Against the Holy Scripture." We want to demonstrate the weakness of the "sermon" here.

Let us first give an overview of the content. Van Baalen quotes twelve texts, apart from the reference to the book of Jonah. The brother gives no exegesis (interpretation of scripture) at all. He does not go into a single concept. The concept of grace, which is certainly the main issue, he does not discuss. Also, the brother never goes into the related concepts of goodness, mercy, kindness, and so forth. He does not give any explanation of a text, unless we must accept as the brother's explanation what he sometimes says about a text. Much less does he even somewhat work out any of the fundamental ideas of scripture that stand in close connection with the subject. Concerning the image of God, sin, the development of sin, election and reprobation, and so forth, the brother makes no mention; he simply quotes twelve texts. At times he says something about a text, at times nothing at all, and at times he merely refers to a text without even quoting it.

Without saying anything about them, the brother quotes the following texts: Psalm 33:5; 65:11; Luke 6:35; 1 Kings 21:27–29; Acts 14:16–17; Genesis 31:4–7; and Psalm 105:14–15. Without quoting them, the brother refers to the following texts: Ezra 1:2–3; John 1:4; and Romans 2:4–5. He does say something about Matthew 5:45 and Romans 1:24, 26, 28, but he does not give anything that can claim the title of scriptural interpretation.

This method is condemned from the Reformed standpoint as totally reprehensible. It is an easy way of getting something from scripture and seeming to prove it to the simple folk. The writer who uses such a manner of giving proof from scripture naturally needs to devote very little study to his subject. The method has the intention of reaching its goal very easily, so that with a single text it moves anyone out of the way. But for anyone who piously considers this method, it is very weak and does not supply any proof. A Baptist uses the same method to demonstrate that infant baptism is condemned, and an Arminian that God wills all men to be saved and therefore there can be no mention of personal election in scripture. The fact is that the scripture forms an organic whole. Therefore, you cannot treat all the parts as standing loosely next to each other.

It is also very peculiar that Van Baalen's method is that of the old Scholastics and of the Methodists and pietists from the eighteenth and the beginning of the nineteenth centuries. Kuyper writes,

> The manner in which the Scholastics ordinarily brought up proof from Holy Scripture consisted almost in the citation of this or that specific statement appearing in this or that verse of holy scripture. Now the reformers are not known to be

completely free of this method; indeed, they make much use
of this method; but not one of the reformers uses this method
exclusively. They compare scripture with scripture. They look
for an *analogia fidei* [analogy of faith]. They are constantly
trying to penetrate deeper into the organic life of the scriptures. Whoever has even hastily paged through Voetius' writing
(*"Quousque se extendat autoritas Scripturae"* [How far does
the authority of scripture extend itself?]) at once perceives the
much more correct standpoint on which the theologians of
that time had set themselves. But insofar as the teller of this
legend (previously named) was similar, as in the eighteenth
and the beginning of the nineteenth centuries, this unscientific
method gained more and more entrance, especially under the
influence of pietism and Methodism. Few thoughtful people
among the simple believers promoted so odd a notion of holy
scripture. Such people then deemed that scriptural proof had
been supplied when one quoted a specific verse from holy
scripture that literally and fully expresses what is asserted.
It is a strict requirement that...releases you from all further
inquiry, and as long as you just cite the scripture, no one will
ask whether your citation is taken from the Old or New Testament, whether it was said by Job's friends or by Job himself,
or whether it appears as an absolute or with an application to
a specific case. The Bible is then your codex, the concordance,
your index, and with the help of that index you can cite from
the codex whenever it sounds right.

The absolute reprehensibility of this method hardly requires
any explanation.[61]

The quotation above applies precisely to the chapter of Van
Baalen's pamphlet "Against the Holy Scripture." His quoting of a few
texts, many of which have nothing to do with our subject, is unworthy
of the brother. Over against the passages the brother quotes, other

61 Abraham Kuyper, *Encyclopaedie der Heilije Godgeleerdheid* [Encyclopedia of
holy theology], 2nd ed. (Kampen: Kok, 1909), 2:518–19.

passages can be mentioned that clearly refute his notion. His position is that God actually wants to show grace, goodness, and mercy to the reprobate in this life. He sends grace to them, is graciously inclined toward them, and lavishes goodness upon them.

Now we will not ask how the brother reconciles this idea, which would be an explanation of the text "He is kind unto the unthankful and to the evil" (Luke 6:35) or of the text "He maketh his sun to rise on the evil and on the good, and sendeth rain on the just and on the unjust" (Matt. 5:45), with any Reformed thinking. But we would like to ask how he would reconcile this with Psalm 92:5–7: "O LORD, how great are thy works! and thy thoughts are very deep. A brutish man knoweth not; neither doth a fool understand this. When the wicked spring as the grass, and when all the workers of iniquity do flourish; it is that they shall be destroyed for ever."

Note that the last clause expresses God's purpose, which he accomplishes. He carries it out himself. He makes the wicked spring forth; he makes the workers of iniquity flourish. This means that he makes them great in earthly gifts, in rain and sunshine, in money and goods, and in honor and influence. God does that with the purpose of destroying them forever. Scripture says that here. Scripture is not talking about the thoughts or ways of a man but most certainly about the thoughts of God. It is concerned with the depth of the riches of the knowledge and the ways of God, which are past finding out.

Do not say that this belongs to the hidden things of God, for holy scripture reveals this to us here and wants us to know it. God's word wants us to understand that the Lord enriches the wicked with earthly blessings in order to destroy them forever. How would you reconcile this with your explanation that God lavishes goodness upon the reprobate, that he truly intends to bless them and is favorably inclined toward them?

The same thought is also expressed in Psalm 73, where the concern is over what you would call general or universal grace [*algemeene genade*]. But the poet complains that he has very little of it; the ungodly have everything. This too is a thoroughly scriptural idea, is it not? That so-called universal grace is not very common. This is what scripture teaches. So it was with Asaph. The ungodly had rest, peace, and prosperity in the world. Their eyes stood out with fatness. There was no end to their wealth and prosperity. But with Asaph it was just the other way around. His chastening was renewed every morning. This now grieves the poet. He murmurs against it. He does not understand it. It seems as if there is no knowledge in the Most High.

But soon Asaph goes into the sanctuary of God and sees that contrast in an entirely different light. He sees two things. Concerning himself, he sees that God tightly holds his right hand and guides him by his counsel in order afterward to receive him in glory. Concerning those ungodly men, he sees that God does exactly the opposite. Peace and prosperity are never blessings for the ungodly and are not intended by God as such. They are not proof that God looks down upon them in kindness and wants to bless them in his favor. On the contrary, "Surely thou didst set them in slippery places: thou castedst them down into destruction. How are they brought into desolation, as in a moment! They are utterly consumed with terrors" (Ps. 73:18–19). You must understand that these "slippery places" in this context are the earthly wealth and prosperity in which God has set them and through which he casts them down into destruction. This is the same thought as in Psalm 92.

Once more: how do you reconcile this scriptural notion, which appears again and again, with your idea that God is actually good to the reprobate? Do not immediately say again, brother, that this is rationalism, which wants to reconcile everything and bring it toward a unity of thought, because that does not apply here. It is not rationalism to compare scripture with scripture and to look for the *analogia scripturae* (analogy of scripture). Scripture does not have all kinds of absurdities and contradictions, but most certainly it has one root idea. Scripture certainly does not say in one place that God lavishes goodness on the same men whom it tells us in another place God casts into destruction through those gifts. It is a question of scriptural interpretation here, brother.

In connection with a few passages that appear to teach that God actually lavishes goodness on and is favorably inclined toward the reprobate, we point out, first, that God actually is good to unthankful and wicked men. We also are such men. God's people are such. By nature we are all unthankful and, in principle, enemies of God. God is filled with eternal goodness toward those unthankful and wicked men, and he loved them even when they were yet enemies. He is so good that he gives Christ unto death for them, actually grants them his grace, and causes all things to work together for their good. In that goodness he grants them all good things, even though he may lead them in ways of suffering and oppression, of persecution, slander, and death. Even those apparently evil things are always evidences to them of God's goodness, because he seeks their good in both time and eternity. Therefore, goodness is essentially a concept no different from grace. If anything, goodness expresses the same idea as grace in an even stronger way. But it is goodness upon his people that works only for good to his people and even comes upon them while they are still unthankful and wicked.

Second, God's people live together with the reprobate in this world until they are separated in the day of judgment. They live in the same world and receive the same gifts. Those gifts are God's gifts, revelations of his goodness. The goodness of God, his grace and love, which is meant for his people and is a blessing for his people alone, is thoroughly revealed also to the reprobate ungodly. Outwardly they receive everything God's people receive. They receive even more, because among the people of God are ordinarily not many noble or rich men. But all of this merely works the ruin of the ungodly. It is not that God intended it to be otherwise but did not accomplish his purpose. Rather, it was God's idea and his great wisdom to work their ruin through those gifts. Thus you can also understand that the ungodly man is responsible for his own ruin. The goodness of God revealed to him in the good gifts has only made him more wicked. He has polluted all of it through sin, and therefore his guilt is all the greater.[62]

---

62 The same idea is true with respect to the word, which is also a revelation of God's grace and comes not only to the elect, but also to the reprobate. Thus, the reprobate also have the revelation of God's grace, which was intended to give life only to the elect. It is therefore not Reformed to say that God intends the reprobate to receive grace. Our fathers very clearly taught the opposite in Canons of Dordt 3–4, error 5. The offer of grace does come to all in this world wherever elect

Third, the child of God, in whose heart is the life of God and in whom God has perfected his love, now also loves and blesses his enemies out of that living love, even as God loved him when he was yet an enemy—something that nevertheless does not mean that he now loves God's enemies too. The word of the poet pertains to them: "Do not I hate them, O LORD, that hate thee?...I hate them with perfect hatred" (Ps. 139:21–22). This principle is repeatedly expressed in holy scripture, was taken up in the law of Israel (Deut. 13:6–11), and later was professed by the Savior in Luke 14:26: "If any man come to me, and hate not his father, and mother, and wife, and children, and brethren, and sisters, yea, and his own life also, he cannot be my disciple." God's people, on account of the love wherewith God loved them, can have mercy upon their enemies, but they cannot love the enemies of God.

The observation that this chapter in Van Baalen's pamphlet attests to a much too superficial interpretation of scripture pertains also to the texts that speak about Ahab's repentance. If one does speak of general grace, it is something entirely different from what is related there. Besides, the brother simply quotes without going into any explanation. We would still have to know the character of Ahab's conversion and how it is connected with the second message Elijah has to bring to the king. That [second] message really comes down to this: when the Lord sees that Ahab goes before his face in sackcloth and ashes, afraid from the prophet's first message, the prophet now announces to the king that the proclaimed evil will come upon his house not in his days, but in the days of his son. All of this had to be explained, but Van Baalen merely gives the quotation.

___

and reprobate live organically together, but grace always remains particular from God's side. The one good word is a savor of death unto death and a savor of life unto life, although it is according as God gives grace or does not give grace with the preaching of that word.

So it truly is with all things. According as God gives or does not give grace with his gifts, all things work unto blessing or unto curse. See the references to Psalms 73 and 92 above. So it is also with suffering. Suffering in and of itself is an evil, but with grace suffering becomes a blessing for God's people. Therefore, we do speak of a general revelation of God's grace, goodness, kindness, mercy, and so on, and of good gifts, which all men receive, but not of general grace. Righteous and ungodly men have everything in common in this world, except for grace.

If we enter into the matter, it is completely clear. Ahab has sinned dreadfully. God thunders in his ears that he will punish him with the utter desolation of his house. Ahab's house will be eradicated from Israel. A final judgment is thus announced: utter desolation.

However, one must understand two things. First, scripture teaches that the Lord does not execute such a final judgment unless evil has become fully ripe. The measure of unrighteousness must become full. This pertains to the end of the world and to various judgments in the course of history, such as the flood and the destruction of Sodom and Gomorrah and of Jerusalem, which are types of the end. If the Lord causes someone to be cut off, the measure of unrighteousness is full.

Second, it is also a scriptural idea that fear before an announced judgment is evidence that this evil has not yet become ripe. Ahab was afraid at the first message. He trembled before the fearful judgment of God and went around in sackcloth and ashes. Therefore, Elijah must announce that the evil on Ahab's house will indeed come, but not until the days of his son—something that certainly does not mean that grace is shown to Ahab at the expense of his son, but rather that the evil in Ahab's house will then have become fully ripe. Then this judgment will be executed.

Also, the meaning Van Baalen attaches to "gave...up" and "gave...over" in Romans 1:24, 26, 28 is not the scriptural thought. The brother simply adopts Kuyper's explanation of these passages, which is that the phrases mean that God first restrained sin, held the process of sin in check, and then left the operation of sin to itself.

We have many objections to this explanation. First, it is a completely unscriptural and un-Reformed idea that God leaves something to itself, even if it pertains to sin. God never stands around, looks on, and watches something develop, to put it crudely.

Second, there is no mention of such restraining at all in the context. Paul develops the idea that there has been a revelation of God's eternal power and Godhead in nature since the beginning of the creation, and furthermore, that man could be acquainted with this revelation because of natural light. But man has become foolish in the depravity of his heart, has refused to recognize God as God, and going from bad to worse, has portrayed God as a beast and creeping thing. The waters have coursed quickly in the heathen world. There was no restraining. Thus the context does not mention any restraining of sin.

Third, Van Baalen's explanation also contradicts the text he quotes from Acts 17, which clearly expresses that God let the heathen walk in their own ways.

Fourth, the expression "gave...over" never means that God leaves something to itself, but rather it denotes a positive act of God whereby God seizes something and delivers it over. This same word is used for the giving over of the Son unto death (Rom. 4:25), the Son's giving up of himself (Gal. 2:20), the self-sacrifice of Christ to God for a sweet-smelling savor (Eph. 5:25), and the men who have given up their lives for the name of the Savior (Acts 15:26).

We could continue. Nowhere does the word mean a restraining, but everywhere it denotes a positive act of giving over. So also is it in Romans 1. According to the righteous judgment of God, as punishment for their sin of not wanting to recognize him but having portrayed him as a man, a beast, and a creeping thing, God seizes the heathen and plunges them deeper into uncleanness. Giving over does not mean that God stands by and does nothing more, but rather it looks to a very positive and righteous act of God's rejection.

It is not our concern here to go into the book of Jonah at length. The history is the same as Ahab's conversion. Nineveh was also frightened at God's thundering voice that announced utter destruction. Therefore, Nineveh is spared for a while. It is well-known how the city was destroyed some years later. But apart from that, it simply will not do to deal with the book of Jonah as Van Baalen does. Jonah is prophecy, is it not? You will never understand the right meaning of the book when you treat it as merely a piece of history.

Why is the book of Jonah prophecy? Why is Jonah a type of Christ in his burial and resurrection? Why must Jonah go to Nineveh? Why not to Babylon? How is Nineveh, in distinction from Babylon, Sodom and Gomorrah, and Jerusalem, an image and type in the holy scriptures? You see, we must have the answers to all of these questions to give proof for a scriptural idea from the book of Jonah. The brother does not do that.

But you certainly cannot speak of *universal* grace in connection with something that occurs within a single city, can you?[63]

We can leave the chapter "Against the Holy Scripture" as well. The brother has imagined the matter concerning us to be much too easy. He evidently started from the idea that it was a foregone conclusion that Danhof and Hoeksema were erring spirits who understood neither the confessions nor scripture, or who used both in a rationalistic manner. The opposite is true, brother. We want to understand the scriptures and build along purely Reformed lines. If you think that by quoting twelve texts—some of which have nothing at all to do with the matter, most of which you do not even explain, and others of which you pass by with a single word—you can set us aside and present the doctrine of common grace as crystal clear, you are indeed mistaken. Your chapter is unworthy of a Reformed exegete of scripture. Your cry, "Once again, acknowledge that you have erred," is well-intentioned and much appreciated, but also very misplaced.

---

63 Nineveh stands at the peak of the heathen world and pictures the heathen world as God's people must soon be gathered out of it. This is the difference between the meaning of Nineveh and of Babylon. Babel is the whore, a picture of the reprobate, antichristian world, from which God's people have to separate themselves. Nineveh is a picture of the world as it is temporarily spared by God in his long-suffering, as the gospel is preached to that world, and God's people must be gathered out of that world before the end can come. However, all of this will first come to pass after Christ will have been in the heart of the earth for three days and then raised up. This is why Jonah is the picture of Christ who dies, enters into the heart of the earth, arises, and is preached to the world of which Nineveh is a picture.

CHAPTER 6

A SAD CONCLUSION

xcept for the questions Van Baalen thinks he must put to us and
seems to think must be resolved by us, the brother concludes his
pamphlet with a chapter claiming to demonstrate that our view
is Anabaptist.

After all that we have read and criticized up to this point, we did
not have high expectations for this chapter. Van Baalen never tried to
form an accurate depiction of our view, which he thought was "single
track" and rationalistic. Hence the two chapters that followed, which
were supposed to demonstrate that with our view we oppose scripture
and the confessions, were a complete failure. Proceeding now to this
chapter, we did not expect that Van Baalen would make it clear that
we are Anabaptist.

Even though we did not have high expectations, we are still disappointed by the brother. His attempt to smear us with the paint of
Anabaptism is definitely sad from almost every viewpoint. We will
explain the reasons for our disappointment.

Van Baalen begins once again with his resentment of our attack of
Janssen. Clearly the brother intends to defend Janssen with this pamphlet. We will not get into that matter; it is truly finished. Van Baalen
will certainly have to be much bolder if he hopes to advance the cause
of Janssen. It simply amazes us all the more that our church papers
have so highly recommended this pamphlet. Especially Beets ought
to be rebuked for this. He even thought it should have been written
in English. He offers no criticism. Gratuitously this veiled defense of
Janssen is again recommended to the people!

The first section of Van Baalen's chapter serves merely to inform

our people that Hoeksema once wrote in the *Banner* challenging someone to show that he is Anabaptist. Van Baalen says he will gladly take
that challenge. Now *that* we can accept.

The content of the chapter amounts to this. Van Baalen's conviction is that an Anabaptist can indeed be a Christian. No one should
think, then, that Danhof and Hoeksema no longer belong to Christendom. We are thankful for that. But an Anabaptist, so writes the
brother, is not a Reformed man. He does not belong to our churches.
We heartily agree with that as well.

Furthermore, Van Baalen says that the main characteristic of an
Anabaptist cannot be identified with a single word. The question, what
actually makes an Anabaptist an Anabaptist? cannot be answered so
easily. Not all Anabaptists thought alike. There were many differences
of opinion among them. They did not all think alike even concerning
such things as the incarnation of the Word or polygamy. Therefore,
if Danhof and Hoeksema are accused of Anabaptism, one must not
think that this accusation implies that these brethren also are inclined
to polygamy or defend it. Also, according to Van Baalen, Danhof's
claim went much too far when he wrote that the Anabaptists actually
did away with the scriptures, especially the Old Testament.

So, according to Van Baalen, Louis Berkhof is also wrong. Berkhof
wrote on "The Spectre of Anabaptism" in the *Witness* and intended to
leave the impression that there are absolutely no Anabaptists among
us, because no one among us agrees with the Anabaptists in everything. But this means nothing. According to Van Baalen, Berkhof just
wants to lull our church to sleep. He says, "There is no fire in the city!
Just go back to bed! Rest easy!" Brother Van Baalen says "no thanks"
to that. He does not want to go to bed before he is certain there is no
fire. Now that is certainly commendable of the brother. But a citizen
who continually screams "fire," whereas he only sees the moon shining
through the trees, and who gets the citizens of the city out of bed with
his "fire" cry, will eventually become quite a nuisance.

The main characteristic of an Anabaptist, which is so difficult to
find, has indeed been found by Van Baalen. For him it resides in one's
interpretation of grace. If the brother can just demonstrate that we

think exactly like the Anabaptists on the doctrine of grace, the prosecution has won and we stand forever branded as Anabaptist. To this endeavor Van Baalen devotes what follows in this chapter. Therefore, it is important to pay close attention. If the evidence that the brother provides is conclusive, we stand condemned. If it is no evidence, the endeavor is a failure.

What is the Anabaptists' view of grace? Van Baalen gives two sentences in which the chief characteristic of that view must come to light. "All salvation is from grace, but that grace is common to all. Insofar he (Adam Pastor) goes along with Hoffman."[64] "This universal call presupposes the power to answer it. The cause of one's damnation never lies with God. Many claim that they have insufficient grace to accept the gospel, and thus they are unwilling to use what they have."[65]

Note well, reader, that in the whole chapter, these are the only two quotations in which Van Baalen traces the Anabaptists' view of grace. These two sentences give the characteristic view of the Anabaptists on the doctrine of grace. Read them once again. What is the main characteristic in these sentences? Most certainly the Anabaptists held to the view of the Remonstrants and denied the doctrines of free grace and of election and reprobation. Apart from that, there is nothing distinctive in these sentences.

Van Baalen says that we differ radically from the Anabaptists on this point. "Fairness demands that we emphasize this point of difference. For the Anabaptists it was the one grace that was offered but not accepted, so that the sinner did not will to be saved. For Danhof and Hoeksema it is the one grace that is offered but cannot be accepted, so that the sinner cannot be saved."[66] Apart from this there is nothing distinctive in the sentences Van Baalen quotes. Everyone will assent to that. Both Pastor and Hoffman universalized saving grace. We do not agree with this distinction; we differ radically from it.

What has Van Baalen proven? Up to this point his argument is that

---

64 Van Baalen, *Denial of Common Grace*, 80. Van Baalen quotes Dr. Dosker, who wrote about the Anabaptist Adam Pastor. Melchior Hoffman (1495–1543) was an Anabaptist prophet and visionary in northern Germany and the Netherlands.—Trans.
65 Ibid., 81. This is also a quotation from Dosker's work.—Trans.
66 Ibid.

the main characteristic of Anabaptists is their view of grace; Danhof and Hoeksema differ in principle from the Anabaptists on this point. The conclusion [of Van Baalen] is that both brothers are Anabaptist.

But our conclusion is that Van Baalen proves the exact opposite of what he wanted to prove. So far the endeavor of this chapter is a complete failure.

We have still more criticism. Van Baalen writes, "And for Danhof and Hoeksema it is the one grace that is offered but cannot be accepted, so that the sinner cannot be saved." This sentence is evidence of Van Baalen's thoughtlessness and inaccuracy in writing. Certainly we have never said that grace can be offered but not accepted and that the sinner cannot be saved. Van Baalen does not mean it that way either. What he meant is undoubtedly that the sinner cannot accept grace and be saved of himself, even though it is preached to him.

Further, we would like to ask whether Van Baalen's view is different. One gets the impression that he also condemns that view of grace. That view, brother, is indeed Reformed. You should not write that Danhof and Hoeksema think of it so, but rather that this is the only Reformed position ever to exist. We think also of the way Van Baalen quoted "God wills that all men be saved," and we ask, is there not something wrong with you too, brother? Is not something wrong also with your position regarding election and the total inability of natural man? This makes such a strange impression.

But we are not to the end of the chapter. After Van Baalen has proven that we differ radically from the Anabaptists on the doctrine of grace, and thus, according to his own judgment, his attempt to brand us as Anabaptists has failed completely, he comes at it from another side. Once again he chants by way of the little "world flight" ditty that we are Anabaptists. To say this is only because of our doctrine of grace was not good enough. Therefore, this: "But both have this in common, that they know of only one grace, and therefore they utterly condemn the world and cannot see any good in it."[67]

Van Baalen did not demonstrate that this was actually the view of the Anabaptists. It was not implied in the quotation from Dosker. But

---

67 Ibid.

we will grant that this is true. The question is, does it apply to us? Will brother Van Baalen ever demonstrate this?

We would like to take the word *world* in the sense in which you take it, namely, in the approximate sense of nature. (You surely will not take it ill of us that we condemn the "world" in the sense of the wicked, which "world" scripture always warns us against?) We ask, brother Van Baalen, where have you heard us say that we want to go out of the world? You will exert yourself in vain if you look for something resembling that in anything we have written. Where have you heard us claim that we must avoid all civic institutions, that we must not occupy any governmental office, or that we may not wage any war?

That seems to be roughly Van Baalen's presentation of our view, as appears from his quotation of Rev. Westerbeek van Eerten.[68] However, the brother can be assured that this is absolutely not our view. Our position is just the opposite. We do not want to go out of the world at all; our intention is not to abandon any area of life. We have called God's people to occupy the entirety of life. However, we want this people of the Lord, his covenantal people, not to forsake or deny her God in one single domain. His people are called to live out of grace in every domain—out of the one grace through which they were incorporated into Christ and through which they love God, so that they keep his commandments.

This is what we have written and preached, and Van Baalen could certainly have known this. In fact, in the *Banner* of June 12, 1919, we wrote, "Also, the child of the kingdom does not go along with this identification with the world as he strives to manifest himself in every domain of the life of that world. This is indeed his clear calling. In industry and commerce, in science and art, in state and society, the citizen of the kingdom may never fail to manifest himself by drawing back into the narrower sphere of the church as such. Then he would have to go out of the world, whereas it is his calling to be in the midst of it."

"World flight" therefore does not apply to us, brother, as you will certainly now admit. If you take "world" in the sense of "nature," you will certainly see that we do not separate nature and grace but wish to

68 Ibid., 81–82.

live everywhere out of grace. If you take "world" in the sense of "the wicked," we do not take flight, but we fight the good fight until the very end so that no one may take our crown.

So up to page 82 of his pamphlet Van Baalen still has not proven anything. With this before our minds, we note that he leaves a most strange impression, which we would rather not describe, when he asks, "Now does the reader want even more proof?"[69] The author apparently thinks he has given more than enough evidence. Whatever else could be added would be redundant. There is so much proof that we are Anabaptist that the author can be generous in providing it.

Our answer to that question would have been, "Yes, brother, we have not had any yet. It still has to come. You have not proven anything except for the opposite of what you wanted to prove!" But the reader demands the proof. We will check this proof very closely.

Kuyper wrote that the doctrine of common grace is "of paramount importance exactly for the present juncture of time." He says that this doctrine is an "indispensable part of the Reformed confession." He says he has "proven that particular grace cannot do without common grace for a moment, and demonstrated how the great work of God's grace in Christ presupposes the fruit of common grace in all things."[70]

Good, brother! We will not criticize any of that now. But what do these quotations have to do with your subject, *The Denial of Common Grace: Reformed or Anabaptist?* Nothing, am I right? We have come to the middle of page 83; still no proof.

But now comes something that looks like proof. Bavinck wrote, "The second ones [Anabaptists] despise *gratia communis* and know of nothing but grace."[71] This does not apply to us either. We despise nothing. When Bavinck writes that the Anabaptists despise *gratia communis*, he refers to the natural gifts that the Anabaptists despised. This

---

69 Ibid., 82.

70 Quotations from Kuyper's *Common Grace*, in ibid., 82–83.

71 Herman Bavinck, *De Algemeene Genade* [Common grace] (Grand Rapids, MI: Eerdmans-Sevensma, n.d.), 19; see also Herman Bavinck, "Common Grace," trans. R. C. Van Leeuwen, in *Calvin Theological Journal* 24, no. 1 (April, 1989): 38–65. The quotation occurs on page 53 of this translation: "The Anabaptists scorn the *gratia communis* [common grace] and acknowledge nothing besides grace."—Ed.

has nothing to do with our view. The second phrase of this sentence applies to us even less. It is not true that we have "nothing but grace." You can surely sense the essential difference between the view rendered by the words "he knows of nothing but grace" and the view stated with "we know of only one grace." Therefore, even if a word from Bavinck was decisive proof, this still does not apply to us.

We are at the bottom of page 83. Still no proof... The chapter is coming to an end. With the greatest suspense the reader asks, "Is the proof still coming?"

Yes, of course! There are still two quotations from Kuyper. The first quotation: "And with just one more small step you merge imperceptibly with the Anabaptist viewpoint...Then science becomes unholy."[72] This is a disappointment: it does not apply to us. We do not take that small step, nor does it lie within our way of thinking. We do not consider science unholy, only unbelieving science. We wish to live out of grace and keep God's commandments also in the domain of science.

The second quotation: "This Anabaptist standpoint (the shunning of everything in the world as absolutely sinful) that is still defended in many circles under the name Reformed would have never been accepted if the confession of common grace had lived continuously in the midst of the churches."[73] We have already clearly demonstrated that we never preached this Anabaptist shunning. We have preached the scriptural notion of separation from the wicked world.

Still, apart from this, the proof so greatly sought after that we are Anabaptist is not in this quotation either. Just pay attention, reader. In the words quoted above, Kuyper says that whoever maintains the viewpoint of common grace is kept from Anabaptist shunning.

Whoever believes in common grace is not an Anabaptist. But it is not stated that all who do not believe in common grace are Anabaptist. Just read the quotation one more time. That is how it appears. Everything that walks on two feet is not a horse. But everything that does

---

72 Van Baalen, *Denial of Common Grace*, 83.
73 Ibid., 83–84.

not walk on two feet is not yet proven to be a horse. There is a lack of logic and distinction here.

Again all this is concluded with the call to repentance: "Once again, acknowledge that you have gone astray." Now, brother, we have gone astray. We have wandered about in your pamphlet. We have come back from it with a sigh of relief!

For yourself and also for us, brother, (for we do still feel a sort of solidarity and joint responsibility as preachers in the same denomination) if you ever write again, conduct a more thorough study, consider your subject a bit better, and then produce better work. We still refuse to believe that this is the best you can offer.

ANSWERS TO QUESTIONS

Having come to the end of his pamphlet, Van Baalen thinks he must ask us several questions, which, it seems to him, call for resolution.

We do not feel obligated to answer every question the brother thinks he must ask us, and we are a bit too busy to spend much time on this. But we will oblige him. Therefore, we give the following brief answers.

First, Van Baalen wants us to explain the love that existed between a certain Hector and his wife, according to an ancient Greek poet. The occasion for this question is obviously Van Baalen's misunderstanding. He thinks Danhof might have remarked somewhere on the occasion of a classical examination that natural love outside the boundaries of grace is always bestial. This is not the case. The question was whether we sing in the Song of Solomon of natural love or of the love of Christ and his church. In response, Danhof claimed that natural love is never a type of the love between Christ and his people in holy scripture. The love between a husband and wife as it originally existed before sin is a picture of the everlasting. After the fall there is still natural love outside the boundaries of grace, but it was corrupted by sin, and instead of love for God's sake, it has now become love for its own sake.

Does not article 24 of the Belgic Confession say that without justifying faith man never does anything except out of self-love and fear of damnation?[74] Natural love, in its principle corrupted and torn away from God, actually develops into bestiality and whoredom. Therefore, that love is a picture of spiritual whoredom, while love in the area of

---

74 Belgic Confession 24, in Schaff, *Creeds of Christendom*, 3:410–11.—Ed.

regeneration can again become a type of the bond between Christ and the church.

Explain the love between Hector and his wife in some other way, Van Baalen, always in agreement with the Reformed confession.

The second question has to do with products of classical antiquity viewed in the light of our position. Let it suffice to refer the brother to what we quoted above—Canons 3–4.4, Belgic Confession 24, and Calvin's judgment on this.

In the third question the brother writes that we have accused Calvin, Bavinck, Kuyper, Warfield, Vos, and others of Arminianism. Our answer is that we have defended principles; we have never gone against persons. In this regard and based purely on what you wrote in your pamphlet we do have doubts about whether you, Van Baalen, are not tainted with this corrupt error. Prove with the confessions that we have doubted you unjustly.

In the fourth question we are asked to explain the behavior of Pharaoh's daughter, who drew Moses out of the water. The brother says that this was surely a good deed apart from faith. We want to ask Van Baalen this same question in the light of scripture and the confessions. The scripture says, "Whatsoever is not of faith is sin" (Rom. 14:23). The confessions teach that without faith no one ever does anything but out of love for himself. This is quite clear to us. Pharaoh's daughter wanted the beautiful little child. She felt drawn to that particular child. She did not save every little Hebrew who was drowning in the river. We do not read either that she went to Pharaoh to show him the horror of his command, do we? She wanted to make that beautiful little child her son. If by and by that little child does not want to be called her son, he is in danger of his life. Therefore, human mercy may very possibly be sin before God.

The last question is really more of a threat than a question. The brother threatens that if we do not yet see the bad consequences of our view, he will be compelled to write another pamphlet in which he will make clear to us that we are unable to preach well with our view.

Here is our answer: Write another pamphlet, brother. There is definitely need for a more grounded and convincing work.

ALONG
PURE PATHS

A Response to Concerned Brothers

———————⟫◇⟪———————

HENRY DANHOF
AND
HERMAN HOEKSEMA

TRANSLATED BY MARVIN KAMPS

Introduction to *Along Pure Paths*

The pure paths referred to in the title and described in the content of this foundational writing for the Protestant Reformed Churches are those of churches that confess and live the sound Reformed doctrines of the creeds. They are not the paths followed by the Christian Reformed Church in her adoption of the doctrine of a common grace of God. Against such paths, this treatise warns.

Henry Danhof and Herman Hoeksema wrote this booklet at the height of the controversy over common grace in the Christian Reformed Church, sometime between December 1923 and the meeting of the Christian Reformed synod in June and July 1924 that would adopt the theory of common grace as official church dogma. The booklet was the authors' response to criticisms of a book they had written a little earlier, titled *Sin and Grace.* In the book, they had both criticized the theory of common grace as taught by Abraham Kuyper and explained their views of the development of sin and of the particularity of God's grace.

Along Pure Paths clarifies the issues in the common grace controversy. The three main issues are whether God is gracious to the reprobate ungodly, whether the natural (unregenerated) human can do good works, and whether scripture teaches a restraint of sin by a working of grace in the hearts of unregenerated humans.

Danhof and Hoeksema insisted that their adversaries address these issues not by looking about in society or by appealing to impressive scientific and literary achievements of unbelievers, but by the teaching of scripture and the Reformed confessions. Once again, the authors warned that the theory of common grace, which many of the leading lights in the Christian Reformed Church were defending, would, if adopted, promote the worldliness of thinking and of life already evident in that church at the time.

The appearance of this booklet prior to the synod of 1924 left the Christian Reformed Church without excuse when it adopted the unconfessional theory of common grace and subsequently disciplined the ministers who rejected common grace in their uncompromising confession of particular grace. The judgments that God has brought, and is today bringing, on that church are just: Harold Dekker and the heresy of universal atonement; Harry Boer and the denial of double predestination; Howard Van Till and the attack on creation, as also the questioning of the inspiration of the Bible in Genesis 1–3; the world conformity of women in church office; Edwin Walhout and making the Christian religion dance to the tune of unbelieving, evolutionary scientism (biblically, "the world"); and much more besides.

Compelling in *Along Pure Paths* is the authors' treatment of scripture. They refute all the alleged biblical evidence for common grace put forward, necessarily weakly, by the advocates of common grace. They advance the overwhelming, and conclusive, testimony of scripture everywhere against the theory of common grace.

Haunting is the lament over former friends and coworkers in the ministry of the Christian Reformed Church, who once shared the deep concern of Danhof and Hoeksema but then, under pressure, turned on them, in league with the bitter enemies of the two witnesses to particular grace, total depravity, and the antithesis.

—David J. Engelsma

FOREWORD

lthough the authors of this publication present a preface, the
undersigned members of the publication committee considered
it important to call the reader's attention to some related matters. The intent of this note will become evident as one reads.

A response is required to the critical evaluation and condemnation
made by many of Danhof and Hoeksema's book *Sin and Grace*, which
set forth in a somewhat expanded form the Reformed concepts of sin
and grace and exposed the misconceptions and errors of their opponents.[1] This response is especially necessary because the common grace
question will be placed before synod.

Furthermore, as the preface will briefly mention, a strong organization has been established that will offer the two ministers, who have
been attacked and discourteously treated by the ecclesiastical press,
lawful support in their struggle for the truth. The publication committee of the Reformed Free Publishing Association is responsible for the
publication of this pamphlet. Should the Lord will and the lives of the
ministers and of the association members be spared, the committee has
plans for a second publication to inform fully and to enlighten all who
love the truth, treasure the purity of doctrine, and seek the salvation of
the church concerning the significant doctrines about which there are
differences of opinion among us.

The publishing association does not consider its task completed,
however, with these preliminary plans. It hopes in the not-too-distant
future to execute its plan to present to the world a periodical each
month.

---

1   *Sin and Grace* was originally published in Dutch as Danhof and Hoeksema, *Van
    Zonde en Genade*. The English translation is Henry Danhof and Herman Hoek-
    sema, *Sin and Grace*, ed. Herman Hanko, trans. Cornelius Hanko (Grandville, MI:
    Reformed Free Publishing Association, 2003).—Trans.

We envision a periodical that will provide instruction and assistance in a simple and appropriate manner. It will treat in an orderly fashion every matter of interest in the development of the truths of holy scripture according to established and truly Reformed lines of thought, without pursuing the many divergent paths that lead away into error. As much as possible it will provide light so that all may have a right understanding of the Christian's life on earth, to the honor of God and his name. The publication committee hopes to give further information about this in the near future.

Everyone who feels in his heart kinship with this organization established for this purpose, and who would publicly take a stand for the cause of the Lord in this way, is kindly invited hereby to contact one of the following members of the board of the Reformed Free Publishing Association.

—The publication committee

C. Van Ellen, chairman
1110 Dunham St.
Grand Rapids, Mich.

Arthur Wyma, secretary
711 Delaware St.
Grand Rapids, Mich.

J. C. Moerman, treasurer
R.R. 3
Kalamazoo, Mich.

R. H. Timmer, asst. treasurer
610 Dolbee St.
Grand Rapids, Mich.

W. Verhill
858 Kalamazoo Ave.
Grand Rapids, Mich.

Ralph Wolthuis
1807 South Burdick St.
Kalamazoo, Mich.

PREFACE

For various reasons the authors of this brochure consider it necessary to present again to our ecclesiastical public this writing, which is chiefly a response, further to enlighten them regarding the theory of common grace and the related question that has become a point of disagreement.[2]

In general we are pleased with the reception of our latest book, *Sin and Grace*. Superficially considered, this may sound strange, since many turned against us. However, on closer examination one can understand that we are actually satisfied and thankful for the reception of the book.

First, under God's blessing we were privileged to concentrate the attention of many on the viewpoint that is well-known in our fellowship by the name common grace. This is of great value in itself. Nothing is as discouraging for a preacher as a sleepy audience; nothing so disheartening as the failure of an instructor to gain and to keep the attention of his students; and surely there is nothing so deflating for a writer as his writings lying unread in the bookstore. This was not the case for us. People have given much attention, from whatever perspective, to what we wrote. Even though many did not immediately agree with us, we were very encouraged to draw the attention of almost the entire church on one point of her doctrine.

Second, we are thankful that many of our people not only understood the central issues that must serve as the guiding principles for

---

2 The brochure is a response to various Christian Reformed ministers who were defending the doctrine of common grace and attacking Danhof and Hoeksema for opposing common grace. The brochure identifies three of these defenders of common grace as Keegstra, Van Baalen, and Beets. All were prominent in the Christian Reformed Church.

The "related question" was whether the natural man is capable of doing what is good.—Ed.

the development of this part of our Reformed truth, but also were convicted of the truth of them as we presented it.

People should not forget that what is presented in our ecclesiastical papers absolutely does not give a faithful portrayal of the situation as it lives in the bosoms of our people regarding the question about which they [the vocal and ardent defenders of common grace] write. As was to be expected, the pen that enlightened the church public was entirely in the hands of those who do not agree with us. Because of this our ecclesiastical press does not faithfully reflect the thinking of our people on this question. Many people throughout the churches are becoming convinced that according to Reformed foundational principles, the lines cannot be drawn any differently from what we do. Even though they do not agree with us in everything, the majority feels that the problem confronting us is not really solved by an appeal to Abraham Kuyper.

In light of all the public opposition, these facts engender thanksgiving and hope for the future. For surely it is our purpose to fight not for the sake of fighting or to display our knowledge, but for the sake of God's truth and the salvation of his church, especially that part where he has given us a place. From that perspective we also take great joy in the initial fruit of our work.

Third, we are thankful for the criticism. The nature of the case is that there would be criticism; we did not imagine it differently and prepared ourselves for a severe struggle. How could it be any other way when on the basis of scripture and the confessions, we oppose Kuyper and Bavinck on this point? Therefore, we are not amazed by the criticism.

Still, something in the content of the criticism and in the present resulting circumstances gives satisfaction and hope. Even after a long and broad discussion in the ecclesiastical papers, people recognize that no one can place against our position a well-worked-out viewpoint that offers peace to the churches. Some, such as Van Baalen, may not sense this at all, yet in general it is the testimony of the facts. Our people sensed that it was easier to turn the pen against us than to develop positive truth that would satisfy and could stand the test of holy scripture according to our Reformed conception of the truth. This no one did, least of all Van Baalen. No one could prove that our viewpoint conflicts with the Reformed confessions. Some have tried this. Some have claimed success. But this is not true, as we hope to demonstrate in this brochure. Also no one could prove that the doctrine of common grace may be identified as Reformed dogma.

All these things have moved us to thanksgiving and given us courage for the future. We hope therefore to continue this struggle, even as we now do in the following pamphlet.

The brothers who have registered their objections surely expect a response from us, or they will conclude that their criticisms were decisive and unanswerable. The brothers who are in full or partial agreement with us will be looking for a further defense of our viewpoint and additional light on the subject. Aside from the present struggle many questions still have to be answered. We hope to commit ourselves to this task in the future according to the measure of strength and means that the Lord gives us.

We make one more introductory observation that chiefly concerns the manner of the struggle and the means we find necessary to use. At first we intended to publish an answer in *De Wachter*. We wrote an article and sent it to the editor [Keegstra] but found no receptivity there. The editor immediately disagreed with the first part of our answer because it contained something against Janssen. The editor sent the article to the publication committee. A few weeks later, it was returned to us with a request that we change it. We could not do that. Besides, we were informed that a long discussion [concerning the theory of common grace] in the church paper was not deemed desirable.

Such occurrences make it unpleasant and impossible to write in our church papers. *It is offensive to write for a magazine when the editors have the right to censor what we write! Whatever we write we sign and we are responsible for what we write!*

Consequently we abandoned the idea of writing in the church papers and decided to present our answer in a brochure. Many brethren offered us support in this endeavor. They have organized as a publication committee, first to publish our brochures and perhaps later to present to the public a more regular written witness, should this prove desirable. Should the way unto this end be opened for us and should it be that our only responsibility is to write, we think it is necessary to take up this work.

In conclusion, a few comments are necessary about what we wrote in our "Friendly Request."[3] We wrote that we deemed the theory of common grace un-Reformed and unbiblical. In response to our witness, some of the brothers have become inflamed and viewed it as a charge against many brothers who believe in common grace. Some even think it was incumbent that we present a formal indictment against all who believe in general grace.

All of this, however, rests on a misunderstanding. First, above all it must not be forgotten that we believe that a general grace doctrine is extra-confessional. The confessions do not address it. We have often expressed this opinion. Second, the theory of common grace as developed by Kuyper cannot be harmonized with the confessions. Far from accepting the idea that the principles, or elements, of a general grace doctrine can be found in the confessions, we consider the theory to conflict with what we have inherited from our fathers. In that sense we have used the term *un-Reformed*. In our judgment the doctrine of general grace is not only extra-confessional, but also so diametrically in conflict with the confessions that it cannot form an integral part of them.

This preface is already too long. Let us say it one more time: it is not our purpose to create division and conflict, but only to seek the cause of God's truth and the true well-being of God's church on earth. According to our deepest convictions, the theory of common grace leads us away from the truth of God's word and from the explicit confession of our churches.

Certainly we are willing to be corrected if we err. But then the brothers who intend to do this and who oppose our position must come with clearer testimony and stronger arguments than we have had until this time. At least so far we are unshaken in our convictions.

Having as our only purpose the Lord's cause and will, we therefore continue onward in our struggle for our convictions, come what may.

—The authors

---

3   This writing cannot be identified.—Ed.

CHAPTER I

SURVEY
AND DISTINCTIONS

For the sake of clarity, it seems appropriate to divide this brochure into separate chapters according to the various matters at issue. One would naturally envision us to follow the path of the brothers who have opposed us or raised objections in writing and to answer them point by point. Then we would dedicate a separate chapter to answer each one: Keegstra, Van Baalen, Beets, and the rest. However, this would lead to endless repetition of essentially the same arguments. Further, this would frequently divert the reader's attention from the issue and create confusion instead of clarity.

Therefore, we have chosen a different order of proceeding. In the struggle now taking place some central questions have been more or less touched on and treated by nearly every author. Regarding these central issues of controversy we hope to provide an answer to the brothers in light of scripture and the confessions.

At the outset it can only be advantageous to be reminded again of the various questions in the dispute. So much has been written that is not only irrelevant, but also obscures the issue. Before anything else, we may well ask, what is the conflict really about?

The first question is, is there grace separate from Christ that is bestowed on both elect and reprobate?

Remember, the issue is not whether God loves all his creatures. About this we all agree. In our judgment, it is properly emphasized (because it is our view as well) that the covenant with Noah, which includes all creatures, is the actual covenant of grace. The Lord loves all the works of his hands, upholds them temporally, and will glorify them presently with the children of God and cause them to enjoy their freedom.

One should not alter the question and ask if God has favor toward the *unconverted*. This is done as well, and the obvious consequence is that the point of disagreement is obscured more and more. It is of no purpose to substitute for the word *reprobate*, or *ungodly*, the word *unconverted*. The reason is obvious. Unconverted persons could very well be elect persons and not reprobate. One may not say of all the unconverted that God in his eternal counsel hates them, although of the reprobate one can say this. Therefore, the question may not be presented this way.

It is not superfluous to reiterate that the issue is not whether God bestows good gifts on all the children of men. Some of the brethren apparently write with this idea. They present our position as if we believe there is nothing good in the whole world. Not only have we never asserted this, but also we have always positively denied it. We have continually taken the position that in this dispensation the elect and the reprobate have everything in common. It is not only true that the reprobate also receive rain and sunshine, money and possessions, and gifts and talents from God; but it is also true that the elect participate in the sufferings of this present time and temporally endure the sufferings that the entire creation endures because of sin.

The issue concerns only and exclusively whether elect and reprobate in this life, in and with all these things they have in common, receive grace from God. The two issues are: first, whether God in this dispensation is gracious to the reprobate, has a favorable attitude toward them, and in his favor bestows all these things on them; second, whether in and through all these things, God actually causes an operation of his grace to go forth upon the reprobate, so that things are real blessings to them.

Those who think it is their duty to defend general grace maintain that God has a favorable attitude toward the reprobate and bestows all these things in his favor and that these things are real blessing to them. We deny this.

In this booklet we hope to treat the disagreement among us by first letting our opponents speak and then setting forth and defending our own viewpoint in harmony with scripture and the confessions. Concerning this point the editor of *De Wachter* observed that since we know so very little about God, it was inappropriate to speak (as we did) in such absolute terms regarding God's attitude toward the reprobate and the ungodly. Others have said that we formed our own opinion of who God is and then out of that preconceived, man-made, and perhaps rationalistic conception of God have deduced our entire viewpoint. Let it be emphasized that that is not our method.

We want to know God as he has revealed himself in his word and to accept that revelation without any hesitation concerning election and reprobation. We do not want to go beyond the revelation of scripture, nor have we ever done that. It is then very peculiar that the brothers continually complain that we provide very little direct scriptural proof, but yet they have not attempted even once to refute those allegedly few scriptural proofs. However, we will let the scriptures speak to the issues of disagreement and defend our position only on the basis of scripture and the confessions.

The second major question is, can the natural man still do good? This question as well must be more carefully limited in our thinking, if we are profitably to speak about it.

Both sides in this dispute readily grant that the natural man can perform no *spiritual* good by himself and in his own strength; both grant that outside of the grace of regeneration there is no grace applied to him that would enable him to perform spiritual good. Note, however, that the brothers who maintain common grace in great measure lack clarity regarding this so-called spiritual good. In general they seem to use *spiritual good* in approximately the same sense as *saving good*. The meaning then seems to be that the natural man of himself cannot perform any act of faith. He is unable in and of himself to convert to Christ and thus to embrace him by faith. In addition, he is unable to bring forth fruits of faith and thankfulness. Members from both sides are completely in agreement concerning these matters.

In the judgment of our opponents the truth that man is wholly incapable of himself to accomplish any saving good is a truth that is also definitely established. However, these brothers persist in continuing the battle regarding what they identify as saving good. None of the brothers has definitely established that one would be unable to preach the gospel in a sound Reformed sense without believing in common grace, although some have more than once made this claim. However, this only creates confusion of concepts. Both sides also acknowledge that *without some grace* the natural man is wholly incapable of any good and inclined to all evil: he absolutely cannot do any good.

But the difference between us concerns whether there is a certain operation of God's grace upon each man, including the reprobate, through which he is placed in a position to perform works that are essentially good. This latter idea is taught by those who believe in general grace. One may then differ concerning how he presents the operation of this common grace. One may explain in different ways this good that the natural man does. But it is certain that only in the following manner is the question presented accurately: the natural man outside of regeneration and Christ receives grace from God through which he can perform works that are morally good according to God's judgment. This we deny with all the strength that is in us.

This question, we must not forget, must also be resolved in the light of scripture and the confessions. Our experience is that our opponents appeal repeatedly in this connection to other sources than scripture. They look around in the world, call our attention to all the good deeds that the worldly man performs, and then ask us whether we have the courage to deny that all these are good works in the judgment of God. They point to the arts and science and to the grand development of modern man; or they turn to the accomplishments of the heathen from ancient Greece and display before us the poems of heathen origin; and they ask if all these realities can be called good works not in the natural, moral sense, but good before God. This entire method of reasoning we absolutely reject. On this point as well, we will limit ourselves exclusively to the utterances of scripture and the confessions.

If the scriptures teach a grace that empowers the spiritually dead sinner to do good before God, we will gladly submit to that instruction. But if scripture directly and clearly teaches that this is not the case and expresses exactly the opposite, our opponents will have to bend in submission to scripture. Then they will no longer twist the expressions of sacred scripture to fit sinful judgments about what they observe of natural man's activities in the world. We must evaluate the latter in the light of scripture.

The third question is, does sacred scripture actually teach a restraint of sin? This question is frequently so twisted and blurred in various ways and so erroneously presented that no one is sure what the issue is actually about. A little clarification here is not superfluous.

The issue does not concern whether God rules the deeds of men through the disposition of his providence. About this we all agree. Others have properly explained this fact. They have constantly said that we deny that God in his providence maintains and in his power rules over all wicked men and devils so that they cannot move or resist his will even for a moment. Yet this is not the case. Concerning this truth both sides in the dispute are in hearty agreement. God rules over the evil deeds of the reprobate and of devils according to his good pleasure. This whole idea has absolutely no connection to the issue before us.

Nor is it the question whether the sinner is bound to and restricted by various means in the execution of sinful deeds. No one denies that the police officer must thwart a thief, if he can prevent him, in order to stop his breaking and entering. Not only is sinful man frequently restrained by the authorities from executing evil deeds, but he is also bound to and limited by various means, powers, times, places, and circumstances. This entire question can be ruled out of consideration.

However, the question is whether there is an operation of God's grace in the heart of the natural man that restrains sin in its development. This restraint of the working of sin unto the spiritual and moral corruption of humanity is viewed as beginning immediately after Adam's fall in paradise. God administered common grace to Adam as a spiritual emetic by which he partially vomited the poison of sin. In this way the corrupting development of sin in Adam was immediately arrested.

Keegstra thinks that we unjustly presented Kuyper's proposition in *Sin and Grace*. This is essentially not the case at all. Suppose we would grant to Keegstra that Kuyper did not intend to teach that there was poison in the tree of knowledge of good and evil but that it was his aim to speak of the poison of sin. Yet this would not essentially change anything according to Kuyper's proposal. When man ate of the tree of knowledge, the poison of destruction that would cause death would by itself begin to work without any punitive act of God.

> Death viewed in connection with eating from the tree of knowledge can be understood in two ways: either as a punishment that was threatened, or as a consequence that would result from the act itself. If death is required for treason, it is a threatened punishment, for men do not die from the act when they commit high treason. But when I say, "Don't eat that Prussian blue, for you will die of it," there is no mention of punishment in itself, but only the warning that this poison is deadly, and that whoever swallows it will die from it.[4]

Death, according to Kuyper, is not to be viewed as a punitive act of God upon the sinner, but as an inherently necessary consequence that arises from sin as poison.

Moreover, God's prophecy to man, "If you eat of that tree you will die," does not mean, "Then I will kill you," but it means, "Then you will die of your own doing." When man ignores this warning, God stands ready with his general grace and causes it to work as an emetic by which the destruction—not all of it but only part—is spewed forth. This is the earliest restraint of sin. If anyone can conclude differently from Kuyper's common grace, we are gladly willing to be instructed. But we cannot accept the mere assertion, lacking all proof and demonstration, that we have misrepresented Kuyper.

If, according to Keegstra's representation of Kuyper, we view sin as poison, man in paradise by common grace vomited forth part of the poison of sin. Then there is only one possible conclusion: sin would have totally corrupted man if general grace had not intervened between man and sin. Man as he now exists, with the restraining operation of common grace begun in paradise, is not totally corrupt. The

---

4 Kuyper, *Common Grace*, 1:209.

restraining operation of common grace, initiated in paradise against the corruption in the human heart, continues to work until God withdraws it. Besides, there is not only such a restraining work of grace in the heart of each man whereby he does not become wholly corrupt, but also this operation influences the whole organic and social life of our generation in connection with all things, so that sin cannot develop as quickly as it otherwise would. In other words, by virtue of the restraining operation of general grace, the development of sin is out of step with the organic development of the human race in connection with all things.

Also this question will have to be discussed in the light of scripture and the confessions. If sacred scripture teaches that death is not God's punishment of sin on the transgressor but that it necessarily comes forth of itself as a consequence of sin, and if this is the representation also found in the confessions, we will submit to it with all our hearts. If scripture teaches that man vomits up the destruction-causing poison by an operation of God's grace, and if our confessions teach the same thing, we will confess it as well, for truly we bow before scripture and we love the Reformed confessions. If scripture and the confessions teach an ongoing restraint of the developmental process of sin, which restraint proceeds from God as a gracious operation on the heart of every man and on the organic whole of things, we do not want to maintain anything else but the testimony of scripture. But if the testimony of scripture positively opposes all these things, we will stay the course in our struggle and continue to instruct our people to the contrary, because this concerns God's truth and the certainty of his covenant with us.

CHAPTER 2

GRACE FOR
THE REPROBATE?

To the question whether there is grace for the reprobate our opponents answer affirmatively. This question must always be understood according to our explanation in the previous chapter. Our response to this question is negative.

Our opponents point to the following as proof of their position.

Van Baalen instructs us first and foremost by an appeal to Maccovius concerning the difference between hatred according to God's good pleasure and hatred proceeding from wrath. When we read in holy scripture, "Esau have I hated," this is hatred of God's good pleasure. This means that God has hated the creature with a negative hatred in his eternal counsel, without consideration of his sin. It means nothing more than that God has not chosen that creature. But the hatred of his wrath is directed against the creature who actually has become a malefactor. It is the hatred wherewith he rejects and condemns the disobedient creature because of his guilt.

From this distinction by Maccovius, Van Baalen teaches that we are able "in some measure to understand how God, without being in conflict with himself, can hate man with a negative hatred that consists in not writing his name in the book of life, and yet God can bless that man with temporal blessings that consist in a curbing of his sin, so that he does not make himself worthy of the punishment that falls upon devils."[5]

Further, Van Baalen points to the following texts of scripture:

---

5   Van Baalen, *Novelty and Error*, 117.

The earth is full of the goodness of the LORD. (Ps. 33:5)

Thou crownest the year with thy goodness; and thy paths drop fatness. (Ps. 65:11)

But love ye your enemies, and do good, and lend, hoping for nothing again; and your reward shall be great, and ye shall be the children of the Highest: for he is kind unto the unthankful and to the evil. (Luke 6:35)

That ye may be the children of your Father which is in heaven: for he maketh his sun to rise on the evil and on the good, and sendeth rain on the just and on the unjust. (Matt. 5:45)

And it came to pass, when Ahab heard those words, that he rent his clothes, and put sackcloth upon his flesh, and fasted, and lay in sackcloth, and went softly. And the word of the LORD came to Elijah the Tishbite, saying, Seest thou how Ahab humbleth himself before me? because he humbleth himself before me, I will not bring the evil in his days: but in his son's days will I bring the evil upon his house. (1 Kings 21:27–29)

God repented of the evil, that he had said that he would do unto them; and he did it not. (Jonah 3:10)

But it displeased Jonah exceedingly, and he was very angry. And he prayed unto the LORD, and said, I pray thee, O LORD, was not this my saying, when I was yet in my country? Therefore I fled before unto Tarshish: for I knew that thou art a gracious God, and merciful, slow to anger, and of great kindness, and repentest thee of the evil. Therefore now, O LORD, take, I beseech thee, my life from me; for it is better for me to die than to live. (Jonah 4:1–3)

Who in times past suffered all nations to walk in their own ways. Nevertheless he left not himself without witness, in that he did good, and gave us rain from heaven, and fruitful seasons, filling our hearts with food and gladness. (Acts 14:16–17)

God blessed Noah and his sons, and said unto them, Be fruitful, and multiply, and replenish the earth. (Gen. 9:1)

As for Ishmael, I have heard thee: Behold, I have blessed him, and will make him fruitful, and will multiply him exceedingly; twelve princes shall he beget, and I will make him a great nation. But my covenant will I establish with Isaac. (Gen. 17:20–21)

Ye shall not afflict any widow, or fatherless child. If thou afflict them in any wise, and they cry at all unto me, I will surely hear their cry; and my wrath shall wax hot, and I will kill you with the sword. For that is his covering only, it is his raiment for his skin: wherein shall he sleep? and it shall come to pass, when he crieth unto me, that I will hear; for I am gracious. (Ex. 22:22–24, 27)

Whoso findeth a wife findeth a good thing, and obtaineth favour of the Lord. (Prov. 18:22)

Or despisest thou the riches of his goodness and forbearance and longsuffering; not knowing that the goodness of God leadeth thee to repentance? But after thy hardness and impenitent heart treasurest up unto thyself wrath against the day of wrath and revelation of the righteous judgment of God; who will render to every man according to his deeds. (Rom. 2:4–6)

As may be expected from Van Baalen's proofs, the other brothers who have written about this subject do not have much to add. Not all the brothers would be willing to subscribe to all these texts as proof for grace upon the reprobate. However, some of the brothers have additional texts as proofs.

Apart from that, we still must say from the heart something concerning De Jong's opposition. We find it strange, apart from the question of common grace itself, that De Jong so aggressively agitates and writes such a long series of articles concerning this subject. It seems strange that he feels so troubled concerning us and that he can write and speak so critically. Naturally, it is in one sense understandable that he could be somewhat fearful that because he worked cooperatively with us for a time on the *Witness*, he will come under suspicion of denying the doctrine of common grace. But is such a long series of articles necessary to cleanse him from our stain?

Besides, considering what we heard from De Jong when we worked together, we would certainly have expected him to turn the sword of his pen against other enemies. After all, De Jong's soul was always filled with sorrow concerning the corruption of Pelagianism in the church and the corruption in our seminary. We expected from De Jong a pitched battle against other enemies instead of us. But De Jong turned against us, and he did that when (we do not say because) so many others think it is their duty to turn against us now. All of this would be understandable if the brother really had such a great burden as he tries to evidence in his writings. But we could find very little of a great burden. We carefully saved his articles and have perused them all again. We were amazed that one could write so much and say so little!

De Jong presents the following biblical proofs for the issue under discussion:

Then Jesus beholding him loved him [the rich young ruler]. (Mark 10:21)

Let favour be shewed to the wicked, yet will he not learn righteousness: in the land of uprightness will he deal unjustly, and will not behold the majesty of the LORD. (Isa. 26:10)

The LORD is good to all: and his tender mercies are over all his works. (Ps. 145:9)

Whatever else, it has become clear that De Jong teaches a grace on the reprobate. He writes, "This leaves space remaining for the revelation of God's general grace, and in such a way that we can still speak with Calvin of *God's love* toward nonbelievers." This last expression could lead to misunderstanding, but we want to take it in the sense that De Jong, according to the context, perceives of nonbelievers as reprobate.

Daniel Zwier has only one text: Isaiah 26:10.

Berkhof has written concerning "The Favor of God toward the Unconverted." Since this is not about our subject, we will not treat his article in any detail. It would lead us too far afield. However, it is not permissible to change the word *reprobate* into *unconverted*, because there surely are many unconverted who are elect. We have spoken personally with the professor about this, and he promised to correct that error in a future article. In a second article Berkhof has done that, but in such a way that he places the fault for the misunderstanding at our door. This too is done unjustly. It is clear from our whole book that we used the word *ungodly* in the sense of reprobate, not unconverted. That this use is biblical is plain from many texts of God's word, which we will quote later. For the rest, we will not go further into this. It would only create confusion.

Beets has also written against our conception of reprobation. One does not really know what to do with this brother. He writes so much, so effortlessly, so fluently, and with great emotion. Besides, he writes about everything in our church paper. He recommended the book of Bultema. Later he was satisfied with the condemnation of that book. Then he recommended *The Coming of the Lord* by Dr. Snowden, which advocated a postmillennial position that is even worse [than Bultema's premillennial position in his book]. Finally, Beets thought that postmillennialism was the real Reformed position, after he was confronted concerning his recommendation of Snowden's book. It seems that anything and everything passes muster with him.

People are often amazed about what Beets writes. It is the same with his public speaking. He speaks effortlessly and for any kind of audience. The *Grand Rapids Press* recently reported on a speech by Beets at the YMCA, in which he clearly set forth how God fought for the Allies and against the Germans—so much so that God caused the wind to turn in the battle of Ypres at just the right moment and to blow the poisonous gas back into the faces of the Germans! One nearly gapes in astonishment.

His articles now cause the same reaction. They concern what the American public would possibly think of our conception of reprobation, which we claim to be the best. He writes that the American public would read what article 1 of the Belgic Confession and Psalm 145:9 say, and then they would ask, should God be depicted as we have done? People will doubt that all of this can be harmonized with human responsibility. Judging according to the example of Jonathan Edwards, Beets is convinced that such "sentiments" as ours should not be broadcast. Approvingly he appeals to Kuizenga, who calls us "hard-boiled," which expression is certainly to be attributed to our lack of personal possession of common grace. Besides, Beets claims that he carefully investigated whether as good citizens, we had written our names in the registry of voters so that we could vote. Since one of us had registered and the other had not, Beets could draw no conclusion. He merely observed that it was illogical for the one brother to vote. All this made an impressive series of articles in the *Banner*!

But if you ask for proof from scripture and the confessions, Beets does not have much to offer. What he does provide is the following. He calls our attention to a quotation from the conclusion to the Canons of Dordt.

> Finally, this Synod exhorts all their brethren in the gospel of Christ...to regulate, by the Scripture, according to the analogy of faith, not only their sentiments, but also their language, and to abstain from all those phrases which exceed the limits necessary to be observed in ascertaining the genuine sense of the Holy Scriptures, and may furnish insolent sophists with a just pretext for violently assailing, or even vilifying, the doctrine of the Reformed Churches.[6]

He quotes from article 1 of the Belgic Confession: "[God] is eternal, incomprehensible, invisible, immutable, infinite, almighty, perfectly wise, just, good, and the overflowing fountain of all good."[7]

Beets also quotes Psalm 145:9: "The LORD is good to all: and his tender mercies are over all his works."

Keegstra has also written about this subject, but he presents nothing more than what the other brethren have presented from scripture and the confessions. We do not mean that the editor of *De Wachter* would subscribe to all the texts quoted above as proofs for God's grace to the reprobate, but only that we have not been confronted with other texts as proofs from him.

---

6 Conclusion to the Canons of Dordt, in Schaff, *Creeds of Christendom*, 3:597.—Trans.

7 Belgic Confession 1, in ibid., 3:383–84.—Trans.

We think we have now mentioned and identified all the proofs of our opponents. If we have overlooked something, let no one take this oversight amiss. There will always be opportunity to correct this failure.

How must we respond to all of this? The best method, it seems to us, is first to present our proof texts and after that to investigate whether it is appropriate, according to the method of Van Baalen, to let these so-called parallel texts stand next to one another as humanly irreconcilable and as representing two different lines of thought. This also will have to be demonstrated from scripture.

We call attention first to Romans 9:13 in connection with Malachi 1:2–4. "Jacob have I loved, but Esau have I hated." The apostle's statement is a quotation from Malachi, who clearly explains what God's hatred, the hatred of his good pleasure, means for Esau and his generations.

2. I have loved you, saith the LORD. Yet ye say, Wherein hast thou loved us? Was not Esau Jacob's brother? saith the LORD: yet I loved Jacob,

3. And I hated Esau, and laid his mountains and his heritage waste for the dragons of the wilderness.

4. Whereas Edom saith, We are impoverished, but we will return and build the desolate places; thus saith the LORD of hosts, They shall build, but I will throw down; and they shall call them, The border of wickedness, and, The people against whom the LORD hath indignation for ever.

Obviously these texts explain one another, especially when we recognize the distinction that Van Baalen quotes from Maccovius: a distinction between a hatred of God's good pleasure and a hatred of God's wrath. It is not at all clear why Van Baalen points to this distinction and what he really means by it. In connection with the question before us, this distinction proves nothing. Van Baalen has convinced himself that we proceed from an ultra-supralapsarian position and that if others want to agree with us concerning our view of common grace, they would first have to take that supra viewpoint.

Supralapsarianism and infralapsarianism have to do with the order of God's decrees, and in this connection especially with reprobation.

The supralapsarian Maccovius faced the following questions: In the decree of reprobation did God have the reprobate in view without any consideration of sin? Or in the decree of reprobation did God have in view a fallen race of humanity? Maccovius' position was the first view; the fall follows reprobation in the decree. When he was challenged in this matter, and wanted to remove the apparent severity of the decree of reprobation, he explained that one must distinguish between the hatred of good pleasure and the hatred of wrath. However, that does not change anything regarding the present issue.

The specific question that confronts us is, does God historically and in this world love the reprobate and bestow grace on them? This question does not concern the order of God's decrees, but God's attitude in history toward the reprobate, that is, as actually existing reprobates. What is the significance of Maccovius' distinction from this perspective? That the reprobate, who were the objects of the hatred of the good pleasure in God's counsel, in history also actually become ungodly, are dead and remain in sins and iniquities, and thus become the objects of the hatred of wrath.

Whether one agrees with Maccovius' supra position or with Bogerman's infra position does not alter the issue in any way.[8] From the infra viewpoint one would simply say that God in his counsel had the reprobate before him as already fallen and that he let them remain in that fallen condition. Here as well, the reprobate are dead in sin and iniquity in history and are the objects of the hatred of wrath. With a view to common grace, it is a matter of complete indifference whether one is supra or infra.

From this viewpoint it is of great importance to compare Romans 9:13 with Malachi 1:2–4.

---

8   In his booklet *Novelty and Error*, a vigorous defense of common grace and an attack on particular grace, Van Baalen brought up Johannes Maccovius—an ardent supralapsarian at the time of the Synod of Dordt—against Danhof's and Hoeksema's rejection of common grace. Danhof and Hoeksema saw this appeal as a tactic to relate denial of common grace to the supralapsarian view of predestination. Danhof and Hoeksema flatly denied the notion. Rejection of the theory of common grace has nothing whatever to do with the debate among Reformed theologians between supralapsarianism and infralapsarianism.—Ed.

Edom, whom God hated in the counsel of his good pleasure, appears historically as the ungodly nation, "the border of wickedness," and therefore also as the nation against whom the Lord sets himself in history, the nation upon whom he has indignation now and unto all eternity (Mal. 1:2–4). It is a riddle to us how anyone could drag common grace into an explanation of Malachi 1. Yet this is exactly what Van Baalen must do to advance somewhat his position that God actually loves and bestows grace on the reprobate who, historically, are the ungodly.

If we remember the connection between the hatred of good pleasure and the hatred of wrath, both of which can very well be maintained from the position of either infra or supra, we can also better understand the language of scripture. Then the issue can be presented in the following manner. First, the reprobate historically are always the ungodly; they become nothing other than the ungodly and actually commit nothing other than ungodliness. Second, in this way they also unquestionably become the objects of the hatred of wrath. Thus the question is specifically, if you take these reprobate in a historical sense, and thus as ungodly, as haters of God and as those who are thinking about sin and are serving sin, does God love these reprobate persons? The scriptures must provide the answer to this question. Malachi 1:2–4 answers conclusively in the negative. Moreover, that is also the current thought of holy scripture.

Consider the following texts:

1. Blessed is the man that walketh not in the counsel of the ungodly, nor standeth in the way of sinners, nor sitteth in the seat of the scornful.
2. But his delight is in the law of the LORD; and in his law doth he meditate day and night.
3. And he shall be like a tree planted by the rivers of water, that bringeth forth his fruit in his season; his leaf also shall not wither; and whatsoever he doeth shall prosper.
4. The ungodly are not so: but are like the chaff which the wind driveth away.
5. Therefore the ungodly shall not stand in the judgment, nor sinners in the congregation of the righteous.

6. For the LORD knoweth the way of the righteous: but the way of the ungodly shall perish. (Ps. 1:1–6)

4. He that sitteth in the heavens shall laugh: the Lord shall have them in derision.
5. Then shall he speak unto them in his wrath, and vex them in his sore displeasure.

9. Thou shalt break them with a rod of iron; thou shalt dash them in pieces like a potter's vessel. (Ps. 2:4–5, 9)

4. For thou art not a God that hath pleasure in wickedness: neither shall evil dwell with thee.
5. The foolish shall not stand in thy sight: thou hatest all workers of iniquity.
6. Thou shalt destroy them that speak leasing: the LORD will abhor the bloody and deceitful man.

9. For there is no faithfulness in their mouth; their inward part is very wickedness; their throat is an open sepulchre; they flatter with their tongue.
10. Destroy thou them, O God; let them fall by their own counsels; cast them out in the multitude of their transgressions; for they have rebelled against thee. (Ps. 5:4–6, 9–10)

2. The wicked in his pride doth persecute the poor: let them be taken in the devices that they have imagined.
3. For the wicked boasteth of his heart's desire, and blesseth the covetous, whom the LORD abhorreth.
4. The wicked, through the pride of his countenance, will not seek after God: God is not in all his thoughts.
5. His ways are always grievous; thy judgments are far above out of his sight: as for all his enemies, he puffeth at them.
6. He hath said in his heart, I shall not be moved: for I shall never be in adversity.
7. His mouth is full of cursing and deceit and fraud: under his tongue is mischief and vanity.

8. He sitteth in the lurking places of the villages: in the secret places doth he murder the innocent: his eyes are privily set against the poor.

9. He lieth in wait secretly as a lion in his den: he lieth in wait to catch the poor: he doth catch the poor, when he draweth him into his net.

10. He croucheth, and humbleth himself, that the poor may fall by his strong ones.

11. He hath said in his heart, God hath forgotten: he hideth his face; he will never see it.

12. Arise, O LORD; O God, lift up thine hand: forget not the humble.

13. Wherefore doth the wicked contemn God? he hath said in his heart, Thou wilt not require it.

14. Thou hast seen it: for thou beholdest mischief and spite, to requite it with thy hand: the poor committeth himself unto thee; thou art the helper of the fatherless.

15. Break thou the arm of the wicked and the evil man: seek out his wickedness till thou find none.

16. The LORD is King for ever and ever: the heathen are perished out of his land.

17. LORD, thou hast heard the desire of the humble: thou wilt prepare their heart, thou wilt cause thine ear to hear:

18. To judge the fatherless and the oppressed, that the man of the earth may no more oppress. (Ps. 10:2–18)

The LORD trieth the righteous; but the wicked and him that loveth violence his soul hateth. (Ps. 11:5)

1. The fool hath said in his heart, There is no God. They are corrupt, they have done abominable works, there is none that doeth good.

2. The LORD looked down from heaven upon the children of men, to see if there were any that did understand, and seek God.

3. They are all gone aside, they are all together become filthy: there is none that doeth good, no, not one.

4. Have all the workers of iniquity no knowledge? who eat up my people as they eat bread, and call not upon the LORD.

5. There were they in great fear: for God is in the generation of the righteous. (Ps. 14:1–5)

Their sorrows shall be multiplied that hasten after another god; their drink offerings of blood will I not offer, nor take up their names into my lips. (Ps. 16:4)

13. Arise, O LORD, disappoint him, cast him down: deliver my soul from the wicked, which is thy sword;

14. From men which are thy hand, O LORD, from men of the world, which have their portion in this life, and whose belly thou fillest with thy hid treasure: they are full of children, and leave the rest of their substance to their babes. (Ps. 17:13–14)

26. With the pure thou wilt shew thyself pure; and with the froward thou wilt shew thyself froward.

27. For thou wilt save the afflicted people; but wilt bring down high looks. (Ps. 18:26–27)

8. Thine hand shall find out all thine enemies: thy right hand shall find out those that hate thee.

9. Thou shalt make them as a fiery oven in the time of thine anger: the LORD shall swallow them up in his wrath, and the fire shall devour them.

10. Their fruit shalt thou destroy from the earth, and their seed from among the children of men.

11. For they intended evil against thee: they imagined a mischievous device, which they are not able to perform.

12. Therefore shalt thou make them turn their back, when thou shalt make ready thine arrows upon thy strings against the face of them. (Ps. 21:8–12)

Because they regard not the works of the LORD, nor the operation of his hands, he shall destroy them, and not build them up. (Ps. 28:5)

Many sorrows shall be to the wicked: but he that trusteth in the LORD, mercy shall compass him about. (Ps. 32:10)

The face of the LORD is against them that do evil, to cut off the remembrance of them from the earth. (Ps. 34:16)

1. Plead my cause, O LORD, with them that strive with me: fight against them that fight against me.
2. Take hold of shield and buckler, and stand up for mine help.
3. Draw out also the spear, and stop the way against them that persecute me: say unto my soul, I am thy salvation.
4. Let them be confounded and put to shame that seek after my soul: let them be turned back and brought to confusion that devise my hurt.
5. Let them be as chaff before the wind: and let the angel of the LORD chase them.
6. Let their way be dark and slippery: and let the angel of the LORD persecute them.
7. For without cause have they hid for me their net in a pit, which without cause they have digged for my soul.
8. Let destruction come upon him at unawares; and let his net that he hath hid catch himself: into that very destruction let him fall. (Ps. 35:1–8)

12. The wicked plotteth against the just, and gnasheth upon him with his teeth.
13. The Lord shall laugh at him: for he seeth that his day is coming.

35. I have seen the wicked in great power, and spreading himself like a green bay tree.
36. Yet he passed away, and, lo, he was not: yea, I sought him, but he could not be found. (Ps. 37:12–13, 35–36)

1. Why boasteth thou thyself in mischief, O mighty man? the goodness of God endureth continually.
2. Thy tongue deviseth mischiefs; like a sharp razor, working deceitfully.

3. Thou lovest evil more than good; and lying rather than to speak righteousness. Selah.
4. Thou lovest all devouring words, O thou deceitful tongue.
5. God shall likewise destroy thee for ever, he shall take thee away, and pluck thee out of thy dwelling place, and root thee out of the land of the living. (Ps. 52:1–5)

But thou, O God, shalt bring them down into the pit of destruction: bloody and deceitful men shall not live out half their days; but I will trust in thee. (Ps. 55:23)

3. The wicked are estranged from the womb: they go astray as soon as they be born, speaking lies.

6. Break their teeth, O God, in their mouth: break out the great teeth of the young lions, O LORD.
7. Let them melt away as waters which run continually: when he bendeth his bow to shoot his arrows, let them be as cut in pieces.
8. As a snail which melteth, let every one of them pass away: like the untimely birth of a woman, that they may not see the sun.
9. Before your pots can feel the thorns, he shall take them away as with a whirlwind, both living, and in his wrath.
10. The righteous shall rejoice when he seeth the vengeance: he shall wash his feet in the blood of the wicked.
11. So that a man shall say, Verily there is a reward for the righteous: verily he is a God that judgeth in the earth. (Ps. 58:3, 6–11)

5. Thou therefore, O LORD God of hosts, the God of Israel, awake to visit all the heathen: be not merciful to any wicked transgressors. Selah.
6. They return at evening: they make a noise like a dog, and go round about the city.
7. Behold, they belch out with their mouth: swords are in their lips: for who, say they, doth hear?

8. But thou, O LORD, shalt laugh at them; thou shalt have all the heathen in derision.
9. Because of his strength will I wait upon thee: for God is my defence.
10. The God of my mercy shall prevent me: God shall let me see my desire upon mine enemies.
11. Slay them not, lest my people forget: scatter them by thy power; and bring them down, O Lord our shield.
12. For the sin of their mouth and the words of their lips let them even be taken in their pride: and for cursing and lying which they speak.
13. Consume them in wrath, consume them, that they may not be: and let them know that God ruleth in Jacob unto the ends of the earth. Selah.
14. And at evening let them return; and let them make a noise like a dog, and go round about the city.
15. Let them wander up and down for meat, and grudge if they be not satisfied. (Ps. 59:5–15)

But God shall shoot at them with an arrow; suddenly shall they be wounded. (Ps. 64:7)

1. Let God arise, let his enemies be scattered: let them also that hate him flee before him.
2. As smoke is driven away, so drive them away: as wax melteth before the fire, so let the wicked perish at the presence of God.

6. God setteth the solitary in families: he bringeth out those which are bound with chains: but the rebellious dwell in a dry land.

21. But God shall wound the head of his enemies, and the hairy scalp of such an one as goeth on still in his trespasses. (Ps. 68:1–2, 6, 21)

22. Let their table become a snare before them: and that which should have been for their welfare, let it become a trap.

23. Let their eyes be darkened, that they see not; and make their loins continually to shake.
24. Pour out thine indignation upon them, and let thy wrathful anger take hold of them.
25. Let their habitation be desolate; and let none dwell in their tents.
26. For they persecute him whom thou hast smitten; and they talk to the grief of those whom thou hast wounded.
27. Add iniquity unto their iniquity; and let them not come into thy righteousness.
28. Let them be blotted out of the book of the living, and not be written with the righteous. (Ps. 69:22–28)

   See Psalms 73, 78–79, 83, 89, 91–92, 94, 97, 101, 105, 109, 118–19, 136, 144–45, 147, and 149.

32. For the froward is abomination to the LORD: but his secret is with the righteous.
33. The curse of the LORD is in the house of the wicked: but he blesseth the habitation of the just. (Prov. 3:32–33)

2. Treasures of wickedness profit nothing: but righteousness delivereth from death.
3. The LORD will not suffer the soul of the righteous to famish: but he casteth away the substance of the wicked. (Prov. 10:2–3)

24. The fear of the wicked, it shall come upon him: but the desire of the righteous shall be granted.
25. As the whirlwind passeth, so is the wicked no more: but the righteous is an everlasting foundation.
26. As vinegar to the teeth, and as smoke to the eyes, so is the sluggard to them that send him.
27. The fear of the LORD prolongeth days: but the years of the wicked shall be shortened.
28. The hope of the righteous shall be gladness: but the expectation of the wicked shall perish. (Prov. 10:24–28)

20. They that are of a froward heart are abomination to the LORD: but such as are upright in their way are his delight.

31. Behold, the righteous shall be recompensed in the earth: much more the wicked and the sinner. (Prov. 11:20, 31)

There shall no evil happen to the just: but the wicked shall be filled with mischief. (Prov. 12:21)

The righteous eateth to the satisfying of his soul: but the belly of the wicked shall want. (Prov. 13:25)

9. The way of the wicked is an abomination unto the LORD: but he loveth him that followeth after righteousness.

29. The LORD is far from the wicked: but he heareth the prayer of the righteous. (Prov. 15:9, 29)

Every one that is proud in heart is an abomination to the LORD: though hand join in hand, he shall not be unpunished. (Prov. 16:5)

But the wicked are like the troubled sea, when it cannot rest, whose waters cast up mire and dirt. There is no peace, saith my God, to the wicked. (Isa. 57:20–21)

God is jealous, and the LORD revengeth; the LORD revengeth, and is furious; the LORD will take vengeance on his adversaries, and he reserveth wrath for his enemies. (Nahum 1:2)

He that believeth on the Son hath everlasting life: and he that believeth not the Son shall not see life; but the wrath of God abideth on him. (John 3:36)

18. The wrath of God is revealed from heaven against all ungodliness and unrighteousness of men, who hold the truth in unrighteousness;

24. Wherefore God also gave them up to uncleanness through the lusts of their own hearts, to dishonour their own bodies between themselves.

26. For this cause God gave them up unto vile affections: for even their women did change the natural use into that which is against nature. (Rom. 1:18, 24, 26)

Therefore hath he mercy on whom he will have mercy, and whom he will he hardeneth. (Rom. 9:18)

God resisteth the proud, and giveth grace to the humble. (1 Pet. 5:5)

All of the above quotations are completely different language from that of common grace. God, who is light and in whom there is no darkness at all, hates the reprobate; his soul is filled with abomination toward him; he turns against the reprobate and resists him, is furious with him, persecutes him, and destroys him. The belly of the reprobate God fills with hidden treasure and causes his curse to abide in the reprobate's house. God gives him over to the lusts of his heart and flesh, and God's wrath abides on him. Scripture speaks this way of the ungodly reprobate as he lives his life on earth in wickedness. Without any further explanation it will have to be acknowledged that the Bible overwhelmingly testifies throughout against the position that the other brothers have tried to prove with a few texts, that God in this life loves and shows grace to the wicked, to the reprobate, to the sinner apart from Christ.

The question arises whether the Bible teaches both, and whether we will have to let these two ideas stand next to one another in unreconciled conflict. Van Baalen says he prefers it this way. Then we would have to accept that God loves and blesses the reprobate outside of Christ; that he is extremely furious with him but is also overflowing in his kindness toward him. (To our amazement, Van Baalen thinks he has to criticize this use of the word *overflowing*. We say his criticism is to our amazement, because we thought surely he knew his Dutch better.[9]) Is that perhaps the right opinion?

In answer we first observe that our opponents, whom we identify

---

9   The Dutch word is *tieren*, which can mean "to rave, to rant, to rage," or "to thrive, to flourish, to be luxuriant." The basic idea is that of overflowing or abundance. The context determines the nature of that abundance and overflowing in either a positive or a negative sense.—Trans.

as those who so happily promote a general grace, most certainly are completely silent about the one side of these two unreconciled ideas. The emphasis falls exclusively on general grace. Second, we do not deal here with a mystery, but with an absolute contradiction. The one excludes the other. To hate and to love, to be indignant and to be abounding in goodness, cursing and blessing, to abominate someone and to love him—these exclude one another. We would keep silent if God's word actually taught both and if there were no possibility of reconciling the texts we have quoted and the texts our opponents advanced. This is not the case whatsoever, in our opinion. Nowhere does the Bible say that God blesses and bestows grace on the reprobate, that is, the ungodly. That is our conviction. For support of that position we present the following.

First, many of the quoted texts do not really say anything about God's attitude toward the reprobate ungodly. To these belong the following texts: "The earth is full of the goodness of the LORD" (Ps. 33:5). Definitely, we would say; but the ungodly are not the objects of this goodness according to the explicit statement of scripture, and this text does not say that they are either. The same is true of Psalm 65:11: "Thou crownest the year with thy goodness; and thy paths drop fatness." Here too the ungodly are not mentioned, and there is no mention of God's attitude toward them.

What Van Baalen quotes from Exodus 22:22, 27 proves exactly the opposite position than he intends, for the Lord says in that passage that he is filled with wrath toward and punishes those who defraud the widow and the poor among his people. Those who defraud are thus the ungodly.

We do not know how much weight Van Baalen ascribes to Proverbs 18:22: "Whoso findeth a wife findeth a good thing, and obtaineth favour of the LORD." But, taken seriously, it certainly then allows for no doubt, that the poet of Proverbs does not here intend all wives, taking into consideration what he says about the brawling and foolish wife [Prov. 21:9; 25:24], as well as that he did not find one [woman] in a thousand [Eccl. 7:28]. Truly, we maintain that anyone who has an ungodly or wicked wife would not imagine that he had been favored by the Lord.

We consider also Genesis 9:1: "And God blessed Noah and his

sons." We regard this as God's organic covenantal blessing of his people. There is, moreover, not the least bit of proof that among the sons of Noah there is even one reprobate, Ham included. The sin Ham committed is no proof that he was reprobate. Ham was certainly punished in the curse that fell on his son, but he himself was never cursed. The curse fell on Canaan.

The text from 1 Timothy 4:10, "God, who is the Saviour of all men, specially of those that believe," we explain as an expression of God's providence by which he upholds all men temporally in organic connection with all things.

Second, in the texts regarding Ahab and Nineveh the final punishment, the total destruction, was postponed. By that postponement we are taught that God did not complete it until the measure of iniquity was full. Ahab's house bore the evil in his son, and Nineveh was laid waste forty years later.

Concerning the blessing Ishmael received, Van Baalen and others think that this event may be simply explained as a blessing of common grace. One reasons then that Ishmael was reprobate, that God had nonetheless promised to bless him, and that consequently it is as clear as crystal that God can also love the reprobate, because he indeed blessed Ishmael. The argument appears so solid that one cannot in any way dislodge it. Against this reasoning a response seems impossible.

This supposed certainty is more often the case when people simply quote a text off the cuff to prove a certain proposition. Lately this has been done frequently to prove that the doctrine of common grace is the truth. One is easily inclined to lay hold on a passage of scripture and, without any further investigation, quote it as a proof for what he desires to prove. Such a proof, superficially considered, can appear clear and compelling. Yet when the text is more closely examined, it soon looks much different. It will become apparent that this is the case with regard to the so-called proof of Ishmael.

What is the real situation? Abraham prays for Ishmael. He says, "O that Ishmael might live before thee!" According to the entire context, this prayer does not intend to ask for a little common grace or earthly good for Ishmael, but it very definitely refers to the promise of the covenant. Abraham found it so difficult to accept the idea that he would still have another son that he said in his heart, "Shall a child be born unto him that is an hundred years old? and shall Sarah, that is ninety years old, bear?" (Gen. 17:17). The prayer of his lips for Ishmael follows in the next verse. The prayer therefore refers to the promise of the covenant, which was ordained for Isaac according to God's plan. Immediately Abraham receives God's answer: "As for Ishmael, I have heard thee: Behold, I have blessed him" (v. 20). From these facts it is already apparent that one cannot, without anything more, identify Ishmael as reprobate and regard the blessing of Ishmael as a blessing of common grace. The whole context of this passage, as well as the entire representation of scripture, conflicts with such an explanation.

But there is more. Genesis 25:13–15 names the sons of Ishmael according to the order of birth. The firstborn of Ishmael was Nebajoth; after that Kedar, Adbeel, Mibsam, and the others. When we read Isaiah 60:3–7 in conjunction with this, we receive a different impression of the blessing on Ishmael. There we read of the entering of the heathen into the promise of the covenant, which had been given to Isaac:

3. And the Gentiles shall come to thy light, and kings to the brightness of thy rising.

4. Lift up thine eyes round about, and see: all they gather themselves together, they come to thee: thy sons shall come from far, and thy daughters shall be nursed at thy side.

5. Then thou shalt see, and flow together, and thine heart shall fear, and be enlarged; because the abundance of the sea shall be converted unto thee, the forces of the Gentiles shall come unto thee.

6. The multitude of camels shall cover thee, the dromedaries of Midian and Ephah, all they from Sheba shall come: they shall bring gold and incense; and they shall shew forth the praises of the Lord.

7. All the flocks of Kedar shall be gathered together unto thee, the rams of Nebaioth shall minister unto thee; they shall come up with acceptance on mine altar, and I will glorify the house of my glory.

If we read the Bible in its unity, instead of merely quoting a text that appears suitable to prove our position, we arrive at an entirely different perspective from what Van Baalen offers concerning the blessing of Ishmael. The blessing relates to Ishmael's generations. In Isaiah 60 we are taught very clearly that God thought of Ishmael, he heard the prayer of Abraham, and he caused the son of Hagar to enter the glory of the covenant. When the heathen enter into the blessing of the covenant with Israel, at the forefront of this host stands Ishmael in his sons Nebajoth and Kedar when they rise up to worship at Jerusalem. Thus we explain these matters on the basis of sacred scripture.

Van Baalen treats 1 Timothy 4:10 too casually, as he must to cement his proposition to this text. He wants to prove his assertion that God loves the reprobate. This verse distinguishes between believers and all men: "we trust in the living God, who is the Saviour of all men, specially of those who believe." It says that God is the preserver (*soter*) of all men. Van Baalen says that the word *preserver* always has a favorable significance, so very clearly God is favorable to all men, including the reprobate.

We stated that Van Baalen's explanation too easily accepts what needs to be demonstrated. It says that *soter* (preserver or savior) always has a favorable meaning. However, it does not say what the favorable significance is. In the abstract it could be that we do not understand *soter* in the text to mean *savior* in the ordinary sense, but as *provider* or *preserver* in the sense that God temporally keeps and supports all men. Then the word would relate to God's providence.

Understood this way, there would be no hidden proof for Van Baalen's proposition, namely, that God bestows grace on the reprobate. However, this explanation of *soter* does not fit. It does not agree with the usual meaning of this word in scripture and is not true to the idea of the text. Then the text would say that God is the preserver, or keeper, of all men, chiefly of believers. But this makes no sense. *Soter* (preserver) should be understood in the ordinary sense of savior. Then the text means that God is the savior of all men, specially of believers. (*But* is in the translation not in the original.[10])

---

10 The Dutch *Staten Bijbel* uses the word *maar* (but).—Trans.

However, is it acceptable to say that God is the savior of all men? Why does the apostle add "specially of those who believe"? Does not this line of reasoning run stuck?

The solution is in the meaning of the Greek word *malista* translated as "specially." It is a word that does not always have precisely the same meaning. It is translated as "chiefly," "primarily," "particularly," and "especially." *Malista* has the sense of "to speak more specifically and in this text it can be translated in a way that does justice to the meaning of *soter* (savior).

We let *savior* have its ordinary meaning without sailing off into Arminian waters. The Arminian explains the text this way: God wants to be the savior of all men, but it depends on man's free will whether he accepts salvation through faith. That teaching we cannot accept.

However, if we read the text this way, "God is the savior of all men, particularly [more definitely] of believers from all men," this would be a very good explanation. So it was with Israel in the old administration. God is the savior of all Israel, and yet this obtains only for the remnant according to the election of grace. In the new dispensation salvation obtains for all men in contrast to Israel as a nation, yet it applies only to believers, or elect, from among all men. The meaning of this verse, explained in the light of all scripture, is that God is the savior of all men, namely the believers from among all men.

That our explanation harmonizes with the Bible's general thought and manner of speaking is not difficult to demonstrate. In the old covenant the whole house of Israel is often mentioned in general, while it is nonetheless very clear that only spiritual Israel is intended. That this is possible arises from the fact that not everyone who is of Israel is Israel. The seed of the flesh is more numerous than the spiritual seed.

The prophets speak of the house of Israel in general. God is a preserver of Israel. Strictly understood, God is the savior only of Israel in a spiritual sense, that is, of the elect in Israel. If we understand this, we can also comprehend how scripture can speak in such different ways to and about Israel. For example, consider Isaiah 42:24–43:4:

24. Who gave Jacob for a spoil, and Israel to the robbers? did not the LORD, he against whom we have sinned? for they

would not walk in his ways, neither were they obedient unto his law.

25. Therefore he hath poured upon him the fury of his anger, and the strength of battle: and it hath set him on fire round about, yet he knew not; and it burned him, yet he laid it not to heart.

1. But now thus saith the LORD that created thee, O Jacob, and he that formed thee, O Israel, Fear not: for I have redeemed thee, I have called thee by thy name; thou art mine.

2. When thou passest through the waters, I will be with thee; and through the rivers, they shall not overflow thee: when thou walkest through the fire, thou shalt not be burned; neither shall the flame kindle upon thee.

3. For I am the LORD thy God, the Holy One of Israel, thy Saviour: I gave Egypt for thy ransom, Ethiopia and Seba for thee.

4. Since thou wast precious in my sight, thou hast been honourable, and I have loved thee: therefore will I give men for thee, and people for thy life.

See also Isaiah 63:7–9 and Hosea 2:23 in connection with Romans 9:26. Concerning these latter texts, one should pay attention to Paul's application to all nations of what Hosea prophesies concerning the ten tribes. Those who were not God's people become in the new dispensation God's people. This spiritual reality does not mean that the ten tribes are again accepted, but that the heathen enter into Israel's tents. Just as God was the preserver of Israel in the old dispensation, which strictly understood means the preserver of believers and elect in Israel, so in the new dispensation God becomes the preserver and savior of all men, which means the savior of believers from among all men.

According to our conviction 1 Timothy 4:10 should be explained in this manner. One then does no violence to the words of the text and at the same time remains consistent with the current thought of holy scripture.

Naturally Van Baalen is free to give a different explanation of 1 Timothy 4:10. If he has a better one, let him present it. But he does not give any explanation. To excuse oneself of the duty to explain a somewhat difficult word of scripture by stating that a word always has a favorable meaning is too easy. However, he will have to give an explanation that more faithfully than ours does justice to the meaning of the words and is in harmony with the current thought of scripture. He cannot have a principal objection to our explanation. In any case, there is no proof for his position in this text.

Van Baalen appeals to Romans 2:4–5: "Despisest thou the riches of his goodness and forbearance and longsuffering; not knowing that the goodness of God leadeth thee to repentance? But after thy hardness and impenitent heart treasurest up unto thyself wrath against the day of wrath and revelation of the righteous judgment of God." The essence of Van Baalen's explanation of these verses is that God is plenteous in mercy toward the reprobate. God shows this goodness to the reprobate to lead him to conversion. This is God's revealed will. But the reprobate resists God's mercy and by doing so gathers to himself the treasures of wrath.

We do not agree with him. First, we do not believe that election and reprobation are hidden realities. As an absolute abstraction, it is certainly true that we do not know who is elect and who is reprobate when they are considered naturally without any regard to their works. But election and reprobation as such, the truth that God wills not to save all men, is not hidden but is revealed. Yet Van Baalen says, "For they should not have reasoned on the basis of the hidden things, election and reprobation."[11]

Second, we do not agree with Van Baalen's claim that God's revealed will is that all men be saved, provided they convert. If all men would convert, they would be saved. But the Bible does not teach that God wills all men head for head to be saved and that salvation depends on the will of man to convert himself. Following Van Baalen's ideas, we get two tracks, and the one track is definitely Arminian.

---

11 Van Baalen, *Novelty and Error,* 137.

A Reformed explanation of Romans 2:4–5 is possible. The text discusses God's overflowing goodness that leads to conversion, which definitely is saving goodness. We especially note that there is no mention of common grace in the text. Many texts that have no connection to the doctrine of common grace are quoted again and again without careful analysis to oppose the truth of particular, saving grace. This text speaks of saving grace, for it leads to conversion. It does not say that it can or will lead to salvation if this or that is true, but only that "goodness" leads to conversion. However, this goodness does so only for the elect. It never leads other persons to conversion.

Both the elect and the reprobate live under revelation, under the preaching of this goodness; they both live under the dispensation of a goodness that leads to conversion. The reprobate also comes into contact with this revelation of God's goodness toward his people. The consequence is that he despises that goodness in his sin and unconverted heart. That is and remains his guilt. That others do not despise this goodness is due to God's grace. That the sinner by nature does this is not God's fault but his own fault. Consequently he gathers to himself the treasures of wrath.

It is noteworthy that our opponents completely ignore the confessions regarding the significant point of the common grace theory: does God in this life overflow in goodness toward and bestow favor and grace on elect and reprobate? If we have not completely overlooked this, our opponents have not quoted even one part of the confessions to prove their point. We are not saying that they have not attempted this. Certainly Van Baalen and other brothers quoted Canons 2.5, 11 and 3–4.8–9 that deal with the external calling. Van Baalen quoted these passages because he thinks the preaching of the gospel to everyone without distinction is a proof of God's goodness toward the reprobate. Van Baalen resolutely maintains the Arminian line! The external call must be a proof of common grace. The address of the external call to everyone is a proof that God loves the reprobate.

We would say, "from the claw, the lion."

We want to reason with Van Baalen according to the Reformed

line of thought about these spiritual truths. We would say, "Brother, do you not believe with us that the elect come to salvation finally and exclusively by the grace of God alone?

Besides, we want to ask you in all seriousness, "If God loves the reprobate and shows his love in the external call to salvation, but no one can come unless God draws him, what is that love, grace, mercy, or however you may identify it that from God's perspective can draw, but does not draw, and of which the consequence is that those who are called receive more severe judgment?" We really want to ask Van Baalen this question, yet it will not profit because he will simply appeal to his double-track system and jump over to the other line. That is very easy to do. Van Baalen's one line is Arminian and the other is Reformed. However, on these two tracks no train can run.

The confessions do not speak of a calling to the reprobate, but simply of a calling to all men. The external call cannot be brought to the elect alone, but it is brought to all men as the elect are reached through the gospel. Naturally that calling is a serious call. It is an emphatic call to repentance and conversion. In and through the preaching of the gospel, God overflows in goodness and graciousness to his people alone, for the elect are called only through his goodness.

The reprobate also live under and hear the general external calling in the preaching. But they live under the preaching and despise God's goodness so that they gather to themselves the treasures of wrath. That is not God's fault but their own.

We definitely agree with this testimony and believe that all these matters were treated at Dordrecht in 1618–19. Common grace was not included there in the discussions.

We call attention to the official Reformed confessions and in particular to the Heidelberg Catechism:

Will God suffer such disobedience and apostasy to go unpunished?

By no means; but he is terribly displeased with our inborn as well as actual sins, and will punish them in just judgment in time and eternity, as he has declared: *Cursed is every one that*

*continueth not in all things which are written in the book of
the law, to do them.*[12]

Here is stated the dreadful wrath of God in time and eternity. Punishment in time is mentioned, with temporal punishments consonant with the temporal administration. Eternal punishment is mentioned, with eternal punishment consonant with eternity. Christ alone brings change to this dreadful reality. Where does common grace fit in?

The only thing remaining is the matter of rain and sunshine. About this matter we want to say the following:

First, these realities stand in precisely the same relationship as all other things. Both God and man make use of rain and sunshine. In themselves rain and sunshine are good, or fit, instruments. Leaving out of consideration any particular divine purpose and relationship to the reprobate and ungodly, if God reveals himself by the means of rain and sunshine to the evil and the good as they interact in mutual relationships, these things are a revelation of God's love and goodness in his relation to the creature.

The texts from Matthew 5 and Luke 6 do not speak to the matter of God's specific relation to the ungodly as ungodly. In Luke 6:35 we read that God "is kind unto the unthankful and to the evil." This refers chiefly to the children of God, who by nature are unthankful and evil but are still objects of God's goodness in Christ.

Rev. Ghysels so emphatically rejects this explanation that he does not account it worthy of a response. However, we still hold this explanation to be valid. We ask him not to be so hasty to condemn our explanation.

In the context we read that Jesus cried out, "Woe unto you," to the rich, to those who were full, to those who laugh as the world. Thus he cried out to the ungodly in contrast to the children of the kingdom of Christ, who are blessed. Further, the main thought is that God's children must reveal the living God in their lives by their love for their enemies, for God does the same with them. He is overflowing in goodness to them not because they show so much love to him, but

---

12 Heidelberg Catechism Q&A 10, in Schaff, *Creeds of Christendom*, 3:310.—Trans.

notwithstanding that they are unthankful and evil. Luke 6 does not mention rain and sunshine. Nor is it the heart of Matthew 5:44–45: "I say unto you, Love your enemies, bless them that curse you, do good to them that hate you, and pray for them which despitefully use you, and persecute you; that ye may be the children of your Father which is in heaven: for he maketh his sun to rise on the evil and on the good, and sendeth rain on the just and on the unjust."

The love wherewith God loves those who did not love him is the possession of the children of the kingdom alone. Only they can reveal this love because it has been poured into their hearts. They only are the children of the most high God, and they are that through the love wherewith God loved them when they were still enemies.

Apart from this, God still reveals his goodness to all men in each and every one of his good gifts that the righteous and the wicked have in common in their mutual coexistence. Just as it is with God's saving word, as a revelation of God's grace in an objective sense to all who live jointly under the preaching of the word, so too rain and sunshine are a revelation of God's goodness in the general sense.[13]

However, the question is, does God through these external gifts bless and cause his grace to be enjoyed by the ungodly as the wicked reprobate? That will have to be made clear from the sacred scriptures.

Second, one must be cautious with reasoning in generalities about rain and sunshine. The shining of the sun and the falling of the rain do not always happen according to definitely established laws of nature. Scripture does not teach that they do. According to the Bible God sends timely rain or withholds it. Sometimes he sends rain that washes everything away, then rain at the time of harvest or a devastating, torrential downpour. He does not send rain to every city or on every section of the land. Sometimes he rains down hail and fire. Sometimes he sends gentle rain on his deteriorating inheritance; then again he is

---

13 By "objective sense" Hoeksema means that the preaching of the gospel makes known the grace of God to all in the audience, regardless that some are not, subjectively, the objects and recipients of this grace. Similarly, rain and sunshine in themselves display the goodness of the Creator, regardless that rain and sunshine are not a blessing to all upon whom they fall or shine.—Ed.

for his people a protection against the rain. Sometimes there is also burning heat immediately after the rain.

This was the case in the old dispensation, and it is the same way now. The farmer will tell you what a difference this makes for particular crops and for men, animals, and society. Rain makes plants grow to maturity and causes them to bloom, but it also destroys. Rain has many and varied advantageous and disadvantageous consequences mainly for the plant world and by extension for the life of man and beast and for the whole earth.

There is perhaps a more varied influence on the entire kingdom of creatures from the sunshine than from the rain. The sun is a lovely image of Christ's righteousness, but it also burns and scorches, and then it is a figure of oppression and persecution. Whatever has the spirit of life and the power of life the sun colors and brightens, but whatever is weak and dying shrivels under the sun's scorching rays. It purifies the air but causes various toxic vapors to arise. The sun's rays have varying influences and effects on the sick according to the nature of the affliction, the time of the year and day, the shuttering of windows, the wind, the clothing, and the like.

Stated briefly, rain and sunshine and whatever is associated therewith have a very dissimilar effect and influence, an operation that is extremely antithetical in this dispensation. In the midst of and under the influences of these realities live the evil and the good, the unrighteous and the righteous. Therefore, it is unacceptable to speak about common grace in connection with all this. The real question is, what does God do with all of this regarding the righteous and the ungodly, respectively, as the elect and the reprobate? They are all means or instruments that the creature definitely uses, and they are used by God as means to execute his counsel.

Third, does God cause all these things—rain and sunshine, personal properties and houses, money and possessions, gifts and talents—to be blessings for the ungodly, the reprobate, in their temporal and historical existence? That is, does he bestow grace, favor, and goodness on the enemy of himself and his people by means of all these things?

The Bible gives a very clear answer to this question. We have appealed to Psalm 73 and Psalm 92 in this regard. In Psalm 73 Asaph at first stares himself blind at all of the things of this world and does not see any difference between the righteous and the wicked in the reception of these things. Still worse, he sees that while the righteous are plunged into suffering and affliction, the wicked prospers, and in his evil he flourishes and knows no sorrow. But when Asaph goes into the house of the Lord he sees the very same realities much differently. Affluence and pleasure for the wicked are slippery places on which God places him and on which he hastens to destruction. To be fattened for the day of slaughter is truly not to receive grace. In Psalm 92 this is expressed more strongly, for the psalm teaches that God causes the wicked to prosper so that he will be destroyed unto all eternity.

Therefore, we must not look in scripture for two different lines or two entirely different conceptions that decisively exclude one another and let them stand in irreconcilable conflict. We must let the mutual coherence of the entire Bible speak to us. Scripture teaches that God hates the ungodly; that God's soul is filled with abhorrence because of him; that God's wrath abides on him; that God causes his curse to dwell in his house; that God resists him and is very furious with him; that there is in God's good gifts in this temporal dispensation a revelation of God's mercy and goodness to all his creatures, among whom also the wicked lives; and that God works discriminately in these things toward the righteous and the wicked, the elect and the reprobate. When the ungodly lives in the midst of God's good gifts, this does not diminish the fact that God's wrath and curse rest on him and even dwell in his house. Whatever may be common to all, God's grace never is.

Finally, what must be said about the rich youth whom Jesus respected and loved (Matt. 19:16–22)? We would not consider this text worth a special discussion if it were not quoted so often as a proof for common grace. Yet there is no such proof in it, and it cannot be a proof because there is nothing common in this incident. It concerns only one young man. How the Messiah could thunder against the ungodly you may read in Matthew 23.

Various explanations can be given of the Messiah's love for the rich young man. First, the explanation could be that the Savior, according to the flesh an Israelite, loved that Israelite who had walked externally in the paths of the covenant. Yet another explanation of Jesus' love seems possible. Above all we should not forget that the young man came to Jesus not to tempt him, but in all earnestness of soul with the question on his lips and in his heart concerning eternal life. Second, the young man did not in that moment enter into the kingdom of heaven, but he did go away with a *heavy* heart. Third, Jesus explains this situation when he says to his disciples that it is scarcely possible for the rich to enter the kingdom of heaven—so difficult that it is easier for a camel to enter the eye of a needle. When the disciples react in bewilderment, the Savior says that what is not possible with men is possible with God (vv. 23–26).

If we take all of this as a whole and read again that Jesus loved this young man, we are inclined toward the explanation that this young man later returned and by the wonder of God's grace became a recipient of the eternal life about which he had inquired. The camel then goes through the eye of the needle. It is not impossible that we encounter this young man again in Joseph of Arimathea. At any rate, there is certainly no proof to be found in the text for common grace to the reprobate.

In our opinion we have finished the first part of our task. It can no longer be thrown in our faces that we have not quoted any proof for our position that God does not have a favorable attitude toward the reprobate, historically existing as ungodly and the enemy of God, but that he hates him.

Each one may judge the strength of our scriptural proofs in comparison with those of our brothers who oppose us.

We conclude with the claim that the Bible teaches no common grace of God on the wicked and the righteous. They have all things in common in this life, except grace.

CHAPTER 3

CAN MAN
BY NATURE DO GOOD?

This is the second question requiring our attention. Our opponents will speak first regarding their proofs for their position that man by nature can do good. Then we will present our viewpoint along with the necessary proof from scripture and the confessions.

Van Baalen's presentation is not that the unregenerate sinner is able by his own strength either to will and to choose the good or not to will and not to choose the good that earthly life presents. No, he teaches emphatically that man, without regenerating grace, is able to do moral good *because God forces him to do it.* We let Van Baalen speak regarding his view:

> Man's nature is wholly corrupt. Yet the unregenerated man does good in the sense of civil righteousness.
>
> Sometimes that good, as moral good, assumes such a character that we would be inclined to say, "The man who did that is positively not 'unable to do any good and inclined to all evil.'" Nevertheless, we still have to maintain this Reformed confession in regard to the man who does good.
>
> How can this be? There are different kinds of good.
>
> Man can do good because man *must* [do good] by virtue of an instinct implanted in his nature. In this sense the animal does good, since it acts according to the ordinance, or law of life, that God created for that animal. In this sense man often performs the good. He must. His nature forces him. That means God forces him to do it. But in this doing of good there is no merit.

However, may we speak of moral good in connection with the unregenerate man?

Yes, because God has established all sorts of laws for man. God has established not only a law of existence for animals, but also a moral law. If man acts in accordance with God's moral law, to that extent his deed is good. It is a deed in harmony with his ordinance.

Yet man does that out of many secret motivations: shame, fear of punishment, and consideration for his health. He does not do it to the honor of God's name, that is, out of faith. He cannot do that in his own strength, since he is and continues to be "dead in sin and trespasses" until and unless God regenerates him. The good he does is positive good as far as it is in accord with the rule of God's law. Therefore, we call it good or civil righteousness.

However, it is not perfectly good. Consequently, it does not merit anything. Yet the good the natural man does merits nothing from another perspective.

If we ask, how can the nature of man do anything good? Is it not wholly corrupt? The answer is, most assuredly it is, but God works in that sinful nature so it brings forth the good. This does not mean that God changes the nature. He does not make it better. But he forces it into a somewhat different direction than it wants to go. Therefore, it does not arrive at the destination that it has chosen, namely, at a complete development of and a breaking forth into only evil. It arrives at a position somewhat between completely evil and completely good.

This divine intervention we call an activity of God's common grace (*gratie* in distinction from *genade*, or saving grace). Therefore, whatever good the sinner does comes from God.

However, that it still remains sinful is due to the activity of the sinner, who will need to have more than "restraining grace" to do what can be identified as acceptable by a holy God.[14]

---

14 Van Baalen, *Novelty and Error*, 36–37.

General grace takes nothing away from all of this. It never places the sinner in a position to do good *before God*. It never allows the sinner to do any *spiritual* good. It changes nothing in the nature of man. It only forces man to act in many respects according to the law of God, even though these works are against his own will and are not done to the honor of God.

How can these truly good deeds in themselves (good, because they were done according to God's law) be spiritual good, since they proceed from wrong motives? The manifestation of these may be good, yet the motive spoils everything. Hence it is that man suppresses in unrighteousness the light of nature, unless saving, heart-renewing grace intervenes.[15]

We conclude that Van Baalen's doctrine is that the natural man of himself cannot do nor does any good at all; that he is dead in sin and trespasses; that God forces man against his will to do the good; and that this good is not spiritual good, but truly moral good.

Van Baalen presents the following as proof for his position:

> God blessed them, and God said unto them, Be fruitful, and multiply, and replenish the earth, and subdue it: and have dominion. (Gen. 1:28). [The proof is hidden in the idea that man always complies with this creational imperative.]

> By me kings reign, and princes decree justice. (Prov. 8:15)

> Samuel said to all the people, See ye him whom the LORD hath chosen, that there is none like him among all the people? (1 Sam. 10:24)

> Solomon's builders and Hiram's builders did hew them, and the stonesquarers: so they prepared timber and stones to build the house. (1 Kings 5:18)

> Go to the ant, thou sluggard; consider her ways, and be wise: which having no guide, overseer, or ruler, provideth

---

15 Ibid., 74.

her meat in the summer, and gathereth her food in the harvest. How long wilt thou sleep, O sluggard? when wilt thou arise out of thy sleep? (Prov. 6:6–9 compared with Prov. 10:5)

He that gathereth in summer is a wise son: but he that sleepeth in harvest is a son that causeth shame. (Prov. 10:5)

The lord commended the unjust steward, because he had done wisely: for the children of this world are in their generation wiser than the children of light. (Luke 16:8)

Therefore shall a man leave his father and his mother, and shall cleave unto his wife: and they shall be one flesh. (Gen. 2:24 compared with 1 Cor. 7:14)

For the unbelieving husband is sanctified by the wife, and the unbelieving wife is sanctified by the husband: else were your children unclean; but now are they holy. (1 Cor. 7:14)

7. Ask, and it shall be given you; seek, and ye shall find; knock, and it shall be opened unto you:

8. For every one that asketh receiveth; and he that seeketh findeth; and to him that knocketh it shall be opened.

9. Or what man is there of you, whom if his son ask bread, will he give him a stone?

10. Or if he ask a fish, will he give him a serpent?

11. If ye then, being evil, know how to give good gifts unto your children, how much more shall your Father which is in heaven give good things to them that ask him? (Matt. 7:7–11)

3. For rulers are not a terror to good works, but to the evil. Wilt thou then not be afraid of the power? do that which is good, and thou shalt have praise of the same:

4. For he is the minister of God to thee for good. But if thou do that which is evil, be afraid; for he beareth not the sword in vain: for he is the minister of God, a revenger to execute wrath upon him that doeth evil. (Rom. 13:3–4)

1. I exhort therefore, that, first of all, supplications, prayers, intercessions, and giving of thanks, be made for all men;
2. For kings, and for all that are in authority; that we may lead a quiet and peaceable life in all godliness and honesty. (1 Tim. 2:1–2)

Put them in mind to be subject to principalities and powers, to obey magistrates, to be ready to every good work. (Titus 3:1)

I will bless them that bless thee, and curse him that curseth thee: and in thee shall all families of the earth be blessed. (Gen. 12:3)

30. The LORD said unto Jehu, Because thou hast done well in executing that which is right in mine eyes, and hast done unto the house of Ahab according to all that was in mine heart, thy children of the fourth generation shall sit on the throne of Israel.
31. But Jehu took no heed to walk in the law of the LORD God of Israel with all his heart: for he departed not from the sins of Jeroboam, which made Israel to sin.
32. In those days the LORD began to cut Israel short. (2 Kings 10:30–32)

Van Baalen presents the following confessional proof:

And being thus become wicked, perverse, and corrupt in all his ways, he hath lost all his excellent gifts which he had received from God, and only retained a few remains thereof, which, however, are sufficient to leave man without excuse; for all the light which is in us is changed into darkness.[16]

---

16 Belgic Confession 14, in Schaff, *Creeds of Christendom*, 3:398–99.—Trans.

There remain, however, in man since the fall, the glimmerings of natural light, whereby he retains some knowledge of God, of natural things, and of the difference between good and evil, and discovers some regard for virtue, good order in society, and for maintaining an orderly external deportment. But so far is this light of nature from being sufficient to bring him to a saving knowledge of God, and to true conversion, that he is incapable of using it aright even in things natural and civil. Nay farther, this light, such as it is, man in various ways renders wholly polluted, and holds it [back] in unrighteousness; by doing which he becomes inexcusable before God.[17]

God is under no obligation to confer this grace upon any... With respect to those who make an external profession of faith and live regular lives, we are bound, after the example of the Apostle, to judge and speak of them in the most favorable manner; for the secret recesses of the heart are unknown to us.[18]

We have faithfully quoted all the proofs Van Baalen presented for his position that God forces the natural man to do good works and that these deeds are moral good.

Y. P. de Jong has also written concerning this question. We have tried to find somewhat definite lines of thought in this brother's writing, so that we can reproduce in a few sentences the points of difference between us. However, we are unable. We have asked ourselves, does De Jong teach that the natural man is able to do moral good? What is the civil righteousness, or moral good, that God compels one to perform? What is the relationship to virtue and external order? What does De Jong understand by total depravity? The brother still owes us a clearly delineated response.

If he represents a third school of thought, distinguished from Van Baalen and ourselves, he certainly fails to demonstrate where that school of thought leads. It does not appear to have a definite direction. It appears that De Jong gains wiggle room for the operation of

---

17 Canons 3–4.4, in ibid., 3:588.—Trans.
18 Canons 3–4.15, in ibid., 3:591.—Trans.

God's general grace by vague expressions concerning total depravity and civil righteousness, as demonstrated by the following:

> What is the Reformed doctrine of man's inability to do good? The answer must be that man is spiritually dead by nature; that he lacks true love toward God and his neighbor; that therefore true love cannot be the motivating principle of his life, by which he is determined and led in his thinking, speaking, and doing. [De Jong's language is extremely weak and negative. Scripture and the confessions use much stronger language: not that man lacks true love, but that he hates God and his neighbor, is an enemy of God, and contemplates hostility; that he is perverted in all his ways, godless, and corrupt. This is the language of scripture and the confessions. If De Jong would adopt this language, much of his wiggle room would fall away.]
>
> Further, total depravity implies that the sinner can do no spiritual good and in all his life allows himself to be led by inclinations and desires that are directed to an inferior good compared to God and that find their purpose in man. [We have the same objections to this language. "No spiritual good" is De Jong's language. Our confessions teach that man *is wholly incapable of doing any good and inclined to all wickedness.* Scripture and the confessions teach that the natural man seeks not an inferior good, but sin. Here as well, the wiggle room falls away, should De Jong decide to use the language of scripture and our confessions.]
>
> Subsequently, this confession of man's total inability implies that in the final analysis man is always hostile toward God. [We believe the testimony of scripture when it says, "The carnal mind is enmity against God" (Rom. 8:7). We make the same observation as before. "In the final analysis" is the language neither of scripture nor of the confessions. This expression should be dropped. Then the wiggle room falls away as well.][19]

---

19 Y. P. de Jong, *Christian Journal* (Thursday, March 6, 1924).

Van Baalen does not talk this way. He is clear and definite. One is able to take a position contrary to him. One cannot do that with De Jong, because he is weak and extremely vague, and thus he gains the desired wiggle room.

In regard to the so-called good, which De Jong also addresses, the very same weakness and vagueness shows up.

> Total depravity does not include the idea that each man is as bad as he can be. He can degenerate from bad to worse. Nor does this doctrine obligate one to hold that the sinner retains no knowledge of God in his conscience...
>
> Nor does this doctrine of total inability commit one to the idea that the sinner is deprived of attributes that are attractive to man and that, according to human judgment, are definitely beneficial...
>
> Besides, no one claims by the confession of man's total depravity that all the forms of sin come to manifestation in each and every sinner. Such cannot be the case, because the one sin sometimes excludes the other sin, for example, greed and prodigality.[20]

De Jong says a little later, "Man has not become the same as a fallen angel; and the earth, though indeed cursed, has not become a hell, but after the flood it has become a stage on which life and death, sin and grace, Christ and Satan, wrestle with one another for dominance in this dispensation."[21]

Still later he says, "It is the fruit of God's long-suffering and of his benevolent goodness, that is, of his general grace, that this half-way depravity came to be: man has not become a fallen angel nor the earth a hellish sphere."[22]

The last quotation seems to teach that without common grace man would have been changed into a fallen angel and the earth into a hellish sphere. Whether De Jong actually meant that, we do not dare to say. Yet he literally says it.

---

20 Ibid.
21 Ibid.
22 Ibid.

In the following paragraph De Jong summarizes the material he attempted to make clear above:

> The result was that something happened, call it a sort of half-way depravity that came to be. [De Jong apparently does not much care how this reality is identified.] This is a circumstance that makes possible human history, in which God interacts with man as far as necessary, so that sin does not break forth into full, everlasting death. Man is not completely wild; there is still a certain love for the truth and a general, vibrant sense of justice; external virtue is still preferred to vice, and in this way human society is not dissolved, but on the contrary, science and art can develop and prosper.[23]

We do not dare to make a definite conclusion from all this material regarding De Jong's position concerning the natural man. Does he teach that the natural man does moral good, even though he does no spiritual good? If yes, then what is the difference between the two kinds of good? How is it possible for the natural man to do moral good? Is the possibility explained by the little remnants of natural light or by a source outside of man, since man is absolutely incapable of doing any good? We prefer to leave the matter as De Jong expressed it. His product is completely lacking in any proof from scripture and the confessions, except for his appeal to the mercy of Pharaoh's daughter and the rich youth whom Jesus loved.

Keegstra does not have much on this point. He mentions that there is shame in the natural man and how it must be explained from our viewpoint. He only makes a few observations, but does not develop a specific position.

Beets also passes by this point in silence. At least, we could not find anything, except what he quotes from Kuizenga. However, Kuizenga reasons not from scripture and the confessions, but from what he thinks he discerns of actual life. He does not understand how there could possibly be science if the natural man can do nothing good. We have no desire to go into this because it does not relate to the question

---

23 Ibid.

before us. We are obligated to reason on the basis of God's word, and it is inappropriate to enter into a discussion with anyone who is not ashamed to pour out his heart in street language and describe another believer as hard-boiled.

We therefore have to treat only Van Baalen's presentation. His doctrine is that God forces the natural man to do good deeds, and in this manner the natural man can perform moral good.

This viewpoint occurs frequently in his writings, and he never offers another. Van Baalen has surpassed his master in this regard. Kuyper struggled to escape the consequence of his common grace doctrine. The consequence is simply determinism and fatalism, and Kuyper had to arrive there as well. Sometimes he did. However, he preferred to speak of the wonder of God's general grace bestowed immediately after the fall, through which man's inclinations were improved and he was restored to a spiritual condition that enabled him to will and to do the good.

Van Baalen is different. He summons courage and says, "God forces the sinner toward moral good against his will, and although it is not the sinner's act but God's deed, nevertheless I claim that the sinner apart from regenerating grace performs moral good. Danhof and Hoeksema know that as well, but they will not acknowledge it. That is their sin."[24]

We do not agree with Van Baalen that God forces the natural man against his own will to do moral good. Our objections are two. Such a forced act is not moral good, precisely because it is compelled and is contrary to the will. Such a deed is not an act of the sinner but of God. Considered as an act of God, it is of course good; yet it is not from any perspective a morally good deed of the sinner. In our judgment a doctrine of that kind always merits the charge of fatalism and determinism.

---

24 What appears within the quotations marks seems to be a summary of Van Baalen's doctrine on pages 36–37 of his *Novelty and Error*. Van Baalen does state that God "forces it [the depraved nature of the ungodly, unregenerate person] in a somewhat different direction than that in which it itself wills to go." The result, according to Van Baalen, is that the nature of the godless, unregenerated human "produces the good."—Ed.

Van Baalen grants as much. He makes precisely the same judgment as we do. He understands very well that God's forcing a man to perform a certain deed is plain fatalism.

> No, it was not grace that the Roman said, "I will crucify you."
> No one has ever claimed that it was. Nor was it the act of God
> that the Roman said, "I will crucify you." It concerned the act
> of God, and it concerned grace; for it was definitely grace that
> that heathen knew better. It was not saving grace, but it was
> by God's favor that that heathen knew better and could have
> known better. *Whoever denies this falls into fatalism, or, if you
> will, into determinism, which is un-Reformed; for then God
> forces a man to sin.*[25]

Here Van Baalen very correctly says that the teaching that God forces one to sin is fatalism or determinism and thus un-Reformed. The same holds just as much when one is forced to do the good. We insist that the claim that God forces a man against his will to do the good is fatalism or determinism, which is un-Reformed. Let one be wholly free to choose whatever name he wishes to give such an act, it remains fatalism or determinism, which is un-Reformed.

Please do not misunderstand us. We do not claim that Kuyper and Van Baalen want determinism. We prefer to think that Van Baalen has written these things in good faith and that he actually does not understand the issues. Yet that does not add to or alter the facts. His representation, his doctrine, is fatalistic or deterministic. Theologically this is un-Reformed, and philosophically it is un-Reformed. One will have to choose.

We see only three possibilities. First, one can choose and follow the lead of Pelagius: the natural man is not completely corrupt, is not without the ability to do the good, and is not inclined to all wickedness. Then one has a ground for the proposition that man can do moral good. If only one would admit that this is his position, each of us would know where the other wants to go. Second, one can agree with Van Baalen and say that God forces the by-nature totally

---

25 Van Baalen, *Novelty and Error*, 129. The emphasis is added.—Trans.

depraved person to do the good even though it is against his will. This position is very clear, and each one knows where it leads. It destroys the moral nature of the natural man. Then one is a determinist. Third, one can maintain that the natural man is totally depraved and wholly incapable of doing any moral or spiritual good. This position is also very transparent. One then has taken the position of scripture and the confessions, which will become clear from what follows.

Not one of the texts Van Baalen quoted proves that the natural man performs a morally good deed, and even less that God forces man to do a morally good deed. Van Baalen simply makes conclusions. He has necessarily supposed a proof where none exists when he concludes from the different passages that Saul, Jehu, the unjust steward, and so on performed moral good. Nowhere does sacred scripture distinctly teach this. Just place what scripture explicitly teaches in contrast to Van Baalen's claim. The difference is readily apparent.

1. The fool hath said in his heart, There is no God. They are corrupt, they have done abominable works, there is none that doeth good.
2. The LORD looked from heaven upon the children of men, to see if there were any that did understand, and seek God.
3. They are all gone aside, they are all together become filthy: there is none that doeth good, no, not one. (Ps. 14:1–3)

9. What then? are we better than they? No, in no wise: for we have before proved both Jews and Gentiles, that they are all under sin;
10. As it is written, There is none righteous, no, not one:
11. There is none that understandeth, there is none that seeketh after God.
12. They are all gone out of the way, they are together become unprofitable; there is none that doeth good, no, not one.
13. Their throat is an open sepulchre; with their tongues they have used deceit; the poison of asps is under their lips:
14. Whose mouth is full of cursing and bitterness:
15. Their feet are swift to shed blood:

16. Destruction and misery are in their ways:
17. And the way of peace have they not known:
18. There is no fear of God before their eyes. (Rom. 3:9–18)

5. For they that are after the flesh do mind the things of the flesh; but they that are after the Spirit the things of the Spirit,
6. For to be carnally minded is death; but to be spiritually minded is life and peace.
7. Because the carnal mind is enmity against God: for it is not subject to the law of God, neither indeed can be.
8. So then they that are in the flesh cannot please God. (Rom. 8:5–8)

For whatsoever is not of faith is sin. (Rom. 14:23)

2. Wherein in time past ye walked according to the course of this world, according to the prince of the power of the air, the spirit that now worketh in the children of disobedience:
3. Among whom also we all had our conversation in times past in the lusts of our flesh, fulfilling the desires of the flesh and of the mind; and were by nature the children of wrath, even as others. (Eph. 2:2–3)

17. This I say therefore, and testify in the Lord, that ye henceforth walk not as other Gentiles walk, in the vanity of their mind,
18. Having the understanding darkened, being alienated from the life of God through the ignorance that is in them, because of the blindness of their heart. (Eph. 4:17–18)

For we ourselves also were sometimes foolish, disobedient, deceived, serving divers lusts and pleasures, living in malice and envy, hateful, and hating one another. (Titus 3:3)

Doth a fountain send forth at the same place sweet water and bitter? (James 3:11)

For the time past of our life may suffice us to have wrought the will of the Gentiles, when we walked in lasciviousness, lusts, excess of wine, revellings, banquetings, and abominable idolatries. (1 Pet. 4:3)

28. Even as they did not like to retain God in their knowledge, God gave them over to a reprobate mind, to do those things which are not convenient;
29. Being filled with all unrighteousness, fornication, wickedness, covetousness, maliciousness; full of envy, murder, debate, deceit, malignity; whisperers,
30. Backbiters, haters of God, despiteful, proud, boasters, inventors of evil things, disobedient to parents,
31. Without understanding, covenant-breakers, without natural affection, implacable, unmerciful. (Rom. 1:28–31)

All of these texts strongly express the opposite of what Van Baalen teaches regarding the moral good of the natural man and God's alleged forcing man to do good. They also condemn De Jong's attempted distinction regarding two ethically different kinds of good. The Bible does not have anything whatsoever to say about this.

What do the confessions teach?

Are we so far depraved that we are wholly unapt to any good, and prone to all evil?

Yes; unless we are born again by the Spirit of God.[26]

Can we ourselves make this satisfaction?

By no means; on the contrary, we daily increase our guilt.[27]

But revolting from God by the instigation of the devil, and abusing the freedom of his own will, he forfeited these excellent gifts, and on the contrary entailed on himself blindness of mind, horrible darkness, vanity, and perverseness of judgment; became wicked, rebellious, and obdurate in heart and will, and impure in [all] his affections.[28]

---

26 Heidelberg Catechism Q&A 8, in Schaff, *Creeds of Christendom*, 3:310.—Trans.
27 Heidelberg Catechism Q&A 13, in ibid., 3:311.—Trans.
28 Canons of Dordt 3–4.1, in ibid., 3:587–88.—Trans.

There remain, however, in man since the fall, the glimmerings of natural light, whereby he retains some knowledge of God, of natural things, and of the difference between good and evil, and discovers some regard for virtue, good order in society, and for maintaining an orderly external deportment. But so far is this light of nature from being sufficient to bring him to a saving knowledge of God, and to true conversion, that he is incapable of using it aright even in things natural and civil. Nay farther, this light, such as it is, man in various ways renders wholly polluted, and holds it [back] in unrighteousness; by doing which he becomes inexcusable before God.[29]

And being thus become wicked, perverse, and corrupt in all his ways, he hath lost all his excellent gifts which he had received from God, and only retained a few remains thereof, which, however, are sufficient to leave man without excuse; for all the light which is in us is changed into darkness, as the Scriptures teach us, saying: *The light shineth in darkness, and the darkness comprehendeth it not:* where St. John calleth men darkness. Therefore we reject all that is taught repugnant to this concerning the free will of man, since man is but a slave to sin.[30]

We believe that, through the disobedience of Adam, original sin is extended to all mankind; which is a corruption of the whole nature, and an hereditary disease, wherewith infants themselves are infected even in their mother's womb, and which produceth in man all sorts of sin, being in him as a root thereof; and therefore is so vile and abominable in the sight of God that it is sufficient to condemn all mankind.[31]

After presenting his proofs from the confessions, Van Baalen suddenly appears to have changed his position. He had declared that he was definitely in favor of the doctrine that the natural man is totally depraved and that God forces him to do moral good. Moral good

---

29 Canons of Dordt 3–4.4, in ibid., 3:588.—Trans.
30 Belgic Confession 14, in ibid., 3:398–99.—Trans.
31 Belgic Confession 15, in ibid., 3:400.—Trans.

does not arise from man's nature but is an act of God. However, this doctrine the brother could not find in the confessions. The confessions do not teach determinism; the confessions always maintain human responsibility. The confessions do not speak of God's forcing anyone. But Van Baalen now discovers in the confessions a "double track" and thus allows the good that the natural man performs to issue readily out of man's nature, out of "the image of God in the broader sense."

Listen to what he says regarding article 14 of the Belgic Confession.

What do we have here? It presents not a single-track theology, but truly a double-track theology. It teaches the position that man is totally depraved; he is depraved in all aspects of his being and in all his faculties. No light is found in man. He has lost all his good gifts. That is one track on which the line of our reasoning must proceed. The Belgic Confession emphatically maintains this truth, because scripture teaches it.

The other track, however, is not lacking in the Confession's instruction. [We expect Van Baalen to identify from the confessions the track that proves that God forces man to do something. Yet now Van Baalen changes.] There are small remnants. Remnants of what? Remnants of all his excellent gifts.

What are these excellent gifts? The image of God in man. This article speaks about them. Man has lost all of them, but has kept small remnants of them. These small remnants are what Reformed men have identified as the image of God in the broader sense. In the narrower sense the image of God is knowledge, righteousness, and holiness. These spiritual powers man lost. Man's mind and will are totally depraved, but the image of God in the broader sense man kept. It is a remnant thereof. Therefore, it is something good, and man can see the good, and the remnant of the image of God deprives man of every excuse.

We must insist on this track as well. The Confession does that, but not by forfeiting the first track. Nor must we forfeit the second track for the first. The question is not whether we can reconcile both, but the question is, does the Confession teach both?[32]

Our response is, first, it has not yet become clear how a train can run safely on two tracks. Two rails, yes, that we can understand. But how a train can safely proceed on two sets of tracks, two tracks that run in diametrically opposite directions, we do not understand. One cannot perceive of such a possibility even if the trains are merely thought and reasoning. It is a riddle how one can answer, "Yes, this is possible," without forfeiting the right to respond honestly by saying, "No, that is impossible." If to deny that a train can run on two tracks that run at the same time in opposite directions is "rationalism," we are willing to stand guilty on this point.

Second, we will demonstrate that Van Baalen now has three tracks. First, the Reformed track is that man is totally depraved and incapable of doing any good. Second, the track of determinism is that God forces the totally depraved man to do moral good. Third, the Pelagian track, which Kuyper called the ethical line, is that natural man does good by virtue of the small remnants—the image of God in the broader sense. Thus man is not forced but does good by his own nature.

Third, neither Belgic Confession 14 nor any other Reformed confession present a double track, for they teach that man's natural light is darkness, and he defiles it in many ways in natural and civil things and holds it down in unrighteousness. Therefore, the confessions teach a single track—the first track.

Fourth, Hepp condemned Van Baalen's statement as double-track theology. No, Hepp says, the image of God in the broader sense is not to be attributed to general grace.[33]

Fifth, Kuyper in his better days wrote the following regarding the small remnants:

Now we come to the question: what is to be said about the remnants [rudera]? Man is in all his ways depraved, but retains "only a few remains" [of his excellent gifts], as article 14 of the

---

32 Van Baalen, Novelty and Error, 157–58.
33 Valentijn Hepp, De Reformatie (February 29, 1924).

Belgic Confession teaches. Surprisingly, the ethicists agree with the Belgic Confession, but they forget what immediately follows: "for all the light which is in us is changed into darkness." These remnants are enlarged when viewed through a magnifying glass, and the small remnants in the end become the whole man.

In opposition to that position, the Confession teaches concerning these remnants that in the *nature* of man nothing good remains, for man by nature is wholly sinful and is neither intellectually nor volitionally empowered to do good; but that these remnants nevertheless obtain in regard to the substance. Nature and substance are distinguished in this way: nature is *quod nascitur* (the working); substance is that out of which work is wrought. The depravity of the will does not mean therefore that the *voluntas* (the ability to will) became *noluntas* (inability to will; man did not lose his will); but that the operation of the will always runs in the negative; man's willing is faulty. The confusion of these two concepts gives occasion to see, as do the ethicists, a sinner's hand that can grasp the cord, or with the Lutherans to reduce man to a mute block of wood or stone...

The Confession originally called these remnants *scintillae* (sparks or faint traces), but in the translation followed by the Synod of Dordt that word was replaced by *vestiga* (footprints), which provides the much clearer understanding that we must have. *Vestigium* (footprint) indicates that a person has been there, but that the person left. Therefore, if we say that there is to be observed in us a footprint of God's righteousness, this does not mean that a portion of that righteousness still remains in us, but means exactly that there is nothing remaining in us of that righteousness.

The Roman Catholic Church at the Council of Trent in the fifth session taught in opposition that the original righteousness and knowledge was only diminished and weakened in strength. It is still there but is limited and weakened. Against that idea our fathers said in opposition, "There is nothing left of it; everything is dead, corrupt, and depraved; we can see only that a fire had once burned there, that there had been righteousness." Therefore, immediately at the mention of the small remnants, the Confession states, "*For* all the light which is in us is changed to darkness." Rome said, "There still burns a little light." On the contrary our church declared, "Everything is darkness." We must constantly read the Confession as written against Rome. Although it may appear at first unclear, "for" is in its rightful place.[34]

Van Baalen must therefore maintain his deterministic presentation that God forces man against his will to do good deeds. No matter how much he prefers several tracks on which he causes not one train but several trains to run, the most recent track he will have to abandon. The Confession is single-track Reformed and provides absolutely no proof for Van Baalen's doctrine that God forces the sinner against his will to do morally good deeds. Holy scripture as well contains no proof for his position. We will put to the test one of Van Baalen's proofs and let the reader do the same with the other quotations.

We need proof that God forces the dead sinner to do moral good. Consider the alleged proof Van Baalen cites in his appeal to Jehu. What did Jehu do? He wiped out the family of Ahab. That deed was in harmony with the command Jehu had received. Did Jehu do an ethically good deed? It would have been good if he had chosen God's side and had wasted Ahab's house out of hatred for the sin of that family and out of love for God. Did Jehu do that? He absolutely did not. He was guilty of taking another's life (Hosea 1:4). Besides, he walked in the sins of Jeroboam. His deed was not morally good. However, did God force Jehu against his will? God did not do that. It was in complete harmony with Jehu's sinful will, driven by sinful ambition, to root out the whole royal generation of Ahab. The entire history of this event testifies to this. Proof for Van Baalen's position is not found at all.

We intend by this brief analysis to end our discussion of this

---

34 Abraham Kuyper, *Locus de Peccato*, in *Dictaten Dogmatiek* [Dictated dogmatics] (Grand Rapids, MI: B. Sevensma, 1910), 84–86. The emphasis is added.

question. One does not discover in scripture or the confessions any support for the claim that the natural man can do what is morally good; much less is there support for the position that God forces him to do it. It has amazed us immensely that others think it is necessary to oppose us constantly with weapons that cause one to recall the swords and shields of the Remonstrants. True, there is a difference. The reasoning is not exactly the same on this point. Van Baalen does not want the doctrine of Pelagius, but he maintains nothing other than divine coercion and sacrifices the sinner's freedom. Those who see in the institution of government God's common grace also hold to the notion of coercion.

Although with differences regarding the particulars, the majority want an element of material freedom for the natural, unregenerated man to choose and to do the good. The one limits such freedom strictly to the so-called natural life and says that the sinner only in his relations with other people has a free will and the ability to fulfill the laws God has laid down for society. The other is less emphatic but proposes the common grace doctrine in connection with the preaching of God's word. He wants common grace in order to maintain the well-meant offer of grace and salvation to all men, including the reprobate. Supposedly no preaching is possible unless one proceeds from the notion that somehow God wills that all men head for head and soul for soul be saved.

All this is astonishing. We have always thought the matter of free will and all that pertains to that subject were decisively decided for Reformed people at Dordrecht. We thought too that Kuyper with his common grace had focused his attention on natural life. Next to the absolute antithesis in the spiritual realm he placed the idea of fellowship in the realm of the earthly and natural: state, society, art, science, and so forth. He attempted to find a basis for social cooperation between believers and unbelievers in natural life, and he thought he discovered it in common grace—God's gracious operation in the heart of the natural, unregenerate sinner, whereby the sinner becomes qualified to do positive good before God in the spheres of earthly life.

From that viewpoint we have contemplated the issues. Earlier we received a stimulus to do that from the many writings of the brothers who are pushing common grace, but most recently we received even greater stimulus by our investigation of Janssen's instruction in our seminary. Janssen logically applied the principles of Kuyper's common grace theory. In our opinion, the common grace theory gave him an apparently Reformed basis for his views about scripture and his exegesis of scripture. We maintain that it is impossible to demonstrate the truth of this alleged basis. We maintain as well that Janssen properly comprehended Kuyper's position. Therefore, it pains us greatly that others turned against us and made everything revolve around the issue of the free will of the sinner, instead of demonstrating that Janssen's position was the proper application of common grace. Once again we plead: let us discuss common grace from historical-confessional and biblical-logical viewpoints. Then at least we need not immediately charge one another with heresy. A condemnation on confessional grounds, as concerns us, is out of the question.

We stand by our answer: man is wholly incapable of doing any good. That is the language of the confessions and of the Bible. To contend that the natural man can do good is Pelagian. To contend that God forces him to do good is determinism.

In addition, what is civil righteousness? It is that the sinner sees the divinely appointed relations, the established laws, the instruments of societal life, and the like. He recognizes their appropriateness and usefulness and uses them for his own purposes. If he makes fairly decent use of them, the result is an activity that shows formal agreement with God's laws. This is civil righteousness regarding virtue and external order. If the attempt fails, as is often the case, civil righteousness is lacking and what obtains is the opposite thereof.

The sinner's basic error, however, also regarding the external order of society, is that he neither seeks God nor purposes to please him. On the contrary, he seeks himself and intends, in fellowship with other sinners, to maintain with the whole world its sin of opposition to God in everything he does. This is sin. Besides, in real life this has evil consequences for him and his fellow creatures. His specific treatment of his fellow man and fellow creatures occurs according to the same rule and with similar consequences. In this way sin constantly develops and corruption abounds. Still there continues to be a relatively formal, proper activity according to the laws God has established. However, through these efforts the natural man never achieves moral good.

This is our position.

Who will venture to explain these matters differently?

CHAPTER 4

NO RESTRAINT
OF SIN IN ITS DEVELOPMENT

The question confronting us is whether there is an operation of common grace in the heart of the unregenerate individual and in his communion with his fellow man and fellow creatures, an operation that began in paradise and continues throughout history until God is pleased to withdraw it. Our opponents claim this is true. We deny it.

Van Baalen gives the following proofs for his position:

Is it not true that God obstructs, checks, restrains, and curbs evil, yet still permits it to develop organically?

The three forms of unity teach this reality.

In whom [our Father] we do entirely trust; being persuaded, that he so restrains the devil and all our enemies, that, without his will and permission, they cannot hurt us. (Belgic Confession 13)

We believe that our gracious God, because of the depravity of mankind, hath appointed kings, princes and magistrates, willing that the world should be governed by certain laws and policies, to the end that the dissoluteness of men might be restrained, and all things carried on among them with good order and decency. (Belgic Confession 36)

But the good Shepherd, who loves his flock and for whom he has given his life, has wondrously and continuously put down the raging of their persecutors at the right time and by his outstretched arm; and he has

exposed and nullified the crooked ways and the deceitful counsels of seducers, demonstrating by both that he
is truly present with his church. Of this reality we have
a clear proof in the history of godly Caesars, kings, and
princes, whom the Son of God has time and again moved
to help his church, filled them with a holy zeal for his
house, and by their obedient service has…suppressed the
turbulence of tyrants.[35]

These quotations condemn the brothers' second position.
Indeed, the quotations contradict their position that sin always
develops organically and that man's organic place in time and
history, not the restraining operation of God's grace, is the reason all men do not commit every sin.[36]

Van Baalen cites the following proofs from scripture:

"God said unto him [Abimelech] in a dream, Yea, I know that
thou didst this in the integrity of thy heart; for I also withheld
thee from sinning against me: therefore suffered I thee not to
touch her" (Gen. 20:6).

In 2 Thessalonians 2:6 we read that the antichrist is withheld, that is, checked or suppressed. Verse 7 is clear that this
does not relate to the organic development of things, as if he
could not come until sin had organically developed: "For the
mystery of iniquity doth already work: only he who now letteth
will let, until he be taken out of the way." Read this in connection with 2 Thessalonians 2:11–12: "And for this cause God
shall send them strong delusion, that they should believe a lie:
that they all might be damned who believed not the truth, but
had pleasure in unrighteousness." [Van Baalen's meaning is that
God checks the coming of antichrist. God intervenes by sending a special power of delusion where earlier he had restrained

---

35 Preface to the Canons of Dordt, in *Acta of Handelingen der Nationale Synode…
te Dordrecht 1618 in 1619* [Acts of the national synod in Dordtrecht 1618–1619]
(Utrecht: Den Hertog's, n.d.), 291.—Ed.
36 Van Baalen, *Novelty and Error*, 154–55.

sin's development by preventing the coming of antichrist. The thought is expressed that the truth with which the then-living people had come into contact through the preaching is *love for the truth*. They are guilty because of their unbelief, their failure to accept the well-meant offer of the truth, and therefore they will be punished with a spirit of delusion. They will go lost because of their rejection of the well-meant offer and their choice to seek pleasure in unrighteousness.]

"He suffered no man to do them wrong: yea, he reproved kings for their sakes; saying, Touch not mine anointed, and do my prophets no harm" (Ps. 105:14–15).

"The Lord bringeth the counsel of the heathen to nought: he maketh the devices of the people of none effect. The counsel of the Lord standeth for ever, the thoughts of his heart to all generations" (Ps. 33:10–11).[37]

Y. P. de Jong also wrote concerning this in the *Witness* of December 1923. He had the same proofs as Van Baalen, except De Jong discovered a proof in God's warning to Laban in a dream not to harm Jacob (Gen. 31:24). For the rest, De Jong added nothing new to what Van Baalen has written. Beets also quoted nothing new; Keegstra did not either. We have before us all their proofs.

Our answer is that Genesis 31:24 is not proof that the development of sin is checked by the operation of common grace in the heart of man and in the history of men. It is not difficult to prove this contention. We begin with the Belgic Confession concerning divine providence:

We believe that the same God, after he had created all things, did not forsake them, or give them up to fortune or chance, but that he rules and governs them, according to his holy will, so that nothing happens in this world without his appointment; nevertheless, God neither is the author of, nor can be charged with, the sins which are committed. For his power and goodness are so great and incomprehensible, that he orders and executes his work in the most excellent and just manner even when the devil

---

37 Ibid., 139–41.

and wicked men act unjustly. And as to what he doth surpass-
ing human understanding we will not curiously inquire into it
farther than our capacity will admit of; but with the greatest
humility and reverence adore the righteous judgments of God
which are hid from us, contenting ourselves that we are disciples of Christ, to learn only those things which he has revealed
to us in his Word without transgressing these limits.

This doctrine affords us unspeakable consolation, since we
are taught thereby that nothing can befall us by chance, but by
the direction of our most gracious and heavenly Father, who
watches over us with a paternal care, keeping all creatures so
under his power that not a hair of our head (for they are all
numbered), nor a sparrow, can fall to the ground, without the
will of our Father, in whom we do entirely trust; being persuaded that he so restrains the devil and all our enemies that,
without his will and permission, they can not hurt us.

And therefore we reject that damnable error of the Epicu-
reans, who say that God regards nothing, but leaves all things
to chance.[38]

We say from the heart yes and amen to this beautiful article of the
Confession. It affords us an inexpressible comfort in the battle, as it
did for our fathers. It is the strength of the Christian's life, and it causes
him to be the conqueror in the battle with the powers of darkness.

The explanation that draws common grace out of this article
simply cripples this article. What does it truly express? Does it teach
common grace to the elect, reprobate, and devils alike? Does it teach
an operation of grace upon all, including the ungodly and devils? The
answer is, absolutely not! This article treats God's providence. One
should not forget that the people of God speak in this article. God's
people confess not common grace but God's providence.

How does providence function in this world of sin and grace? Concerning God's attitude, does providence operate out of God's common
grace to all men? No, article 13 teaches that God causes his providence

---

38 Belgic Confession 13, in Schaff, *Creeds of Christendom*, 3:396–98.—Trans.

to operate out of the motive of grace toward his people. Thence it extends outward in love over his people, but conversely it turns against the ungodly and devils. What we believe is exactly and powerfully confessed in this article. That is the inexpressible comfort of the article for the people of God.

But, you ask, does the article not teach a restraining of the process of sin by common grace, for it says that God holds in check devils and evil men?

There is no common grace in the article, but it plainly expresses that God's providence rules and cooperates in the deeds of enemies and devils so they cannot always execute their hostile plans. What is spoken of is an operation not of grace, but of God's great power. The process of sin is not arrested, but God controls the deeds of sinful men. He does this not out of the motive of common grace, but out of the principle of grace and love toward his people.

Certainly if God strikes dead one hundred fifty thousand raging enemies outside of Jerusalem's gates, they do not capture Jerusalem. If God visits Pharaoh and his house with plagues, no one touches Sarah. If God drowns Pharaoh and his army in the Red Sea, Israel is not utterly destroyed. Or to use an example of Beets, if Charles V is prevented at just the right moment from turning against the Reformation because God involves Charles in several wars, the pope cannot through him realize his evil plan. All that is as plain as day and it is not common grace. The drowning of Pharaoh and his whole army, dropping the one hundred fifty thousand dead in their tracks, involving Charles V in wars, the plagues on Pharaoh and his royal household for the protection of Sarah—all those are not the operations of grace. Sin was not restrained in any human heart, but only controlled and limited in accordance with God's purposes.

Man sins with his faculties and gifts, means and talents, according to the circumstances and times in which he lives. All of this nevertheless is and remains subject to God's control. Man and his actions are bound to the decree of God's counsel and to his providence. This is even true regarding one's physical strength and the soul's faculties of intellect and will. If God brings to naught Ahithophel's counsel, he protects David; but it is inappropriate to attribute it to an operation of God's grace.

By this explanation we no doubt ease Keegstra's mind, for he thinks we believe that the sinner and his activities are free from God's control, so that the sinner can do whatever he pleases. Thus we will come eventually to a deistic world view.

Our conception is far different. The enemy and the devil and his angels are in good hands—the power of our heavenly Father. We deny a restraining of sin through an operation of grace on the ungodly, which spiritually improves them, and we maintain article 13 of the Belgic Confession.

This explanation resolves the difficulty of article 36 of the Belgic Confession. The government is an institution of God just as marriage is. These and similar institutions are means and instruments for man. Divine authority invested in government officials can be employed for good and evil. This is not only possible, but also such things happen. Government officials can enact good or evil laws; they can punish certain flagrant malefactors and murder the righteous. They can advance the cause of God's kingdom and oppose his kingdom. All this actually happens. The government officials' use of the power entrusted to them is defined and modified by their spiritual and moral capacity.

It is true also that the dissoluteness of individual citizens is always inseparably bound to government controls. A certain order and definite direction in society is created through the enactment of laws and the punishment of transgressors of those laws. The process of sin, nevertheless, is not in any sense restrained, nor is there through the authorities any operation of grace in the hearts of the citizens; even less does the government qualify its citizens to perform any positively good works. Nor may it ever be forgotten that the government can, comparatively speaking, punish only a few sins.

Finally, the government's sword has been almost consistently turned against those who faithfully confess God's name. Consider the fearful struggle of ancient Israel against the sevenfold world power of the old dispensation, the persecutions of the first three centuries, and the struggles during the Reformation. That all abundantly substantiates the claim that government's use of authority throughout history has frequently, if not generally, been turned against Christ, his cause, and his people.

Do not forget the tragedy of Golgotha. Pilate had power. He bore the sword. He was certainly obligated to use the sword against evil doers. He had the power to crucify Christ or to release him. He repeatedly expressed his awareness that the Savior was free of any guilt. Nevertheless, he gave the Messiah over to be crucified. So Christ was given over by the determinate counsel of God and put to death by the hands of unrighteous men. Take note of that fact. If you speak of the restraint of sin, of the process of sin in history, you are not finished when you have pointed to the government's calling, that is, what it is *obligated* to do. But the question involves as well what government actually *does* with the entrusted power and the responsibility laid on its shoulders.

We believe that this is understandable language and is in complete harmony with the Belgic Confession.

What remains of Van Baalen's scriptural proofs? Nothing whatsoever.

Regarding Abimelech in Van Baalen's quotation of Genesis 20:6,[39] our answer is that there was no sin in Abimelech's heart that could be restrained, because he did not intend to sin. There was no operation of grace in Abimelech. As in the example of Pharaoh, God had simply brought Abimelech into a physical situation through which he was

---

39 Van Baalen had appealed to Genesis 20:6, concerning God's withholding King Abimelech from sinning against him in the matter of taking Sarah as his wife. This text was supposed to prove a restraint of sin in the ungodly by a common grace of God. Danhof and Hoeksema replied that, in fact, Abimelech had no intention of sinning in this matter, as God acknowledged in verse 6: "thou didst this in the integrity of thy heart." So obsessed were the leading theologians with common grace that they avowed a restraint of sin where in fact no sin was. One might add to Danhof's and Hoeksema's argument here against a restraint of sin by a common grace of God that God's providential government of would-be sinners, preventing them in some instances from carrying out their wicked desires, is not at all the same as the teaching of common grace that there is a work of grace in the heart of the unregenerated sinner, keeping him from sinning by some influence of love for God in that heart. Somewhere Hoeksema remarked that the Christian Reformed synod of 1924 could not distinguish a spiritual work of grace upon the heart from the deterrence of the commission of a crime by a policeman on his beat.—Ed.

unable to perform the deed. There is nothing common in that instance. If we assume that Abimelech was not a child of God, which is not plausible, the motive of God's act by which he prevented Abimelech from touching Sarah lies in Sarah. God reveals his grace toward his people in this history and shows the source of his providence in its operations. This working of God through which he prevents men from touching women who belong to others is entirely common, but not among the ungodly. The issue is whether there is a general operation of God's grace in the heart of the natural man, by which the development of sin is restrained, is it not?

Regarding 2 Thessalonians 2:6 our response is that this is not an easy text. No doubt Van Baalen would agree. Conclusive exegesis of this text in its specifics we will not attempt to offer.

Nevertheless, the text definitely does not prove an operation of common grace. Leaving aside in what aspect the antichrist is checked, there is no doubt that Paul does not refer to an operation of grace through which the power of the antichrist will become temporarily less sinful. When Paul speaks of that which restrains the antichrist, he refers to a specific person, as is clear from the phrase "until he be taken out of the way." "He" does not refer to antichrist, but to the person whom the apostle thinks restrains antichrist, as is obvious from the next verse. After the one who restrains the antichrist is removed from the scene, the antichristian powers will be revealed for the first time, which the Lord will consume with the Spirit of his mouth. In the days of the apostle there was a specific person who stood in the way of the full revelation of the antichristian power.

There is no mention of a restraint of the antichrist from the viewpoint of sin in its development, but of the prevention of the revelation of his power before the appointed time. He desires to reveal himself as extremely powerful over the whole world. He wants to exalt himself above all that is called God. He wants to sit in the temple of God, pretending that he is God (v. 4). The activity of the antichrist, the striving of the power of unrighteousness and all its activity, has as its goal to arrive as soon as possible at the full revelation of his power. In that desire and striving he is restrained. He was checked in Paul's time and is today. He is checked by specific persons and by wars, pestilences, famine, revolution, death, and the like. God has everything at his disposal to restrain the antichrist in the development of his power, so that he is unable to reveal himself sooner than God's appointed time.

Along these lines we prefer to explain this difficult text. We proceed in the line of scripture (cf. Rev. 6). Certainly in 2 Thessalonians 2 there is no mention of a power of grace that arrests the development of sin. One should not forget that verse 7 teaches exactly the opposite of what the brothers imagine they can draw from this text: "for the mystery of iniquity doth already work." Unrighteousness worked then, is working now, and works throughout all the ages. Yet the antichrist cannot arrive at the revelation of his power sooner than God wills, and that will be when the mystery of iniquity will have labored to the very end in connection with the development of all things.

Regarding Psalm 105:14–15: "He suffered no man to do them wrong: yea, he reproved kings for their sakes; saying, Touch not mine anointed, and do my servants no harm" and Psalm 33:10–11: "The LORD bringeth the counsel of the heathen to nought: he maketh the devices of the people of none effect. The counsel of the LORD standeth for ever," our response is that these texts teach the same as article 13 of the Belgic Confession. There is no general grace in them, but God's favor toward his people. There is no nonsaving grace toward the heathen, but a punishment of kings and a nullifying of the counsels of the ungodly against God's people. Think of Pharaoh in the Red Sea, Amalek, all the kings who were killed for the sake of Israel, and the military might that the angel of the Lord struck dead in front of Jerusalem's gates. Consider further all the deeds the ungodly world does to harm and to suppress the cause of the Lord. Most definitely, God brings their counsels to naught—not in grace but in wrath; not through the operation of grace by which he restrains sin, but through his almighty power and wisdom.

Thus nothing remains of all these apparent proofs for common grace. We still insist that sin progresses in the history of the world. The one sin of Adam in paradise develops along the line of the organic development of the human race. Immediately after the fall Adam could sin very little. Life was restricted. Consider all the stealing, murder, adultery, declarations of war, attempted ruination of scripture through higher criticism, and all the social and political sins and crimes that have happened in our modern times. One simply could not speak of all that evil in connection with Adam. It is impossible, not because sin was restrained by general grace, but because Adam formed the root of the human race.

As the human race developed and the life of man in the world became richer and much more inclusive, sin developed. Each one personally sinned with the means of and in harmony with the place God designated for him in the human race. All this is under the all-controlling providence of God, who executes his counsel through all these realities and remains righteous, while the whole world becomes worthy of condemnation before him. This is our position, and it has not been refuted by anyone. In this way we can continue to uphold all the scriptural texts that exclusively testify of the universal depravity and ungodliness of the natural man.

Our response is finished. We believe we have answered fairly well all of our opponents' arguments. We will leave it as is for the present, but this is not our last word. In the future we will continue to write and speak about this question and will treat different questions related to our position. We hope that soon the stubborn attempts to condemn us as heretics will end. We could then more peacefully do positive work. Achieving this purpose—not conflict—is our objective.

We will not let ourselves be intimidated by anyone. We will not be scared away by Dr. Hepp either. He finds us immodest. We think it immodest that he so rudely became involved in our struggles in the United States. We find it even less polite that he presumes to be an appointed judge of our affairs. We decline his attempt with thanks. We believe that in our book [Along Pure Paths] we have politely answered his brochure. If the brother wishes to write again, it is fitting that he only engages in the arguments and does not presume to be an arbitrator in a dispute.

Once again, we will not be intimidated by anything, so that we can perform our callings in relation to the matter of common grace.

We are deeply convinced that Kuyper erred.

We are also deeply convinced that our churches must be warned and called back from a wrong track. Where, according to our convictions, the battle concerns God's cause and the salvation of his church, we will continue to fight now and in the future with all the strength and means the Lord our God may be pleased to grant us.

FOR THE SAKE OF JUSTICE AND TRUTH

A Message of Clarification and Direction

HENRY DANHOF
AND
HERMAN HOEKSEMA

TRANSLATED BY MARVIN KAMPS

Introduction to *For the Sake of Justice and Truth*

The content of this pamphlet is varied. Written in the early summer of 1924 (there is reference to a magazine article dated May 1924), the pamphlet takes note of criticisms of the authors' book *Sin and Grace* and of a flurry of protests against them and their teachings against common grace, directed to the upcoming Christian Reformed synod of 1924.

In view of a number of "instructions" to the synod requesting examination of Danhof and Hoeksema concerning their orthodoxy, they (the two authors of the pamphlet) said that a study of the theory of common grace ought to precede any examination of them concerning their orthodoxy or heterodoxy in the matter of the theory of common grace. Danhof and Hoeksema urged a thorough study by a committee of synod that would include representatives of all existing views on common grace, including the supporters of the recently condemned Ralph Janssen.

Danhof and Hoeksema wanted free, open discussion of the doctrinal issue. In the pamphlet they pleaded with the synod that was to meet soon not to formulate and adopt a dogma of common grace.

To all of that reasonable proposal and plea, the synod would pay no attention. Indeed, it would not permit discussion of the issue even in the form of Hoeksema's defense of himself and his thinking regarding common grace before the synod that was deciding the issue.

The pamphlet's treatment of the various unbrotherly and disorderly attacks on Danhof and Hoeksema exposes the determination of influential ministers in the Christian Reformed Church to destroy the two ministers ecclesiastically. They succeeded. By means of the keys of the kingdom—church discipline—they wickedly deposed Hoeksema and Danhof from their sacred office and unjustly cast them out of the Christian Reformed kingdom of heaven. This means that the Christian Reformed Church has their blood on its hands to this day and therefore stands under the woe pronounced by Jesus upon all church assemblies that, in disregard of justice and truth, persecute those who confess the truth and walk in righteousness. "That upon you may come all the righteous blood shed upon the earth, from the blood of righteous Abel unto the blood of Zacharias son of Barachias, whom ye slew between the temple and the altar" (Matt. 23:35).

Especially in the chapter advertising the forthcoming publication of a magazine—the *Standard Bearer*—that would appear in October 1924, Danhof and Hoeksema bared their souls regarding their zeal for sound, Reformed, Christian doctrine and their desire for a holy, antithetical, Christian walk in all spheres of earthly life.

That the Christian Reformed Church could condemn this theology and cast out such ministers is appalling. That it did explains the subsequent history of the Christian Reformed Church and its present apostate condition.

—David J. Engelsma

FOREWORD

The publication committee of the Reformed Free Publishing Association now offers to the brothers and sisters in the Christian Reformed Church and to other interested fellow Christians the second brochure that we promised would follow *Along Pure Paths*, which was favorably received and enjoyed by our brothers and sisters, had their approval, and occasioned their thanksgiving.

In this brochure we first give a historical clarification of the question among us regarding common grace. Second, since it has been made a controversial matter by one of our opponents, we specify the issue in more detail in the same manner as it has been placed on the synodical agenda and will be placed before synod. Third, we include Hoeksema's protest to synod and its explanation. Last, we give the reasons that led to the initial, successful efforts for the publication of a monthly magazine, and we set forth clearly the principles of the content of this periodical that constitute its foundational concepts.

Along Pure Paths, published by the Reformed Free Publishing Association, was praised for its calm manner of instruction, its clear content, its easily understandable style, and its attractive external appearance. In this new pamphlet, which we believe is necessary, the authors furnish us with a good work that is not in the least inferior to the previous, although the nature of this apology is somewhat different.

The reporting of several facts concerning the common grace struggle in the papers and in ecclesiastical gatherings is sufficient for the honest and unprejudiced reader—who may not "be on top of the situation" concerning the formal process and the attitude of the attackers—to recognize the crooked paths "the other side" here and there has chosen to follow. The protest, which forms the content of the third chapter of this brochure, gives sufficient introduction to indicate a "dreadful confusion of things" by the brothers who think that the authors of this pamphlet "should no longer be active" as ministers of the divine word in the Christian Reformed Church.

The authors deservedly reprimanded Rev. E. J. Tanis for his cowardly and unmanly game of hide-and-go-seek when they repeatedly came to him seeking an apology and reconciliation for his rash and unreasonable attacks and his attempt to blacken their names. Then the two pastors, often mistreated for their defense of the truth, spoke an earnest word and gave an appropriate witness that would make a lasting impression concerning the future struggle for the truth on the minds of those who fear God and seek their courage from him.[1]

By reading this public and urgent petition to our ecclesiastical bodies, which rule in regard to doctrine and execute justice and promote the truth, and by a calm consideration of the historical events sketched in connection with our proposed agenda, may a return to the old paths be advanced and the faith of God's people be strengthened in their God and King.

We thank God for the Spirit, who is the guardian of his word, and for those still present among us who guard the purity of doctrine.

—The publication committee
G. Vos
G. Van den Berg
W. Verhil
A. Van Tuinen
J. H. Van der Vennen
G. Van Beek

---

1   There is reference to this reprimand in chapter 4 of this work, *For the Sake of Justice and Truth*. Evidently, Danhof and Hoeksema reprimanded Rev. Tanis for his criticism of their intentions to found a magazine—the *Standard Bearer*—that would defend and develop the Reformed faith over against the weaknesses and errors of the Christian Reformed Church. The content of the proposed magazine would be the "witness" that is spoken of.—Ed.

CHAPTER I

HISTORICAL EXPLANATION OF THE ISSUE OF COMMON GRACE

S everal years ago we began to make known our profound concern regarding the unity movement of the spirit of our age
in the various European countries, as well as in America, not
entirely excluding Reformed circles, and we insisted that the antithesis
be placed more emphatically on the foreground in opposition to the
synthesis.[2] We feared the danger of slogans, distinctions, and classifica-
tions, such as "the fatherhood of God and the brotherhood of man";
"religion and culture"; "thus we are one with the world, and we have
our cultural task not as believers, but as *humans*"; "let there be antithesis in the spiritual realm out of the root of regeneration and synthesis
in the area of this natural life"; "from now on it will be our calling to
make the souls of the people of this nation receptive to the doctrine
of common grace"; and the like. In particular we were apprehensive
about the changed mood and attitude toward life among the younger
generation, also in Reformed circles.

Between the older and the younger generation is especially this
difference: the first have retained a certainty or conviction in the
authoritative word of God for their spiritual perspective of and attitude toward life, while the latter speak of a probability or likelihood,
according to a standard of authority found in general human opinion.
By means of independent scientific investigation and an unfettered,

---

2   The "unity movement," no doubt, is a reference to the ecumenical movement that
culminated in the founding of the World Council of Churches in 1948. The origin
of this movement is usually given as a missionary conference in 1910. Danhof and
Hoeksema foresaw and forewarned of the deadly ecumenical consequences of the
doctrine of a common grace of God.—Ed.

comparative study of differing religions, they look for systems and propositions that will enable them to put together a position that will satisfy the demands of public opinion. This naturally exercises an influence upon one's view and study of scripture.

Justifiably then there is talk in our circles of a "changing of the tide in Old Testament scholarship." People couple Bible with Babel. They place next to one another Greece and Israel, Athens and Jerusalem, Plato and Isaiah, and the wisdom of this world and the foolishness of the cross and present Christendom as the synthesis of the nations. "Each nation has brought stones for the erection of Christendom. Greece and Jerusalem have contributed the greater portion for this work."[3] This stream of thought fills us with dread. In our judgment, this striving for synthesis must inevitably lead to theoretical and practical world conformity.

We desire to live in accordance with scripture and in scripture's light to pay attention to the signs of the times. If people are watching the events of the day, they recognize that our entire human interaction stands in the sign of the synthesis in a deeper and more mysterious sense. Men live out of the idea of the unity of the nations. Political salvation is sought in a worldwide covenant between nations. Holy scripture teaches that in society and in social concerns things will develop toward a world organization. Meanwhile, especially in the area of labor, almost everything is now regulated by laws that have international approval. Finally, with the agreement of the majority, various social reforms that affect the rearing of children, the instruction in the day schools, morality, and religious worship are being introduced.

If the majority of people and the authorities reckoned with God's will and his word, there would be very little to say against this. People would have to be concerned only with the freedom of the individual. After all, the children of Adam's generation are all one in the essence

---

3 Although the authors do not provide the author and source of this quotation, they are obviously quoting a contemporary Christian Reformed theologian. The quotation clearly indicates the spiritual thinking that was driving the movement of common grace in the Christian Reformed Church in the early 1920s.—Ed.

of their natural existence. The bond of human fellowship necessarily draws one to the whole.

Yet that is impossible, for the children of men are spiritually two. They live out of a twofold spiritual life-principle. In addition, the majority of people are not God-fearing. God's people are a small sheepfold. And the authorities often act contrary to God's ordinances. Leaving out of consideration the thoughts of the flesh, which is enmity against God, if God's people under these circumstances yield to this pressure for unity of natural fellowship and solidarity of the human race, they will distance themselves from their fundamental spiritual principle of life. Then the antithesis will be obscured, and they will live the life of the world that has turned from God. This is unavoidable when one travels the path of synthesis.

At the very least this will be true at the end of this dispensation. According to God's word the true service of the Lord will continually diminish. Certainly a pretense of godliness will remain, but ungodliness will be multiplied and the love of many will grow cold. Evil times are coming. The man of sin must be revealed, and then Gog and Magog and their immoral company will come. Only after that will the last hour strike, and complete deliverance from all the power of the enemy will be realized.

Believers must remind one another of this truth. They must be urged to exert themselves unto ultimate perseverance in this spiritual battle. The believer should know not what mere men have to say or what they wish to be, but he must know what God wills him to do and allows. To attain that, one must have insight into God's word and an earnest determination not to depart from it. The will to live a self-denying life is also necessary. Only those who are willing to lose their life for Christ's name's sake will find it. One must not fear self-examination either. We must pay very careful attention to the errors of our hearts and the perversity of human life. Our entire lives—inclinations, plans, desires, thoughts, words, and actions—must arise from the root of regeneration, which is the principle of true love.

Whoever would be the friend of the world is the enemy of God. The believer is the friend of God and therefore an enemy of the entire kingdom of darkness. Consequently he must reveal himself to be that kind of person in this present world, with sincere trust in God and with his eye fixed only on God's word. His life's task is to take to heart the cause of the Son of God. He is of the party of the living God. God's child is God's friend.

This controlling thought of the covenantal conception we have tried to develop in a series of articles, lectures, and particularly in its most fundamental implications in Danhof's pamphlet *The Idea of the Covenant of Grace*. We have placed on the foreground of our world-view the idea of the absolute antithesis. We have done this especially in opposition to the present unremitting, zealous promotion from various sources of a perspective on the relationship between God's people and a world that lives in enmity toward God, which viewpoint in our judgment may not be ours. That was in 1919 and earlier.

Henry Danhof delivered the lecture entitled "The Idea of the Covenant" in Grand Rapids, Michigan, at the request of the general pastors' conference. The lecture was given with the understanding that on the following evening, June 5, 1919, Rev. J. Groen would give a similar lecture for the same audience in which he would sketch the fundamental elements of the synthesis line of thought. In this way people could gain a clearer understanding of the relationship between the church and the world. Because Rev. Groen was ill his public lecture was impossible then.

We could not execute the schedule of events we had chosen. A second conference was scheduled by common consent, but no one was willing to be the speaker. Up to the present such a speech has not been given. No one has concisely, systematically, and theologically explained, according to strict biblical principles and lines of thought, the fellowship of the believer with the unbeliever. The synthesis line of thought has not been presented. People had great praise at that time for our weak attempt to explain our relationship to God and to the world, which is the enemy of God, along the line of the antithesis. A negative critique of our position was entirely lacking. This was also true a year later when our lecture was published.

This silence may not be taken as proof of sincere agreement with everything we said. However, we did not anticipate any opposing declarations when we claimed that no one would have thought to criticize us concerning what we had written or spoken prior to the synod of 1920. The historical facts testify too clearly to that assertion, were it not for the issues in regard to Janssen.

Let us explain more carefully the historical facts. The synod of 1918 appointed Herman Hoeksema as associate editor for the rubric "Our Doctrine" in the *Banner*, and at the synod of 1920 he was reappointed to that position. No one up to that time had demonstrated or even claimed that there was any difference, even in the slightest degree, between his writings of the first two years and the second two years. It is also true that there was no mention of any criticism of Hoeksema's articles before 1920, while at the synod of 1922 from Classis Hudson the following instruction was introduced: "The Synod take care that no significant aspects of doctrine are denied in the articles of the rubric 'Our Doctrine' in the *Banner*, as occurs now."

The synod could not deal with this instruction, because Classis Hudson presented no proof for what it had claimed. But what is the explanation of this unique phenomenon? What could have occasioned submitting an instruction of this kind? One cannot answer this question decisively, but one can point to certain specific facts.

In 1919 a petition was presented to the curatorium [theological school committee] for an investigation of Janssen's instruction. The curatorium agonized over the matter, without satisfying the actual request. Subsequently the same petition was submitted to the synod of 1920. The synod did not satisfy the actual petition but was content to make a judgment on a few symptoms the four professors had mentioned in their petition. The synod judged, in accordance with that standard, that Janssen could and should be vindicated as professor. Yet no peace resulted from that decision. Soon thereafter, various persons demonstrated that neither the curatorium nor the synod had satisfied the petition for an investigation of Janssen's instruction in the seminary. At the same time it was shown by quotations from student notes, which have become increasingly well-known, that an investigation was very necessary.

Rev. Herman Hoeksema also did this investigation. He did not condemn Janssen, but he made known his objections or difficulties with Janssen's instruction and asked that those be removed.

In his answer to Hoeksema, Janssen did not address the problems that were raised but attacked Hoeksema with the accusation of being un-Reformed. According to Janssen, Hoeksema could not judge his instruction, because Hoeksema did not have a pure understanding of doctrine but was Anabaptist. After all, Hoeksema denied universal grace. Hoeksema, however, would not be diverted from the right path of action but continued to insist on an investigation of Janssen's instruction.

Meanwhile, ecclesiastical action was not neglected. At the autumn assembly of Classis Grand Rapids West, the consistory of Broadway Avenue Christian Reformed Church submitted a protest against the decision of the synod of 1920 and requested classis to endorse it and send it to the next synod. The classis appointed a committee to prepare advice for classis, but because of internal differences that committee could not present its official report on time. However, the four members whom the committee had selected to evaluate and explain the Janssen matter from formal and material perspectives and from positive and negative perspectives submitted separate reports.

Danhof's report was submitted first and was on time. He rejected Janssen's position and the principles governing his teaching. Some time after the deadline of April 1, 1922, G. Hoeksema submitted his report. It touched on the same points but defended the professor and criticized Danhof's report. Although the classical committee in the Janssen case did not officially adopt Danhof's report, copies of it were distributed to Janssen and his friends without the committee's permission and without Danhof's knowledge and approval.[4] The substance of G. Hoeksema's report was published in *Religion and Culture*. Since then Danhof has been defamed by the name Anabaptist.

The matter became continually more complicated. Meanwhile, at the earnest insistence of no fewer than eight classes, the curatorium took the matter in hand. It granted Janssen vacation for a year and

---

4   Ralph Janssen *De Synodale Conclusies* [The synodical conclusions] (1923), 32–33.

appointed a committee to investigate his instruction and to report its findings by the middle of February 1922. Danhof and H. Hoeksema were appointed to the seven-member committee. The committee submitted majority and minority reports. On the basis of that investigation, the curatorium judged "that such teachings are unsatisfactory and not desirable for our school." This decision was sent to the synod of 1922. The final outcome of the synodical investigation, on the basis of the aforementioned reports, was that the synod decided by an almost unanimous vote to depose Janssen on the grounds of insubordination and not being Reformed in doctrine.

That placed the defenders of Janssen in a very difficult position. The professor had originally suggested that only a very few in our circles adhered to the errors of Anabaptism, of whom H. Hoeksema and H. Danhof were the chief advocates. Those few individuals, whom Janssen claimed were un-Reformed, could not understand and were incompetent to evaluate his instruction, because he proceeded along pure paths. Janssen thought the Christian Reformed Church desired to remain faithful and pure in doctrine. But this latter idea became increasingly difficult to maintain when the group of objectors became more numerous and finally when the churches by synodical declaration decided concerning Janssen's instruction completely in the spirit of the suspicions of the four professors, the opinions of H. J. Kuiper and H. Danhof, the majority report, and the judgment of the curatorium.

Sometime before the synod of 1922, Janssen submitted to the curatorium objections against the instruction of the four professors. In his judgment Berkhof was not free of rationalism; Heyns' covenantal view was in error; and F. M. Ten Hoor and S. Volbeda were Anabaptists and essentially no different in their teachings from Hoeksema and Danhof. All of them were Lutheran in their view of scripture. The root of all those errors had its source in Ten Hoor, who did not have a sound view of common grace. Was he not a fierce opponent of Abraham Kuyper? All the others had been influenced by Kuyper in the pernicious error of sixteenth-century Anabaptist doctrine. Even Volbeda was guilty, although he had gained the highest academic degree in theology at Amsterdam.

However, after carefully investigating these things, the curatorium declared that the matters Janssen brought were not subject to the Reformed confessions and that the instruction of the four professors could not be called un-Reformed. It was apparent that Janssen had to conclude, since the members of the curatorium were leaders of our people, that two conflicting lines of thought existed in our ecclesiastical communion and that it was absolutely necessary to expose this fact. Janssen did this in his *De Crisis in de Christelijke Gereformeerde Kerk in Amerika*.[5] He claimed that two separate streams of thought had existed in our church fellowship for a very long time, and this had reached such a point of development that it could not be ignored. In a relatively short time the churches had arrived at "an inexpressibly great crisis." In opposition to the un-Reformed position of the four professors and some preachers, such as H. J. Kuiper, H. Hoeksema, and H. Danhof, and some members of the curatorium who were committed to the Anabaptist doctrinal error—the denial of common grace—only a few of the faithful raised the banner of Reformed doctrine regarding general grace.

Under such circumstances how could anyone express Reformed ideas in a report, while lacking awareness of the new generation with a new mentality and many more needs than the former generation? Janssen wrote in that spirit. The four professors and four pastors answered him in their *Waar het in de Zaak Janssen om Gaat* (The issues in the Janssen case).[6] They pointed out that the issue was not the doctrine of common grace but the instruction of Janssen and that "when the synod of 1922 condemned the instruction of Dr. Janssen, one party did not condemn the other, but the church condemned as un-Reformed the instruction of one of her professors." And that is what happened.

Now what? According to the position of Janssen and his friends, the conclusion was unavoidable that the Christian Reformed Church had run aground in a sickly, Anabaptist swamp and that the faithful had no choice but to be the "faithful who grieved her spiritual

5   Ralph Janssen, *De Crisis in de Christelijke Gereformeerde Kerk in Amerika* [The crisis in the Christian Reformed Church in America] (Grand Rapids, MI: Grand Rapids Printing Co., 1922).
6   The four professors were L. Berkhof, W. Heyns, F. M. Ten Hoor, and S. Volbeda. The four ministers were H. Danhof, Y. P. de Jong, H. Hoeksema, and H. J. Kuiper.—Ed.

condition." That had been done before, after all. They had mumbled about it for a while. Chicago had been deemed an appropriate place for the opening of a seminary. People should trust that truth and justice would prevail in the end. One would then have to attempt to awaken the people from spiritual drowsiness. Was anything more obvious than that Janssen would write more pamphlets?

His first publication appeared in November 1922 under the title *Het Synodale Vonnis en zijne Voorgeschiedenis Kerkrechtelijk Beoordeeld,* in which Janssen argued that the synod in his case did not act according to the general "common grace principles of justice and morality for ecclesiastical justice" and "for ecclesiastical practice."[7] His main attack was not directed toward Hoeksema and Danhof, although Janssen repeatedly asserted that they denied aspects of Reformed doctrine and deduced the logical consequences of their teaching from their leaders, the four professors. He said their position did not differ essentially from the position of Ten Hoor, Heyns, Berkhof, Volbeda, and perhaps a dozen other preachers who were named.

Janssen specifically attacked H. J. Kuiper, H. Keegstra, and J. Manni, mentioning their unjust ecclesiastical government and immoral behavior. In Janssen's judgment, the church sinned "against better knowledge."[8] That almost all the delegates of synod either denied or failed to appreciate the doctrine of common grace was nothing but lies and deceit. Janssen quoted from article 36 of the Belgic Confession with specific application to Kuiper: "We detest the Anabaptists... who...would subvert justice...and confound that decency and good order which God hath established among men."[9]

This brochure did not have much impact. That it would have much of an impact was impossible, for Janssen's condemnation involved nearly all the delegates of synod. Besides, the grounds he presented could not withstand the test of examination, as was demonstrated in *De Wachter.* At the same time a strange and unexplained phenomenon

---

7   R. Janssen, *Het Synodale Vonnis en zijne Voorgeschiedenis Kerkrechtelijk Beoordeeld* [The synodical judgment and its prehistory, criticized in light of the Church Order] (Grand Rapid, MI: M. Hoffius, 1922).

8   Ibid., 22.

9   Belgic Confession 36, in Schaff, *Creeds of Christendom,* 3:433.

occurred. Janssen thought it was necessary to say all these things *after* the synod made its decision and he had left the synodical meeting.

The same holds true of Janssen's brochure *The Synodical Conclusions* published in September 1923. The broader circle of our people did not notice that brochure, and the rubric "Book Reviews" did not mention it. What purpose could it have served? Once again Janssen made his judgment according to the standard of common grace. According to him, if the synod had made its decision on the basis of common grace, it would have arrived at a different conclusion in evaluating his instruction.

We agree with Janssen's assertion, but the synod did not do that.

On the contrary, according to Janssen, "The decision originated from the statements of an errant preacher [Danhof]. After that, it resulted from the declarations of preachers who held errant views, many of whom were personally prejudiced against Janssen, such as H. Hoeksema, H. Danhof, H. J. Kuiper, and J. Manni (the majority section); and later the synod adopted the declarations of an errant, outrageous, prejudiced subcommittee."[10]

The issue concerned specifically the position of one professor at our theological school [Calvin]. In Janssen's opinion the issue was that in his work as professor he was committed to the position of science that common grace provided him and that Danhof in his evaluation of Janssen's instruction was committed to the position of faith in holy scripture as God's infallible word. It is therefore a difference between Janssen's position and Danhof's position. When more sharply defined, the difference amounts to this: Hoeksema and Danhof maintain that the position of science, which Janssen claims is provided by common grace, is not only denied him as a theological professor in our school, but is also impossible because the ground for the position—common grace—is lacking. The synod could therefore evaluate Janssen's instruction and condemn it without touching the issue of whether or not common grace exists—which is exactly what it did.

Likewise, although Janssen accused many others, such as Ten Hoor and Volbeda, of Anabaptist doctrinal error, they could continue

---

10 Janssen, *Synodical Conclusions*, 33.

to say that they did not identify with Abraham Kuyper's way of thinking regarding common grace. Yet they did not deny the existence of a common grace. In the abstract that could be the case, and the synodical decision could be maintained. Meanwhile, Janssen should withdraw his accusations of Anabaptist error, spiritual weakness, and being un-Reformed. The difference between Janssen and us concerns the ground of one's perspective on science.

Some friends of Janssen seemed to have sensed this. Although in the autumn of 1922, J. K. van Baalen could not judge concerning the instruction of Janssen, and consequently was unsure about the justice of synod's verdict concerning that instruction, he at least chose for himself, from his perspective, the certain for the uncertain. But he is convinced that the denial of common grace is Anabaptist and that those who deny common grace cannot purely preach the gospel. This must be the consequence, even if the congregations where they preach the word do not perceive this. Van Baalen therefore calls specifically to them to repent of the error of their ways.

The accused preachers, Danhof and Hoeksema, however, had the boldness to offer Van Baalen their provisional answer in *Not Anabaptist but Reformed*. They threw the ball back to him. They answered, no, the preaching of the gospel cannot rest on the foundation of universal grace, since such a position necessarily would lead to Arminianism and Pelagianism, in each case to a doctrine of a Christ for all men, head for head and soul for soul objectively, and consequently to semi-Pelagianism. Also in the preaching of the whole word of God, emphasis must be placed on the negative side of divine predestination—reprobation. The whole counsel of God must be preached. Although preachers are obligated to treat the subject of reprobation with great wisdom, one may not make himself guilty in any way of rejecting reprobation, as happens all too frequently in practice.

In our circles the issue of common grace is reduced to the doctrine of man's free will. Perhaps this is what caused Valentijn Hepp, professor at the Free University in Amsterdam, to think of a misunderstanding. Certainly it is a real misunderstanding when anyone confuses common grace with free will in the unregenerated sinner. We did not have such a misunderstanding, and therefore Hepp had no right to write of misunderstanding in relation to us.[11] Undoubtedly there was misunderstanding among some persons, and Hepp had the right to point that out. He should have heard us first and then discussed the issue of common grace with us, which is the point of contention. That discussion should have been in light of what he had written.

But that did not happen, even when we published our book *Sin and Grace* and Van Baalen answered us with his *Novelty and Error*. Even after that, Hepp continued to evade the question and arrogantly and high-handedly set himself up as a negotiator and an adviser. No one actually received any benefit from his efforts, except those who saw no chance for a good solution to the matter and therefore were inclined to adopt another's advice, especially if it was offered free of charge by a professor from the Free University.

To this group belongs Zwier who did not want more than one synodical committee for the Janssen issue.[12] Apparently neither did the editorial staff of the *Witness*, because as some are saying and as Hepp said, the issue has not been thoroughly searched out. This group offers nothing definitive, and neither does Hepp. The synod would not be permitted to give its committee a definite assignment, and the committee apparently would have to build its case from the ground up.

Yet others do not share this opinion. In certain circles some reason that whatever common grace may be, it does not change anything regarding the issue from a church government viewpoint. They claim that the issue can very well be left provisionally undecided. The fact is, there is common grace, even though it has not been proven. Hoeksema and Danhof boldly deny common grace. Based on that viewpoint of common grace, it is completely justified to conclude that they cannot be orthodox in their preaching of the holy gospel.

What is the hesitation? Anyone can file an ecclesiastical complaint against Hoeksema and Danhof and subsequently take the appropriate action if the accused do not repent. If it becomes necessary to judge,

---

11 Hepp, *Misunderstanding.*—Trans.

12 Daniel Zwier, "*Niet te heet van stal loopen*" [Don't walk off like a hothead], *Witness* (May, 1924).

the synod can decide that common grace is biblical, ask the brothers if they confess such a doctrine and preach in harmony with it, and depose them from office if they refuse to confess that doctrine and preach it. Then the church can labor peacefully to establish a more refined and ecclesiastical formulation of the dogma of common grace. This could be done in many different ways; the manner is unimportant. The most important thing is to do this as soon as possible, for there is turmoil and unrest in our churches. It is our duty above all to restore the peace of the churches.

People are apparently in agreement that Danhof and Hoeksema deserve to be deposed from office because of their persistent denial of the existence of common grace. However, the opposition against them has been obviously transferred to various individuals who regard themselves as called to take the first step. Perhaps differing methods of proceeding give a better guarantee of achieving the predetermined goal. However, people are rising against Hoeksema and Danhof in various ways, about which we will give more details later.

The issue concerning common grace originally was forced to the foreground by the pressure of the Janssen case. There was a fundamental difference regarding Janssen's basis for his so-called scientific position out of which he gave theological instruction to his Reformed students. We have demonstrated how men expressed the original issue of common grace and how it led back to the matter of man's free will.

We will, however, continue to maintain that the synod of 1618–19 settled the matter of the sinner's free will. Likewise, we will continue to maintain that on the so-called scientific viewpoint of Janssen, even though he has it rest a thousand times on the foundation of the so-called common grace, there simply cannot be any mention of any essentially Reformed theology.

Nevertheless, now we are confronted with the theory of common grace, particularly as it is represented by Abraham Kuyper. In essence there is no other theory, even though men claim there is. We contend that Kuyper's theory cannot stand the test of scripture and the confessions. We reserve the right to draw the line differently from Kuyper. People may differ with us or offer other positions, but if they accuse us of being un-Reformed, they should walk the path of honesty and honor. If they do not do that, they are responsible for the consequences of their actions.

Finally, we call attention to the most recent fruit of our labors, the brochure *Along Pure Paths,* for your further study of the subject of common grace and of our perspective on specific points that have slowly come to the foreground in the discussions. In this brochure we respond to almost everything mentioned in the critiques. If people exclude for now the matter of man's free will, which was settled long ago, what is there left that can be used to indict us? We deem that sort of dealing extremely dangerous. We need to have studious endeavor, not ecclesiastical procedures. Yet people at once want to send objections, requests, and instructions to synod. Therefore, we will have to reckon with that reality.

CHAPTER 2

COMMON GRACE
BEFORE SYNOD

We are opposed in different ways. Some brought charges and attempted to initiate ecclesiastical action against us at the consistory, classis, and synod. In our presence but without our approval, others directed a request to synod with the approbation of classis. Others are planning to come to synod with various instructions.

Van Baalen took the lead. Perhaps there was a reason for that. His book *Novelty and Error* remained unanswered for a time. The authors [Hoeksema and Danhof] of the book *Sin and Grace* sought an opportunity to respond to the criticism of their book, which in the fall of 1923 had come from various persons in a short series of articles in *De Wachter* under the heading "Brief Response." To Hoeksema and Danhof's great amazement and disappointment, there was no room in *De Wachter* for them to respond to that critical series. Besides, at the beginning of 1924 pens began to write anew.

We decided to postpone the writing of a new brochure, so that we could respond to both the old and the new critics. Possibly that caused Van Baalen to surmise that we would make him wait for a response. However, Van Baalen relayed to us in late January that he planned to submit to our consistories objections to our public preaching of un-Reformed and unbiblical ideas. In his letter, dated January 22, 1924, he spoke of his objections, *which others shared*, against our un-Reformed doctrine; and he demanded, "You take back your un-Reformed utterances and slanderous remarks regarding Dr. Kuyper, Dr. Bavinck, and a host of your fellow preachers."

Van Baalen's "Document of Objection," which contained five grievances, arrived in early April. For various reasons the others had withdrawn from a cooperative effort. Van Baalen assured us that his "Document of Objection" was completely his own work and that he had not passed it around, although he had distributed a similar one.

> Our first grievance concerns the claim of Rev. Danhof and Rev. Hoeksema that God is never gracious, favorable, or has an attitude of goodness toward the reprobate.
>
> Second, the above-mentioned erroneous conviction proceeds from another error against which the undersigned must express his earnest objection. Danhof and Hoeksema place election and reprobation on one line and conceive of both as proceeding in the same manner out of God's counsel.
>
> Third, Danhof and Hoeksema deny that God restrains, suppresses, or curbs evil and sin.
>
> Our fourth objection is directed against the position that the unregenerate can do absolutely no good.
>
> Our fifth objection against the public ministry of Danhof and Hoeksema relates to the superficial and unwarranted manner in which they accuse many officebearers in our church and in the sister church in the Netherlands of not being doctrinally Reformed and of world-conformity in their striving to let their light shine before men that they may glorify the Father who is in heaven.

In his document Van Baalen demanded our consistories to deal with us regarding these objections and allowed the consistories thirty days to accomplish this. That requirement was made with a view to the classical gathering in the middle of May.

The consistories of Eastern Avenue in Grand Rapids and of Kalamazoo First in Kalamazoo hastened to arrange a meeting of the combined consistories on April 22. Van Baalen was informed that he would be able to talk to the accused brethren there and then appear with his remaining objections at the a combined consitory that evening. It was commonly agreed that this schedule was the most desirable, and everyone hoped Van Baalen would find it acceptable. However, that was not the case. According to his letter, Van Baalen did not want to debate with Danhof and Hoeksema, and even less did he desire to maintain his objections against them in the presence of their consistory members. He was willing, so he wrote later, to explain in more detail his document to the consistories without the pastors being present. Yet the consistories were obligated to act on Van Baalen's petition in regard to their pastors.

Meanwhile the meeting of Classis Grand Rapids West was upon us. Van Baalen appeared there with the request that classis take action regarding his document against Danhof, which Van Baalen had submitted to Danhof's consistory. The question was whether that document could be declared admissible under the circumstances described above. That question was not answered. But Danhof and Van Baalen agreed to discuss the five points of Van Baalen's protest, and if any objections remained to go together to the consistory of Kalamazoo First.

The dialogue took place the next day. The result was that Van Baalen did not drop even one of his objections and concluded that he would have to reflect more on it. The question was, when could he appear before the consistory? They decided on the following Wednesday when the officebearers would meet again at the gathering of Classis Grand Rapids East. This gathering decided to set the date [for Van Baalen's appearance before the consistory of Kalamazoo] as Monday evening of the following week. On that occasion, Danhof asked Van Baalen to discuss with him the remaining points of disagreement, since Van Baalen had reflected on their previous discussion, and after that discussion a week ago nothing had happened. Van Baalen did not relent concerning any of the points of disagreement, but he promised to visit Danhof in his home before the consistory meeting.

This meeting was indeed held. About 4:30 p.m. on Monday, Van Baalen appeared at Danhof's door. Van Baalen was asked again to discuss his remaining objections. Danhof did not want to press for a second meeting or further discussions, because there was no time for that. He asked Van Baalen to put his objections in writing. But this was unacceptable to Van Baalen. He said that Danhof's explanation concerning the objections when they had discussed their differences had completely put his mind at ease. However, in his judgment, Danhof's explanation did not harmonize with what he had presented earlier as portrayed in Van Baalen's protest document. Danhof then proposed that Van Baalen bring *that* point to the consistory. Van Baalen did not want any part of it. He wanted to bring the original protest to the consistory, but not the results of their discussion.

They presented the status of the matter to the consistory. Danhof's oral explanation had given Van Baalen peace of mind, but he thought that the explanation did not harmonize with what Danhof had written. Although the discussion between Van Baalen and Danhof had taken place, they could not decisively prove to the consistory the accuracy of their presentation. Danhof expressed his opinion and desire to repeat the same explanation at an agreed upon time and place in the presence of three witnesses appointed by the consistory. These witnesses would keep a written record of what was said so that the disagreement could be resolved rightly and Danhof's character could remain untouched. The consistory judged Danhof's desire to be very fair and decided to ask Van Baalen to approve it. Van Baalen refused, appealing to his right, granted by classis, to call for a special meeting of the classis. He would pursue the issue at classis, even though he had refused to discuss that point of difference before the full consistory.[13]

The matter remains this way until the present. If Van Baalen is still permitted to call a special gathering of the classis, the consistory would have to protest that action. The fairness of the above-mentioned desire [of Danhof] does not allow for any doubt in that regard.

At the meeting of Classis Grand Rapids East the matter took a different turn. Its final decision was that Van Baalen had to bring his protest document to the consistory. Van Baalen gave notification of his rejection of that decision, and his protest will consequently come to synod.

At the same meeting of Classis Grand Rapids East some objections

---

13 "That point" is the alleged difference between what Danhof had earlier said or written about Van Baalen's theology and what Danhof said to Van Baalen in their private meeting.—Ed.

regarding common grace were sent back to the consistory, as well as "instructions from the consistory of the Christian Reformed Church at Kelloggsville, Michigan," identified as the pastor's overture. Although his overture was about common grace, just like Van Baalen's protest document, it differed in form. Rev. M. Schans asked the classis to approve his document and to forward it to synod as the instruction of classis.[14]

This overture put to the background the essential matter of common grace. Above all Schans wanted the synod to demand the pastors, Danhof and Hoeksema, to explain various points of doctrine in more detail and to test by God's word and the confessions some expressions in their writings. When that was done Schans desired the synod to weigh the desirability of expanding the confessions regarding the doctrine of common grace. If such expansion was deemed advisable, a committee should be appointed to study what scripture and the confessions say regarding common grace and to test in the light of scripture what notable Reformed theologians taught regarding that doctrine. Therefore, Schans acknowledged the possibility that scripture and the confessions do not contain the doctrine of common grace and that the teachings of notable Reformed theologians concerning it could not endure the test of God's word. Notwithstanding, Schans wanted Hoeksema and Danhof to be examined and deposed from office first to restore the rest and peace of the churches.

Our protest against such treatment and the altered final decision of classis in this matter will go to synod. Here we are confronted with the attempt to condemn us without synod's judgment on the issue of common grace. If that question must first be decided, there would not really be any prospect of a judgment of synod concerning the persons of Danhof and Hoeksema. It [the overture of Schans] was clearly all about their persons; it was not about finding a solution to the problem of common grace. Against such a shocking twisting of these matters, we must protest with all that is in us. Nor may we let the matter stand merely with a naked protest, no matter how powerful it may be. This

14 Rev. Martin Schans was the minister of Kelloggsville Christian Reformed Church from 1917 to 1924.—Ed.

protest is presented separately in another place [in chapter 3 of this booklet, *For the Sake of Justice and Truth*].

In addition to the protest and the overture mentioned above, and about which we must presently make a particular observation, other separate instructions concerning common grace were submitted to the next synod. At least one other protest was so closely related to this question that we want to note it here. We have in mind Rev. Quirinus Breen's "Protest against the Conclusions of the Synod of 1922 in the case of Dr. R. Janssen, Material Part." That protest is not against us but is directed against synod. Yet the matter is so intertwined with the different instructions, protests, and overtures that only a little knowledge about it is necessary to understand that the present common grace controversy and the Janssen matter are related to one another like two drops of water, and they stand or fall together.

The instructions to synod in the matter of common grace are the following:

1. Whereas, the doctrine of common grace is absolutely denied by two ministers of our church in their book *Sin and Grace* and since the agitation caused by this is detrimental to the spiritual development of the church; therefore, Classis Hackensack asks synod to declare that such a denial is contrary to scripture and to our Reformed doctrine; further that synod appoint a committee to make a thorough study of this matter and enlighten the church.—Classis Hackensack

2. Since in our judgment the position regarding general grace, as it appears in the book *Sin and Grace*, conflicts with our forms of unity, we feel ourselves aggrieved. Therefore, we request synod to investigate this matter.—Classis Sioux Center

3. With great interest and deep sorrow Classis Hudson, having taken note of the bitter conflict in our churches concerning the doctrine of general grace and considering that it belongs to the authority of synod to decide doctrinal differences and to preserve doctrinal purity in the

churches, decrees to petition the next synod to take such measures as under the leading of the Holy Spirit can assure the maintenance of the pure confession regarding the idea of general grace and if necessary to explain it in detail and thus restore rest and peace in the bosom of the church.—Classis Hudson

4. Let synod appoint a committee to subject the issue of general grace to careful biblical, historical, theological investigation to arrive at a definite formulation of this aspect of doctrine.—Classis Muskegon

5. Let synod in earnest consideration express itself or appoint a committee of investigation in the matter of the doctrinal question pending in our churches, namely the doctrine of general grace.

Grounds:

1. Inasmuch as the doctrine of general grace is preached in our churches and is denied by others in such a way that the one position definitely excludes the other.

2. Because this question works unrest in the churches.—Classis Grand Rapids West

The same holds true regarding the above instructions as with the various protests and overtures; namely, they turn matters upside down. They assume as already proven what should be the result of an investigation. Why would anyone appoint an inquiry committee, if the point in question has already been decided? The matter is already settled!

Let it be observed that the issue between us is not about subordinate points of common grace, so that we can stand united on the position of common grace. But the argument touches exactly on whether or not general grace even exists. If in the formulation of a protest or an overture people unintentionally proceed from the idea of the existence of common grace, by that action they condemn those who deny the existence of common grace. What this means for the party [that denies the existence of common grace] in the contemporary issue among us— if synod should adopt an instruction or overture formulated in such a manner—does not need to be indicated more fully and specifically. Such a decision would strike an irreparable breech in the fellowship among our churches and those who deny the existence of common grace. The synod may not countenance such carelessness.

In our judgment the next synod must not in the least venture to make a pronouncement about common grace, since the matter is not yet ripe for that to be done. Whether synod should appoint a committee of inquiry we will not address now. However, if synod would decide to appoint a committee, it should be very careful that its mandate to the committee does not include a ruling on the matter under consideration. For example, synod is not permitted in its mandate to the committee to state, in agreement with the request of Classis Hackensack, that a denial of the existence of common grace violates scripture and the confessions. If synod did that, it would settle the essential issue. For the same reason synod should not make the instructions from Classis Sioux Center its own. No less may it declare what the real point in question is. If synod did that, the matter would be settled from synod's perspective, if only provisionally and conditionally.

Understand us well: synod may decide this matter for itself. That is its right and privilege, and in the end, its duty; but it must not signal at the outset its judgment in a mandate to a study committee regarding the real issue. That would make the work of such a committee entirely superfluous. And this concerns also the ultimate goal at which the instruction of Classis Muskegon, and relatively that of Classis Hudson, requests the synod to aim. That purpose was specifically to arrive at a definite formulation of the doctrine of common grace.

Such a committee cannot be given direction unless synod's mandate to the committee assumes the existence of common grace. Yet if synod's mandate contains this assumption, it harbors within it the decisive resolution of the present differences in our fellowship regarding this doctrine. Then an ecclesiastical break between the parties cannot be prevented.

This is also the case if synod would adopt the instruction of Classis Grand Rapids West without altering it. This instruction proceeds from the assumption not that some in our churches teach a doctrine of common grace (for we do not in any way deny that), but that some teach general grace as if it were official Reformed doctrine. Then the conclusion cannot be avoided that those who deny the existence of common grace would be unable to preach the Reformed faith fully and positively. Consequently, the synod might point to the fact that some in our churches teach common grace and others do not; but without prior investigation they may not attach the seal of Reformed orthodoxy to the one or the other. Should synod wish to work by means of a committee, it is proper that the committee first report to synod concerning the real point in question, so that synod can express its final judgment on the basis of the authorized investigation and according to the submitted advice.

If synod follows this path, it would appoint a committee with the general mandate to make a thorough study of the fundamental issues from all perspectives concerning everything that relates to common grace. The first and direct purpose of that study would be to educate. In our judgment, detailed particulars need not immediately be presented. In this way there would be a chance that at the synod of 1926 something could be reported. In practice this method would have the great advantage of using the united and sharpened spiritual and intellectual powers, which men now use to oppose one another, toward a shared and positive purpose. This would be true if synod is concerned for a relative proportion. There should not be only two groups on such a committee, but at least four or five (more or less) synodical delegates who represent the different perspectives and definite lines of thought found in our fellowship and who are concerned with the life of our churches and the instruction at our school.

That procedure would also give Breen a splendid opportunity to withdraw the protest he plans to present before the synod. If the brother continues with his protest as it is now, we fear that we will necessarily lose him as well. In that protest he maintains almost everything that Janssen taught in our school and that was condemned as un-Reformed by the synod of 1922. If the synod continues to maintain its judgment regarding the instruction of Janssen, it is difficult to see how Breen can preserve his fellowship with our churches, or our churches with him. Also here [with regard to Breen] it is fitting that a division be prevented, if at all possible. It will be possible only if we can discuss and study the question of common grace together, because Breen, just as Janssen, bases his ideas chiefly on the theory of common grace.

We certainly recognize that people can condemn Breen, as they did Janssen, without reference to the doctrine of common grace. That is possible, we say, and can be done on good grounds, but it will bring no peace to the churches. This is all the more true because Breen and others are of the opinion that we, Danhof and Hoeksema, who deny the existence of common grace, had such great influence on the synod of 1922, so that our novel perspective—and in their opinion errone-ous ideas—regarding the Janssen case finally became the position of the synod. For this reason men from that side think that the condem-nation of us, which people are demanding, would bring a reversal of the synodical decision in the matter of Janssen's instruction and the restoration of his name and reputation for the injustice done to him. Contending that the matter was not that way—as we have repeat-edly and candidly testified with an eye focused on the honor of our synod—makes no difference concerning the practical aspect of the present problems in our fellowship. The friends of Janssen have and are giving that interpretation to what happened. An end would come to that misrepresentation if some of their representatives could be granted membership on a synodical committee.

In brief, the profit of such a method of dealing with the issue would be uncommonly great. We therefore do not oppose the naming of such a committee with a mandate of that kind.

In the same breath we add that synod would act more wisely if it left the study of common grace to personal initiative. The time is certainly not ripe for the formulation of a new Reformed dogma. If anyone deems the time to be ripe, he should first concentrate on the idea of the covenant. We live spiritually out of the covenantal concep-tion, even if it is with uncertainty and the lack of definite and clear understanding; and for that [formulating a definite conception of the covenant], life principles and various elements are found in our confessions. At the same time, men operate along one historical, foundational, and positive line.

All of that historical, confessional structure cannot be maintained regarding the theory of common grace. It is not true that the Lord's church in its spiritual, heartfelt life, in the service of her King, will or can consciously walk and work according to that theory. This theory during the last twenty-five years, apart from its appearance on the extremely distant horizon, has shown itself to the church very vaguely and without clear lines of characterization.

Surely this theory may and must be explained to the church, but the solution to the real question in an ecclesiastical sense is not thereby brought closer to realization. In no period of history or any instance has there been an expansion of our confessions regarding this point. Why then must we have a synodical committee? The consistory, classis, and synod are ecclesiastical judicial bodies. Certainly they are called to decide doctrinal issues. But if they would do that, ideas, opinions, theories, and positions must fall under the terms of the Reformed confessions, or if things are ripe for that men must formulate a new dogma. The latter no one has yet done with a single one of the conceptions that reign among us. The synod of 1922 rejected a request to test the theory of premillennialism by scripture and the confessions because synod judged premillennialism to be unrelated to salvation. Even before that time, the curatorium declared regarding the different views of the four professors, against whom Janssen had brought charges, that their doctrinal teachings could not be called un-Reformed, because for some of them nothing, and perhaps for others a few scattered elements, could be found in the confessions.

Does anyone imagine that we are truly ready to proceed with the formulation of a new Reformed dogma of common grace? Let us act soberly and for a moment take note of the tremendous, long-lasting struggles of the church of all ages to arrive at even a somewhat definite conception of the eternal truths revealed in God's word. If it must come to the formulation of a new Reformed dogma, it would be preferable to cast us out so the Christian Reformed Church would not commit such foolishness.

CHAPTER 3

HERMAN HOEKSEMA'S PROTEST AGAINST CLASSIS GRAND RAPIDS EAST

To the synod of the Christian Reformed Church
To be held June 1924 in Kalamazoo, Michigan
Esteemed fathers and brothers,

The undersigned considers it necessary to protest some of the decisions of Classis Grand Rapids East taken at its gathering on May 21, 1924, in connection with an overture that was laid on the classical table as an instruction in the name of the consistory of Kelloggsville, Michigan.

My protest is threefold.

First, I protest the way Rev. Schans brought his so-called overture, which is really a protest, to classis, which classis declared admissible.

Second, I protest the way classis acted on that overture and its decision to forward a part of it to synod.

Third, I protest the content of point B of Schans' overture that has been forwarded with point C to synod in the name of the classis.

The explanation of the first part of my protest is that Schans felt burdened, in cooperation with others, to prepare an overture, in which he directed a threefold request to classis and through it to synod. First, he requested synod to investigate the undersigned (and Danhof) with a view to their orthodoxy on the general offer of the gospel, election and reprobation, God's restraint of sin, civil righteousness, human responsibility, and the providence of God and his government of all things. Second, Schans requested that after the completion of that personal investigation, the writings of the undersigned and of Danhof be examined and various expressions be tested in relation to some biblical texts and some confessional expressions. Third, Schans wants synod to appoint a committee to study the doctrine of common grace according to scripture and the confessions. Schans' first request was not adopted by classis, but it is necessary to call attention to it to defend my protest against the action of the classis on this point.

Schans had his so-called overture adopted by his consistory as an instruction to classis, although it was not signed by the consistory or the clerk of consistory, but only by Schans. Furthermore, Schans published his overture, which contained cloaked charges against myself and Danhof, and disseminated it to the public. Besides, a few days before classis met, through the classical stated clerk, Schans sent copies of his overture to all the members of all the consistories of our classis, without notifying me or my consistory.

I have laid bare on the floor of Classis Grand Rapids East all of my objections against that entire method. However, the classis did not want to hear me, approved of all that by their silence, received the overture as legally before the classis, and treated it as such.

The points of my first protest are twofold.

First, classis declared admissible an overture to have us dealt with as pastors (subjecting us to an examination on the above-mentioned points is dealing with our persons), although in connection with his overture, neither Schans nor his consistory visited us or our consistories. It is certainly not in harmony with Reformed church government to permit the examination of a pastor on the floor of classis or synod while bypassing or ignoring his consistory. That the classis nevertheless allowed this, although it did not send that portion of the overture to synod, is hierarchy.

Second, Schans published his overture on his own authority and allowed it to be sent to all the members of all the consistories of our classis, before the classis could declare its opinion regarding the admissibility of his so-called overture. Maintaining such a method of operation would lead to monstrous ecclesiastical hierarchy. Every protestant would then have the right to act in the same way as Schans. Without informing the person or his consistory and without waiting for the judgment of classis on the admissibility of his protest, one could have his protest published and forwarded to all the consistory members in the classis. We complained about this on the floor of classis, but the classis did not sustain our objection.

The explanation of the second part of my main protest is that classis decided not to forward point A of Schans' overture to synod. A substitute motion, which had already been prepared, as evidenced by the typewritten form in which it appeared at classis, was made and adopted. The brief content of that substitute motion was to send points B and C of the overture to synod.

Point B interrogatively set forth many different charges against us. It requested synod to examine our writings, or more accurately some statements in our writings, and to test them by some scriptural texts and parts of the Reformed confessions. From all perspectives the content had the character of a protest.

When point B was to be discussed, we almost begged the classis to treat that material item by item on the floor of classis. We claimed and demonstrated how untrue the content was. We offered to debate every aspect of point B with one classical delegate or with three or six delegates appointed by classis for that purpose. Nothing helped. The delegates did not want any discussion. They wanted to forward point B without discussion, and they did that. In the presence of hundreds of witnesses, most of whom were members of the Eastern Avenue congregation, the delegates dared to commit the injustice of refusing to discuss with me the issues raised. Instead they forwarded to synod a document that was really a protest. The majority of the classical delegates were unable to explain what they had sent to synod.

Against that treatment I am protesting. Certainly Schans should have discussed point B with us before bring it to classis. He should also have brought point B to the consistory meeting.

Specifically my protest is against the emphatic refusal of classis to discuss the content of its instruction to synod.

The third part of my protest is against the content of point B. The classis did not want to treat that material. At this time we submit it to synod.

In this section Schans quotes many expressions from our writings in the *Banner*, various brochures, and our book *Sin and Grace*.

The statements relate to the following points of doctrine: God's grace toward the reprobate ungodly, election and reprobation, the restraint of sin, the good works of the natural man, human responsibility, and God's government in relation to all things.

I have especially two objections to this part. First, out of many hundreds of pages of material, Schans laid before the synod a few statements taken out of context, and he wanted synod to make a declaration about them. Second, Schans did not want those statements tested by the whole of scripture and the confessions, but according to a few texts of God's word and a few quotations from the confessions.

The first part of Schans' second section deals with our denial that God gives grace to the reprobate, historically identified as the ungodly. Schans quotes some expressions from our writings to show this. He then asks them to be tested against a few scriptural texts and some confessional statements. He requests the judgment of the synod on those quotations from our writings.

Schans completely forgot that all the quotations from our writings concern common grace, that is, whether or not there is a common grace of God to all men. This will become very clear if the context of the quoted statements is examined. That Schans completely forgot this is evident from his referral to the external calling of the gospel. Does Schans want to identify that as common grace? Is the preaching of the gospel common to all men? Following this path of reasoning, the issue between us about common grace is shifted to the question that was settled at Dordt in 1618–19.

The texts to which Schans appeals do not answer the question, does God give grace to the *reprobate*? They speak only of God's mercies over all his works or of the external call of the gospel that comes to all who hear it. The texts are Psalm 145:8; Luke 6:35; Isaiah 45:22; Ezekiel 33:11; Luke 14:17–18, 24; Acts 13:46; and Matthew 22:9.

The same is true of the confessional statements that Schans quotes. They are Canons 2.5 and 3–4.8–9. These articles also treat the external call of the gospel that comes to all to whom the gospel is preached. Let Schans demonstrate not by logical schemes but by our writings that we have ever opposed and denied the external call to everyone who comes under the preaching of the gospel. What does that have to do with common grace? We wrote about that issue. Further, we readily acknowledge that this whole section of Schans' overture (3–6) makes a very bad impression on us. We doubt if Schans agrees with what our fathers taught concerning particular grace in Canons 2, error and rejection 6. There is a distinctly Arminian odor that cleaves to Schans' entire attempt to brand us as heretics.

To test our claim that God does not give grace to the reprobate, historically existing as the ungodly, synod must have completely different texts. We refer to the texts quoted in *Along Pure Paths* (25–34).

The second point of Schans' protest treats our perspective concerning election and reprobation. Apparently he objects to our teaching that there is not only a saving operation of God according to the line of election, but also a *similar* (not to be confused with *same*) operation of wrath and rejection according to the line of reprobation.

The texts Schans quotes on this point are Deuteronomy 29:29, Ezekiel 33:11, Romans 9:15, and Ephesians 1:4. The articles of the confessions to which he appeals are the Belgic Confession article 16 and Canons 1.7, 15.

Our response is that we do not speak of hidden things, but only about things that God has revealed to us in his word. Schans needs to appeal to other texts, such as Romans 9:18 and Malachi 1:2–5. In addition, see the texts quoted in *Along Pure Paths* (25–34). We have no objection to the articles quoted from the confessions, nor does Schans prove that he has the right to assert that we object to those articles. Apart from that, it seems strange that Schans opposes the doctrine that there is not only a saving operation, but also a divine operation of rejection and wrath, the latter directed toward the reprobate, historically identified as the ungodly.

Third, Schans objects to our denial of the restraint of the process of sin by common grace. He wants the synod to test this denial—or preferably the statements that he quoted from our writings—against some scriptural and confessional statements. He appeals to Genesis 20:6, Psalm 105:14–15, 2 Thessalonians 2:6–7, and Belgic Confession articles 13 and 36.

Our response is that these texts do not mention a restraint of sin by common grace, but they speak of God's government over the ungodly in such a manner that God protects his people so the ungodly cannot harm them (*Along Pure Paths*, 14–17, 77–83).

Fourth, Schans refers to our denial that the natural man does good. On page 10 of the overture, he attempts to present our convictions as if we also deny civic righteousness. Schans wants our viewpoint examined on the basis of 2 Chronicles 10:30, Romans 13:3, 1 Peter 2:14, Canons 3–4.7, and the Belgic Confession.

Our response the synod can find in *Along Pure Paths* (12–44, 50–73). Besides, we doubt very seriously that Schans stands squarely on Reformed principles when he clearly teaches that an evil tree, apart from regeneration, brings forth good fruits.

In Schans' fifth point it is evident to what extent he prefers his logical schemes to the clear language of what we have written. He quotes a few statements that he thinks relate to the doctrine of human responsibility. When he reads those statements, Schans is unable to suppress the question "whether the responsibility of man is not diminished or set aside and whether God is the author of sin" (11–12).

My answer is, why does Schans not quote from our writings instead of speculating on the basis of his erroneous conclusions? Is what we wrote years ago in the *Banner* and more recently in *Not Anabaptist but Reformed* in Schans' estimation not sufficiently clear? Or was it too clear for his purposes? Or has he never read our books, pamphlets, and articles but only quoted a few expressions for his own purposes? We wrote:

Thus far we have strictly maintained the all-encompassing character of God's decrees on the one hand and the moral freedom and responsibility of man on the other hand.

We have firmly refused to diminish the power and sovereignty of God or to grant that man is in any way able to destroy the counsel of God. To do this would deal the death-blow to our Reformed doctrine. God is and remains absolutely sovereign. His counsel has never been destroyed, nor changed, nor led aside by any deed of men or devils. All of history, evil included, is an unfolding of the counsel of the Almighty.

On the other hand, we have just as emphatically maintained the responsibility of man. The accusation of determinism, sometimes brought against the Reformed confessions, we have cast far from us. Man is a creature who acts freely. What he does, he does consciously and willingly. He is and remains free in the formal sense.

Although these two lines of God's counsel and man's moral freedom and responsibility might run parallel insofar as our eye can see, and as McCosh expresses it in his *The Divine Government*,[15] we will still hold fast to both of these truths on the basis of scripture without compromise or surrender. It may be freely granted that we are dealing with a mystery here. The question how God maintains his irresistible counsel over against his moral creatures; how it is possible for God to cooperate with these moral-rational beings so that his counsel is worked out and their responsibility still maintained, may ultimately put us in a dilemma. But this does not mean that we simply abandon one of the two horns of the dilemma and delude ourselves into believing that we have the truth in only one of the horns. We must emphatically hold fast to both.[16]

We expressed on the floor of classis that we do not understand Schans' sixth point concerning God's government. No one attempted to enlighten us. We do not understand what Schans is driving at or what his objection is. According to Schans, do we too frequently coordinate the kingdom of darkness with the kingdom of light? Are both presented as being God's institutions? Thus he continues on page 13 of his overture. All this goes far beyond our capacity to understand. We gladly explain that we have not in any way coordinated the kingdom of darkness with the kingdom of light but have always antithetically set them over against one another. We would be willing to set forth an

---

15 McCosh, *The Method of Divine Government, Physical and Moral.*—Ed.
16 Hoeksema, *Banner* (June 17, 1920); Danhof and Hoeksema, *Not Anabaptist but Reformed*, 28.

explanation regarding all Schans' objections, but we also declare that we do not understand from where in our writings Schans derives such nonsense. He fails to explain himself on this point.

Finally, I have an observation and a request. If the synod decides to treat this protest, which has never been discussed with me or with my consistory and which the classis also refused to discuss but simply forwarded, I request of synod that Schans be held responsible for his protest and that he be required to debate me on the floor of synod regarding all the points of his protest.

Beseeching the leading of the Holy Spirit for the delegates of the synod in all the matters that may be brought before you, I remain respectfully,

Your brother in Christ,
H. Hoeksema

CHAPTER 4

PLANS FOR THE PUBLICATION
OF A MONTHLY PERIODICAL

Brothers, people are finding fault with you down to the soles of your shoes!" So our friends recently cautioned us. Yes indeed, against that nothing can be said.

You remember that we mentioned some time ago our future plan to publish a monthly magazine and that we were offered support for that effort by the Reformed Free Publishing Association. You ask, what evil could possibly be seen in that? Yes, the proverb is true: people judge others by themselves. It has happened once or twice before—to which we have alluded—that "a notable document" in the wrong hands turned out all right. "In order to cultivate a more faithful, healthy, biblical worldview in our churches," people think they are justified to work secretly through "a number of previously chosen pastors and members of our church," with the purpose "of coming to a collaborative protest against the unjust manner in which Janssen was attacked, and the way the entire matter has been handled since the synod of 1920, and also to protest against the synod of 1922 regarding its action of deposing the professor from office."[17] People spoke boldly in that connection of an unjust judgment and an unecclesiastical and unfair treatment; notwithstanding, the synod almost unanimously condemned the instruction of Janssen.

This entire movement to recruit protestants has correctly been branded a very serious danger to the unity of our church. Since this

---

17 Quoted here are supporters of Janssen, defending evil tactics on behalf of his defense. However, the same people criticized Danhof and Hoeksema for planning a magazine to promote the Reformed faith against common grace.—Ed.

secret rousing of the spirits became public, the wind has apparently lain down. The movement evidently could not endure exposure to the light of justice.

But what is this! The papers announce that a powerful organization of brothers will "offer support by all lawful means to the pastors Hoeksema and Danhof, who are treated discourteously by the ecclesiastical press, in their struggle for the truth."[18] Well, well, is that not precisely the same thing as the secret movement to recruit protestants against the synodical decision in the case of Janssen, who was condemned a short time ago in the *Witness*?

Certainly there are many points of difference. That was a secret movement directed against an already-decreed judgment of the synod. On the contrary, we are dealing with an announcement of a society for the publication of a periodical.

Even so, the author of "Timely Topics" in his simpleness draws his bow.[19] He calls it "raising money to defend Hoeksema and Danhof." He states further:

The *Standard-Bulletin* brought us the startling news yesterday that an organization was being established to raise funds and to initiate propaganda for the defense of Rev. Hoeksema and Rev. Danhof. Their fearless testimony on behalf of fundamental Reformed truth has aroused formidable opposition within the Christian Reformed Church and has endangered the ecclesiastical position of the two men. So it is claimed.

The majority of us would no doubt like to believe that this movement does not meet the approval of Hoeksema and Danhof. I know that the former, and possibly the latter, after the last synod earnestly denounced a similar movement to wage propaganda for a former professor of our seminary. To be

---

18 No source was given in the original. This is a general reference to what was evidently being said in the various periodicals circulating in the Christian Reformed Church about the creation of the *Standard Bearer*.—Ed.

19 "Timely Topics" was evidently a column in one of the Christian Reformed periodicals of the day. The author was the Christian Reformed minister E. Tanis, who was active in the promotion of the theory of common grace and aggressive in opposition to Danhof and Hoeksema.—Ed.

consistent, the brethren are compelled to take the same stand toward this latest agitation.

It is certainly an unscriptural and un-Reformed method. When other brethren question the soundness of our views, we should not recourse to propaganda but should appeal to the established church courts—classes and synod. This movement is revolutionary and can result in nothing but evil for the agitators and for those against whom the agitation is launched. Let us hope that Hoeksema and Danhof will have the courage to nip this thing in the bud. Such an attitude will command the respect of the whole church.

The movement, moreover, is premature. The synod has not yet taken a position in respect to the teachings of the two brethren. The followers of these brethren ought to have enough confidence in the strength of their position and in the justice of synod to abide [wait for] the synodical meeting.[20]

We have heard that men authorized to speak have attempted to inform Rev. Tanis, but up to this time have been unable to find him at home. Consequently, he can count on a visit in the very near future. He should take this as notification that they will be speaking to him. It will be made exceedingly plain to him that one cannot immediately act on first impressions. At the same time his attention will be emphatically directed to the publications, year after year, of several periodicals in our circles, for instance, *Religion and Culture* and the *Witness*.

Should *we* be the only ones who do not have the right to write and to publish a brochure, a book, or a monthly magazine? Since when?

Without waiting for an answer from Tanis, at this time we joyfully announce that sufficient support has been guaranteed for us to proceed with the publication of a periodical with relative freedom and appropriate speed. This periodical will be dedicated to the development of the truths of scripture according to the present circumstances of our people in this country, in a manner fitting for the proper development of interested and sympathetic members of the Reformed churches. All

---

20 No reference was given in the original.—Ed.

the particulars concerning the time and manner of the appearance of the magazine have not yet been worked out, but we will inform you in the near future of developments.

The support of which we have often spoken is not limited to merely the moral and financial aspects of this endeavor. More active participation has been promised. Not everything will be written by two or three individuals. We will not address in our writing only a few or only one group, nor will we limit ourselves only to the subject of common grace.

The latter is absolutely not our purpose. On the contrary, it is our purpose to instruct the Reformed child of God and to enable him to live a full, deep, all-encompassing Christian life for his Lord in every relationship, in every area, and in every sphere of life. We are afraid of dividing life, which is organically interrelated, into separate realms, as not only happens on the basis of common grace, but also must happen by virtue of a pressing necessity if one would be logically consistent. Therefore, in the past we have indicated the danger contained in that doctrine for God's people, and we will continue to do so in the future.

God's word demands the whole man for Christ. The believer does not have a twofold task in this life: a special task as a Christian and a general cultural task in fellowship with all men as human beings. This simply would be impossible. Man, also regenerated man, is one organic whole; he cannot live in one area of life out of this principle and in another area of life from a different principle. If one proposes the theoretical possibility of this, the result will necessarily be deception of oneself and others. According to our sincere conviction the doctrine of common grace must lead theoretically and practically to world conformity. Therefore, we have denounced the principle of this theory.

It is our firm conviction that this applies as well to what Hepp says about the principle of the theatrical play *Saul and David* by Querido, recently performed among our people in the Netherlands:

> If the foundational principle of this play would permeate and influence our whole life, our Reformed people would become spiritual weaklings, our Free University would die of shame, the Anti-revolutionary party would be struck with paralysis,

"Patrimonium" and with it all social action would be transferred to unbelievers, and our Netherlandic Calvinism would belong to the past; it would cease to exist. [21]

We are not implying that this principle has effectively influenced our people's lives.[22] We maintain that our people as a whole, with some exceptions, have never lived consciously and deliberately out of that principle. Even though Hepp considers himself justified to use such language to oppose Dr. Prof. F. J. J. Buitendijk—who "enjoyed" the production of that play and in the historical context of Hepp's critique recently resigned from the editorial staff of De Reformatie—we use this language specifically to oppose all who want to see us deposed from office because of our position on common grace. We will continue to underscore this threatening danger, come what may.

Yet that [the danger of world conformity promoted by the theory of common grace] is not the only danger against which we warn, but also an integral part of our task is to identify all dangers for the Reformed believer. We will not limit ourselves to just one area of concern or to the discussion of sporadic phenomena in our identification of erroneous theories and practices, but we will trace as far as possible the principles from which they sprout. We will also attempt to develop positively the themes of God's word along established lines concerning related aspects of human life. For example, in our evaluation of the ideas of theatrical art, we will attempt to give our very best in connection with the faculties of imagination in man as God's image bearer. In connection therewith we will take into consideration what others have said about theatrical art.

Yet we will not merely subordinate ourselves to the judgment of "the wisdom of Greece." But in our judgment a serious effort should be made in our circles to remove from our necks the oppressive yoke of the old heathen philosophers and artists, which harms us in our

21 Valentijn Hepp, De Reformatie (April 25, 1924).
22 The authors do not identify the "principle" of which they speak. In light of the context, this "principle" must be that of world conformity on the part of Reformed Christians—the very error that Danhof and Hoeksema were opposing in their struggle against the theory of common grace.—Ed.

view and evaluation of the productions of the sciences and the arts, especially in connection with our religious convictions and fundamental principles of moral life, as well as for educational reasons. We must stand in the freedom with which Christ has made us free. For too long the heathen have ruled over the inheritance of the Lord.

We Christians let ourselves be influenced far too often through theories that are nothing but the laws of men, and we neglect to penetrate into all the fullness that we have in our head, Christ Jesus. Not uncommonly we are ensnared anew by the yoke of bondage. We are deceived especially in the area of middle and higher education by vain philosophy and the fanciful mirroring of the mind of the flesh, and perhaps even more deceptively influenced by the norms: rules and prescriptions of the wisdom of this world regarding education and culture; the enjoyment and evaluation of the beautiful, the good, the true; and the promotion of justice, mercy, love, and virtue.

Informed people outside of our circles say,

> The ancient Athenians were history's best example of a nation that over-educated the intellect at the expense of the heart. No society since time began produced greater men than the Athens of Themistocles, Pericles, and Demosthenes; yet few civilized communities have produced less worthy men. Except for Socrates and a mere handful of others, the great figures of Greek history combined an almost unbelievable intellectual dishonesty and moral indifference with the most brilliant accomplishments to which the human mind has yet soared. What there was of Greek religion was totally devoid of a moral phase. That deficiency was supplied only in a very limited degree by Greek philosophy. Like a beacon light, their example should warn Christian America against the danger of permitting the schools to continue a course of instruction that omits a phase of education that is of vital importance to the citizens of a self-governed country.[23]

On the contrary, in our circles one frequently hears talk of the "divine" Plato, and people dare to equate the life of Socrates with

---

23 No reference was given in the original.—Ed.

Christ's life. Besides, for almost every principle of science and art, people calmly refer to the old heathen world of Greece and Rome. In our judgment, this may not happen. As Bible believers we must learn to view and evaluate the old heathen world and the present world of heathendom and nominal Christendom all around us in the light of and according to the measure of God's word. To that end we intend to labor.

We want to let scripture speak. We must bind ourselves to it through the Holy Spirit. Philosophical reasoning, no matter how apparently neutral and learned it may be, is not fit to be preferred over scripture. We are called to subordinate heart and mind to scripture's judgment. God's word must instruct us regarding God, ourselves, and the world of the creature around us. Apart from the Bible we possess no fountain from which we can draw knowledge. Neither does nature, next to or independent of holy scripture, give us any essential knowledge of God, as he would have us know him and as he must be known. Article 2 of the Belgic Confession does not teach this either. To this fact we hope to point in the future.

The revelation in God's word is not merely more detailed, but also is a further and higher revelation than that in creation. Before the fall, therefore, revelation was necessary and was given to man. Man had to know God's thought, will, and law not only in and from the creation, but he also had to know them in relation to creation. How could he have behaved in any other way than from the principle of free, earnest love toward God as prophet, priest, and king? Man as God's image bearer, as God's vice-regent over all creation, and as God's friend and covenantal family member must know God's will, must know everything God thought to do according to his sovereign counsel with and regarding his creatures as well as through them. God's friend must know what his Friend did.

We hope in the future to dwell at length and expansively on this glorious covenantal idea. We must learn to know God from his revelation and utterances to man regarding himself and in opposition to the word of deception by the devil, the adversary of God. In this way we will walk the antithetical line. It must become so very clear to us from

God's revelation that God is God, as well as that God is one. We must never permit even for a moment any power, no matter who or what it may be, to place itself above, next to, or even under God, because in reality that power does not exist.

Our reasoning may be directed only toward actually existing, divine reality. In our presentation and reasoning we must initiate the process with mind and will as God's image bearers and as his covenantal people. In a most particular manner this applies to the antithesis that God has placed between good and evil. We must assimilate this antithesis into our consciousness and desire to hold it in love and deny and hate Satan's opposing position. In so doing we are actively of the party of the living God; we are followers of God as dear children.

If we proceed on this antithetical basis, we will not adopt the so-called scientific viewpoint of creation and scripture and many considerations regarding human factors, general historical authorities, heathen religions, monumental revelations, and the like. But we will hold to a Bible-believing conception of God's revelation. Following the antithetical line, we take our stand on a different position, proceed from a different principle, and follow an entirely different line of commitment. Our questions will be directed to God. We seek in a measure to understand how all things in creation and re-creation are of, through, and unto God. All things are for his sake, and they cause us to know God and lead us to God. Then in some measure we will sense that all creatures must be an organic unity, that there must be a close connection between creation and re-creation and between this earthly dispensation and the eternal future, and that Christ from the foundation of the world, in his fellowship with his believing people, is pictured in the symbolism of earthly things: light, sun, morning star, lion, grain of wheat, vine, good shepherd, door of the sheepfold, water, food, glory, joy, and humanity—the man, prophet, priest, king, and the first Adam.

Concerning these and similar matters we wish to write. In close connection, we will treat what must be derived from this regarding man's place in creation, the kingship of man and of Adam, and man's dominion and governance before and after the fall. We will also let the

light of God's word fall on article 36 of the Belgic Confession. Therefore, all sorts of questions relating to the home, society, and civic life
will be treated. We will seek to shed light on problems and to resolve
them according to the demand of God's revelation and the require-
ments of the life of God's people.

We will take the position of scripture to accomplish that. Let there
be no misunderstanding. We do not mean that we will proceed merely
from the thought that the Bible is the authoritative word of God. No,
we will try to view things from the vantage point of the biblical writers. We will not go to Babel to ask concerning the origin of scripture,
and we will not knock at the door of the wise of Athens for light and
instruction regarding the revelation of our God. We will set ourselves
next to Moses in the wilderness and next to John on the isle of Patmos.
From their mouths we want to learn what God says of himself, of his
counsel and plan for the creation, man, the covenant, Satan, temptation, the fall of man, the placing of enmity, the Mediator, the organic
development of things, the two seeds, the battle of the ages, the people
of God in opposition to the kingdom of man, the antichrist, Gog and
Magog and their immoral company, the final catastrophe, the renewing of all things, and the eternal dispensation.

We will not attempt to give a philosophical view of all world
events, but we will try in some measure to depict the line of the history
of revelation. In order to go forth with confidence in the right way, we
must know what God is doing and consequently what is happening,
what is fermenting and working in the congregation and in the unbelieving world as a reaction to the Spirit's working. We must carefully
try to differentiate between many sounds and colors. Briefly stated, we
must understand the speech of God.

The Bible must teach us. In it God must speak to us. Our world-
view and conception of life must be in harmony with its testimony. The
Bible must teach us about sin and grace, cursing and blessing, reprobation and election, and destruction and blessedness. Scripture's view
of nature must be ours. Our seeing and knowing must be formed in its
prophetic light. Apart from scripture we know nothing with certainty.
In God's word we have the standard for judgment and evaluation of

all things and all conduct. Only scripture knows what is good and what is evil. It judges concerning the hidden life of our hearts and teaches us to know the real life of the nations of the world. Without scripture we would walk amid riddles. But in its light we see the light. Because of its illumination we need not limit our judgment concerning man to merely his external activity, but we can also know the deeper causes and motivations of his heart.

Therefore, we must pay very careful attention to scripture's speech, also when it speaks to us in types and symbols, in sounds and colors, in forms and numbers. Its measures and weights and quantities and calculations purpose to instruct us. Its signs and wonders, dreams, visions, portrayals, and symbols display the work of the God of the covenant, cause us to know his will, and point out to us the way. By faith in God's word we understand the origin of things and their further existence after death, as well as their calling and ordained end. The Bible causes us to know man, the significance of the fall, and man's restoration in Christ.

In the Bible we not only listen to the cry of rebellion and of those suffocating in destruction, but we also hear the cry of the new life and of eternal joy and amazement. In this way we learn from the Bible to know the purpose of the earthly paradise, of the ark of salvation, of the temple of shadows, of the spiritual dwelling place of the Lord, and of God's eternal tabernacle. In its light we see the line of demarcation between holy and profane, clean and unclean, the inheritance of the Lord and the fellowship of the children of disobedience. The contrasts of scripture are also sound. Cain and Abel, Enoch and Lamech, Noah and his contemporaries, Abraham and the king of Sodom, Jacob and Esau, Israel and the sevenfold world kingdom ["seven heads" in Rev. 13:1] of Egypt-Babylon-Rome, the church and anti-Christendom, and the heathen powers of Gog and Magog must all be viewed in the light of scripture. Then we understand their relationships.

Our ears must be cupped to hear the lament and jubilation of the children of men on the earth, even as scripture gives us to hear them. It must cause us to see the identifying difference between the suffering of the saints and that of impenitent sinners. The Bible must also teach us to distinguish between the mark and battle insignia of the King of kings on the foreheads of God's children and the sign of the beast on the right hand of merchants and followers of the prince of darkness. This must be taught us in our present time and regarding our practical walk of life. Only then do we walk safely.

Our purpose is to walk in the light of scripture. Unto that end we want to labor by means of a magazine. We will gladly apply the lines of Reformed thought to the points enumerated above, upon which in our judgment we [ministers and theologians in the Christian Reformed Church, among whom Danhof and Hoeksema were included] do not now shine the full light of God's word. People should not take amiss this latter statement. It is our firm conviction that there are such points. In addition, we firmly believe that as the day of the Lord and the hour of persecution for God's people draw closer, the knowledge of God's word will be multiplied and there will be light, so that we will not have to stumble and fall.

All of the points enumerated here will not be addressed. That is unnecessary. We hope from time to time to place them with great care on the foreground. Nevertheless, we point to one thing now, namely, that in life's outward manifestation man may not be divided into two, or that he could cease to use everything that stands at his service and through that to make his influence felt; or that he can live out of two principles—regeneration and general grace in fellowship with all men.[24] That is impossible! Believers and unbelievers are of one root in their natural existence in Adam, but spiritually they are two and therefore cannot walk together or work together from their separate spiritual, ethical source of life. Therefore, we want to work zealously for a life lived out of the root of regeneration, in all areas of life, in every relationship, at every opportunity, and by using every means at our service: gifts, faculties, positions, institutions, and influences. We do not tolerate any halfheartedness or practical dualism in the life of God's child.

---

24 Here Danhof and Hoeksema warn against two distinct errors. One is world-flight—not using all things earthly that serve humans. The other is trying to live from two different principles—special, saving grace in worship and common grace in everyday, earthly life.—Ed.

This is the essential difference between us and the men of the *Witness*, as well as the reason for our independent action. We believe there is no essential basis for cooperation of believers and unbelievers in a good sense, not in any common grace worked in the heart of the sinner by a wonder of God immediately after the fall, nor in something the sinner retained after the fall. The men of the *Witness*, however, apparently prefer not to express an opinion. In light of their unwillingness, we find it necessary to withdraw as coworkers and to leave the consortium.

Understand what we say. No one forced us to do this. No one has any objection to working jointly, our opinion is that to work together properly there must be unity of conviction. Nor do we want attributed to others an opinion that only *we* have. If we must suffer for our opinions, as appears to be the case, we want to bear that suffering and not cause it to be the lot of others. We eagerly want to develop further our concepts, on account of their extreme importance for the practical life of God's people in this world. Although our salvation does not depend on it in a narrow sense, yet our attitude toward the world is determined in large measure by it.

In addition, the circumstances of the Janssen case make it necessary for us to explain our position in more detail. We cannot continue to take a halfway stance, and neither can others. We also understand very well that the friends of Janssen will not sit still either. The synodical decision had to be repealed. In order to achieve that, the first attack had to be directed toward us. That was anticipated, as we indicated. So it happened. Friend and foe attacked us with weapons borrowed from Arminianism. That was unfair. For the time being, however, we must be satisfied with such treatment. In our public witness we must labor defensively to a certain degree.

We hope this will change after synod meets. Insofar as it is in our power, we will labor positively and constructively. We will not break off from the church unless it becomes absolutely necessary. Full emphasis will be laid on what is essential. We will not purposely be silent about the chief issues. We intend to cause the authoritative grip of God's word to be felt all along the line of human activity. Conflict therefore cannot be excluded anywhere.

We intend to place the spiritual, moral antithesis on the foreground. We will do this especially in certain areas where, in our judgment, false teachings and viewpoints rule in our fellowship and erroneous practices have infiltrated. We will be engaged in this as well when such concepts and viewpoints to one degree or another have a Reformed character. We will address various related points of the Belgic Confession, such as article 36, and synodical utterances. We will write in such a way that we give no occasion for lawful criticism of our writings.

We hope and pray that people will not attack us on points concerning which we all are in complete agreement, as they have done in the most recent past. But if they are intent on doing that, we will still go our own way. We will do this more specifically if the principles Janssen employed in his instruction are sooner or later surreptitiously reintroduced and officially sanctioned. Our protest continually opposes that.

Finally, let it be said that amid the changing circumstances, we hope to know the times and the seasons, and we will from now on direct our attention chiefly to those who in principle understand us and want to fight this fight with us in the strength of the Lord. We will enter into the closest possible fellowship with them for our mutual edification in faith, hope, and love. For their encouragement and comfort, we quote the words recently addressed to us by a friend.

> It is good, from time to time,
> To sharpen one another,
> And with single-minded diligence
> To cast away the stones
> That obstruct our way,
> To stride forth with courage.
> Such unites God's children
> Of every tongue and time.

> We fight for God's truth and God's justice.
> Ours is the crown of honor laid away,
> Which God will give to us in grace,
> Not only to us, but also to a great number

Who have, with us, in this hostile world
Laid hold on God's inerrant word.
The Lord preserves the soul of him who loves him,
But he destroys those whom he deems ungodly.

CALVIN, BERKHOF, AND H. J. KUIPER

A Comparison

HERMAN HOEKSEMA

Introduction to *Calvin, Berkhof, and H. J. Kuiper*

T
he purpose and value of the booklet *Calvin, Berkhof, and H. J. Kuiper* are that it demonstrates from one of John Calvin's prominent books—*Calvin's Calvinism*—that the first point of common grace of the Christian Reformed Church, with specific reference to a well-meant offer of salvation, not only has no backing in Calvin, but also is condemned by the reformer as Pelagianism.

The title of the booklet mentions Louis Berkhof and H. J. Kuiper because those two leading Christian Reformed theologians were noisily enlisting the Geneva reformer in support of universal grace in the preaching of the gospel. They were publicly charging that Hoeksema's rejection of a well-meant offer was a fundamental departure from Calvin and Calvinism. Berkhof was also regarded as the main author of the three points of common grace adopted by the Christian Reformed synod of 1924.

The booklet addresses what is either a deliberate falsehood or an inexcusable misconception on the part of the proponents of the well-meant offer, to the present day: with their rejection of the well-meant offer, the Protestant Reformed Churches have become hyper-Calvinists—outside the tradition that comes down from the theology of John Calvin. Those who are guilty of the lie or misconception, as the case may be—God judges!—have never read *Calvin's Calvinism*. This is the work of Calvin that Hoeksema appeals to in the booklet. If the Reformed proponents of a well-meant offer have read the book, they are careful not to refer to it in their polemics.

Yet once more, in the booklet Hoeksema makes plain that the issue in the controversy over the well-meant offer is not whether God unfeignedly calls all who hear the gospel, reprobate and elect alike, to believe in Jesus Christ, with the external call of the gospel. He does. But the issue is the doctrine of the Christian Reformed Church—and of Berkhof and Kuiper—that the external call is grace to the reprobate, that is, the teaching that God has an attitude of love toward the reprobate ungodly, sincerely desires their salvation, and in this (obviously saving) grace offers them salvation.

Hoeksema charged that this doctrine is sheer Arminianism and Pelagianism. It denies predestination. Although Hoeksema never used the terminology, the well-meant offer is (playing off the charge of *hyper*-Calvinism) *hypo*-Calvinism, that is, literally, below Calvinism, failing to come up to the standard of Calvinism; in fact, a fundamental deviation from Calvinism.

In writing of Berkhof, Hoeksema could not refrain from sounding a personal note. To the end of his life, Hoeksema felt the wound of the turning on him by the Christian Reformed theologian. Berkhof was his respected professor in seminary. Berkhof officiated at Hoeksema's wedding. Prior to 1924 Berkhof had freely spoken to Hoeksema of the need to address the spread of Arminian theology in the Christian Reformed Church. When the efforts of Berkhof and the three other professors at the Christian Reformed seminary to condemn the higher critical views of Ralph Janssen were foundering, it was Hoeksema who came to the rescue, thus making himself the object of hatred on the part of Janssen's many and powerful defenders in the Christian Reformed ministry.

Addressing Berkhof, Hoeksema wrote, "For the same teachings contained in *Calvin's Calvinism* you have persecuted Danhof and myself, and you did not rest until we were expelled from the communion of your church. At the time you became friends even of your enemies to unite with them in expelling those who were your friends and brethren in the faith. You are responsible before God, before whose judgment seat we will have to appear together."

But those hurtful personal dealings with a former student, friend, and colleague were not the worst. "The worst [was that] you assumed leadership in the church to introduce the Arminian three points, the first of which is so plainly condemned by the teachings of John Calvin.

A large part of the church, already strongly inclined to turn into Arminian paths, as you well know, has followed you. For their following and their further deviation from the truth of the word of God you are responsible. So serious is this matter."

The booklet *Calvin, Berkhof, and H. J. Kuiper* originally was a series of articles in the *Standard Bearer*. Hoeksema began the series in volume 6, number 1 (October 1, 1929): 24. He concluded the series in volume 6, number 7 (January 1, 1930): 164–68.

At the end of the pamphlet, as at the conclusion of the series in the *Standard Bearer*, Hoeksema promised that he would make "other remarks" concerning Calvin's powerful treatises on predestination and providence in his book, *Calvin's Calvinism*. Hoeksema fulfilled that promise in subsequent issues of volume 6 of the *Standard Bearer*. Those other remarks were his response to the charge by his Christian Reformed critics that he was guilty of using "strong language" in his exposition of Reformed doctrine. In a series of articles titled "Calvin and Strong Expressions," Hoeksema demonstrated not only that Calvin used strong expressions in defending the truth of the sovereignty of God, but also that Calvin used the very same strong expressions for which his Christian Reformed adversaries condemned Hoeksema.

—David J. Engelsma

PREFACE

The content of the pamphlet hereby offered to the public is not personal, as the title might suggest. But the purpose of the pamphlet is to set forth the Reformed view of the truth, as defended by John Calvin, in opposition to certain Arminian tendencies and tenets that the Christian Reformed Church officially adopted and that Prof. Louis Berkhof and Rev. H. J. Kuiper now zealously defend.

From the outset we claimed that in officially adopting the first point of common grace (the doctrine compared in this pamphlet), the Christian Reformed Church departed not only from fundamental and confessional Reformed theology, but also from the historical Reformed line. The notion may always have been afloat in Reformed circles that God is gracious in the preaching of the gospel, conceived as a general and well-meant offer of salvation, to all who hear it. The truth is that this and similar ideas are not direct fruit of Reformed thinking but have been imported from the camp of the Pelagian and Arminian enemy. Because we refused to subscribe to these imported errors we were expelled from the ministry and fellowship of the Christian Reformed Church.

To testify against this doctrinal error and unrighteous deposition from our office is our solemn duty before God and an obligation of true love to the church and the brethren in whose midst we labored in the past. The republication of *Calvin's Calvinism* by the Sovereign Grace Union offered a new means to this purpose, and gladly I made use of it by drawing a comparison between Calvin's teaching and that of the first point as defended and explained by Berkhof and Kuiper.

Originally this comparison appeared in a series of articles in the *Standard Bearer.* I am grateful to the seminary students through whose efforts I am now able to offer to the reading public the same material in pamphlet form.

May our covenantal God use this testimony as a humble means for the maintenance and furtherance of his cause in the world.

—Herman Hoeksema, 1930

The reader may know that on my recent trip to Europe, I came into contact with some brethren of the Sovereign Grace Union in London, England, particularly with Rev. Henry Atherton, the general secretary of that union, and his people of Grove Chapel. I had the privilege of spending a Sabbath in their midst and of ministering the word of God to them in two worship services. It is not my purpose to write about this Union. Let me say, however, that the leaders of the Christian Reformed Church cannot agree with the principles of this Union, especially with those of Atherton and his church. They are strict Calvinists who emphasize the very truths the Christian Reformed Church denied in its declarations of the synod of Kalamazoo in 1924.

To mention only one important matter, Atherton and his people emphatically deny that the preaching of the gospel is a well-meant offer of salvation on the part of God to all who outwardly hear the preaching. Time and again Atherton emphasized to me that grace is never an offer and the preaching of the gospel cannot be God's offer of salvation to all. They believe in predestination, and they preach it without reservations. If Atherton were a minister in the Christian Reformed Church, it would cast him out as it did me. I consider it best for everyone concerned that there is clear understanding of this matter, for such is the simple truth.

Although I cannot write a lengthy review of it at this time, I urge the reader to secure the recent publication of the Sovereign Grace Union entitled *Calvin's Calvinism*. This is a work written by John Calvin in his mature years, in which he deals particularly with the subject of predestination. The book was first published in 1552, was translated into

English for the first time in 1856, and was reprinted and published by the Sovereign Grace Union.[1]

As a work of his later years devoted to the subject of predestination, the book offers a fuller, clearer, and riper view of Calvin on this subject than his *Institutes*. The Christian Reformed Church cannot agree with what he wrote in this book. The leaders of that church departed far from Calvin and the Calvinist faith.

I was surprised to hear that Berkhof wrote a very favorable review of the book. How can Berkhof harmonize the following quotation from Calvin with the first point of 1924 and everything Berkhof wrote to defend the view that the gospel is an offer of salvation, even to those who are lost?

> Pighius will confess that there is need of illumination to bring unto Christ those who were adversaries to God; at the same time he holds fast the fiction that grace is offered equally to all, but that it is ultimately rendered effectual by the will of man, just as each one is willing to receive it.[2]

How do Berkhof and those who agree with him judge the following doctrine of Calvin?

> With reference to his hardening men's hearts, that is a different way of God's working...because God does not govern the reprobate by his regenerating Spirit. He *gives them over to the devil and leaves them to be the devil's slaves,* and he so overrules their depraved wills by his secret judgment and counsel that they can do nothing but what he has decreed.[3]

---

1 John Calvin, *Calvin's Calvinism: The Eternal Predestination of God [and] The Secret Providence of God,* trans. Henry Cole (London: Sovereign Grace Union, 1927). The Reformed Free Publishing Association has revised and reprinted the Sovereign Grace Union's edition as *Calvin's Calvinism: God's Eternal Predestination and Secret Providence together with* A Brief Reply *and* Reply to the Slanderous Reports, ed. Russell J. Dykstra, 2nd ed. (Jenison, MI: Reformed Free Publishing Association, 2009). All references to *Calvin's Calvinism* are to the second edition.

2 Ibid., 40.

3 Ibid., 283–84. The emphasis is Hoeksema's.—Ed.

Notwithstanding all your vain talk about it, the truth is that a "heart of flesh" [Ezek. 11:19] and a "new heart" [Ezek. 36:26] *are not promised to all men promiscuously,* but to the elect peculiarly, in order that they might walk in the commandments of God.[4]

Surely the synod of 1924 would have discovered these passages in Calvin's work, and having found that Calvin is "Reformed, albeit with a tendency to be one-sided,"[5] it would have cast him out of the Christian Reformed Church.

I will review these matters when time allows. It is my purpose only to recommend that our people secure and read this book. The Sovereign Grace Union did a good work when they reprinted it.

---

4   Ibid., 280–81. The emphasis is Hoeksema's.—Ed.
5   *1924 Acts of Synod of the Christian Reformed Church Held from 8 June to 15 July, 1924, in Kalamazoo, MI,* trans. Henry De Mots (Grand Rapids, MI: Archives of the Christian Reformed Church), 147. The phrase in quotation marks, which Hoeksema proposes as the judgment of the Christian Reformed synod of 1924 on John Calvin, was the judgment of that synod on Danhof and Hoeksema by official decision.—Ed.

CHAPTER I

THE "INCIVILITY"
OF THE LOVE OF THE TRUTH

do not intend to compare the three men whose names appear in the title of this work. But my purpose is to make a comparative study of their views, doctrines, and convictions as clearly expressed in their writings.

I will not compare their teachings from every viewpoint and regarding every detail. It is particularly their attitudes toward the free offer of salvation in connection with the doctrine of predestination and sovereign grace that I expect to investigate. I will not compare the views of each man individually, for that would lead us nowhere. I have a definite purpose. I would like an answer to a definite question that concerns us all—Calvin, Kuiper, Berkhof, the undersigned, and all our readers and hundreds more.

That particular question is, do Berkhof and Kuiper in everything they have publicly taught in recent years follow John Calvin's conception of a certain free offer of salvation to all men? If they do, I do not hesitate to admit that I do not. If Calvin holds to the general and free offer of salvation to all men promiscuously in the sense in which Berkhof and Kuiper do, I must depart from Calvin.[6] This is *my* interest in the question I propose to answer.

---

6   Hoeksema does not here admit that Calvin may have taught a well-meant offer of salvation as did the Christian Reformed Church in 1924. It is the burden of this booklet to demonstrate that Calvin rejected a well-meant offer to all humans. But Hoeksema declares—and it is worthy to note that he does so—that *if* Calvin taught the well-meant offer, Hoeksema takes issue with Calvin. Hoeksema was no blind follower of men, not even of great, godly men. But Hoeksema will show from *Calvin's Calvinism* that Calvin rejected the heresy that God is gracious to all who hear the gospel, desiring to save them all, and in this desire making to all an ineffectual offer.—Ed.

However, if Berkhof and Kuiper in their writings on this subject depart from Calvin, they should cease appealing to him and his views as if they agreed with him, and they ought not to recommend his works, particularly *Calvin's Calvinism*. They ought frankly to admit that they condemn Calvin on this point, as they did and do me. This is *their* interest in the matter.

If it is not true that John Calvin held to a gracious and general offer of salvation on the part of God to all men, Berkhof and Kuiper ought not to present him as if he did. His name ought to be cleared from the indictment of teaching any such Pelagian errors. That is *Calvin's* interest in the matter. During this investigation the atmosphere regarding certain matters will probably be cleared, the truth will shine more clearly and brightly, and we will all be edified. That is the interest of *all our readers* in the matter and of many more who ought to be our readers.

So I will compare Berkhof and Kuiper with Calvin.

What is the occasion for this comparison? The first is the publication of *Calvin's Calvinism*, which sets forth Calvin's views on predestination, related doctrines, and the secret providence of God. It is the work of Calvin's mature years, which in my estimation adds to the value of the book.

The second is a particular paragraph in Berkhof's review of this work.

These treatises are indeed valuable productions of the great reformer. It is true that sometimes while reading them we feel that [Calvin] is hardly civil to his opponents. He certainly does not speak of them in terms of endearment. But in this respect his polemics simply reflect the spirit of the age. The one thing that stands out very clearly in these treatises is that Calvin is eminently scriptural in his representations. He bases his teachings on the word of God, and is always ready to apply to them the touchstone of scripture. Moreover, in the deep things of God he has no desire to go beyond the plain teachings of the Bible and rebukes those who attempt it. He is willing to go as far as the word of God does, but not farther, and does not hesitate to admit that the doctrines of predestination and divine providence raise problems that he cannot solve. Time and again he indignantly repudiates the idea that in teaching the doctrine of predestination he makes God the author of sin and renders the free offer of salvation impossible. He has no patience with those who want preachers to be silent regarding these great doctrines for fear they might be injurious to some. At the same time he desires that these doctrines be taught with care and discretion.[7]

Third, both Berkhof and Kuiper are great defenders of the three points. If Berkhof is not the father of them, he certainly is one of their foster fathers, and he published a pamphlet in their defense. Kuiper preached and published three sermons on these points, in which he made many statements that are still fresh in my mind because of their glowing enthusiasm for the doctrine that God freely offers salvation to all men and earnestly desires their salvation. Also these statements should be compared with the teachings of John Calvin on this subject.

I will start with the paragraph quoted from Berkhof's book review and call special attention to the part that speaks of Calvin's view of the free offer of salvation and of his timidity to enter into the deep things of God. We want to know exactly Calvin's view on these matters and whether or not Berkhof rightly interprets Calvin.

Before entering into this, I must speak of other matters that impressed me when I read Berkhof's brief appraisal of Calvin's book. Berkhof makes statements concerning Calvin's treatment of his opponents. "[Calvin] is hardly civil to his opponents. He certainly does not speak of them in terms of endearment." The professor attributes this feature of Calvin's treatises to "the spirit of the age." It was the custom of the time to treat opponents in that fashion.

Now it may be admitted that Calvin handles his opponents without the gloves of a superficial civilization. He thoroughly enters into their reasoning and enervates their every argument. In doing so he does not spare them and is little careful what he calls them. We would

---

7   Louis Berkhof, *Banner* (July 26, 1929).

probably speak of our "honorable opponent" and write with utmost respect, although we do not mean a word of it; we do not think our opponent is honorable at all, and we have no respect for him whatsoever. Calvin surely does not write that way; he calls a spade a spade. Some very interesting illustrations can be quoted from his work to substantiate this statement.

> Since the trouble that this vain mortal [Servetus] endeavored to cause us reaches unto you also, it is just that you should partake of the blessed fruit that God brings out of it.[8]

> Yet, that the object of this impure and abandoned one [Servetus] was not only to blot out all knowledge of God's election from the minds of men, but also to overturn his power is clearly manifest from those mad dreams of his that you possess in your public records.[9]

> Passing by this fellow in silence, the reason we enter into the battle with the other two—Albertus Pighius and Georgius the Sicilian—is, as we will explain, twofold. This ignorant pettifogger could bring forth nothing but what he obtained from these two sources, and so would make what was bad in them worse and worse. To contend with him, therefore, would have been a contest cold and profitless. Let our readers be content with one proof. With what cavils Pighius and Georgius would darken the first chapter of Paul to the Ephesians has been shown in its proper place. They indeed were ignorant and disgusting, but the folly of this worthless being is fouler still, for he blushed not to babble his nonsense in your Senate and venerable assembly; and not only this, but dared to defend with pertinacity what he had thus blattered in folly.[10]

> I propose now to enter into the sacred battle with Pighius and Georgius the Sicilian, a pair of unclean beasts, by no means

---

8 Calvin, *Calvin's Calvinism*, 9.
9 Ibid., 11.
10 Ibid., 12.

badly matched. Though I confess that in some things they differ, yet, in hatching enormities of error, in adulterating Scripture with wicked and reveling audacity, in a proud contempt of truth, in forward impudence, and in brazen loquacity, the most perfect likeness and sameness will be found to exist between them, except that Pighius, by inflating the muddy bombast of his magniloquence, carries himself with greater boast and pomp, while the other fellow borrows the boots by which he elevates himself from his invented revelation.[11]

Yet this ape of Euclid [Pighius] puffs himself off in the titles of all his chapters as a first-rate reasoner.[12]

Now as I proceed, it will be my object not so much to consider what Pighius says, nor in what order he says it, as to take care that this worthless fellow be prostrated and buried under the ruins of his own desperate impudence.[13]

If there had been one grain of the fear of God in Pighius, could he ever have dared thus insolently to call God to order?[14]

Pighius, indeed, can pour out the flood of his characteristic loquacity with all the ease in the world, and without one drop of sweat at all. But that his tongue might have full play, he seems always to take care to wet himself well with wine so that he may be able to blow forth at random, and without any check of shame whatever, those blasts of abuse that first fill his two swollen cheeks.[15]

Some small space must now be found for dealing with Georgius of Sicily. All things connected with this miserable creature are so insipid, vain, and disgusting that I feel ashamed to spend any time or labor in his refutation.[16]

---

11 Ibid., 16–17.
12 Ibid., 78.
13 Ibid., 82.
14 Ibid., 96.
15 Ibid., 121.
16 Ibid., 144.

It is no wonder that the more audacity this worthless fellow betrays in wresting the Scriptures, the more profuse he should be in heaping passages on passages to suit his purpose, seeing that he does not possess one particle of religion or of shame that might restrain his headlong impudence.[17]

I could easily multiply these illustrations from Calvin's work, but these will suffice.

Certainly these are not terms of endearment, and in our present conception of civilization, they are not civil terms. Calvin must be severely condemned if our present civilization is a true standard for treating the enemies of the truth of God. It means little when Berkhof attempts to excuse Calvin by saying that Calvin's uncivil expressions reflect the spirit of his time. Men were more brutal and uncivilized then than they are today, and Calvin was no exception. But I seriously question that as a proper explanation of the cutting words Calvin uses to address and describe his opponents. If there were even an element of truth in that, the fact is the polemics of others were not always characterized by the same lack of civilization the professor finds in Calvin's writings. Consider in the following passage the smooth language of one of Calvin's opponents, of one "calumniator," as Calvin calls him:

You are a man, John Calvin, now known throughout almost the whole world. Your doctrine has many favorers and supporters, but it has also many enemies and opponents. For myself, being one who earnestly wishes that there were but one doctrine, as there is but one truth, and who greatly desires to see all men agree, if it were possible, in that one doctrine, I have thought that you ought to be informed, in a friendly manner, of those things which are everywhere spoken against your doctrine; that if false, you might refute them and might have an opportunity of sending your refutation to me so that I might be able to make a stand against your adversaries. And I ask that you would frame your refutation of such arguments as may be plainly understood by the people.[18]

17 Ibid., 154.
18 Ibid., 230.

Surely this attack on Calvin is clothed throughout in very refined and civil language. Read the following to see how Calvin answers the calumniator:

> As far as you are concerned, poor masked monitor, I derive some consolation from the thought that you cannot be ungrateful towards the man who has treated you with much greater kindness than you deserved at his hands, without betraying at the same time your foul wickedness against God. I know quite well that there is no sport more grateful to your academics than the rooting out of all faith from the hearts of the godly by casting a shade of doubt over all that they hold dear. And the sweet pleasure that you derive from all those revilings that you direct against the secret providence of God is apparent from the very point of your pen, however much you strive to hide your base gratification. But I summon you and all your fellows before that tribunal on which the judge of heaven sits, from whose mouth the blast and the bolt shall one day fall upon you all and lay you prostrate. I trust, however, that I myself, before I am done, shall make your insolent speaking against God to be as loathsome to the feelings of all good and godly men as they are inwardly gratifying to your own heart.[19]

These quotations make clear that not everyone carried on polemics in the same "uncivil" language as John Calvin's. His opponent's language throughout is smooth, sweet, and polite. He does not call Calvin names but treats him with apparent respect. This shows that you cannot explain Calvin's language from the spirit of his time, unless you picture Calvin as less polished and civilized than his average opponent. This certainly cannot be said of the Genevan reformer. It is also clear that Calvin does not change his style one whit because of the sweetness and politeness of his adversary's language. Calvin immediately attacks him with the severest language and invokes the bolts of God's judgments on him and his friends to lay them prostrate.

---

19 Ibid., 231–32.

What then is the explanation of Calvin's form of writing? I would explain it from a very firm conviction regarding the truth. Calvin did not doubt. He was strong in the faith. He did not intellectually philosophize about the truth for the sake of mental enjoyment and exercise of his logical faculty, but he was deeply convinced of the truth of what he wrote. He believed the word of God and was assured that his doctrine was the true representation of the truth of God's word. Still more, Calvin loved the truth of which he wrote, and he had a personal part in it. Calvin's heart was filled with reverent love of God and the fear of his name. Calvin embraced the truth with all his heart, and in it he clung to his covenantal God, the glory of whose name meant so much to Calvin.

It follows and is evident from all his writings that Calvin regarded his opponents who attacked the truth of predestination and of the sovereign grace of God as enemies of the truth of God, which they were. According to Calvin's conviction these men slandered the name of his God. They were wicked, base fellows, ungodly men, who possessed no grain of religion and of the fear of God. Calvin, who could endure so much concerning his honor and name, did not hesitate to express his contempt and holy hatred against those enemies of his God. I am convinced that these are the deeper and nobler motives behind the reformer's "uncivil" language.

Hardly civil?

What is civilization that speaks in endearing terms when the enemy attacks the truth and name of God, and the language should be in holy wrath? What does it mean to express our highest esteem and respect for opponents of the truth when there is not a grain of such respect in our hearts? Is this a bit of ungodly hypocrisy? Surely the theory of common grace can cover this wicked hypocrisy, according to which we are often more concerned with our honor and the friendship of man than with the honor and friendship of God. Common grace has already so blinded the eyes of many that they would even criticize the profound love of God expressed by the psalmist in Psalm 139, where he emphasizes that he hates those who hate his God and are his enemies. It is a small wonder that in our age of humanism, self-love, and the honor of men rather than of God, we stumble over Calvin's language that calls the enemies of God by their true names, rather than feigns esteem for them.

My general second remark is that one almost receives the impression that Berkhof's book review of *Calvin's Calvinism* in the *Banner* was chiefly a warning to be careful and not to enter too audaciously into the deep things of God. Oh, Calvin is so careful! He almost seems to devote his work chiefly to defending the free offer of salvation in light of the doctrine of predestination. He appears almost timid in his care not to express himself too boldly on the subjects of election and reprobation, as if they were the subjects on which Calvin wrote, and as if such was his chief purpose. Nay more, as if there were even one iota of Berkhof's theory of a free offer of salvation on the part of God in the whole work.

One feels how the wind blows in Berkhof's book review. It appears that the three points were before his mind when he wrote. One receives the impression that he was thinking of 1924, of the Protestant Reformed Churches, and of the corruption of the doctrine of Calvin and of the Reformed faith by the Christian Reformed Church in its three declarations. Then that church, very politely and civilly, without giving the ministers an opportunity to defend themselves and the truth, wickedly expelled those who faithfully defended the truth of the sovereign grace of God in opposition to the adopted theory of common grace. Berkhof must have met many passages in *Calvin's Calvinism* that flatly contradicted the doctrine that under his leadership was adopted by the church in the now famous three points. Now he desperately tries to read into *Calvin's Calvinism* the "whitewashed Calvinism" of the three points. Now he emphasizes that Calvin is careful not to go beyond scripture and defends a free offer of salvation in the sense of the first point of 1924.

Grace to all in the preaching of the gospel, is it not, Professor? Grace also to the reprobate in the proclamation of salvation in Christ? God's earnest desire to save not only the elect, but also all men? This is what you mean by a free offer of salvation. This is what Kuiper preached in his sermons on the three points.

You maintain that that corruption of predestination is the doctrine of Calvin? We will see.

I assure you that the publishers of the book will be amazed when they hear that *Calvin's Calvinism* makes such a strange impression on some Reformed (?) leaders in America. The publishers must have nothing of "hawking" Christ, as Atherton called this supposed offer of salvation to all. It surely is not their impression that Calvin believed it. But we will see.

I will quote Calvin extensively on this subject. Fortunately he has a good deal to say on it, so we can obtain a clear conception of his views on the matter. I will also quote what Berkhof and Kuiper wrote on the same subject in connection with the content of the first point of 1924. Then the reader can judge for himself whether the corruption of 1924 is actually the doctrine of the Genevan reformer.

CHAPTER 2

LOUIS BERKHOF AND H. J. KUIPER
ON THE WELL-MEANT OFFER

My comparison will be limited to the teachings of Calvin, Berkhof, and Kuiper with respect to God's so-called well-meant offer of salvation to all men indiscriminately. I will first quote from the writings of Berkhof and Kuiper and then let Calvin speak on this subject.

I will be as objective in representing their views as can possibly be expected. It is not at all my purpose to ascribe any convictions to Berkhof and Kuiper that they do not have. Therefore, I will rarely interpret their statements and will let them speak for themselves in their own words. When I am through presenting their views, they will surely admit that I have not misrepresented their writings and that their teachings are actually as I placed them before the public.

To attain this objective it is necessary to read their writings in the proper light, that is, in connection with the first point of 1924. In the first point the free and well-meant general offer of salvation to all men was mentioned for the first time, and it has been officially accepted by the Christian Reformed Church as a dogma. Both Berkhof and Kuiper published their views in defense of the first point. They agree with the first point. They believe in a free, general, well-meant offer of grace on the part of God to all men without distinction in the same sense in which the first point teaches it.

> Concerning the first point, with regard to the favorable dispo-
> sition of God toward mankind in general, and not only to the
> elect, Synod declares that according to the Scripture and the
> confessions it is determined that besides the saving grace of

God, shown only to the elect unto eternal life, there is a certain kind of favor or grace of God which He shows to His creatures in general. This is evidenced by the quoted Scripture passages and from the Canons of Dort 2.5 and 3–4.8–9, which deals with the general offer of the Gospel; whereas the quoted declarations of Reformed writers from the golden age of Reformed theology, also give evidence that our Reformed fathers from of old have advocated these opinions.[20]

"His creatures in general" means all men, since the first point deals with a favorable attitude of God toward mankind in general, not only toward the elect. Berkhof and Kuiper also admit this. There is then a certain grace of God shown to elect and reprobate indiscriminately. It is not saving grace, the point emphasizes, for this is shown only to the elect.

But the first point does not explain what sort of grace it is. It merely speaks of a "certain" grace. It certainly is a gracious attitude that God assumes toward all men, a gracious inclination of his heart not only to the elect, but also to the reprobate. Whatever he bestows on any man in that attitude he certainly gives in love. This is plain from the declaration, for it speaks of a favorable attitude of God toward all mankind. This is also the meaning Berkhof and Kuiper give to the first point, as is evident from their writings.

Now, what does God indiscriminately bestow on all men? The general offer of the gospel, among other things. Hence the first point teaches that when God has the gospel preached to elect and reprobate, he does so in his grace and loving-kindness, also to the reprobate.

It is unclear what kind of grace the reprobate receive when the gospel is preached to them, because synod's declaration does not explain this. Neither do Berkhof and Kuiper attempt to explain this. They actually admit that the reprobate receive no grace through the preaching of the gospel. However that may be, God bestows grace on them or assumes an attitude of grace toward them in the preaching of the gospel. He loves them somehow; he is gracious toward them. Because he is gracious toward the reprobate, he has the gospel preached to them.

---

20 *1924 Acts of Synod*, 145–46.

If you inquire further concerning what God's gracious attitude toward the reprobate in the preaching of the gospel implies, the first point is again silent.

The only possible conclusion for anyone of sound mind is that God seriously wills the salvation of the reprobate. He is filled with loving-kindness concerning them. In that loving-kindness of his heart he seeks their salvation. Seeking their salvation, he offers them the gospel. The clear teaching of the first point is that God, loving the reprobate and earnestly desiring their salvation, offers them salvation in the gospel of Jesus Christ.

My serious objection to the first point is that it, in spite of all Berkhof's attempts to prove the contrary, is pure Arminianism. God in his grace seriously seeks to bestow salvation on some men through Christ. For this purpose he has the gospel preached to them. But he fails. They are not saved, although God seeks to save them and explicitly has the gospel proclaimed to them. I claim that anyone of sound mind is compelled to conclude that man is stronger than God, but Berkhof and Kuiper are unwilling to do this. The will of man frustrates the gracious purposes of God. Such is the teaching of the first point. And this is rank Arminianism.

Except with respect to the last conclusion [that man is stronger than God], which they are unwilling to draw, Berkhof and Kuiper teach everything I have written above concerning the meaning of the first point. They both hold that God loves the reprobate and is gracious toward them, that in this love and grace he seriously seeks their salvation, and that for this purpose he has the gospel preached to them and Christ offered to them.

The brethren of the Sovereign Grace Union will take note that this is the actual teaching of these men; that this is the official stand of the Christian Reformed Church in America; and that this is also the doctrine Dr. J. van Lonkhuyzen defended in 1924, on the basis of which he urged my expulsion from the Christian Reformed Church.[21]

---

21 Rev. J. van Lonkhuyzen was prominent in the common grace controversy. A pastor in Chicago, Illinois, he was a member of the minority part of a committee to advise the Christian Reformed synod of 1922 regarding Janssen. The minority defended Janssen and his teachings. Van Lonkhuyzen was an ardent proponent of the theory of common grace. After the Christian Reformed synod of 1924, which

I challenge Berkhof and Kuiper to deny the truth of these statements. Gladly will I give them room to do this in [the *Standard Bearer*]. But they will not take up the challenge. It is their doctrine, as it is the plain teaching of the first point. This I will prove from their writings.

Berkhof writes,

> The following link in the argument of synod is this: the general and well-meant offer of salvation is a sign of God's favor toward sinners, is for them a blessing from the Lord. This must emphatically be pointed out, because those who cannot agree with the declaration of synod maintain that the preaching of the word is merely intended as a curse for the reprobate who dwell under such preaching. God does not bless them by this but curses them through it. Insofar as the preaching concerns them, God merely uses it as a means to plunge them more deeply into destruction. Hence preaching is an instrument of his hatred. This is a positively unscriptural thought. The scripture teaches most certainly that we must consider the offer of salvation a temporal blessing also for those who do not heed the invitation.
>
> The following considerations serve to prove this. That God calls the ungodly unto conversion is presented in scripture as a proof that he desires their salvation. [The reprobate are meant here.] In the prophecy of Ezekiel we listen to the voice of the Lord in words that speak of tender mercy: "Have I any pleasure at all [even in any measure] that the wicked should die? saith the Lord GOD; and not that he should return from his ways and live" [18:23]? "For I have no pleasure in the death of him that dieth [he who dies in his sins] saith the Lord GOD: wherefore, turn...and live ye" [v. 32]. These passages teach as clearly as words can that God has no pleasure in the death of the wicked (notice that he does not say "the elect wicked"

---

adopted the theory of common grace as official church doctrine but declined to execute or advise discipline on Danhof and Hoeksema for denying common grace, Van Lonkhuyzen wrote in one of the periodicals that circulated in the Christian Reformed Church, advocating the church discipline of Danhof and Hoeksema for their rejection of common grace.—Ed.

but "the wicked" entirely in general); and the tender calling to them witnesses of his great love for sinners and of his desire to save the ungodly.[22]

The reader will admit that I do not misrepresent Berkhof when I say he teaches that God is filled with saving love for the reprobate sinner as well as for the elect. The passage is emphatic in the expression of this view. Entirely in general, and not specifically regarding the elect, God loves sinners and desires to save them. There is no escape from this conclusion, because this entire argument defends the teaching that God is gracious in the preaching of the gospel to the reprobate and not only to the elect, as was declared in the first point. In no uncertain terms does he condemn the view of the Protestant Reformed Churches: that even though it is God's good pleasure that men preach the gospel in general to all who hear, yet his purpose is to be gracious to the elect only, while it is equally his purpose that the gospel shall be a savor of death unto death for the reprobate. This view that these churches maintain as being the Reformed and Calvinistic view, Berkhof very emphatically condemns.

The reader must keep this in mind. At the same time it is of profound interest, as I compare Berkhof's view with Calvin's on this point, that Calvin in *Calvin's Calvinism* explains the same texts from Ezekiel that Berkhof expounds in the above quotation. Later I will quote Calvin at length. In the meantime I assure the reader that Calvin's exegesis differs essentially from Berkhof's.

I quote another paragraph from Berkhof's defense of the first point so there will be no doubt left that I represent him correctly.

There is still another passage in Ezekiel in which the Lord expresses the same thought in still stronger language, in which he even confirms it with an oath, namely, Ezekiel 33:11: "As I live, saith the Lord GOD, I have no pleasure in the death of the wicked; but that the wicked turn from his way and live; turn

---

22 Louis Berkhof, *De Drie Punten in Alle Deelen Gereformeerd* [The three points, Reformed in all parts] (Grand Rapids, MI: Wm. B. Eerdmans Publishing Co., 1925), 21.

ye, turn ye from your evil ways; for why will ye die, O house of Israel?" Are these not words of tender loving-kindness, in which a father implores his backsliding children [the reprobate] to return to the house and to the heart of the father? Do you listen here, even in the least degree, to the voice of hatred [as if anyone were so insane as to maintain this]? And does not Jesus' lamentation over Jerusalem point in the same direction? Can you imagine anything that surpasses this in touching pathos? "O Jerusalem, Jerusalem, thou that killest the prophets and stonest them which are sent unto thee, how often would I have gathered thy children together, even as a hen gathereth her chickens under her wings, and ye would not!" (Matt. 23:37).[23]

You see, readers, there remains no doubt regarding Berkhof's view. God loves the wicked, elect and reprobate. He is filled with most tender mercy toward them. His heart longs to save them all without exception. In the most touching words of profound pathos, he cries over them when they do not heed his tender calling. This is the grace the reprobate receive. However strong and filled with longing to save this grace is, it does not save. It is vain, for the reprobate do not heed the tender call of their gracious Father.

And Kuiper? He teaches the same doctrine, as a faithful son of the church that adopted the three points, except he would have us believe that it is a mystery that God wills and does not will the salvation of the reprobate.

By far the most serious objections raised against the three points concern the first of these, specifically the *general offer of the gospel* [that is, God offers the gospel to the reprobate *in his grace*]. The objection is that synod has virtually committed itself to the Arminian doctrines of the general atonement and free will.

This objection is as absurd as it is serious. So far as we know, the only argument in support of this astounding charge is that God cannot sincerely offer salvation [*in his grace*] to

---

23 Ibid., 21.

reprobate sinners, unless Christ has actually paid for their sins and they have a will that is free to choose the salvation offered to them. Our answer is that this does not follow at all. [One could expect a sound argument to prove that this does not at all follow, but there follows instead a hopeless appeal to mystery.] It is true that *human logic cannot fully harmonize* the doctrine of election and reprobation, of a particular atonement, and of man's total depravity (which implies that our will by nature is free to choose only the evil but not the good) with that of the general offer of grace. But does this mean that both cannot be true? There is not one doctrine of Holy Writ that does not involve us in intellectual difficulties. Think of the mystery of the one being and the three persons, of divine sovereignty and human responsibility, of divine providence and human freedom, of original sin and the sinlessness of Christ, of the union of the two natures in the one divine person of Christ.[24]

To prove the contention that scripture teaches this gracious, general offer of salvation, Kuiper refers to Ezekiel 33:11; Matthew 23:37; Luke 14:15–21, 24; and 2 Peter 3:9.

Clearly Kuiper is of the same conviction as Berkhof regarding the first point of doctrine. Notice how, on the basis of this doctrine, Kuiper preaches to his congregation:

Let us emphasize the fact that *your conception of God* depends upon your answer to the question whether God shows any favor to the reprobate. A certain Christian has well said: "Our God is a just God, but not a cruel God." He has no pleasure in the misery of any of His creatures. He sends the wicked *earthly* blessings as the fruits of His kindness, in order to convince them of His sincere willingness to bestow upon them the *greater* gift of salvation in Christ. God is just and stern, but

---

24 H. J. Kuiper, *The Three Points of Common Grace: Three Sermons at Broadway Avenue Christian Reformed Church* (Grand Rapids, MI: Wm. B. Eerdmans, 1925), 11–12.

He is not harsh and cruel. He is not a God who reveals to a large part of humanity nothing but His wrath. Even the reprobates are His creatures, the works of His hands; and in His goodness and grace He lavishes blessings upon them as long as they live, even though they perish in their sins. Thus He magnifies His love as well as His wrath in the reprobate; even as He glorifies His justice as well as His grace in the redeemed. Neither can you maintain the sincere offer of salvation to *all* who hear the gospel, unless you accept the truth which is formulated in the first point of synod. If God assumes no attitude of favor to the unthankful and evil, he cannot sincerely offer them the blessings of redemption. Then what our Confessions say cannot be true: "He has most earnestly and truly declared in His Word what will be *acceptable* to Him; namely, that all who are called (by the gospel) should comply with the invitation." It is true that God has from eternity chosen some to eternal life, and rejected others. But it is just as true that He sincerely offers salvation to all who hear the gospel. The fact that we with our finite minds cannot fully harmonize these two truths should not make us hesitate to accept both. Both are clearly revealed in Holy Writ. There is no one here in the audience who can say, "God hates me." Suppose you knew that you will ultimately be lost; even then you could not say, "God does not care for me." The gospel we preach is a gospel for sinners—for all sinners. It is glad tiding also for you. God has no pleasure in your death but therein that you turn and live. He hates your sins, but He does not hate you. He invites you to come to Him and be saved. That very fact will make your punishment doubly deserved if you should be lost. You will never be able to say, "I have not tasted God's goodness and grace; I have never experienced His love." You will have to say, "I have spurned His love, rejected His grace; and now there remains for me a righteous judgment, a well-deserved wrath whose flames will burn forever and ever"[25]

---

25 Ibid., 15–16.

The reader will agree that I do Kuiper no injustice but present his views correctly when I say that he believes and teaches that God loves the reprobate, earnestly desires their salvation, and has the gospel preached to them to seek and to save them. If you bring the indictment of Arminianism against Kuiper for such teaching, he appears horrified and amazed and calls you absurd because you draw conclusions that do not follow. However, being at a loss how further to defend himself, he hides behind the pretext that it is all an unsolvable mystery. Nevertheless, you must believe that God loves whom he hates, that he seeks the salvation of those whom he never intends to save, that he blesses whom he curses, and that he seriously invites those to whom he forever shut the door of his kingdom in sovereign righteousness. Such is a true representation of Kuiper's views, himself being our witness, for he will not deny this. He will not reply that I have done him an injustice.

The saddest feature of all is that Kuiper maintains that this is the only Reformed view and that all other views are essentially fatalistic. He will expel out of the Reformed church all who do not subscribe to his logical contradictions and enigmas.

> One of the most serious aspects of the present denial of the doctrine of Common Grace is the denial of the general offer of salvation. It robs the gospel of its evangelical note [by evangelical note the writer means the preaching that the gospel *is for all sinners*]. It is bound in time to create an attitude of religious passivism and fatalism which has been the curse of every church where the preaching of election was not counterbalanced by the sinner's responsibility [the old, baseless accusation that all enemies of the truth of sovereign grace brought against its defenders: *ex ungue leonem*] and of God's sincere offer of salvation to all without discrimination.[26]

Thus are the views of Berkhof and Kuiper on the first point. One gets the impression that they err in good faith, hard though it is to believe this of men with sound minds. Sometimes it appears that they

---

26 Ibid., 13. "*Ex ungue leonem*" is a Latin proverb that means from the claw one recognizes the lion.—Ed.

do not understand their own speech. For instance, in Kuiper's book we also find the following quotation from Calvin, cited in support of the theory that God earnestly desires the salvation of all who externally hear the gospel: "For there is a universal call, by which God in the external preaching of the Word invites all, indiscriminately, to come to him, even those to whom he intends it as a savor of death, and an occasion of heavier condemnation."[27]

Yes indeed, that is Calvin's doctrine. For some who hear the gospel God intends it as a savor of death and an occasion for heavier condemnation.

That is our churches' doctrine. God will have the gospel indiscriminately preached to all who hear. He will save his elect by preaching and harden the reprobate by it. With a free conscience before God and all who hear us, we declare that thus we believe and preach and always did preach.

But that is not the doctrine of Berkhof and Kuiper. Let no one be deceived! They do not teach that God will have the gospel preached to some of the reprobate *in order that* it may be a savor of death to them. On the contrary, they hold that God offers Christ to the reprobate in his grace to them, earnestly desiring their salvation. This view they make the basis of their preaching.

If the views of Berkhof and Kuiper on this subject have become clear, and they and the reader will admit that I have done them no injustice, I am satisfied. For I have no other purpose than to get at the truth of the matter, to clear the sky of misty clouds of poisoned gas that have been cast over it.

We desire to know who—they or we—are in agreement with the great Genevan reformer. If they are, we will still maintain our view, for we are deeply convinced that it is the truth of the word of God; but we will not call Calvin our spiritual father. If they are not in agreement with Calvin, we would like to compel them to disavow Calvin, to expel him from their fellowship as they did us, and to claim Arminius of Leiden as their great teacher.

Suppose that England's Calvinists, the men of the Sovereign Grace Union, be judges in this matter.

27 Ibid., 12.

CHAPTER 3

JOHN CALVIN ON THE OFFER
(THE EXTERNAL CALL)

The general and well-meant offer of salvation is a sign of
God's favor toward sinners.
—Louis Berkhof

He sincerely offers salvation to all who hear the gospel.
—H. J. Kuiper

A man must be utterly beside himself to assert that this promise is made to all men generally and indiscriminately.
—John Calvin

A common practice with such is to address their auditory
thus: "I offer you Christ." I do not believe that any man who
can use such language is a converted man.
—William Parks, *Sermons on the Five Points of Calvinism*
(Sovereign Grace Union, 1929)

What was Calvin's view with respect to a general offer of salvation, well-meant on the part of God to all who hear? On this
Berkhof and Kuiper lay so much stress that they refuse to live
in the same church fellowship with those who deny it.

Was it Calvin's conviction also that when the external call of the
gospel comes to elect and reprobate alike, it is a sign of God's grace
to them all? Did he also believe, like Berkhof and Kuiper, that in the
external preaching of the gospel we must see a sign of God's earnest
desire to save everyone who hears it, God's well-meant offer of salvation to everyone? To answer these questions we must quote Calvin.

First we will let the Genevan reformer speak for us on Ezekiel, cited by the synod of 1924 in proof of the first point, of which Berkhof is so fond and on which Kuiper without any doubt agrees with him. In that passage they say there is proof of God's general grace, of the fact that God has no pleasure in the death of any wicked and is desirous to save them all.

This is what Calvin writes:

All this Pighius loudly denies, citing the passage of the apostle Paul, "Who will have all men to be saved" [1 Tim. 2:4]. Referring also to Ezekiel 18:23, Pighius argues thus: That God wills not the death of a sinner may be taken upon his own oath, where he says by that prophet, "As I live, saith the Lord, I have no pleasure in the death of the wicked; but rather that he should return from his way and live" [Ezek. 33:11].

We reply that since the language of Ezekiel is an exhortation to repentance, it is not at all marvelous in him to declare that God wills all men to be saved, for the mutual relation between threats and promises shows that such forms of speaking are conditional. In this same manner God declared to the Ninevites, and to the kings of Gerar and Egypt, that he would do what in reality he did not intend to do, for their repentance averted the punishment that he had threatened to inflict upon them. It is evident that the punishment was announced on condition of their remaining obstinate and impenitent. Yet the announcement of the punishment was positive, as if it had been an irrevocable decree. But after God had terrified them with the apprehension of his wrath and had duly humbled them as not being utterly desperate, he encourages them with the hope of pardon, that they might feel that there was yet left open a space for remedy. Just so it is with respect to the conditional promises of God that invite all men to salvation. They do not positively prove what God has decreed in his secret counsel, but declare only what God is ready to do to all those who are brought to faith and repentance.

But men untaught of God, not understanding these things,

allege that we hereby attribute to God a twofold or double will, whereas God is so far from being variable that no shadow of such variableness appertains to him, even in the most remote degree. Hence Pighius, ignorant of the divine nature of these deep things, thus argues, "What else is this but making God a mocker of men if God is represented as really not willing what he professes to will, and as not having pleasure in what he actually has pleasure?" But if these two parts of the sentence be read in conjunction, as they ever ought to be—"*I have no pleasure in the death of the wicked,*" and *"but that the wicked turn from his way and live"* [Ezek. 33:11]—the calumny is washed off at once. God requires of us this conversion, or turning away from our iniquity [Ezek. 18:23, 30; Ezek. 33:11], and in whomever he finds it, he does not disappoint such a one of the promised reward of eternal life. Therefore, God is as much said to have pleasure in and to will this eternal life as to have pleasure in repentance; he has pleasure in repentance because he invites all men to it by his word. All this is in perfect harmony with his secret and eternal counsel by which he decreed to convert none except his own elect. None but God's elect, therefore, ever do turn from their wickedness. Yet on these accounts the adorable God is not to be considered variable or capable of change, because as a lawgiver he enlightens all men with the external doctrine of conditional life. In this primary manner he calls or invites all men to eternal life. But he brings unto eternal life his own children, only those whom he willed according to his eternal purpose and regenerated by his Spirit as an eternal Father.[28]

This language is plain to all who will understand. Unmistakably the reformer denies that in the passages from Ezekiel there is a general offer of salvation to elect and reprobate promiscuously, a manifest desire to save them all, a revelation of a certain general, or common, grace.

---

28 Calvin, *Calvin's Calvinism*, 87–88.

Calvin affirms what I have often and always taught and written: that insofar as the message is general and comes to all, it is *condition-al*.[29] The offer is eternal life. The condition limiting this offer is turn from your wicked ways.

This condition makes the content of the general message particular. As I have emphasized in the past, a contention my opponents have tried to laugh to scorn, there is a general proclamation of a conditional and particular gospel. He promises *to all who believe* peace and eternal life.

Thus is the plain exposition of Calvin on this passage. He teaches all who hear a *conditional doctrine*: if you turn, you will live.

Because it is conditional, it is also particular, and God in reality promises eternal life only to the elect. According to Calvin, it is quite certain that men do not turn from their wicked ways of their own accord nor by any instinct of nature.[30] It is equally certain that none turn from their wickedness except the elect. Therefore, the content of the externally general message is particular and applies only to the elect of God.

God does not say here that he will save all who hear. He does not express that he is gracious to everyone who outwardly receives the message. He will be gracious only to those who turn from their wicked ways. These are necessarily the elect.

Calvin's exposition is in direct opposition to Berkhof's and to Kuiper's preaching. It is the condemnation of the first point insofar as it appeals to these passages from Ezekiel to prove a certain general grace of God in the general preaching of the gospel.

Notice too that Calvin must have nothing of Kuiper's mystery that God wills and does not will the same thing with respect to the same

---

29 In his earlier writing Hoeksema was less cautious about using the word *conditional* than he became in later years. But he never taught conditions in the sense of an act of the sinner upon which a grace of God that is wider than election depends and by which that grace is delimited. When he used the term, as he did in this passage, it meant the way in which God bestowed the grace of election. Here the *condition* is the way of the sinner's repentance. But always for Hoeksema the promise, well-meant (that is, gracious) offer, and grace have their source in and are governed by election.—Ed.

30 Calvin, *Calvin's Calvinism*, 88.

persons at the same time. Kuiper alleges that this is a deep mystery that we must believe, although we cannot understand it. Calvin replies that only "men untaught of God, not understanding these things," can speak of a twofold will in God.[31]

Note also that there is no truth in Berkhof's statement that Calvin does not attempt to enter into the deep things of God. Calvin is not satisfied with contradictions. He entirely harmonizes the texts from Ezekiel, which deal with the external call to repentance and faith, with the counsel of God until it is clear that there is no conflict at all between the two. God does not profess to will what in reality he does not will. The harmony lies in the general proclamation of a particular truth.

Is it not also a striking phenomenon that the arch-Pelagian Pighius, the opponent of Calvin, quotes the same texts for the same purpose as do Kuiper and Berkhof in defense of the first point of 1924? Pighius quotes them to prove that we may take God at his oath that he does not in general will the death of a sinner. Berkhof writes, "These passages teach as clearly as words can that God has no pleasure in the death of the wicked (notice that he does not say 'the elect wicked' but 'the wicked' entirely in general]; and the tender calling to them witnesses of his great love for sinners and of his desire to save the ungodly."

Berkhof's meaning is perfectly clear. We may take God at his oath that he has a great love for sinners in general and desires to save them all. Thus teaches Berkhof. Thus teaches Kuiper. Thus is the content of the first point.

I conclude that in their exposition of these texts, Kuiper, Berkhof, and the synod of 1924 are in the company of Pighius, the Pelagian, the opponent of Calvin.

I prefer to remain in Calvin's company. And this is the reason they cast me out of the church.

---

31 Ibid.

CHAPTER 4

JOHN CALVIN AGAINST LOUIS BERKHOF
AND H. J. KUIPER

Regarding the texts from Ezekiel 18 and 33, we found that Berkhof and Kuiper do not agree with Calvin. They agree with the Pelagian Pighius in their exegesis of these passages of the word of God.

Berkhof explained that these passages are clear manifestations of the love of God to all sinners, not only to the elect. The texts are clear illustrations of the general and well-meant offer of salvation on the part of God to all men. God earnestly invites them all to come to him and to have eternal life.

This is the implied exegesis of these texts as quoted by the synod of the Christian Reformed Church in 1924, for synod quoted them as proof of the general grace of God to all men as manifested in the preaching of the gospel. Hence I can safely assert that Kuiper would also give the same explanation, for he must abide by synodical decisions, and synod decided that this is the meaning of the texts being considered.

Calvin does not agree with that interpretation. It is the explanation of the Pelagian Pighius, and Calvin opposes him with all his might. Calvin explains that the two parts of Ezekiel 33:11 must not be separated; that if the text is taken as a whole, God promises life only to those who turn from their wicked ways; that therefore the content of the gospel is conditional and particular; that natural man cannot fulfill the condition, but only those to whom God gives the grace of repentance; and that God gives the grace of repentance only to the elect. Thus, according to Calvin, these words do not conflict with the doctrine of eternal predestination. There is no general offer in the text at all. God does not say that he is willing or earnestly desirous to save all men. And there is no mystery whatever. The whole truth is perfectly clear to Calvin's mind.

This difference between Berkhof and Kuiper on the one hand and Calvin on the other is of more than mere exegetical interest. The mere fact that Berkhof and Kuiper differ from Calvin on a pure question of interpretation would not prove at all that they are not in essential doctrinal agreement. But that is not the point.

This instance of differences in their interpretation of a certain text reveals differences in tendency, in principle, in doctrine. Calvin believes only in the truth that grace is particular, that the grace of the gospel is meant only for the elect, even though the preaching of the gospel is general. Hence when his opponent presents a text that apparently contradicts the doctrine of God's election and sovereign grace, he ponders and searches the word of God until he finds the harmony of the truth. He explains those texts that are apparently in favor of general grace and free will in the light of the whole of scripture. But Berkhof and Kuiper actually find in such texts the Arminian doctrine—God earnestly wills the salvation of all who hear the word preached, and the preaching of the word is a manifestation of the grace of God to all. They elicit from scripture the Arminian doctrine of general grace on the part of God, while Calvin adheres to the truth of particular redemption as the fruit of election and sovereign grace.

The differences are in doctrine and in principle, not in exegesis.

The differences between these men will become still more evident if we consider the meaning of a quotation from Calvin mentioned previously.

> It is quite certain that men do not "turn from their evil ways" to the Lord of their own accord or by any instinct of nature. Equally certain is it that the gift of conversion is not common to all men, because this is that one of the two covenants that God promises he will not make with any but his own children and his own elect people, concerning whom he has recorded his promise, "I will write my law in their hearts" [Jer. 31:33]. A

man must be utterly beside himself to assert that this promise is made to all men generally and indiscriminately. God says expressly by Paul, who refers to the prophet Jeremiah, "For this is the covenant that I will make with them. Not according to the covenant that I made with their fathers; but I will put my laws into their mind, and write them in their hearts" [Heb. 8:9–10]. To apply this promise to those who were worthy of this new covenant or to such as had prepared themselves by their own merits or endeavors to receive it, surely must be worse than the grossest ignorance and folly, and the more so as the Lord is speaking by the prophet to those who before had "stony hearts." All this is plainly stated and fully explained by the prophet Ezekiel [Ezek. 11:19; Ezek. 36:26].[32]

This passage is extremely interesting because it raises the question, what do Berkhof and Kuiper mean when they claim that in the promise of the gospel, as presented in the external calling, God earnestly reveals his willingness to save all men? What is the content of their gospel, which they say is for all? Kuiper proclaimed loudly, "The gospel I preach is a gospel for *all sinners*!"

The question cannot be repressed: What gospel does he preach? Does he mean by the gospel the proclamation that Christ has died for sinners and arose, and that now God earnestly invites them to come to him, to believe and repent? In the preaching of the gospel, does he present to his hearers the work that Christ objectively accomplished for us? If he should speak thus, he would present to his hearers a half-truth, which is often more dangerous than a plain lie. It is not the entire truth, it is not the truth fully and correctly stated, if Kuiper should say that Christ died for sinners. He certainly will at all times have to say that he died and arose only for elect sinners and for none other.

It is quite unintelligible how Kuiper can say that the gospel he preaches is for *all sinners*. Notice he did not say that he preached the gospel to all sinners who heard him, but that the very gospel he preached is a gospel for all sinners. Surely in this Berkhof agrees with him.

---

32 Ibid., 88–89.

Let us turn our attention to the question brought before us by the quotation from Calvin.

Does not the gospel contain much more than the preaching of what the Lord did *for* us? Does it not also imply the preaching of the riches of his grace, whereby he applies salvation to all his elect? Does this grace of the Lord Jesus Christ not belong to the promise of the gospel? I am now thinking of the grace of regeneration, whereby in principle we become partakers of the life of the risen Lord; of the grace of effectual calling, whereby we are translated from darkness into light; of the grace of faith, whereby we know that we are justified before God and have peace with him through our Lord Jesus Christ; of the grace of conversion and sanctification, the mortification of the old man and the quickening of the new man; of the grace of perseverance, so that no one can pluck us out of Christ's hand. Do not all these blessings of grace belong to the promise of the gospel? The gospel of our Lord Jesus Christ does not come with a message that he *will* merely save us (of what avail would that be for us, poor, dead, miserable sinners?), but it comes with the very positive glad tidings that he *did save* us and *does save* us even unto the end.

Do Berkhof and Kuiper include all this when they speak of the general preaching of the gospel? Do they mean by the gospel the glad tidings of a Christ not who *will*, but who *does* save to the full; who really atoned for the sin of all the elect; who really gives new hearts to them all; who effectually calls them to faith and repentance; who actually justifies and sanctifies them and holds them in his power so they persevere unto the end?

I take it they do. If they do not, they do not preach the gospel. What would a gospel message mean that did not imply the promise of all the grace of Christ Jesus in the fullness of his riches?

Consider what this means. The gospel they preach is a gospel for *all sinners*. On this they both agree. This implies that they preach that God promises new hearts, repentance, faith, adoption, forgiveness, justification, conversion, sanctification, and perseverance to all who hear the gospel, for all this is surely implied in the gospel.

Plainly they also in this respect depart from Calvin. The great

Genevan reformer does not agree with them, and he expresses his disagreement in the strongest terms. He does not hesitate to assert that a man must be utterly beside himself to claim that God generally and indiscriminately promises these blessings of grace to all men.

Berkhof and Kuiper can draw their own conclusions. How do they feel, I am wondering, about this judgment of Calvin concerning people who claim that the gospel is for all sinners, that God offers salvation in grace to all men, earnestly desiring that all may have eternal life? Note that Calvin writes this in connection with the Pelagian interpretation of Ezekiel 18:23 and 33:11.

Neither is Calvin's language too strong. The folly of maintaining that God promises new hearts to everybody is easily discovered. If God offers the blessing of a new heart to all, if the promises of grace are indiscriminately for all men, why does God not fulfill his promise?

Surely a new heart is entirely the work of God. Man can do nothing toward receiving it. He cannot make himself worthy of it. He cannot get himself into a state of receptivity for it. He cannot even make himself will to receive it. He is incapable of inducing himself even to pray for it. This is true of all men by nature, of all indiscriminately. A new heart is God's work, his gift only and absolutely. Man cannot work for it if God does not bestow the blessing on him; neither can any man resist the operation of God whereby he renews the heart, if it pleases the Almighty to give him a heart of flesh instead of the stony heart. If the promise of the gospel concerning this new heart (not is preached to all who hear, this is self-evident) is given by God to all men without distinction, why does God not fulfill his promise?

Because some do not will to receive it? That is Arminianism. Even then a man must be utterly beside himself to speak thus, for no one is willing to receive a new heart before he possesses it.

More mysteries, perhaps? I fear that Kuiper will answer thus.

But I say with Calvin, nay, but more nonsense! A man must be utterly beside himself to assert that God generally and indiscriminately makes the promise of the gospel concerning a new heart to all men. If God promises this blessing, which he alone can bestow and bestows unconditionally to all men, and does not fulfill the promise, where is God's truth? Is the promise of God brought to nothing? Has his word become of no effect? God forbid! He never made the promise to all, but only to the elect. Kuiper has no right and no calling to present it differently.

Finally, if God promises this blessing to all but does not bestow it on all, where is the general grace in the preaching of the gospel? Certainly Calvin is right. A man must be utterly beside himself to maintain all this.

It is more evident now than before that Berkhof and Kuiper cannot appeal to John Calvin for their views on this point. There is a wide difference too between Calvin and the synod of Kalamazoo in 1924. Anyone who is not utterly beside himself with prejudice will feel constrained to admit this.

But I have not finished. Berkhof also quoted Matthew 23:37 as another proof that God earnestly desires the salvation of all and would have this proclaimed by his ministers. There we read the well-known words, "O Jerusalem, Jerusalem, thou that killest the prophets, and stonest them which are sent unto thee, how often would I have gathered thy children together, even as a hen gathereth her chickens under her wings, and ye would not!"

Berkhof wrote that this text points in the same direction as his explanation of the texts in Ezekiel. It shows that God has no pleasure in the death of any wicked. It witnesses of his great love for all sinners, not only the elect. I do not doubt that Kuiper agrees with him, although I do not have his written word for proof.

The reader will remember how often the protagonists of common grace in recent years have quoted this text.

But what does Calvin say about it? Fortunately this text was also quoted long ago by other Pelagians. I say fortunately, for were it not so, we probably would have no comment of Calvin directly on this passage. But we have not only Calvin's explanation, but also Augustine's explanation. Calvin writes, "What Augustine advanced in reply to them in many parts of his works, I think it unnecessary to bring forward on the present occasion. I will only cite one passage, which clearly and briefly proves how Augustine despised, without reservation, their objection now in question."[33]

---

33 Ibid., 93.

When our Lord complains that though he wished to gather the children of Jerusalem as a hen gathers her chickens under her wings, but she would not [Matt. 23:37], are we to consider that the will of God was overpowered by a number of weak men, so that he who was Almighty God could not do what he wished or willed to do? If so, what is to become of that omnipotence by which he did "whatsoever pleased him in heaven and in earth" [Ps. 135:6]? Moreover, who will be found so profanely mad as to say that God cannot convert the evil wills of men which he pleases, when he pleases, and as he pleases, to good? When he does this, he does it in mercy; and when he does it not, in judgment he does it not.[34]

Striking it is, as all will admit, that even in Augustine's time the Pelagians discovered this text and proof in it for their freewill theory. It is equally evident that Augustine's explanation, quoted by Calvin and adopted by him, differs radically from that of Berkhof.

The interpretation quoted above proceeds from the truth that the divine will is stronger than man's evil will. Thus Matthew 23:37 cannot mean to oppose the human will of wicked men to the divine will of the Son of God, for then it would teach that in the case of Jerusalem the will of men was mightier than the will of God. It follows too that according to Augustine's interpretation it is not the divine but the human will of Jesus to which the text refers.

Thus, again, the interpretation of Calvin and Augustine agrees with mine, not with Berkhof's. I always contended that when Jesus lamented over Jerusalem he spoke according to his human nature. This is plain from the words of Jesus as the culmination of all the prophets. Through those prophets, as well as personally, Jesus often called the wayward children of Jerusalem and would have gathered them as a hen gathers her chickens under her wings. But they would not.

Did the will of men triumph over the will of God? God forbid! "For they are not all Israel, which are of Israel...In Isaac shall thy seed be called" (Rom. 9:6–7). The children of the promise, not the

---

34 Ibid.

children of the flesh, are the children according to election. God willed to gather them, and he actually gathers them unto salvation.

But the will of the prophets, the desire of those who preached the word of God, had always been to gather all the children of their people. According to Jesus' human nature it was no different. Certainly there is pathos in the words, but the pathos is not divine but human.[35]

Clearly thus far Berkhof and Kuiper receive no support from John Calvin. He condemns their doctrine and agrees with the Protestant Reformed Churches.

---

35 To differ with this notion, that according to his human nature Jesus desired to gather all the inhabitants of Jerusalem, does not at all detract from Hoeksema's main point: the genuine children of Jerusalem were the elect among the inhabitants of the city. These Jesus desired to gather. These he *did* gather, despite Jerusalem's opposition. Jesus spoke in the text as the Messiah, whose will, or desire, is the will of God who sent him. The will of God was the gathering not of all the inhabitants of Jerusalem, but only of Jerusalem's genuine children, that is, the elect.—Ed.

CHAPTER 5

JOHN CALVIN
ON DIVINE HARDENING

We must remember the point of the comparison I am making between the views of Calvin, Berkhof, and Kuiper. The great question is not whether the gospel is preached to all those to whom God sends it according to his good pleasure. On this we all agree. The preaching of the gospel by men is promiscuous according to the will of God. Even when that gospel invites those who are hungry and thirsty, those who are weary and heavy laden, the sound of that invitation reaches reprobate as well as elect.

But the great question is, does God have that gospel preached to the reprobate wicked *in his grace*? Do the reprobate actually receive a certain general grace of God when the gospel is preached to them?

I say no, the preaching of the gospel is grace only to the elect. Berkhof and Kuiper say yes, the gospel is God's gracious and well-meant offer of salvation to all men. It is grace also to the reprobate. They claim that their view is Reformed, that it is Calvinistic. This is the reason for investigating Calvin's views on this fundamental question.

More than once I have concluded on good grounds, quoting from *Calvin's Calvinism*, that the Genevan reformer does not agree with Berkhof and Kuiper and that he refuses to be called their spiritual father. He did not agree with their interpretation of the well-known passages from Ezekiel and with their interpretation of Jesus' outcry over apostate Jerusalem. Calvin emphasized that a man must be beside himself to maintain that the promise of a new heart is meant for all men promiscuously. The preaching of the gospel is indeed general, according to John Calvin, but the grace in the gospel is strictly particular. There is no gracious offer of salvation on the part of God to all men.

But I am not through quoting Calvin on this subject. He is very outspoken and definite on this matter. There need be no doubt in our minds as to Calvin's views. All my readers will have to admit this when I have finished. Even Berkhof and Kuiper themselves, I am perfectly confident, will admit that they do not agree with Calvin on this point. I do not know whether they will admit this in public. But whether they do or not, I am confident they can read and understand and conclude before their own minds and hearts that they have departed from the views of the great reformer.

To convince all, I quote Calvin again.

Now let us listen to the evangelist John, who will be no ambiguous interpreter. "But though," says John, "Jesus had done so many miracles before them, yet they believed not on him, that the saying of Esaias the prophet might be fulfilled which he spake, Lord, who hath believed our report? and to whom hath the arm of the Lord been revealed? Therefore they could not believe, because that Esaias said again, he hath blinded their eyes and hardened their heart" [John 12:37–40; Isa. 53:1; Isa. 6:9–10]. Most certainly John does not give us to understand that the Jews were prevented by their sinfulness from believing, for though this be quite true in one sense, yet the cause of their not believing must be traced to a far higher source. The secret and eternal purpose and counsel of God must be viewed as the original cause of their blindness and unbelief. It perplexed, in no small degree, the ignorant and the weak when they heard that there was no place for Christ among the people of God (for the Jews were such). John explains the reason by showing that none believe except those to whom it is given, and that there are few to whom God reveals his arm.

This other prophecy concerning "the arm of the Lord" [Isa. 53:1] the evangelist weaves into his argument to prove the same great truth, and his words have a momentous weight. He says, "*Therefore,* they *could not* believe" [John 12:39]. Let men torture themselves as long as they will with reasoning that the cause of the difference—why God does not reveal his arm equally to *all*—lies hidden in his own eternal decree. The whole of the evangelist's argument amounts evidently to this: Faith is a special gift, and the wisdom of Christ is too high and too deep to come within the compass of man's understanding. The unbelief of the world, therefore, ought not to astonish us if even the wisest and most acute of men fail to believe. Hence, unless we would evade the plain and confessed meaning of the evangelist that few receive the gospel, we must fully conclude that the cause is the will of God, and that the outward sound of the gospel strikes the ear in vain until God is pleased to touch by it the heart within.[36]

This passage is significant, first, because it speaks of the promiscuous preaching of the gospel to men. It concerns the question in dispute among us. Isaiah preached the gospel and only a few believed, so few that he complained, "Who hath believed our report? and to whom is the arm of the LORD revealed?" (Isa. 53:1). Christ preached the gospel. His preaching was reinforced by the performance of many miracles, right before the eyes of the people. Yet also few believed when he preached, even though he performed many miracles.

So the minister of today preaches the gospel, and the result is always the same. Although he cries ever so loudly that the gospel he preaches is for all sinners, yet the result will not be different. Only a certain number will believe the gospel, as long as he does not corrupt it. If he does not preach the pure and true gospel of God in Christ, he may see different results and gather thousands upon thousands. The trouble with this is that God did not gather them. They are "converted" by man not by God.

Second, this quotation of Calvin is significant because it mentions the cause of this unbelief of the multitude and their leaders. How does Calvin explain? Does he say that the gospel Isaiah preached and the gospel Christ preached, together with the miracles he performed,

---

36 Calvin, *Calvin's Calvinism*, 70–71.

constituted a well-meant offer of God to save them all? Does he say that the gospel revealed the grace and loving-kindness of God to all who heard? Does he present the matter as if the preaching of Isaiah and of the Lord revealed the earnest desire of God to save all? Does he leave the explanation of their unbelief entirely with man and his sinfulness?

Far from it! He could not explain the matter thus, because he was bound to the word of God and that word by the evangelist John pointed to an entirely different cause. They *could not* believe! Why could they not believe? Because of their sinfulness? Yes, Calvin says, sinfulness is *a factor*. But it is not *the cause*. The cause is the will of God. He blinded their eyes and hardened their hearts. *Therefore*, they could not believe.

That few receive the gospel is a fact. Calvin concludes that so few receive the gospel because of the will of God. God does not will that all who hear the gospel in its outward sound will believe. This is why they believe not.

If this is the case, there is nothing left of a well-meant and gracious offer on the part of God in the preaching of the gospel. When the gospel is preached, God blinds the eyes and hardens the hearts of some, while he opens the eyes and softens the hearts of others unto repentance. Kuiper talks of mysteries, but he cannot accept as a mystery that God hardens the hearts and blinds the eyes of those to whom he graciously offers the gospel and whom he seriously desires to save.

If he would still maintain that this is his honest conviction and that he can really accept such foolishness as a mystery of God, we will let him have his notions. But he cannot appeal to Calvin.

Calvin believed and expressed without compromise that in and under the preaching of the gospel, there is not only a gracious operation of the Spirit unto salvation, but just as well a hardening operation of God's wrath, so that God does not reveal his arm to all. This excludes grace for all in the preaching of the gospel.

CHAPTER 6

JOHN CALVIN ON GRACE
IN THE PREACHING

Again I call the reader's attention to Calvin's conception of the preaching of the gospel and its significance for those who are not saved—not elect but reprobate. It is not strictly necessary to cite more proof for the statement that Berkhof and Kuiper have departed from Calvin and the historically Reformed line of doctrine when they teach that God is gracious in the preaching of the gospel to all who hear, since the gospel is a well-meant and gracious offer of salvation to all. I believe that I have furnished abundant proof in the quotations already presented.

But I can foresee a possible attempt to enervate my argument by emphasizing that the Genevan reformer speaks of general offers of salvation, of mercy, and of the gospel. It might be alleged that one could not deny the apparent contradiction between Kuiper and Berkhof on the one hand and what I quoted from Calvin on the other hand, but that I did not fully quote him on this subject. Other passages reveal plainly that the great reformer of Geneva also maintained another line of doctrine and taught a general, well-meant offer of salvation on the part of God to all men without distinction. In this way the deceitful impression might be left that Calvin also believed in two lines of truth, flatly opposed to each other and mutually exclusive, and called it a mystery.

It has become general and customary in the Christian Reformed Church to appeal to mystery to hide the old Arminian error that the church defends. When Jan Karel van Baalen, in company with others, exerted himself almost above his power to have Danhof and me expelled from the communion of the Christian church, Van Baalen emphasized that I ran on a single track. He warned against the danger of doing so and taught that we must run on a double track. For the reader who does not remember and cannot verify this statement, I quote Van Baalen words on this point.

> For what is the case? The holy scripture is not *single track*. It is *double track*. There are two lines running through scripture, parallel to each other, like the two tracks of a train. The one track is election and reprobation, the line of God's secret decree. The other line is the accountability of man and the revealed will of God, "who wills that all men shall be saved."[37]

You see the intent of such teaching. On the one hand is God's secret will, which implies that only the elect will be saved and that man can do nothing to effect his salvation. On the other hand is the revealed will, which implies that God wills the salvation of all men. First Timothy 2:4 is quoted in the same sense and with the same purpose as it has always been quoted by all Arminians: "who will have all men to be saved."

This deceitful and general teaching, which is nothing but Arminianism under cover of the Reformed confessions and therefore is more dangerous, is the doctrine of not only Van Baalen, but also of the Christian Reformed Church. In the Reformed churches in the United States, William Heyns is the chief defender and protagonist of this view.

Someone might attempt to show that Calvin held a double-track view of the truth, for he speaks sometimes of a general offer of mercy and of the gospel. Lest someone who does not want to hear the truth makes this mistake, I quote Calvin again as he writes against Pighius.

> One reason (Pighius says) he cannot believe in particular and special election is because Christ, the redeemer of the whole world, commanded the gospel to be preached to all men, promiscuously, generally, and without distinction. But the gospel is an embassy of peace, by which the world is reconciled to God, as

---

37 Van Baalen, *Denial of Common Grace*, 38.

Paul teaches [2 Cor. 5:18–19]. And, according to the same holy witness, it is preached so that those who hear it may be saved.[38]

Such was the difficulty or pretended difficulty of the Pelagian Pighius. The reader will recognize immediately that here we touch on the heart of the question in dispute between Berkhof, Kuiper, Van Baalen, and their confederates and the Protestant Reformed Churches. Pighius' objection to the doctrine of predestination concerned the preaching of the gospel, which is general, promiscuous, and without distinction to all who hear. But how can that be, if you believe in the doctrine of predestination? If God saves only the elect, what is the sense of the general preaching of the gospel? Nay, the objection is more serious still: "the gospel is an embassy of peace" to men. By it God wants to save men. By it the "world is reconciled to God." It follows therefore that grace must be universal—at least as universal as the preaching of the gospel.

Now Van Baalen, Berkhof, Kuiper, and others would answer, we admit everything you say about the preaching of the gospel. It is God's embassy of peace to all who hear. It is his well-meant and gracious offer of salvation to all men promiscuously. "The gospel I preach is a gospel for sinners, for all sinners," says Kuiper.[39] "Who wills that all men shall be saved," quotes Van Baalen. Berkhof appeals to Ezekiel to show that God seriously wills and seeks the salvation of everyone, even of those who are lost.[40] On this they agree. But, these men explain, that is only one side of the truth. That is the one track on which your train of truth must run. There is another side; your train must also run on another track. The other side of the truth is that God does not will that all men shall be saved, but with firm and fixed decree he has limited forever the number who will be saved. That is the other track. If you tell them that the one is the Arminian track, and that your train cannot run in two opposite directions at the same time, they assure you that such is nevertheless the truth. Only it is a mystery.

---

38 Calvin, *Calvin's Calvinism*, 82.
39 Kuiper, *Three Points of Common Grace*, 16.
40 Berkhof, *Three Points*, 21–22, 24.

Does Calvin answer the objection raised against the doctrine of election and reprobation in the same way?

> To this pretended difficulty of Pighius, I would briefly reply that Christ was so ordained the Savior of the whole world that he might save those who were given unto him by the Father out of the whole world, that he might be the eternal life of them of whom he is the head, and that he might receive into a participation of all "the blessings in him" [Eph. 1:3] all those whom God adopted to himself by his own unmerited good pleasure to be his heirs. Now which one of these solemn things can our opponent deny?[41]

Here the reformer begins to answer his opponent by again emphasizing the doctrine of particular redemption. Pighius has asserted that by the preaching of the gospel as an embassy of peace, the world is reconciled to God. Calvin answers, in effect, yes, but the whole world does not mean all men individually and without distinction, but it means the world of the elect, those whom God gave unto Christ out of the world. Then Calvin continues:

> Hence the apostle Paul declares this prophecy of Isaiah to be fulfilled in Christ: "Behold, I and the children whom the Lord hath given me" [Isa. 8:18; Heb. 2:13]. Accordingly, Christ himself declares aloud: "All that the Father giveth me shall come to me, and him that cometh to me I will in no wise cast out" [John 6:37]. And again, "Those that thou gavest me I have kept, and none of them is lost, but the son of perdition" [John 17:12]. Hence we read everywhere that Christ diffuses life into none but the members of his own body. And he who will not confess that it is a special gift and a special mercy to be engrafted into the body of Christ has never read with spiritual attention Paul's Epistle to the Ephesians.
> Hereupon follows also a third important fact: The virtue and benefit of Christ are extended unto and belong to none but the children of God.[42]

---

41 Calvin, *Calvin's Calvinism*, 82–83.
42 Ibid., 83.

Here Calvin establishes from scripture, over against Pighius, that whatever he may allege, he cannot deny the truth of particular redemption. This must be established first. However the general preaching of the gospel may have to be explained, this must stand: salvation is not meant for all, and it is not granted unto all, but only to the children of God. They are the elect. This being firmly established, the reformer is ready to answer the objection of Pighius. Calvin continues: "That the universality of the grace of Christ cannot be better judged of than from the nature of the preaching of the gospel, there is no one who will not immediately grant."[43]

One probably would not expect Calvin to write this. He probably would expect Calvin to write that you cannot conclude from the general preaching of the gospel the universality of salvation in Christ.

In fact, that is exactly what our opponents allege. The preaching of the gospel is one thing. The grace of Christ is quite another. The content of the gospel concerns all. It is a well-meant offer of salvation on the part of God to all without distinction who hear the gospel. These are the two lines you must maintain. They are the two tracks on which your train must run. But you cannot reconcile them. This is a mystery, and you must not enter into the deep things of God. They are secret. The revealed things are for us and our children. These revealed things are, according to Van Baalen, "who wills that all men shall be saved."

Calvin does not reason this way. For him there are not two contradictory lines and opposite tracks in the word of God. That is why he can write, "That the universality of the grace of Christ cannot be better judged of than from the nature of the preaching of the gospel, there is no one who will not immediately grant."[44] But he does not leave the question there. He explains further:

> Yet on this hinge the whole question turns. If we see and acknowledge, therefore, the principle on which the doctrine of the gospel offers salvation to all, the whole sacred matter is settled at once. That the gospel is, in its nature, able to save all,

---

43 Ibid.
44 Ibid.

I by no means deny. But the great question lies here: Did the Lord by his eternal counsel ordain salvation for all men? It is quite manifest that all men, without difference or distinction, are outwardly called or invited to repentance and faith. It is equally evident that the same mediator is set forth before all as he who alone can reconcile them to the Father. But it is as fully well known that none of these things can be understood or perceived but by faith, in fulfillment of the apostle Paul's declaration that "the gospel is the power of God unto salvation to every one that believeth" [Rom. 1:16]. Then what can it be to others but "the savor of death unto death?" as the same apostle elsewhere powerfully expresses himself [2 Cor. 2:16].[45]

Here the reformer explains the principle on which the doctrine of the gospel offers salvation to all. Let me explain in passing that in Calvin the word "offer" does not mean what it expresses in our present-day English. It is a translation of the Latin *offere*, which means "to set forth, to bring to the attention of someone."

What, according to Calvin, is the principle of setting forth salvation to all? Is it an unconditional expression on the part of God that he will save all? Is that the nature of the preaching of the gospel? Can one say, "The gospel I preach is a gospel for all sinners"? Or are the nature and content of the preaching of the gospel particular?

This is the question Calvin raises, and he answers it in the negative. Outwardly the gospel is preached to all who hear, but its content cannot even be perceived or understood except by faith. Such is the declaration of the gospel, for the scriptures do not say that the gospel is God's well-meant offer of salvation to all men. The Bible nowhere uses such Arminian language. The gospel is not an offer but a power of God unto salvation. It is a power of God unto salvation not to all but to those who believe.

Such is the gospel. It is the general proclamation of a particular salvation, as I have always emphasized, a presentation Berkhof ridiculed. He may now ridicule Calvin.

---

45 Ibid., 83.

The Genevan reformer declares that on this question the whole matter turns. See this and you have no difficulty. It is true that the universality of the grace of the Lord can be judged from the nature of the preaching of the gospel, provided this is rightly understood. Salvation is just as universal as the preaching of the gospel declares it to be. But in this preaching there is no unconditional offer of salvation, but the declaration of a power of God unto salvation only to those who believe. Calvin concludes:

Further, as it is undeniably manifest, out of the multitudes whom God calls by his outward voice in the gospel, very few believe. If I prove that the greater part of these multitudes remain unbelieving (for God deems none worthy of his illumination but whom he will), I obtain thereby the next conclusion: The mercy of God is offered [set forth] equally to those who believe and to those who believe not, so that those who are not divinely taught within are only rendered inexcusable, not saved. Some make a distinction here, holding that the gospel is saving to all regarding its power to save, but not in its effect of saving. But they by no means untie the knot by this halfway argument. We are still rolled back to the same great question: Is the same power to believe conferred upon all men?

Paul assigns the reason that all do not obey the gospel. He refers us to the prophet Isaiah: "Lord, who hath believed our report, and to whom is the arm of the Lord revealed?" [Isa. 53:1; Rom. 10:16]. The prophet here, astonished at the fewness of those who believe, seems to cry aloud that it was a thing of the highest shame and reproach that while the word of God was sounding in the ears of all men, there were scarcely any hearts inwardly touched by it. But that so awful a depravity in man might not terrify the contemplators of it, the apostle Paul afterwards intimates, that it is not given to all thus to believe, but to those only to whom God manifests himself [v. 20]. In a word, the apostle in this chapter intimates that any effort or sound of the human voice will be ineffectual unless the secret power of God works in the hearts of the hearers. Of this fact Luke places before our eyes a memorable proof. After he had recorded the sermon preached by Paul, Luke says, "And as many as were ordained to eternal life believed" [Acts 13:48]. Now why was not this same doctrine of Paul received with the same mind and heart by all who heard it? Luke assigns the reason and defines the number of the receivers: "As many as were ordained to eternal life believed." The rest did not believe because they were not "ordained to eternal life." And who is the giver of this disposition of the heart but God alone?[46]

This passage is very significant for the present controversy for more than one reason.

First, it denies the statement that there are two lines in Holy Writ that cannot be reconciled—the mystery that God wills only the elect to be saved and that he earnestly expresses his will to save all men. Calvin must have nothing of such mysteries. When he is placed before the objection that the general preaching of the gospel cannot be maintained in light of the doctrine of particular redemption, he does not avoid the argument but enters into its very heart. Neither does he end up with irreconcilable contradictions that he calls mysteries, but he explains the matter and shows the harmony of God's counsel and the preaching of the gospel.

Second, the quotation is a plain denial of the view that the gospel is a message of peace to all without distinction. It is a power of salvation only to those who believe. Although the outward calling is general, the preaching is conditional and particular.

Third, the quotation is significant because it is a plain denial—that is, plain to all who will perceive and understand—of the statement that the preaching of the gospel is grace also to those who perish. The reformer emphasizes that it is a savor of death unto death to those whose hearts God does not inwardly touch. Moreover, Calvin expresses himself very clearly when he says that the gospel is preached to those who do not believe, not so that they might be saved, but that

---

46 Ibid., 83–84.

they might be rendered inexcusable. According to Calvin this is evidently God's purpose with the preaching of the gospel to those who are lost. But if the preaching of the gospel must be a savor of death to some, a means to render them more inexcusable, where does the grace of God enter into preaching by means of the outward sound, but without the inward voice of the Spirit?

Will Berkhof or Kuiper or both answer, please? You can do so in the *Banner*, if you prefer. Better still, you may have all the space you desire in the *Standard Bearer*. I say "better," because all of our readers do not read the *Banner*, and it would be expedient for them to be acquainted with your replies.

I have shown that you departed from the historically Reformed line, as begun anew and developed more powerfully by John Calvin. I am convinced that you cannot deny the truth of what I have written. If you still think that I have misrepresented either you or Calvin in any respect, will you show the reader in what respect I made such a mistake? And if I presented the matter fairly and truthfully, will you not acknowledge that you have erred?

The matter, you will perceive, is very serious. For the same teachings contained in *Calvin's Calvinism* you have persecuted Danhof and myself, and you did not rest until we were expelled from the communion of your church. At the time you became friends even of your enemies to unite with them in expelling those who were your friends and brethren in the faith. You are responsible before God, before whose judgment seat we will appear together.

But this is not the worst. The worst [was that] you assumed leadership in the church to introduce the Arminian three points, the first of which is so plainly condemned by the teachings of John Calvin. A large part of the church, already strongly inclined to turn into Arminian paths, as you well know, has followed you. For their following and their further deviation from the truth of the word of God you are responsible. So serious is this matter.

Therefore, I charge you before God that you may not keep silent. It is your solemn duty to make plain so all can understand that Calvin teaches that God in the preaching of the gospel is gracious to all, and that this preaching is a well-meant offer of salvation to all who hear the gospel. If you cannot do this, your duty is to acknowledge that you depart from Calvin and that in 1924 you would have thrown him out of your church as you did us.

In conclusion, I cannot refrain from showing what Calvin thinks of Van Baalen's doctrine that God wills that all men be saved. Pighius as well as Van Baalen quoted 1 Timothy 2:4, so we can know how Calvin would have answered this gentleman with whom I would otherwise rather not trouble myself any further.

Calvin writes,

> The difficulty, according to Pighius, that lies in the other place of Paul, where the apostle affirms that "God will have all men to be saved and come unto the knowledge of the truth" [1 Tim. 2:4], is solved in one moment and by one question, namely, How does God wish all men to come to the knowledge of the truth? For Paul couples together this salvation and this coming to the knowledge of the truth. I would ask, Did the same will of God stand the same from the beginning of the world or not? For if God willed or wished that his truth should be known unto all men, how was it that he did not proclaim and make known his law to the Gentiles also? Why did he confine the light of life within the narrow limits of Judea? What does Moses mean when he says, "For what nation is there so great, who has God so nigh unto them as the Lord our God is in all things that we call upon him for? And what nation is there so great, that has statutes and judgments so righteous as all this law that I set before you this day" [Deut. 4:7–8]? The divine lawgiver surely means that there was no other nation that had statutes and laws by which it was ruled like unto that nation. What does Moses extol but the peculiar privilege of the race of Abraham? To this responds the high encomium of David, pronounced on the same nation: "He hath not dealt so with any nation, and as for his judgments, they have not known them" [Ps. 147:20]. Nor must we disregard the express reason:

"Because the Lord loved thy fathers, therefore he chose their seed after them" [Deut. 4:37]. And why did God thus choose them? Not because they were more excellent in themselves than others, but it pleased God to choose them "for his peculiar people" [Deut. 14:2; Deut. 26:18; 1 Pet. 2:9].

What? Are we to suppose that the apostle did not know that he was prohibited by the Holy Spirit from preaching the word in Asia, and from passing over into Bithynia [Acts 16:6–7]? As the continuance of this argument would render it too prolix, we will be content with taking one position more. God, after having lighted the candle of eternal life to the Jews alone, suffered the Gentiles to wander for many ages in the darkness of ignorance, and at length this special gift and blessing were promised to the church: "But the Lord shall arise upon thee, and his glory shall be seen upon thee" [Isa. 60:2].

Now let Pighius boast, if he can, that God wills all men to be saved. The above arguments, founded on the Scriptures, prove that even the external preaching of the doctrine of salvation, which is very far inferior to the illumination of the Spirit, was not made of God common to all men.[47]

A little later Calvin explains that the text Van Baalen cited as proof of his "other track" refers to orders of men rather than to individuals.

I think I gave more than sufficient proof to establish that John Calvin does not sustain the position of the Christian Reformed Church when it expresses in its first point that the external preaching of the gospel is a manifestation of God's grace to all who hear the preaching.

---

47 Ibid., 92–93.

A TRIPLE BREACH IN THE FOUNDATION OF THE REFORMED TRUTH

A Critical Treatise on the Three Points Adopted
by the Synod of the Christian Reformed Church in 1924

———————◆———————

HERMAN HOEKSEMA

Introduction to *A Triple Breach*

Herman Hoeksema published *A Triple Breach* soon after his expulsion from the Christian Reformed Church in 1924–26 and soon after the formation of the Protestant Reformed Churches. The four chapters of the booklet were originally four public lectures.

The booklet was published originally in Dutch as *Drie Scheuren in het Fundament der Gereformeerde Waarheid*. An English translation, *A Triple Breach in the Foundation of the Reformed Truth*, appeared in 1942. The translator is not indicated. It is probable that Hoeksema translated his own work from Dutch into English, especially since the translator took some liberties with the text of the Dutch original. Long out of print, this English translation was reprinted in 1992 by the evangelism society of Southwest Protestant Reformed Church in Grandville, Michigan. The only change from the edition of 1942 was a new foreword in place of Hoeksema's preface. It is the 1942 translation, reprinted in 1992, that is published here with Hoeksema's original preface.

A Triple Breach is Hoeksema's critique—his *devastating* critique—of the doctrine of common grace adopted by the Christian Reformed Church in 1924. He demonstrates that the three points of common grace are not interpretations of the Reformed creeds but "appendages" to the creeds. Chapter by chapter, Hoeksema exposes each of the three points as corruption of the truth of scripture and the Reformed confessions. It was the conviction of Hoeksema, as it is the conviction of the Protestant Reformed Churches today, that the three points of common grace are "deviations from the truth that have far-reaching effects and threaten to undermine the very foundations of the Reformed truth" (Hoeksema's preface).

In the booklet Hoeksema issued a challenge to his Christian Reformed adversaries—Louis Berkhof, Henry Beets, and others—to defend the three points in light of Hoeksema's criticisms of them. They did not respond. The reason was that Hoeksema had conclusively demonstrated that the three points are utterly indefensible by one who claims to be Reformed and therefore is bound by the confessions.

The challenge extended by *A Triple Breach* goes out today to every theologian in the Christian Reformed Church, indeed to every member of the Christian Reformed Church, as also to all others who confess the doctrine of a common grace of God along Christian Reformed lines. None will respond to the challenge. None dares to respond. No defense of the three points as Reformed according to the creeds is possible.

Every member of the Protestant Reformed Churches ought to read *A Triple Breach*. Societies should study and discuss it. The booklet establishes that the existence of the Protestant Reformed Churches was occasioned by persecution of a sound, faithful, Reformed minister for the truth's sake and that this truth was fundamental Reformed doctrine. It will also confirm to the member of these churches that, as a denomination of Reformed churches that uncompromisingly confesses predestination, total depravity, and the antithesis, the Protestant Reformed Churches are true churches of God and necessary.

The work includes some memorable lines, for example, "Regeneration is a wonder, common grace is magical."

An appendix contains the three points of common grace as adopted by the Christian Reformed Church and Hoeksema's succinct expression of the essence of each of them.

—David J. Engelsma

For us it was a matter of conscience when in 1924 we refused to declare ourselves in conformity with the three points of doctrine adopted the same year by the synod of the Christian Reformed Church. We also refused to refrain from making propaganda against those points in the churches, even though on account of this refusal the Christian Reformed Church expelled us from its fellowship. That it was a question of conscience with those who thus dissented and were expelled from the churches has been amply corroborated by the history of the Protestant Reformed Churches since 1924.

Before God and our consciences it was not only impossible for us to subscribe to three doctrinal declarations whose tenets were, according to our firm convictions, in conflict with the word of God and the Reformed standards, but we also considered it our calling to expose before the churches the errors of the three points and to warn our Reformed people against their dangerous tendencies and influence. When therefore Classis Grand Rapids East, in spite of all our efforts to prevent a separation, left us no other alternative than either to sign the three points and promise not to oppose their doctrine openly or to be deposed from the office of minister of the word in the Christian Reformed Church, we chose the latter because before God and our consciences we could do nothing else.

Of this choice we never repented. The more we make a thorough study of the doctrinal implications of the three points and of the arguments in their defense, given by the leaders of the Christian Reformed Church, the firmer our convictions become that they are deviations from the truth that have far-reaching effects and threaten to undermine the very foundations of the Reformed truth.

This conviction explains the publication of this booklet. With a few alterations, it contains a quaternion of lectures on the three points delivered in different parts of the United States.

With the prayer that our God may use this booklet as an instrument in his hands to open the eyes of many to the errors and dangers of the three points and to strengthen their hearts in the truth of his word, we offer it to the interested reader.

—Herman Hoeksema

CHAPTER I

NO INTERPRETATIONS
BUT APPENDAGES

n this chapter I submit to the interested reader a simple, fair, yet very important question. At the same time I purpose to bring before his attention all possible evidence to prove that the question can be answered in only one way.

In putting the question, various assumptions must tacitly be made. First, I will assume that the reader is interested in the truth of the word of God as expressed in the Reformed confessions. It is also his desire that the Reformed truth be maintained, and he is interested in the well-being of the Reformed churches.

Second, I presume that the reader is informed about the existence of the three points. He knows that in 1924 the synod of the Christian Reformed Church formulated three doctrinal declarations. Especially if you are a member of the Christian Reformed Church you will probably consider this a superfluous assumption, for you will ask, what member does not know about the three points? Yet one meets with astounding ignorance in this respect. There are many responsible members of the Christian Reformed Church who know little or nothing about these points. You must not be overly surprised if occasionally you meet one who expresses indignation that the author of this pamphlet formulated the three points and thus departed from the line of the Reformed faith.

Third, I presume that the reader not only knows of the existence of the three points, but also that he is more or less acquainted with their content, is aware of the doctrinal significance of them, understands their tenets, and can discern between the true and the false, between Reformed and un-Reformed.

Assuming all of this to be true, I intend to answer these questions: Are the three points of 1924 *interpretations* of the Reformed confessions or *appendages*, additions to, augmentations of the confessions? Do the three points merely express the content of the forms of unity in a different form, or are they three doctrinal innovations?

The question whether these three points are in harmony with the Reformed confessions I leave alone for the present. It has no direct bearing on the point I wish to discuss. Appendages to the confessions may be Reformed, and the confessions may be augmented in such a way that the augmentation is a further development of the Reformed truth. Amendment of the confessions is possible and proper and must even be considered desirable. But for the present we will not apply the criterion of scripture and the confessions to the three points to discover if they are Reformed.

The sole question before us now is: is the content of the three points contained in the confessions of the Reformed churches, or have the three points been added to the three forms of unity? Are the three points interpretations or appendages? This is an important question.

Leaders of the Christian Reformed Church emphasize that the three points contain nothing new, that they are not three additions or amendments to the confessions but merely further interpretations of what is clearly implied or expressed in the forms of unity. No new confession was drawn up and adopted in 1924, and the existing standards were not augmented. Synod merely interpreted the standards of the Reformed churches, or rather it quoted them, to refute various errors of Danhof and Hoeksema.[1] Such a presentation of the matter was thought to be preferable for more than one reason.

---

1   This is evident from what Berkhof writes. "First...in these points we have no material addition to our confessional standards...Our people may be assured that the synod of 1924 by adopting the three points added nothing to the essential content of our confessions. She only brought forward and formulated a triplet of truths that are clearly implied in our confessional standards and that are partly emphatically expressed therein" (Berkhof, *Three Points*, 5). "In connection with the controversy that has arisen among us, synod only brought forward certain truths that are clearly contained in our confessions or are even emphatically professed therein" (Ibid., 62).

I am unable to understand the courage of the professor to write these bold statements. They are a mystery to me, especially when I consider that in his book on the three points he does not substantiate these statements. Nowhere does he offer any proof for synod's declaration that the preaching of the gospel is common grace, nor does he point out where in the confessions such a doctrine might even be suggested. When he would show his readers where the confession speaks of a general operation of the Holy Spirit that restrains sin, he boldly faces the difficulty and passes on. To substantiate his statements regarding the third point, he wisely quotes only the first half of the Canons of Dordt 3–4. 4. He must have realized that the second half of the same article would certainly disprove his contentions.

In direct examination Dr. C. Bouma testified the following before the Circuit Court of Kent County.

Q. "We have read them [the three points] over and over here. What did synod do? What was the action of synod? What I am getting at is whether it was an interpretation of the confessional standards?"

A. "Most assuredly."

Q. "That is what it was?"

A. "Most assuredly."

Q. "And after synod has made this interpretation what became the duty of all members of the Christian Reformed Church and especially these ministers?"

A. "To submit." ("State of Michigan, in the Circuit Court for the County of Kent, in Chancery. December Term, 1924. Before Hon. Major L. Dunham, Circuit Judge. William Holwerda, Et Al Plaintiffs, Vs. Herman Hoeksema, Et Al Defendants, No. 26695. Grand Rapids, MI. Monday A.M., February 9, 1925," 459.)

Before the same court Professor Volbeda was cross-examined. The attorney inquired into the attitude of the four professors regarding the decision of synod in the Janssen case in 1920. He wanted to know whether they submitted to the decision of synod in that case. Part of the examination follows:

Q. "As I understand it, the Janssen case first came up for consideration by the synod of 1920?"

A. "As far as the synod is concerned, yes, sir."

Q. "And at that time synod made a decision in the Janssen matter?"

A. "Yes, sir."

Q. "And in that decision interpreted and passed upon certain matters of the teachings to the students by Dr. Janssen with relation to doctrine?"

A. "Yes, sir."

Q. "Was that decision of synod in 1920 binding on all members of the denomination?"

A. "Yes, sir."

Q. "Well, I will ask you, doctor, if following that decision of the synod, you, with certain other professors of the college or seminary, joined in publishing a pamphlet protesting against that decision of synod in 1920?"

A. "We did not protest."

Q. "What did you do?"

A. "_____ if you take that in the technical sense of the term."

Q. "Well, what did you do in this pamphlet?"

In this way the three points can easily sink into oblivion. This is deemed desirable. Strange though it may seem, the leaders of the Christian Reformed Church are not eager to be reminded of the three points or to discuss them. Although they formulated the three points and considered them sufficiently important to be a basis for the deposition of ministers, elders, and deacons, yet now they would rather forget the three points. It is considered expedient for the peace of the churches to bury them in oblivion. This burial of the three points is facilitated by presenting them as interpretations of the confessions, while if it were admitted that they were innovations, appendages, additions to the forms of unity, they would have to be brought repeatedly to the attention of the people and of the churches.

For instance, suppose you are called to be an officebearer in the Christian Reformed Church, be it minister, elder, or deacon. In that case, according to the custom of all the Reformed churches, you are requested to sign the Formula of Subscription. By signing the Formula you declare that you agree with the three forms of unity—the Heidelberg Catechism, the Belgic Confession, and the Canons of Dordrecht.

If the three points adopted by the synod of 1924 are virtually new confessions, not contained or implied in the forms of unity, it would

---

A. "We laid the case open, as it had so far progressed before the church at large."

Q. "Did you criticize the action that synod had taken in 1920?"

A. "We expressed our opinion in regard to that decision, yes, sir."

Q. "You expressed the opinion that synod's decision in 1920 was not the correct decision?"

A. "Yes, sir." (Ibid., 481–82.)

Later in the examination the professor testified concerning our case as follows:

Q. "How do you distinguish between the position taken by you in your pamphlet and your position in the Hoeksema matter?"

A. "For one point, in the case of 1920 synod did not interpret the confession."

Q. "What did it interpret?"

A. "It did not expound the meaning of the confession. In the case of 1924 that is the thing that was done; the confession was interpreted, and the sense of the confession as taken by the church was laid down in these three propositions that by this time are familiar. This is one point." (Ibid., 491.)

From these quotations it is very evident that Bouma and Volbeda present the three points as interpretations of the confessions.

be necessary to require every officebearer to sign them separately. If an officebearer should refuse to agree with these points, he would have to be barred from entering his office. But this is never done. Even after the adoption of three points, those who are installed as officebearers sign the same Formula of Subscription, in which reference is made to the same forms of unity as before the synod of 1924. The argument used to defend this omission to require a separate signing of the three points is that they are not appendages but interpretations of the standards. Thus it is possible to circumvent the necessity of requesting church members at meetings of consistory, classis, and synod to express agreement with the three points.

To make this request would no doubt cause trouble. There still are many Reformed people in the Christian Reformed Church who would surely refuse to sign the three points. I could mention by name several who do not agree with them at all.

However, they are not molested because of their attitudes. On the contrary, even though their disagreement with the three points is well-known and they publicly voice objections against them, they are nominated to be officebearers. When a man brings an objection against his nomination and expresses to the consistory his disqualification for service because he does not agree with the doctrine of 1924, his case is easily dismissed. "What difference does it make if you object to the three points? Are they not long forgotten? Who speaks of them? No one will trouble you about your attitude against them, and the consistory does not require you to sign them. You only sign the Formula of Subscription, which does not mention the three points. Therefore, you have no valid objection to your nomination, and your conscience is free!"[2] Thus the peace of the churches is preserved, and the three points are relegated to the land of oblivion. Such officebearers are not to be excused.

I know those who understand very well that the three points are not interpretations of the confessions and that their doctrine conflicts with the content of the Reformed standards. Yet these men remain in the Christian Reformed Church and even become officebearers, although

---

2   Such cases are historical facts, and I could mention names.

they know they are responsible for the doctrine the church adopted in 1924 and for the deposition of thoroughly Reformed ministers, elders, and deacons. Their consciences surely condemn them, for they know the synod of the Christian Reformed Church in 1926 emphatically declared that the three points are interpretations of the confessions and as such must be accepted by all officebearers and members. Although at their installations as officebearers they are not required to sign the three points, these men understand very well that by implication they do that very thing when they declare to be in conformity with the forms of unity as they are interpreted in the three points. Yet it is easily understood that for such officebearers it is easier to silence the voice of conscience when they are not constantly reminded of their personal responsibility for the doctrine expressed by the synod of 1924.

It must not be forgotten that some officebearers do not have in mind the three points when they sign the Formula of Subscription. They imagine that by signing that Formula they express conformity with the standards of the church pure and simple. It may be expected that their number will increase as the history of 1924 recedes into the past. This could never be the case if the three points were properly considered and treated as appendages to the standards, and if at every proper occasion officebearers and candidates for the ministry would sign them.

The question whether it is right and proper for the Christian Reformed Church to be silent regarding the three declarations of doctrine they adopted in 1924 depends on whether or not the declarations are interpretations of the confessions. If they are, the Christian Reformed Church has the proper attitude; if they are not, its attitude is ambiguous and deceptive. Hence the question: are the three points interpretations of the confessions, or are they innovations and appendages to the standards?

First, from a purely formal viewpoint it cannot be maintained that the three declarations of doctrine adopted in 1924 are meant to be interpretations of the Reformed standards. Under what circumstances are interpretations of the confessions necessary? They are necessary only when certain parts of the standards are unclear, or if doubts or different opinions arise regarding the meaning of certain articles of faith. But in 1924 that was not the case at all. There was no request before the synod to explain or to interpret any part of the confessions. There was no difference of opinion with respect to the meaning of any particular article or articles of the forms of unity. The synod was called to consider certain protests against the doctrine of Danhof and Hoeksema, who denied the theory of common grace.

Those two pastors maintained that God is *not* gracious to the ungodly reprobate; that there is *no* operation of grace in the hearts of the reprobate that restrains sin; and that there is *no* influence of grace outside of regeneration that enables the sinner to do good before God. They maintained positively that God's grace is always particular, for the elect only; that the development of sin follows the organic line of the development of the human race; and that the natural man is wholly incapable of doing any good and inclined to all evil.

Those two pastors appealed to the confessions and to the word of God to defend their position, but synod did not interpret those articles and scriptural passages. Instead of interpreting the confessions, synod simply proposed and adopted three declarations of doctrine in which the views of the two accused pastors were denied and condemned. To sustain those three synodical propositions synod merely referred, without any interpretation, to certain articles of the Belgic Confession and of the Canons of Dordrecht and to a few scriptural texts. Synod did not attempt to interpret even one of the articles to which synod referred. Synod merely quoted. The quotations from the confessions were supposed to be sufficiently clear; they needed no interpretation. They were cited to sustain the doctrine of the three points.

From all this it is evident that the three points were never intended to be interpretations of the standards. What is in need of interpretation is not cited as proof for certain doctrinal declarations. The thing explained cannot serve as proof of the explanation, yet the passages that synod quoted to sustain the three points were merely cited as so many proofs. It is sheer nonsense to maintain that the three points interpret their own basis. No more than it can be maintained that the three points are an interpretation of the scriptural passages quoted by synod to prove their biblical character can it be defended that the three points are an interpretation of those parts of the confessions quoted by synod to prove that the three points are in harmony with Reformed doctrine.

Formally, then, the three points are not intended to be interpretations of the confessions.

But, do the three points perhaps *materially* interpret the confessions?

It is perfectly conceivable that although the composers of the three points had no intention to explain but merely to quote the Reformed standards, nevertheless in the three points a further interpretation is offered of certain passages and articles of the confessions, and certain truths clearly implied in these articles are expressed with a new emphasis. Is not this exactly what the synod of 1924 did by adopting the well-known declarations of doctrine?

Let us investigate this matter. In order to carry out this investigation, I will quote the three points and also those passages of the confessions that synod cited for support of the three points.

> Concerning the first point, with regard to the favorable disposition of God toward mankind in general, and not only to the elect, Synod declares that according to the Scripture and the confessions it is determined that besides the saving grace of God, shown only to the elect unto eternal life, there is a certain kind of favor, or grace of God which He shows to His creatures in general. This is evidenced by the quoted Scripture passages and from the Canons of Dort 2.5 and 3–4.8–9, which deals with the general offer of the Gospel; whereas the quoted declarations of Reformed writers from the golden age of Reformed theology, also give evidence that our Reformed fathers from of old have advocated these opinions.[3]

The reader will understand that for the purpose of the present investigation we need not discuss the scriptural passages cited by synod, neither are we now concerned with the quotations from

---

3   *1924 Acts of Synod of the Christian Reformed Church*, 145–46.

Reformed writers. We are especially concerned with the quotations from the standards to which the synod referred under this first point, for we must know whether the three points are a proper interpretation of the standards.

The first quotation is from Canons 2.5:

> Moreover the promise of the gospel is, that whosoever belie-veth in Christ crucified shall not perish, but have everlasting life. This promise, together with the command to repent and believe, ought to be declared and published to all nations, and to all persons promiscuously and without distinction, to whom God out of his good pleasure sends the gospel.[4]

Let us consider whether the first point can be called an interpretation of Canons 2.5. You will immediately concede that there is not even a semblance of similarity between the first point and this article of the Canons. The chief proposition of the first point is evidently that there is a grace of God over his creatures in general. The chief declaration of Canons 2.5 is that the promise of the gospel, together with the demand to repent and believe, must be preached promiscuously and without distinction to all nations and persons to whom God out of his good pleasure sends the gospel.

One has only to read these two propositions to conclude immediately that what is supposed to be an interpretation of Canons 2.5 is not even contained in the article or even suggested by it. By "creatures in general" in the first point we understand God's creation in the organic sense, the whole that God called into existence at the beginning and sustains by his providence. If we take the first point literally, synod expressed merely that God is gracious over all the works of his hands understood organically, that is, without reference to the individual creature. God is good to man and beast and the green herb—to his entire creation.

Let me add that I would not object to the first point and would fully agree with it if synod had confined itself to this chief proposition.

---

4   Canons of Dordt 2.5, in Schaff, *Creeds of Christendom*, 3:586.—Ed.

But this is not the question. The question is not whether I am in conformity with the meaning of the first point, but whether it may be called an interpretation of the confession. Is the declaration of the first point contained in Canons 2.5? Or if it is not literally expressed in it, is the first point implied in Canons 2.5?

Of course your answer is, not at all. The first point speaks of a grace of God; Canons 2.5 speaks of the preaching of the gospel. The first point speaks of "creatures in general"; Canons 2.5 speaks of nations and persons, only those nations and persons to whom God sends the gospel according to his counsel. The notion is absurd that Canons 2.5 literally teaches or implies a grace of God over his "creatures in general." The thought of "creatures in general" was never in the minds of our Reformed fathers when they composed and adopted this article at the Synod of Dordrecht. Of this we can be assured. The chief proposition of the first point, therefore, cannot be considered an interpretation of Canons 2.5.

Those who composed the three points will object that I do not correctly and fairly present the matter. You see, they say that synod never meant to affirm that Canons 2.5 teaches a grace of God over all his creatures. Synod merely cited this article to prove that the Canons teach a grace of God over others than the elect, that is, over other *men*. Even though it may be granted that this article does not speak of a favor of God over all his creatures, synod maintained that it affirmed a grace of God over a wider circle of men that only the elect.

To this I reply that synod must be held responsible for what it actually declared. If synod intended to express merely that God is gracious over other men than the elect, the first point is a poor piece of composition.

For the sake of argument, let us grant that the real purpose of the first point is to declare and teach that God is gracious over the reprobate. If understood in that sense, can it be considered an interpretation of Canons 2.5? Again I answer, in no wise! Taken in that sense, the first point teaches a grace of God over all men promiscuously and without distinction, not only the elect. Canons 2.5 does not mention a grace of God over all men; it merely deals with the preaching of the gospel to all men without distinction.

But, the authors of the three points say that the preaching of the gospel is grace to all who hear the preaching. Thus they say the first point is an interpretation of Canons 2.5. I reply that this is not interpreting but augmenting the confession.

Such a would-be interpretation proceeds from the tacit assumption that the preaching of the gospel per se is grace to all who hear. This surely is not expressed in Canons 2.5. The rest of the Canons makes clear that such an interpretation does not harmonize with the purpose of the fathers of Dordrecht. The Canons were composed for the purpose of opposing the doctrine of the Remonstrants. Therefore, we can be assured that our fathers were very afraid to speak of the preaching of the gospel as general, or common, grace.

Besides, if this had been the fathers' intention, how easily they could have expressed that idea clearly and without ambiguity by declaring, "Moreover, God manifests his grace to all men without distinction in that he wills that the promise of the gospel, together with the command to repent and believe, shall be preached to all nations and persons promiscuously, to whom in his good pleasure he sends the gospel." This, however, they intentionally avoided. I say intentionally, for we can depend on it that the fathers of Dordrecht were perfectly able to express their thoughts in clear language. Instead, they merely affirmed that although God's grace is particular and is bestowed only on the elect, nevertheless God's will is that the gospel shall be preached to all without distinction.

I conclude, therefore, that the first point is not an interpretation of Canons 2.5.

Synod also referred to Canons 3–4.8–9.

As many as are called by the gospel are unfeignedly called; for God hath most earnestly and truly declared in his Word what will be acceptable to him, namely, that all who are called should comply with the invitation. He, moreover, seriously promises eternal life and rest to as many as shall come to him, and believe on him.

It is not the fault of the gospel, nor of Christ offered therein, nor of God, who calls men by the gospel, and confers upon them various gifts, that those who are called by the ministry of the Word refuse to come and be converted. The fault lies in themselves; some of whom when called, regardless of their danger, reject the Word of life; others, though they receive it, suffer it not to make a lasting impression on their heart; therefore, their joy, arising only from a temporary faith, soon vanishes, and they fall away; while others choke the seed of the Word by perplexing cares and the pleasures of this world, and produce no fruit. This our Saviour teaches in the parable of the sower (Matt. 13).[5]

In these articles there is no semblance of an interpretation of the chief proposition of the first point, that there is a grace of God over "his creatures in general." This needs no further elucidation. These articles do not deal with a grace of God over all his creatures or even with God's grace toward mankind in general, but with the preaching of the gospel to those whom God sends the gospel in his good pleasure. Article 8 refers to all who hear the gospel. Article 9 speaks of those who come under the ministry of the gospel but reject it. Therefore, it goes without contradiction that the first point, understood literally, is not an interpretation of these articles.

The only remaining question is whether these articles teach directly or imply that the preaching of the gospel is God's grace to all who hear the preaching.

There are three elements in article 8. First, the calling of the gospel is unfeigned and serious on the part of God for all who come under its ministration. Everyone who hears the gospel can be assured that God seriously and unfeignedly means what he causes to be proclaimed in the gospel. What does God proclaim in the gospel? Does he affirm that he is gracious or will be gracious to all who hear? Does he command his ministers to preach that it is God's intention to save all the hearers? On the contrary, no preacher of the gospel may claim any authority

---

5 Canons of Dordt 3–4.8–9, in ibid., 3:589.—Ed.

to bring such a message. He who presents the gospel in that light does not bring the call of the word but his own philosophy; he corrupts the gospel and makes God a liar. The calling of the gospel is, "Turn ye, and believe in the Lord Jesus Christ. Come unto me, all ye that labor and are heavy laden, and I will give you rest. Ho, every one that is thirsty, come to the waters!" This calling is unfeigned on the part of God. He who hears this gospel has no reason to doubt that he is seriously called.

Second, it is acceptable to God that this calling is heeded and obeyed. To reject the gospel and to disobey the calling is not acceptable to God. He is terribly displeased with everyone who refuses to turn to him and live, with all who despise and reject the gospel.

Third, God promises to all who come and believe in him rest for their souls and life eternal. This promise is not to all without distinction, but to those who will come and believe. No one needs to entertain any doubt as to the sincerity of this promise. He who comes unto God will in no wise be cast out. All who come unto him receive grace and eternal life, for God certainly realizes his promises.

Does all this signify that the serious and glorious gospel—which contains the promise of eternal life to all who believe and rest of soul to everyone who comes to God through Jesus Christ—is God's grace to all who hear the preaching of that gospel and not only to the elect? In other words, can article 8 be interpreted to mean that the proclamation of the gospel is grace also for those who reject it, for the reprobate ungodly? There is not the faintest suggestion of such a doctrine. The declaration of the first point cannot be called an interpretation of Canons 3–4.8.

What about article 9? It teaches that the fault of rejecting the gospel, the sin of refusing to turn, to come to God through Christ and to believe, cannot and may not be attributed to the gospel, to Christ, or to God. The calling of the gospel is sufficiently clear. It speaks unambiguously. It reveals very plainly what is acceptable to God. If anyone refuses to turn to God, he cannot blame the gospel, as if it were not sufficiently clear and rich to lead him to repentance. Nor can the unbeliever blame God for his unbelief, for the Most High clearly reveals to him in the gospel that disobedience and unbelief displease him most terribly and justly. Christ is fully and rightly proclaimed, presented in the gospel, so that the fault of unbelief cannot be sought in him.

The teaching of article 9 is that all the responsibility is the sinner's. The fault lies in his wicked and unrepentant heart, the evil nature, which under and through the preaching of the gospel is revealed to be more terrible. The guilt of the sin of unbelief is only his. Is this the same as the doctrine that those who reject the gospel were always the objects of God's grace in and through the preaching and ministration of the word to them? Does this article even suggest such a thing? The contrary is true. If the gospel manifests the perversity and darkness of the sinful heart and mind, it certainly does not serve this purpose as a revelation of God's grace to that particular heart. It would have been better, according to scripture, that those who reject the gospel had never known the way of righteousness and life. The gospel to them is a fearful judgment. It aggravates their guilt and punishment. They will be beaten with double stripes, for they reveal plainly that they do not will what is acceptable to God. Article 9 does not teach a certain grace of God in the preaching of the gospel for the ungodly reprobate.

Therefore, the first point is not an interpretation of these articles of the Canons but an appendage. It is clearly established that the claim of the Christian Reformed leaders and authors of the three points, that the first point is a further explanation of what is implied and expressed in the confessions, is absolutely false.

A new doctrine was adopted in the first point. It is an addition to the standards. This new doctrine may briefly be formulated as follows: God manifests a certain grace in the preaching of the gospel not only to the elect unto eternal life, but to all without distinction who hear the preaching of the gospel. Or to put it in its briefest form: *The preaching of the gospel is common grace.*

The second point reads as follows:

> With respect to the second point concerning the restraint of sin in the life of individuals and in society, Synod declares that according to Scripture and the Confessions there is such a restraint of sin. This is evident from the quoted Scripture passages and from the Belgic Confession Art. 13 and 36, where

we are taught that God through the general operation of his Spirit, without renewing the heart, restrains sin in its unbridled expression through which remains possible, a societal relationship while from the quoted declarations of Reformed writers from the golden age of Reformed theology it is evident that our Reformed fathers from of old have advocated these opinions.[6]

The passages of the confession to which synod referred in proof of this declaration read as follows: "In whom [God] we do entirely trust; being persuaded that he so restrains the devil and all our enemies that, without his will and permission, they can not hurt us."[7] "God...[is] willing that the world should be governed by certain laws and policies; to the end that the dissoluteness of men might be restrained."[8]

May the second point be considered an interpretation of the parts of the confession quoted by synod? It might easily be understood to teach only that God by his providence governs the devils and the ungodly so they cannot accomplish anything against his will. Yet this is not the teaching of the second point. If it were, I would not object to its doctrine.

The view expressed and adopted by the Christian Reformed Church in the second point is that there is an operation of the Holy Spirit in the heart of every man whereby he is not regenerated, yet he is kept from total corruption of his nature so that he is not as ungodly in his outward life as might otherwise be expected. This is the true meaning of the theory of the restraint of sin as developed in the doctrine of common grace. This also was the question before synod in 1924. That this is the implication of the second point is also evident from its wording. By the general operation of the Holy Spirit there is a certain reforming influence outside of the work of regeneration upon the heart of every man.

This being understood, the question is whether the second point is an explanation of articles 13 and 36 of the Belgic Confession. This question must be answered in the negative.

---

6   *1924 Acts of Synod*, 146.
7   Belgic Confession 13, in Schaff, *Creeds of Christendom*, 3:397.—Ed.
8   Belgic Confession 36, in ibid., 3:432.—Ed.

Very clearly article 13 does not speak of an operation of common grace by the Holy Spirit in the hearts of the ungodly whereby they are somewhat reformed and improved. It speaks of God's providence in connection with the blessed truth of God's power and dominion, even over the instruments and agents of darkness. That this part of the confession speaks of the devils and the ungodly ought to have been sufficient to keep synod from the error of thinking that the article referred to an internal and gracious operation of the Holy Spirit. If synod's interpretation were correct, this article would also teach that there is a reforming influence of the Holy Spirit on the devils, which is absurd. But if synod will not accept such an operation of grace on devils, it will have to admit that article 13 does not refer to such a gracious operation of the Holy Spirit at all, but simply to God's almighty domination, whereby he rules over and governs all things according to his eternal counsel.

This government of the Most High over all things, according to article 13, is divinely motivated not by a certain grace, or favor, over the ungodly, but by his grace and love over his people. Article 13 refers to a very particular grace. Therefore, the second point certainly is not an interpretation of article 13.

The same is true of the quotation synod offered from article 36 of the Belgic Confession. This article does not speak of a restraint of the power and corruption of sin in the heart of the natural man by a general operation of the Holy Spirit, but of an external restraint of certain public sins by the power of the law supported by police power. The plain teaching of this article is that without the power of the magistrates men are not restrained at all, but are dissolute. If there were such an operation of the Spirit as taught in the second point, the police and the sword-power of the magistrates would be unnecessary. But now it is different. Article 36 does not proceed from the assumption of such an operation of grace on the heart of natural man, and therefore it professes the need for laws and police. It is too plainly farfetched when the leaders of the Christian Reformed Church attempt to present the second point as an explanation of article 36 of the Belgic Confession.

Therefore, the second point is also an addition to the confessions

of the Reformed churches. This appendage can be formulated as follows: *there is a general operation of grace of an ethical nature by the
Holy Spirit, by which all men, apart from regeneration, are improved
and reformed to such an extent that they do not break out in all manner of sins.*

Last, I call attention to the third point:

> Concerning the third point, in regard to the doing of so-called
> civil good by the unregenerate, Synod declares that according
> to Scripture and the confessions, the unregenerate, though
> unable to do any saving good (Canons of Dort 3–4.3) are able
> to do civil good. This is evident from the quoted Scriptures,
> and from the Canons of Dort 3–4.4 and the Belgic Confession
> Art. 36, where we are taught that God, without renewing the
> heart, exercises such influence on mankind that it is capable to
> carry out civil good; while from the declarations of Reformed
> writers from the golden age of Reformed theology it is evident
> that our fathers from of old advocated this (same) opinion.[9]

The passages of the confessions to which synod referred in support
of this statement are the following:

> There remain, however, in man since the fall, the glimmerings
> of natural light, whereby he retains some knowledge of God,
> of natural things, and of the difference between good and evil,
> and discovers some regard for virtue, good order in society,
> and for maintaining an orderly external deportment.[10]
>
> Wherefore we detest…all those who…confound that decency
> and good order which God hath established among men.[11]

The third point teaches that the natural man can do good works
before God in civil life. This is exactly what synod meant when it
spoke of civil good. The natural man is able to perform such civil
good by virtue of an influence of God on him that has nothing to

---

9   *1924 Acts of Synod*, 146.
10 Canons of Dordt 3–4.4, in Schaff, *Creeds of Christendom*, 3:588.—Ed.
11 Belgic Confession 36, in ibid., 3:433.—Ed.

do with regeneration. The second and third points are closely related. Both speak of an operation of God and his Spirit on the natural man outside of regeneration. The second point declares that man's nature is somewhat improved by this operation; the third declares that by this operation he is enabled to do good.

It is self-evident that article 36 does not speak at all of such an influence of God on the sinner that enables him to do civil good. The article speaks of the magistrates' power whereby sin is restrained in public life. This article proceeds from an assumption opposite of the basis of the third point. If it were true as synod declared, that an influence of God urges the natural man to do good, the police might be abolished. But since that declaration is untrue, the sword-power is peremptory in society.

The quotation from Canons 3–4.4 is very deceiving because it contains only half of the article, a fact that is more deplorable because the second half of the article makes very evident that synod by a partial quotation corrupted the meaning of the article and changed it into the opposite from what it actually teaches. The second half of the article reads as follows:

> But so far is this light of nature from being sufficient to bring him to a saving knowledge of God, and to true conversion, that he is incapable of using it aright even in things natural and civil. Nay farther, this light, such as it is, man in various ways renders wholly polluted, and holds it [back] in unrighteousness; by doing which he becomes inexcusable before God.[12]

Clearly this article teaches not a certain influence of God on the natural man by which he is somewhat reformed and improved, but natural light and natural gifts that remained in man after the fall. The third point speaks of something the natural man received from God after the fall; the Canons refer to remnants left after the fall. This article emphatically denies that the natural man can do good with the natural light and maintains that he is incapable of using it aright and renders it wholly polluted, even in natural and civil things. However,

---

12 Canons of Dordt 3–4.4, in ibid., 3:588.—Ed.

the third point teaches that the natural man can do good in natural and civil things.

Therefore, the third point is not an interpretation of the confessions but an addition to them. The appendage is that *the natural man can do good in civil things by an influence of God on him that is not regenerative.*

In summary, the Christian Reformed Church formulated and adopted three appendages to the three forms of unity. The first teaches that the preaching of the gospel is general, or common, grace. The second teaches a general operation of grace of an ethical nature by the Holy Spirit, by which all men apart from regeneration are improved and reformed to such an extent that they do not break out in all kinds of sin. The third teaches that the natural man can do civil and natural good by an influence of God on him that is not regenerative.

To assert that these points are in part plainly expressed and clearly implied in the confessions is a false representation, for they are not interpretations but augmentations of the Reformed standards. We can conclude that the three points, even apart from whether they harmonize with the line of Reformed faith and thinking, are deceptive and therefore dangerous declarations.

By adopting them without seeking the advice and consent of the churches, synod assumed a position of hierarchical power and authority above the confessions and greatly impaired the force of them as a bond of unity joining together all who profess and love the Reformed truth. The three forms of unity are clear expressions of the faith of the Reformed churches and as such are a basis on which those churches can and do unite into a denomination. But is not this basis deprived of all force and stability if synod possesses the authority at any time to interpret the confessions in the most arbitrary manner, so that the interpretations of synod declare doctrines that are wholly foreign to the content and intention of the standards? If the broadest gathering of the churches may deal with the confessions so arbitrarily that at any time it may impose on the churches appendages to the forms of unity, these have been debilitated and rendered impotent to serve as a firm basis of union. Then a few theologians are in a position to distort the confessions as they please, and the churches are again placed under the oppressive and accursed yoke of Roman Catholic hierarchy.

Deceptive these three points are as alleged interpretations of the confessions. They are therefore dangerous because every officebearer by implication is compelled to sign these points, although formally and officially he merely declares conformity with the standards of the churches. According to the Formula of Subscription, he merely pledges himself to be loyal to the three forms of unity mentioned by name in that Formula. Honesty on the part of the Christian Reformed Church would require them to augment also the Formula of Subscription so that the three points of 1924 are clearly mentioned therein. Now, however, under the pretext that the three points are not additions to but interpretations of the confessions, every officebearer, whether consciously or not, declares himself to be in harmony with the three points as often as he expresses agreement with the standards of the Reformed churches.

By this self-deception, however, the Christian Reformed Church cannot effectively relegate the three points to the realm of oblivion, nor prevent their influence on the life and faith of the churches. Although in the disguise of alleged interpretations of the confessions, the three points nevertheless exist as real appendages to the standards.

As we will see in the following chapters, the three points are also distortions and corruptions of the Reformed faith. Secretly, and for that reason more effectively, they will complete their work of corruption in the churches until it is too late to save them from drowning in the Arminian waters into which their synod plunged them in 1924. They were immersed while in a state of anesthesia produced by a triple dose of doctrinal morphine, from which, if God does not prevent it, they will not be aroused until it is too late to swim to the safe shore of Reformed truth.

Finally, let it never be forgotten that in 1924 faithful officebearers were deposed from their offices as ministers, elders, and deacons in the Christian Reformed Church because they could not conscientiously sign the three points, and they refused to declare themselves in agreement with the declaration of 1924. These officebearers had promised to be loyal to the Reformed standards, to teach them, and to defend them against all heresies. They are still loyal to these confessions, as no one in the Christian Reformed Church—layman, minister, or theological professor—is able to deny. These faithful officebearers were deposed not because of their nonconformity with scripture and the Reformed standards, but solely because they purposed to defend the standards and to keep them pure from foreign elements and heretical influences. Thus the Christian Reformed Church is the cause of a serious breach among the brethren and has become the occasion for the organization of a separate denomination on the basis of the three forms of unity without the appendages of 1924.

The three points served as an excuse to commit unrighteousness over against the deposed officebearers, and they have served their purpose well. They will very effectively serve their further purpose of destroying the Christian Reformed churches, for they are a triple breach in the foundation of Reformed truth.

CHAPTER 2

ONLY FOR THE ELECT

The augmentation of a certain confession of faith does not necessarily imply that it has been corrupted. It is self-evident that during the true, spiritual development of a church, the need may be felt and begin to assert itself for enlargement of the confessions. Such development and expansion of the confessions may take place in harmony with the fundamental principles of the original confessions and may even be an improvement and purification of them. This can also be applied to the Reformed standards. Although the three declarations that the Christian Reformed Church adopted and alleged to be interpretations of the confessions are not embodied in the original standards, these declarations might be in harmony and agreement with the fundamental principles of the Reformed faith as expressed in the three forms of unity.

If this possibility would prove to be a fact, I would still have serious objections against the procedure the Christian Reformed Church followed in adopting the three points. They certainly should have been submitted to the judgment of the churches before they were finally adopted as being of the same value and force as the Reformed standards. But my chief objection—that these appendages are corruptions of the confessions—would be removed.

This chapter purposes to investigate whether this possibility is true with respect to the first point. I have shown that the first point is an augmentation of and an addition to the standards. The question before us is whether this first appendage is in harmony with the principles of the standards or whether it is a deviation from the line of the Reformed faith.

The appendage adopted in the first point is that God in the preaching of the gospel is gracious to all who hear. More briefly, the preaching of the gospel is common grace.

In order to be entirely fair, it is proper and expedient first to consider, what does the Christian Reformed Church accept as the meaning of the first appendage? I must warn the reader that he will be greatly disappointed if he expects a concise and definite answer to this question from the leaders of the Christian Reformed Church. Their answers are ambiguous and evasive.

This would not be the case if the first point had been adopted by avowedly Arminian churches. Then it would be comparatively easy to obtain an answer to the question. But the first point originated in a professedly Reformed denomination, and the leaders of that denomination most emphatically deny that the doctrine of Arminius is at all embodied in the first point. They emphasize that the Christian Reformed Church firmly believes in the doctrines of predestination, sovereign election and reprobation, particular atonement in Christ, and irresistible and efficacious grace in the application of all the blessings of salvation to the elect only. They plead "not guilty" to the indictment of Arminianism. They even claim not to understand how the Protestant Reformed Churches can honestly accuse them of this heresy insofar as the church maintains the doctrine expressed in the first point. Writes Louis Berkhof:

> The controversy that was carried on had the very usual effect that the very air became impregnated with various false conceptions. Some busy themselves to spread the tale that the three points are three bullets from Arminian canons that shot a terrible breach in our fortifications. The question whether they do so in good faith, we will not discuss. But the fact is that many good people believe presentation, while others, confused thereby, ask the question, what is truth?[13]

> Our church stands as firm as ever in the conviction that Christ died with the intention to save only the elect, although she

---

13 Berkhof, *Three Points*, 3.

recognizes the infinite value of the sacrifice of Christ as being sufficient for the sins of the whole world. He who alleges that synod seeks covertly to introduce the Arminian doctrine of universal atonement becomes guilty of false representations.[14]

It is even emphasized that synod plainly declared in the first point that the saving grace of God is shown only to the elect unto eternal life. Is all this not thoroughly Reformed and free from the taint of Arminianism?

I answer affirmatively. What Berkhof writes in the above citation is undoubtedly Reformed. The same is true of the first point insofar as it declares that the saving grace of God is bestowed only on the elect.

But let us not be deceived by these declarations of soundness in the truth. The first point reminds one of the two-faced head of Janus, a Roman idol distinguished by the remarkable feature of having two faces and looking in two opposite directions. There is a marked similarity between Janus and the first point. The latter is also two-faced and casts wistful looks in opposite directions. The same may be asserted of the attempts to explain the first point by the leaders of the Christian Reformed Church.

The difference is that while the two faces of heathen Janus bore a perfect resemblance to each other, the Janus of 1924 shows two totally different faces. One of his faces reminds you of Augustine, Calvin, and Gomarus, but the other shows the unmistakable features of Pelagius, Arminius, and Episcopius. Your troubles begin when you inquire of this two-faced oracle what may be the exact meaning of the first point. Then this modern Janus begins to revolve, alternately showing you one face and then the other, until you hardly know whether you are dealing with Calvin or Arminius.

The quotations cited above from Berkhof's booklet on the three points show you only the Reformed face of this Janus. If you inquire of him when he turns this face toward you, he says, "The saving grace of God is only for the elect unto eternal life and is bestowed on them alone."

---

14 Ibid., 8.

But compare the following from Berkhof's booklet: "The general and well-meaning offer of salvation is an evidence of God's favor toward sinners, is the Lord's blessing on them." Lest we should misunderstand the professor and imagine that he refers to only elect sinners, he adds in the same paragraph, "Scripture teaches without doubt that we must consider the offer of salvation a temporal blessing also for those who do not heed the invitation," that is, for those who are designated by the word of God as reprobate ungodly.[15]

To prove this assertion the professor continues, "That God calls the ungodly to repentance is presented in the holy scriptures as a proof of his pleasure in their salvation."[16] This may pass as long as you demand no further definition of "the ungodly." No one denies that God has pleasure in the salvation of ungodly men. But when you generalize this and say that God has pleasure in the salvation of *all* the ungodly, that he is willing to save all sinners, you depart from the Reformed line of faith and thinking. I am confident that no Reformed man will deny the truth of this statement. Yet Berkhof departs exactly in this way from the Reformed truth:

> In the prophecy of Ezekiel we may listen to the voice of the Lord in words that testify to his mercy: "Have I any pleasure at all that the wicked should die? saith the Lord GOD; and not that he should return from his ways and live?" And again: "For I have no pleasure in the death of him that dieth [of one who perishes in his sins], saith the Lord GOD; wherefore turn yourselves and live ye." These passages tell us as clearly as words can that God has no pleasure in the death of the wicked. Note that he does not say "of elect sinners," but "of sinners entirely in general. The tender calling we hear therein witnesses of his great love for sinners and of his pleasure in the salvation of the ungodly.[17]

The professor declares in another part of his booklet that it must be evident to anyone who can read Dutch (the professor wrote his booklet

---

15 Ibid., 21.
16 Ibid.
17 Ibid.

in that language) that the first point is not tainted with Arminianism. I
add that it must also be very clear to anyone who can read Dutch that
in the above quotation Berkhof teaches that God's love for sinners is for
all the ungodly, that God is ready to bestow the grace of Christ upon
all sinners. He even emphasizes this when he adds that the Lord in the
prophecy of Ezekiel speaks not of elect sinners, but of sinners "entirely
in general." According to the professor's presentation, this general love
of God and desire to save sinners is declared in the gospel.

If any other meaning can possibly be elicited from Berkhof's words,
I will be glad to receive instruction. His entire argument purposes to
show that the grace of God, the love of God for sinners, and the pleasure he evinces to save them do not apply to the elect only, but to all
men. If this is not the meaning of his words in the quotations cited, I
cannot see that they have any sense at all. However indignant the
professor may appear when I accuse him of Arminianism, he certainly
proves by his words that the indictment is well founded.

Other passages in the same booklet are entirely in harmony with
his defense of a general love of God for sinners and his pleasure to save
them all. Commenting on Romans 2:4, he writes,

> The explanation of this [the riches of God's goodness] must
> be found in the purpose God had in view with this revelation
> of his love. And what was this purpose? Was it to cast the
> ungodly Jews more deeply into perdition? No, but to lead them
> to repentance...But in the case of the Jews the result does not
> correspond to the intention. They hardened themselves against
> the revelation of God's goodness.[18]

If this is not Arminianism and Pelagianism, I cannot read Dutch;
neither do I understand in opposition to what false doctrine our fathers
at Dordrecht formulated the Canons. In the last quoted passage the
professor teaches that God will lead men to repentance, that men do
not want it and harden themselves, and that in this case God's purpose
fails: the result does not correspond to God's intention. If this is not
a defense of the error of resistible grace, language must be extremely

18 Ibid., 27–28.

elusive and deceptive. But this presentation of the matter is wholly in harmony with the professor's view regarding the general love of God toward the ungodly.

The same view the professor expresses again in his interpretation of Genesis 6:3 in connection with the second point: "The Holy Spirit resisted the ungodliness and perversity of those generations that lived before the flood. He sought to check their ungodliness and lead them to repentance....But the Spirit strove in vain; sin increased rapidly."[19]

I am confident that if before 1924 I would have voiced such opinions from a Christian Reformed pulpit under the auspices of a good Reformed consistory, the latter surely would have refused to shake hands with me as a sign of their disapproval.

We may therefore consider it established that the first point teaches that in the preaching of the gospel God evinces his general love to all the ungodly, his pleasure in their lives, and his willingness to save them all. Besides, according to Berkhof, the same point also teaches that in the preaching there is a temporal blessing for all men, also for those who are not saved. He points to the examples of Ahab, who repented and whose punishment was postponed as a result of Elijah's preaching, and of Nineveh, which repented as a result of Jonah's preaching and was temporarily saved from destruction.

This is a minor point and I can dismiss it with a few remarks.

This presentation of the influence of the gospel on the reprobate ungodly is certainly not in harmony with the Reformed confessions. The Heidelberg Catechism teaches that by nature we daily increase our debt, that God is terribly displeased with our original and actual sins, and that he will punish them in his just judgment *temporally* and eternally. Nor is this presentation in harmony with the teaching of the word of God. Temporal blessings under the preaching of the gospel for the ungodly reprobate? May I remind the professor of the terrible curse threatened on the people of Israel if they refused to walk in the way of Jehovah? Will he read Deuteronomy 28? Were not those curses literally carried out on the ungodly nation? The professor may remark that those curses had a typical significance and were threatened on the

---

19 Ibid., 42–43.

people of Israel under the law. I admit it. But are not the professor's examples taken from the Old Testament?

True, final judgment was postponed in Ahab's case. But note, first, that the postponement was not under the preaching of the gospel but under the announcement of most terrible judgment. Second, it was not a postponement of judgment for one who utterly refused to listen to the word of God but for Ahab insofar as he still trembled because of God's terrible wrath. Third, Ahab was not blessed by everything that took place in his case. Ahab's house was not destroyed in his time, but the final execution of judgment was transferred to the next generation. Thus postponement was entirely in harmony with God's righteousness. Final judgment cannot come until the sinner has shown himself to be utterly hard. Ahab still feared and trembled under the announcement of God's judgment. He seemed to be repentant. Hence that God might appear perfectly just and righteous when he judges the final judgment was postponed until the next generation. Fourth, Ahab did not personally escape punishment at all, for he died, and the dogs licked his blood.

All such examples clearly show how desperately the fathers of the three points need some real scriptural proof for their contentions.

Certainly nothing in the word of God contradicts the view that the men of Nineveh were really converted. Not all were converted, but only the elect whom God had in the city at that time for his prophetic purpose. Everything is in favor of such an interpretation. This is evident from Jonah 3:5–9, which describes the conversion of the Ninevites. It is also clear from the Lord's repeated reference to the sign of Jonah the prophet, a sign of Jesus' death and burial and his leaving the nation of Israel to turn to the world with the gospel of salvation. Nineveh is an old-dispensational type of the world from which Christ calls his elect and gathers his "other sheep...which are not of this fold" [John 10:16]. The Savior, in words that leave no doubt as to their meaning, asserts that the men of Nineveh repented through the preaching of Jonah, while the men of his own generation refused to repent through the preaching of one much greater than Jonah. Sound interpretation certainly requires us to understand the word *repentance* each time in the same sense. I maintain that God for his sovereign purpose, chiefly of creating the prophetic sign of Jonah the prophet, had some of his elect in the city of Nineveh at the time of Jonah. They repented through his preaching, and for a time the city was spared for their sakes. Shortly afterward the city was destroyed.

These brief remarks suffice to dismiss the minor question of temporal blessings as a result of the preaching of the gospel. Of much greater importance is Berkhof's assertion, as an explanation of the first point, that through the preaching of the gospel God earnestly seeks the salvation of all men and thus shows grace to all of them. This is the heart of the question. Is such teaching in harmony with scripture and the confessions of the Reformed churches?

We consider this question from two aspects. First, is it in conformity with scripture and the confessions to teach that there is in God the gracious purpose to save all who hear the gospel? Second, do scripture and the confessions teach that such a graciously seeking operation of God proceeds from him through the preaching of the gospel on all who hear?

It ought to be superfluous to prove to any Reformed believer that scripture and the confessions teach exactly the opposite; namely, God's gracious purpose to save the elect only; his righteous and sovereign purpose to leave others in their misery unto damnation; and those who offer a different presentation seek to instill into people the destructive poison of the Pelagian errors.

To substantiate these statements, I refer the reader to the Canons of Dordt, which plainly teach that God has pleasure in the salvation of the elect only; that he purposes to save them and them only; and that he accomplishes salvation objectively and subjectively for them and in them alone. If the first point of 1924 teaches that God earnestly seeks the salvation of all men and that he reveals general grace in the preaching of the gospel to all who hear, it is in direct conflict with the following article in the Canons:

> This was the sovereign counsel and most gracious will and purpose of God the Father, that the quickening and saving efficacy of the most precious death of his Son should extend to all

the elect, for bestowing upon them alone the gift of justifying faith, thereby to bring them infallibly to salvation: that is, it was the will of God, that Christ by the blood of the cross, whereby he confirmed the new covenant, should effectually redeem out of every people, tribe, nation, and language, all those, and those only, who were from eternity chosen to salvation, and given to him by the Father; that he should confer upon them faith, which, together with all the other saving gifts of the Holy Spirit, he purchased for them by his death; should purge them from all sin, both original and actual, whether committed before or after believing; and having faithfully preserved them even to the end, should at last bring them free from every spot and blemish to the enjoyment of glory in his own presence forever.[20]

The well-informed reader will notice that in the following description of reprobation the infralapsarian view is maintained. Yet the article clearly teaches that in God there is the righteous and sovereign purpose, for the manifestation of his justice, to leave some in their misery, not to save them, but to condemn them forever and to punish them for their sins.

What peculiarly tends to illustrate and recommend to us the eternal and unmerited grace of election is the express testimony of sacred Scripture, that not all, but some only, are elected, while others are passed by in the eternal decree; whom God, out of his sovereign, most just, irreprehensible and unchangeable good pleasure, hath decreed to leave in the common misery into which they have willfully plunged themselves, and not to bestow upon them saving faith and the grace of conversion; but permitting them in his just judgment to follow their own way; at last, for the declaration of his justice, to condemn and punish them forever, not only on account of their unbelief, but also for all their other sins. And this is the decree of reprobation which by no means makes God the author of sin (the

---

20 Canons of Dordt 2.8, in Schaff, *Creeds of Christendom*, 3:587.—Ed.

very thought of which is blasphemy), but declares him to be an awful, irreprehensible, and righteous judge and avenger.[21]

This directly condemns the first point as explained by Berkhof, which he interprets as teaching that in God there is a gracious purpose to save all who hear the preaching of the gospel, not only the elect, and that this gracious purpose is plainly declared in the gospel.

> Synod *rejects* the errors of those…Who use the difference between meriting and appropriating, to the end that they may instill into the minds of the imprudent and inexperienced this teaching, that God, as far as he is concerned, has been minded of applying to all equally the benefits gained by the death of Christ; but that, while some obtain the pardon of sin and eternal life and others do not, this difference depends on their own free will, which joins itself to the grace that is offered without exception, and that it is not dependent on the special gift of mercy, which powerfully works in them, that they rather than others should appropriate unto themselves this grace.
>
> Rejection: For these, while they feign that they present this distinction in a sound sense, seek to instill into the people the destructive poison of the Pelagian errors.[22]

Let the reader judge how far Berkhof must plead guilty to the indictment that he instills into the minds of the imprudent and inexperienced this destructive poison of the Pelagian errors under the pretext of making a certain distinction in a sound sense. I freely admit that he does not teach in so many words that the difference between meriting and appropriating must be explained from the free will of man; but I maintain that materially he teaches exactly this when he writes that God's purpose was to save the ungodly Jews, but in their case the result did not correspond to the purpose of God; and when he asserts that the Holy Spirit's purpose was to lead men to conversion, but the Spirit's attempts were frustrated.

---

21 Canons of Dordt 1.15, in ibid., 3:584.—Ed.
22 Canons of Dordt 2, error and rejection 6, in *Confessions and Church Order*, 166.—Ed.

It ought to be plain from the citations from the Canons that the first point, as explained by Berkhof, stands condemned. According to the Canons we may not present salvation in a way that leaves the impression that God graciously purposes the salvation of all who hear. Yet this is exactly the teaching of the first point according to Berkhof's interpretation. Therefore, the Canons unambiguously condemn Berkhof's teaching as Pelagian, and they certainly are not in sympathy with the view that God reveals in the preaching of the gospel his gracious purpose to save all the hearers.

Scripture is no less explicit in its condemnation of this teaching. In proof I could quote the word of God almost at random, but I will limit the quotations to a few passages that plainly deny that according to God's intention the preaching of the gospel is grace to all who hear.

9. And he said, Go, and tell this people, Hear ye indeed, but understand not; and see ye indeed, but perceive not.
10. Make the heart of this people fat, and make their ears heavy, and shut their eyes; lest they see with their eyes, and hear with their ears, and understand with their heart, and convert, and be healed.
11. Then said I, Lord, how long? And he answered, Until the cities be wasted without inhabitant, and the houses without man, and the land be utterly desolate,
12. And the LORD have removed men far away, and there be a great forsaking in the midst of the land.
13. But yet in it shall be a tenth, and it shall return, and shall be eaten: as a teil tree, and as an oak, whose substance is in them, when they cast their leaves: so the holy seed shall be the substance thereof. (Isa. 6:9–13)

Berkhof considers it a terrible doctrine that the gospel is proclaimed as a judgment and curse to the ungodly reprobate. The first point teaches that the preaching of the gospel is always grace according to God's intention. But this passage from Isaiah's prophecy emphasizes that the gospel is preached unto a curse and a hardening of the heart of the reprobate according to God's definitely expressed purpose. Isaiah was called to preach the word of God to the men of his generation so that their eyes would be blinded, their ears would be made heavy, their hearts would become fat, and they would not turn and be healed. In order to save the wheat the chaff must become fully ripe unto rejection through the preaching of the prophet. The captivity of the people and the destruction of the land and the city are the end of Isaiah's preaching, so that he might proclaim salvation and restoration and glory to the remnant according to the election of grace.

Thus also the Savior instructs his disciples in Mark 4:11–12:

11. And he said unto them, Unto you it is given to know the mystery of the kingdom of God: but unto them that are without, all these things are done in parables:
12. That seeing they may see, and not perceive; and hearing they may hear, and not understand; lest at any time they should be converted, and their sins should be forgiven them.

No one will deny that the parables belong to the preaching of the gospel. Was it the gracious purpose of God by means of the parables to save all? In the parables did he earnestly avow a purpose to bring all men to repentance? The contrary is true. The Lord plainly teaches that all these things are done in parables for a judgment and condemnation to those who are without.

These very explicit declarations of the word of God are not contradicted by the following texts to which synod appealed to support the teaching of the first point:

Have I any pleasure at all that the wicked should die? saith the Lord GOD: and not that he should return from his ways, and live? (Ezek. 18:23)

Say unto them, As I live, saith the Lord GOD, I have no pleasure in the death of the wicked; but that the wicked turn from his way and live: turn ye, turn ye from your evil ways; for why will ye die, O house of Israel. (Ezek. 33:11)

In these verses God speaks and swears by himself, and his word is absolutely true and unchangeable. The content of God's oath is that

he has no pleasure in the death of the wicked and that he has pleasure in the conversion and life of the ungodly. It is unnecessary to add
anything more. Although it might be answered from the context, the
question whether the verses refer to elect or reprobate can be left out
of the discussion. God has pleasure in conversion and life. No one
denies this. He has no pleasure in impenitence and death and is terribly
displeased with the impenitent state of the wicked. No one objects to
this. In the same sense that God has no pleasure in the impenitence of
the wicked, he has no pleasure in his death. Conversion and life are
inseparably connected.

These passages do not speak of the preaching of the gospel at all.
They surely contain no offer of salvation nor declare the purpose of
God in the preaching of the gospel with respect to elect and reprobate.
That it is God's purpose through the preaching of the gospel to bestow
the grace of conversion on all who hear is certainly not implied in the
passages. If synod imagines that a general offer of grace is in these
passages, it is most certainly mistaken, for there is no offer whatever.

The first question, whether God through the preaching of the gospel reveals a gracious purpose to save all who hear, can be considered
settled. The first declaration of synod 1924 is in conflict with scripture
and the confessions. The first appendage is not in harmony with the
fundamental principles of the Reformed standards.

Do scripture and the confessions teach that through the preaching
of the gospel a gracious operation of God proceeds on all who hear
the word?

It has always been considered Reformed to maintain that the means
of grace have no power in and of themselves. They are means of grace
only through an operation of the Holy Spirit on the hearts of those who
receive them. This is true of the word and sacraments. Without the gracious operation of the Spirit, the word is not efficacious unto salvation.
No grace and no blessing can proceed from that word as such. In light
of this truth we see that the question above is closely related to the first
point, which declares that God in the general preaching of the gospel,
or offer of salvation, is gracious to all who hear.

If the operation of the preaching on the hearts of the hearers depends on the gracious operation of the Spirit of Christ, according to scripture and the confessions, is there such an operation of grace concomitant with the preaching of the gospel on the hearts of all the hearers? If the confessions deny this and the scriptures declare the very opposite, is it not evident that the first point must be considered a product of the vain imaginations of men?

The Canons teach as follows:

> When God accomplishes his good pleasure in the elect, or works in them true conversion, he not only causes the gospel to be externally preached to them, and powerfully illuminates their minds by his Holy Spirit, that they may rightly understand and discern the things of the Spirit of God, but by the efficacy of the same regenerating Spirit he pervades the inmost recesses of the man; he opens the closed and softens the hardened heart, and circumcises that which was uncircumcised; infuses new qualities into the will, which, though heretofore dead, he quickens; from being evil, disobedient, and refractory, he renders it good, obedient, and pliable; actuates and strengthens it, that, like a good tree, it may bring forth the fruits of good actions.[23]

The point of this article is that when it is God's good pleasure to bestow grace on sinners and show them loving-kindness, God not only causes the gospel to be preached externally to them, but he also actually accomplishes the grace he wants to bestow in the hearts of men and thus efficaciously brings them to salvation under the preaching of the gospel. He accomplishes this only in the elect.

This is emphasized when the Canons reject the errors of those

> who teach that the corrupt and natural man can so well use the common grace (by which they [the Remonstrants] understand the light of nature), or the gifts still left him after the fall, that he can gradually gain by their good use a greater, namely, the evangelical or saving grace and salvation itself. And that in this way God on his part shows himself ready to reveal Christ unto

---

23 Canons of Dordt 3–4.11, in Schaff, *Creeds of Christendom*, 3:590.—Ed.

all men, since he applies to all sufficiently and efficiently the means necessary to conversion.

Rejection: For the experience of all ages and the Scriptures do both testify that this is untrue. *He showeth his word unto Jacob, his statues and ordinances unto Israel. He hath not dealt so with any nation: and as for his ordinances, they have not known them* (Ps. 145:19–20). *Who in the generations gone by suffered all the nations to walk in their own ways* (Acts 14:16). And: *And they* (Paul and his companions) *having been forbidden of the Holy Spirit to speak the word in Asia, and when they were come over against Mysia, they assayed to go into Bythinia, and the Spirit suffered them not* (Acts 16:6–7).[24]

The heart of this article is that the Lord is not ready to reveal Christ to all. Without such a revealing, gracious operation of God the natural man cannot attain to salvation, for he is by nature darkness. Although he comes into contact with the preaching of the gospel, he cannot receive the grace of God by his natural light and gifts. The light shines in the darkness, but the darkness comprehends it not. Such a revealing operation of God does not proceed with the gospel on all who hear, but only on the elect unto eternal life. On this operation, however, everything depends. How then can the first point maintain that the preaching of the gospel is grace to all the hearers and that God purposes to bestow grace on everyone who comes into contact with the gospel? From whatever point of view one considers the first declaration of synod, it clearly conflicts with the standards of the Reformed churches. It can never become an integral part of them.

The word of God is much more emphatic and explicit on this point. It speaks not only of a saving, illuminating, revealing, converting, and quickening operation of God through the preaching of the gospel on the hearts of men, but also emphatically of a hiding and hardening operation of God's righteous wrath under and through the preaching of the same gospel. This can be proven by many texts.

---

24 Canons of Dordt 3–4, error and rejection 5, in *Confessions and Church Order*, 171–72.—Ed.

The Savior thanks the Father that according to his good pleasure, he has hidden these things from the wise and the prudent and revealed them to babes. The context show very clearly that Jesus refers to the actual fruit of his preaching and labors until that moment, particularly in the cities of Chorazin, Bethsaida, and Capernaum. He had preached the gospel of the kingdom to them. The result was that the wise and prudent had rejected it and the babes had received it with joy. How does the Lord explain that twofold result of his preaching? Does he say that God had been gracious to all through his preaching, but that the wise had rejected it? On the contrary, the Savior ascends to the heights of God's good pleasure and explains that God accomplished his pleasure in those who believed. But God hid those things from the wise and the prudent, although the gospel had been preached to them as well as to the others (Matt. 11:25–26).

John 12:39–40 teaches explicitly that the wicked Jews could not believe because God had blinded their eyes and hardened their hearts, so that they should not be converted and healed. Romans 9:18 emphatically asserts that God is merciful to whom he wills and hardens whom he wills. Does not the word of God plainly teach that under the ministry of the word God also gives a spirit of slumber, eyes that they should not see, and ears that they should not hear (Rom. 11:7–10)? The apostle glories that the ministers of the gospel are at all times a sweet savor of Christ unto God, both in those who are saved and in those who perish, whether they be a savor of life unto life or a savor of death unto death (2 Cor. 2:14–16).

I need not quote more texts; scripture is full of similar testimonies. The above proof more than sufficiently shows that the first point is an error and that it is surely an evident untruth that the first point is a mere interpretation of the confessions. It is neither explicitly taught in the standards of the Reformed churches nor implied therein. Nor can the content of the first point be fitted into the whole of the confessions and become an integral part of them. On the contrary, the first point denies the truth that always has been maintained by the Reformed churches and is embodied in their standards: the grace of God in and through the preaching of the gospel is for the elect and for them alone.

In conclusion let us recall the scriptural and Reformed line of the truth. Before the foundation of the world, God in sovereign mercy chose his people unto eternal glory. In their stead and on their behalf he sent his only begotten Son to suffer and die for them vicariously and to reconcile them with God. These elect become partakers of the blessings of salvation merited by Christ only through efficacious grace. These elect he blesses and keeps by the power of his grace so they persevere to the end and no one may take their crown.

God also rejected others to become vessels of wrath fitted to destruction. Some of these he also brings under the preaching of the gospel and even within the pale of the historical development of his covenant, not to be gracious to them, but that in and through them sin may become manifest in all its horror and God may be just when he judges. They will be beaten with double stripes, and it would have been better for them had they never known the way of peace and righteousness (2 Pet. 2:20–21).

The first point of 1924 is an appendage to the confessions and stands in glaring contradiction to the fundamental principles of the Reformed faith. It is well adapted to instill into the minds of the imprudent and inexperienced the destructive poison of the Pelagian errors. Although the leaders of the churches bear the greater sin, all the members of the Christian Reformed Church are responsible for the three points and are duty-bound to reject them as repugnant to sound doctrine.

CHAPTER 3

CONTINUOUS DEVELOPMENT OF SIN

The purpose of this chapter is to determine whether the second point conforms to scripture and the Reformed confessions. The contention that the second point is an interpretation of the confessions, as the leaders of the Christian Reformed Church maintain, is untenable. The second point is also an addition, or appendage, to the confessions. I proved this in the first chapter of this booklet and formulated the addition as follows: there is a general operation of grace of an ethical nature by the Holy Spirit, by which all men, apart from regeneration, are improved and reformed to such an extent that they do not break out in all manner of sins. In none of the Reformed confessions is there a presentation of the truth as expressed in this appendage. Synod appealed to articles 13 and 36 of the Belgic Confession, but without more than a mere semblance of justice.

However, it is not sufficient to prove that the second point is no interpretation of the confessions. As stated before, appendages can be in harmony with the confessions and therefore be Reformed. The Reformed confessions may be enlarged in such a way that they are not corrupted. If it should appear that the second point, although not expressed or implied in the confessions, is nevertheless Reformed, I would not object to accepting its declaration of truth. I would still protest, however, against the way it has been adopted and imposed on the churches.

We now confront the question, does the second point harmonize with the word of God and the Reformed standards? To answer this it is necessary to have a correct conception of the real meaning of the second addition to the confessions. We must understand clearly the teaching of the second declaration of 1924 before determining if it is Reformed or un-Reformed.

To avoid the appearance of evil and to intercept a possible accusation that I arbitrarily impose my interpretation on the second point, I will not confine my examination to the declaration itself, but turn to the Christian Reformed Church for light on the meaning of the second point. No one will dare to say that this is unfair.

But I meet with disappointment, for the same ambiguity and duplicity in the explanation the leaders of that church offered concerning the first point are also revealed in their interpretation of the second. Again we are before the ever-revolving head of Janus, the two-faced idol of the Romans. On the one hand these leaders would maintain the Reformed principle that the natural man is wholly incapable of doing any good and inclined to all evil, unless he is regenerated by the Spirit of God. On the other hand they would make plain that this totally depraved man is not wholly corrupt. The result is that their explanations are necessarily ambiguous and two-faced. No man can serve two masters; no man can successfully hold to two contradictory doctrines.

For proof I refer the reader to the best that is on the market on the three points: the booklet of Berkhof. Notice how he abhors the Pelagian doctrine that there is any good left in the natural man.

> It is really ridiculous that in this connection Arminianism is mentioned. More and more it seems that Arminianism must serve as a bugbear to frighten the people needlessly. The impression has been created that the second point actually teaches that by common grace man is somewhat improved *spiritually*. This would indeed be Arminian. But it is surely puzzling how anyone can read this in synod's declaration. Synod attributes the restraint of sin to the *general operations of the Holy Spirit*, and these, according to Reformed belief, never cause a change in the state of spiritual death of the natural man. They not only fail to quicken him who is spiritually dead, but also they do not bring him one step nearer to life. But something must be added to this. Emphatically synod declared that God restrains

sin through the general operations of the Holy Spirit, *without renewing the heart*. The heart therefore is not renewed; in other words, man in this way is not regenerated. This naturally excludes all thought of spiritual improvement preceding regeneration. Reformed people do not acknowledge a spiritual improvement preceding regeneration. They must have nothing of the notion of preparatory grace. Yet without any semblance of proof, it is alleged that synod adopted the doctrine of such a grace. No, the restraint of sin does not bring man one step nearer to life. It only has reference to the maintenance and improvement of his natural life.[25]

The professor is indignant. I know not who had the sad courage so to arouse his anger by presenting a view of the second point that he considers ridiculous. But I can assure the professor that there is no reason for him to blame me. I always understood quite clearly that the second point does not refer to a *spiritual* change in the sinner. *Spiritual* improvement and *spiritual* good are wrought in man only through the Spirit of the Lord Jesus Christ. I always understood quite well that the second point does not refer to this at all. The good that is supposed to be in the natural man is outside of Christ, has nothing to do with regeneration, and is not wrought by the Spirit as the Spirit of Christ. In fact, my chief objection is that the second point teaches a goodness in man outside of Christ and apart from the work of regeneration. The professor can be appeased. Clearly he maintains the Reformed truth of the total depravity of man.

More emphatically he defends the Reformed view in his description of the natural state of man. He even maintains that the second point proceeds from the assumption and is based on the presupposition that man by nature is wholly corrupt and dead in sin.

This point proceeds on the basis of a very definite presupposition...that man by nature is wholly corrupt and dominated by the principle of enmity against God and the neighbor. He is alienated from God in his inmost soul, and consequently every

---

25 Berkhof, *Three Points*, 38–39.

act of his, even though it might be in harmony outwardly with certain secondary principles of justice, is corrupt in principle as the act of a rebel. Because of sin disharmony rules in the soul of man; a deep moral corruption has taken hold of his whole life. This corruption is not dormant; it develops and causes man to proceed from bad to worse.[26]

I challenge the professor to explain clearly the statement that the second point presupposes the total depravity of the natural man. The second point speaks of a restraint of sin, of a checking of the process of corruption. But how can the process of corruption be checked in anything that is already wholly corrupt? Is it of any avail to add salt to a piece of meat that is thoroughly spoiled and rotten? How then can corruption be checked in a human nature that is wholly depraved? Surely, the second point cannot rest on that presupposition.

The professor's words give the impression that the second point is doctrinally thoroughly Reformed, for it appears to maintain the total depravity of man in strongest terms. We would feel inclined to accept it and give the professor our confidence.

But beware! Janus will presently turn around and show you his other face.

In the restraint of sin the general operations of the Holy Spirit are fundamentally important. [It is deplorable enough for the maintenance of the second point that neither scripture nor the confessions mention this fundamentally important element.] They maintain the glimmerings of natural light that remain in man since the fall and through which he retains "some knowledge of God, of natural things, and of the difference between good and evil, and discovers some regard for virtue, good order in society, and for maintaining an orderly external deportment" [which, however, the natural man, "even in things natural and civil...wholly pollutes, and holds...in unrighteousness." It is strange that the professor seems so averse to quoting Canons 3–4.4 in its entirety.] They cause the seed of external

---

26 Ibid., 35.

righteousness to bear fruit, but do not implant into the heart the seed of regeneration. This operation of the Spirit is not a creative operation, but is moral persuasion. It makes man to a certain extent receptive for the truth insofar as it still influences him from his consciousness. It presents motives to the will, impresses his conscience, makes use of inclinations and desires in the soul, and causes to develop the outward good that still remains.[27]

According to the first presentation, the natural man is totally corrupt and wholly depraved and entirely dominated by the principle of enmity again God and the neighbor. The second point was supposed to be based on the truth of total depravity, but it seems that the professor understood that he cannot do anything with a restraining operation of the Spirit on a totally depraved nature. Now the second point must evidently proceed from an entirely different assumption: man's nature is not wholly corrupt; several good elements remain in it since the fall. In that supposedly corrupt nature the professor discovers the following remnants of good: a seed of external righteousness, receptivity for moral persuasion, receptivity for the truth that operates on him from his consciousness, a will that still can be impressed by good motives, and a conscience that is receptive to good influences and inclinations and desires that the Holy Spirit can use in the restraint of sin—good inclinations and desires—and a remnant of outward good.

I will not attempt to define these terms, but the professor must admit that he does not begin his process of restraining sin and corruption with a nature as entirely corrupt as he first tried to make us believe. Undoubtedly he felt that this would be impossible. Corruption in a wholly corrupt nature cannot be checked. If a totally depraved nature cannot somehow be improved and changed, the case is hopeless.

The professor now gives a different evaluation of the natural man from what he first professed to be the true characterization. He considerably improves the natural condition of the human nature before he allows his process of restraint to commence. He no more proceeds

---

27 Ibid., 37.

from the presupposition that the natural man is totally corrupt and wholly depraved, but he discovers in man, apart from regeneration, a seed of outward righteousness that can generate and bear fruit, a certain receptivity of the truth, and good inclinations and motives and desires. He finds considerable good in the natural man. With such a nature, with these remnants of good, these receptivities, inclinations, motives, and desires, the professor can begin his wonders of restraint. The general operation of the Holy Spirit preserves all this good in the natural man, causes it to develop and bear fruit, and presently you can witness the magic performance of a totally depraved sinner doing good works!

Taking all of the professor's different statements into consideration, we reach three conclusions regarding the real meaning and teaching of the second point. First, the general, restraining operations of the Holy Spirit on natural man are not regenerating, nor conducive to regeneration. The second point, apart from any explanation, emphasizes this very plainly. The professor labored under the impression that I misunderstood the second declaration of 1924 and discovered in it the doctrine that the natural man is spiritually improved without regeneration. He will now see that he is mistaken. He can be assured that I never understood the second point as referring to any spiritual good in the natural man, that is, to the good that is the fruit of the Spirit of Christ. I understand very well that the second point attributes to the fallen nature a good that is *not* of the Spirit of grace. This element constitutes exactly my chief objection against the second point.

Second, there remained in man since the fall many good elements, which the professor comprehends under the term "glimmerings of natural light." There is in man's fallen nature *the seed of outward righteousness*. The reader will understand that this figurative expression can mean almost anything, is very ambiguous and obscure, and would be extremely difficult for the professor to define. What is "outward righteousness"? Is it merely outward conformity to the law of God, without truth in the inward parts? Is it Pharisaism? If it is, must it be considered corrupt? And what is the seed of outward righteousness? Where is it found? In the heart? Then the outward righteousness is also inward. All these remained in man since the fall: *the remnant of outward good, the conscience, good inclinations, desires, and motives, and receptivity for the truth.* They are called the remnants of the image of God in man, and the Holy Spirit appeals to all this good by an operation of moral persuasion.

Third, there is such an operation of the Holy Spirit that influences the nature of every sinner and that is not regenerating but restraining, checking the power of corruption in the nature of the sinner, and thus preserving the good in him. This operation of the Spirit is the efficient cause for the corruption of sin not working through, not totally despoiling the nature of fallen man of all the good still left in it.

We must understand this point clearly. If through the fall the nature of man had become wholly corrupt, if no good had been left in it, there would have been nothing to preserve and to restrain. The corruption of sin would have finished its work. But this is not so. There is a remnant of *original* goodness in the sinner. This remnant would soon be corrupted and these glimmerings of light would quickly be extinguished by the darkening power of sin if the general operations of the Holy Spirit did not exert a restraining and preserving influence on man's depraved nature. Quickly the corrupting influence of sin would have accomplished its work. But according to the second point there is a restraining general operation of the Holy Spirit through which that good in man—*original good* that man retained from the first paradise and that is no *spiritual* good, no fruit of regenerating grace—is preserved from total corruption. This is what the restraint of sin means.

This is not all the Holy Spirit accomplishes by the Spirit's general operation on every man. He does more, according to Berkhof. The Spirit brings outward righteousness and good to development. He causes the seed of righteousness in man, the remnant of original goodness that is still in him, to bear fruit. He does this by moral persuasion. He appeals to the good inclinations and desires in the soul, he presents good motives to the will, he operates on man's conscience. Thus the seed of righteousness develops and bears fruit.

This fruit is the good fallen man performs in his present natural and civil life. He does not come to faith. He does not receive eternal life. He does no spiritual good. He is not engrafted into Christ. He really lives the life of paradise the first, although in a weakened form, a life that is maintained and quickened by the general operations of the Holy Spirit. Thus the natural man apart from Christ can and does perform good works in the world. To a certain extent he lives a good world-life.

Thus, according to Berkhof's interpretation, we must understand the meaning of the second point. The professor will admit that I represent his view correctly and clearly. Neither is another interpretation of this point conceivable.

One question remains. How is it to be explained that original good, that remnant of his original condition in paradise, remains in man since and through the fall? Berkhof does not answer this question, nor is the answer found in the second point. The answer is supplied by Kuyper in his *Common Grace*. He explains that such a restraining, checking, and preserving operation has taken place on the nature of man from the moment of the fall in paradise. If there had not been such a restraining operation of common grace immediately after the fall or concomitant with the fall of Adam and Eve, man's nature would have been totally corrupted then and there. Adam would have turned into a devil, and the earth would have been changed into hell. The life and development of human society would have become impossible.

But the Spirit intervened at once by restraining grace. He did not permit human nature to become wholly corrupt. He left a seed of original goodness in man's heart. Man did not become wholly darkness. He did not fully die. Some light was left him. Some life remained in him. Thus man lives a relatively good world-life in natural and civil things and strives for truth, justice, and righteousness. He is able to do good in this present life.[28]

---

28 Kuyper employs the well-known figure of a person who swallows [the poison] Prussian blue and is given an antidote. When God said in paradise, "The day that thou eatest thereof thou shalt surely die" (Gen. 2:17), that must not be understood as a threat and an announcement of judgment, but as a friendly warning. Man, however, ate of the tree. As someone gives his friend—whom he warned but who nevertheless swallows Prussian blue—an antidote to save his life, so the Lord gave man the antidote of common grace, so that he partly vomited out the corruption of sin and death and did not become wholly depraved.

Thus the meaning and implication of the second point is clearly understood and is set forth according to Berkhof's explanation. He cannot say that I do not understand the meaning of synod's second declaration, and that I incorrectly represent his view of it. By adopting the second point, the synod of the Christian Reformed Church raised the common grace theory of Abraham Kuyper to a church dogma.

Against this view I have several very serious objections on the basis of scripture and the Reformed standards. First, I call attention to certain fundamental principles adopted in the second point that directly conflict with the truth of the entire word of God and with the fundamental line of Reformed thinking. This view is contrary to the truth of God's absolute sovereignty over the powers of sin and death and corruption. It proceeds from a dualistic conception of God and the world, or more particularly, of God and the power of darkness. It represents sin and death as powers next to God, to a certain extent independent of him, powers that can of themselves work corruption. But God checks this power. He restrains a power that exists and works outside of and apart from him.

This is dualism and is contrary to the fundamental conception of the word of God, which always presents God as absolutely sovereign, also over the powers of sin and death and corruption. The corruption of the sinner is spiritual death. This death is no power that operates of itself in man's nature but is God's servant, the execution of God's condemning sentence in man. God inflicted the punishment of death on the guilty sinner in paradise. Death and corruption are powers that can work only through God. But if this is maintained, one cannot speak of a restraining power of the Spirit, for how can God check a power that operates only by his will and through him? The theory of a restraining grace is fundamentally a denial of God's absolute sovereignty. It is dualistic.

Second, this entire conception implies a denial of God's justice. Those who maintain this view want to emphasize that the light, the remnants of good, the outward righteousness that remained in man since the fall, is unmerited grace of God. It is therefore common grace. Very well, but on what basis of God's unchangeable justice does fallen man receive light and life and goodness, this common grace? In paradise God threatened, "The day that thou eatest thereof thou shalt surely die" (Gen. 2:17). If God did not execute this sentence then and there, if he even prevented it, what becomes of the justice of God? To be sure, when the child of God receives remission of sins, redemption, and eternal life, these blessings are unmerited grace. But it must never be forgotten that these blessings have been merited by Christ. To what basis of justice can they point who maintain that natural man outside of Christ receives the blessing of unmerited grace?

Third, the second point is based on the serious error of resistible grace. The operation of the Holy Spirit whereby he would restrain sin is not irresistible. The fact is that corruption and sin are not actually checked but continuously make progress and develop. This was evident in the history of the prediluvian world. This becomes very evident in all history, also in the new dispensation, for the entire development of the world tends toward the realization of antichrist, the final manifestation of the man of sin, the son of perdition.

If you ask how the progress and development of sin are possible if the Holy Spirit restrains sin's corrupting power, those who maintain this view answer that the Holy Spirit finally releases his restraining hold on the sinner and gives him over in unrighteousness. If you ask for what reason the Holy Spirit gives the natural man over in sin, the answer is inevitable: because the sinner resists the restraining operation of the Spirit and goes from bad to worse. The checking power of the Spirit is not efficacious. Man is stronger than God. The Spirit loses the battle with natural man. Or, as Berkhof expresses it, "The Spirit strives in vain. He attempts to check the power of sin and to lead men to repentance, but he strives in vain, he fails."[29] With respect to all these fundamental principles the second point is a deviation from the truth of scripture and the line of Reformed thinking.

But there is more. My chief objection against the second point as interpreted by Berkhof and understood by the Christian Reformed Church is its denial of the total depravity of the fallen human nature. This second point is related to the third as cause and effect. It opens

---

29 Berkhof, *Three Points*, 43.

the way; it creates the possibility for the third point. The third declares that the natural man can do good works, although only in this present life and in the natural and civil sphere; the second points to the good left in human nature through common grace as the source of good works. The second point teaches that the human nature since the fall is not wholly corrupt and totally depraved; it implies that it would have been totally corrupt if the restraining power of common grace had not intervened. Therefore, the second point is a denial of the total depravity of natural man.

Let my opponents show, if they can, that I err. They surely cannot object that I did not interpret the second point correctly and according to its real meaning and implication. I doubt sometimes whether the leaders of the Christian Reformed Church understand the implications of this point. Consider it how you will, the second point always presupposes that some of the original righteousness of paradise is left in man, some moral integrity remains in him, some element of good is preserved, some love of the neighbor, some receptivity for the truth is still discovered in him. If this is not presupposed, there is nothing to keep, to preserve, and to check. For that reason the second point, in which the theory of common grace as expounded by Abraham Kuyper was fully adopted, implies a denial of the total depravity of fallen man.

Berkhof and other leaders of the Christian Reformed Church are insulted that I accuse them of Pelagianism. Berkhof complains repeatedly about this injustice against those who maintain the three points. He even assures his readers somewhat spitefully that such an accusation is ridiculous and suggests that I do not make it in good faith. But I openly challenge Berkhof or anyone else to clear himself of the indictment.

I frankly admit that this accusation would be unjust if I maintained that the second point expressly declares that man of himself can attain to salvation and saving good. This, however, I never asserted. Yet I maintain that the doctrine of Arminius and of Pelagius was in principle adopted in the second point in connection with the first. The first declares that the grace of God is a matter of a well-meant offer to all men, that the preaching of the gospel is common grace. That is Arminian. The main tenet of Pelagianism is the denial of total depravity. Man is inherently good. He did not become wholly corrupt, dead in sins and trespasses through the fall. You can call him ill or dangerously sick but not dead. Pelagianism must have nothing of the doctrine that the natural man is wholly incapable of doing any good and inclined to all evil. This is also the doctrine of the second point.

I admit that there are some points of distinction between rank Pelagianism and the second declaration of 1924. Pelagianism expressly teaches that the natural man by a proper use of his fundamentally good will can attain to the higher and saving knowledge of God. The second point does not teach this in so many words, although the case is left open to suspicion. This will be evident in a comparison of the first point—a general offer of salvation—with the second—a certain receptivity for the truth. I grant that the second point does not expressly maintain that the natural man of himself can attain to spiritual knowledge of God and Christ. But the fact remains that it emphatically maintains that the natural man, by the good remaining in him from paradise since the fall, can live to a certain extent a good world-life before God.

Pelagianism attributes the good left in man since the fall to the character of the fall. Through the fall man did not cast himself wholly into darkness and corruption and spiritual death, so that nothing good remains in him. On the contrary, the will of man remained fundamentally intact, good, and sound. The second point explains the good left in man after the fall by a restraining and preserving operation of the Holy Spirit. The result, however, is in principle the same in both cases: man is not wholly corrupt. Pelagianism explains the good found in every man by an individualistic conception of the race; every man stands and falls as his own master. It denies original guilt and corruption. The second point explains good in natural man, in the race, by a continual preserving and restraining operation of the Holy Spirit. The fact remains, both have in common a postulation of goodness in fallen man and a denial of his total depravity. The second point is in principle Pelagian.

Therefore, what Berkhof writes is untrue: "This point proceeds on the basis of a very definite presupposition...that man by nature is wholly corrupt and dominated by the principle of enmity against God and the neighbor."[30] This presentation is false. I challenge the professor to substantiate his statement and to make clear how corruption can be checked in a nature that is wholly depraved. He will find it an impossible task.

As I have proven, the professor flatly contradicts his statement later when he writes that the seed of outward righteousness and outward good, receptivity of the natural man for the truth, and good inclinations and desires—in short, many good elements—remain in man since the fall, which the Holy Spirit uses by his general operations.[31] The second point is based not on the presupposition Berkhof mentions, but on the directly opposite supposition that the natural man did not become wholly corrupt through the fall. Only on that supposition can there be room for the theory of a general operation of the Spirit by which good is kept from further and final corruption.

I can now define more correctly the real significance and implication of the second appendage to the confessions, as follows: *there is a general operation of the Holy Spirit, whereby the progress of corruption and sin in the human nature is being checked in such a way that the fallen nature was preserved in paradise and is constantly being preserved against total depravity.*[32]

For this declaration, or appendage to the Belgic Confession, synod offered no proof. Article 13 speaks of God's absolute sovereignty and control over devils and ungodly men. God always holds the reins. He directs, controls, and dominates the sinner so that even in his sinful deeds he can only fulfill God's sovereign counsel. He cannot do as he pleases. He is not independent. The Most High holds him in his power. Article

---

30 Ibid., 35.
31 Ibid., 37.
32 It will be evident to the reader that this view tends to obliterate the antithesis and constitutes a proper basis for worldliness. If natural man can actually live a good world-life before God by virtue of the remnants of natural light and goodness left in him from his original state, we must not separate ourselves from the world in natural and civil things to live from a different principle than natural man, but it is our calling to join him and unite with the world to elevate its life. Then you cannot object to the worldly unions but ought to join them; then you must close the Christian schools and unite in improving the public schools, for in all these various domains of life the world also lives a good life before God.

36 of the Belgic Confession that synod quoted refers to the sword power of the magistrates. But nowhere does it suggest a general operation of the Holy Spirit whereby the progress of corruption in human nature is checked. Man is constantly bridled by the Most High, mediately and immediately, in all his actions, but he is always wholly corrupt.

It is more than ridiculous when Berkhof writes, "The second thought expressed in the declarations of synod is that God restrains sin by the general operations of his Spirit. This is not expressed in so many words in our confessions, but may be easily deduced therefrom."[33] Why does not the professor point out how the theory of the general operations of the Spirit can be deduced from the confessions? He considers it an easy matter, yet he fails to make the deduction, although he is well aware that members of the synod of 1924 protested against this expression. However, I safely state without fear of contradiction that the confessions contain no shadow of a suggestion that the fallen nature of man is preserved from entire corruption by the general operations of the Spirit.

Neither do the scriptural passages to which synod referred sustain the declaration of the second point. Synod appealed to Genesis 6:3: "And the LORD said, My spirit shall not always strive with man." The tacit and supposed exegesis of synod is, "My Spirit shall not always check the progress of corruption in man's nature," but this has no sound basis. The exegesis of synod leads to an absurdity, as Berkhof shows plainly on page 43 of his booklet. The Spirit before the flood had not restrained the development of sin at all; the whole race had fast become ripe for destruction. Further, the word *strive* certainly does not mean the same as *check* or *restrain*.

The simple and self-evident explanation is that the Spirit had striven through the word, by the mouths of the prediluvian saints, with the ungodly generation living before the deluge. The result, however, had been not a check of corruption, but hardening of the hearts and further development of sin. The strife of the Spirit would not last forever. The end was approaching. The world would be judged and destroyed in the flood.

33 Berkhof, *Three Points*, 37.

Further, synod referred to a triplet of texts, Psalm 81:12–13; Acts 7:42; and Romans 1:24–26, 28, which teach that God gives the sinner over to all manner of evil, iniquity, and corruption. No exegesis can possibly deduce from these passages the doctrine of a general operation of the Holy Spirit whereby the progress of corruption is checked in the fallen human nature. *Directly* the texts teach exactly the opposite, for to give over is the very opposite of to restrain.

Nor do the texts presuppose a restraint by the Holy Spirit prior to the giving over. Romans 1 teaches very clearly that there is a constant and general manifestation of the wrath of God over all unrighteousness and ungodliness of men, who hold the truth under in unrighteousness (v. 18), and that the wrath of God against the wickedness of men becomes manifest especially in God's giving the ungodly over into worse corruption and deeper mire of sin (vv. 24, 26, 28). The wrath of God manifested in his giving the sinner over is revealed throughout history from its very beginning, according to the chapter, for its cause is that man, knowing God, would not glorify him as God and be thankful.

Hence the chapter teaches exactly the opposite from the declaration of synod. The synod declares *that there is a general operation of grace by the Holy Spirit whereby corruption is checked in the nature of man.* But the first chapter of Romans teaches *that there is a general operation of wrath, revealed by God from heaven, whereby man is given over from corruption into deeper corruption.* Anyone may verify the truth of this explanation by following the reasoning of the apostle Paul in verses 18–32.

Last, synod referred to 2 Thessalonians 2:6–7: "Now ye know what withholdeth that he might be revealed in his time. For the mystery of iniquity doth already work: only he who now letteth will let, until he be taken out of the way." The tacit assumption of synod was that "he who now letteth" is the Holy Spirit who restrains sin so that the man of sin cannot yet be revealed. This explanation is impossible, because scripture would not write of the Holy Spirit, "until he be taken out of the way." Yet this refers to the same person as the expression "he who now letteth." Berkhof in his booklet forgets to mention this text and offers no explanation.

My conviction is that the apostle had in mind a definite person, known to the Thessalonians, who stood in the way of the full realization of the antichristian power and kingdom. We know not, neither need we conjecture who that particular person "who now letteth" was. That person of Paul's time was a type of all those persons, powers, and circumstances that throughout history prevent the realization of the antichristian kingdom before God's time. However, the text certainly does not refer to the Holy Spirit and his general operation whereby he checks the progress of corruption in man's nature.

Other proof synod did not give.

Scripture and the confessions, however, are full of passages that directly contradict the declaration of synod concerning the general operation of the Holy Spirit, whereby the progress of corruption is curbed in man's fallen nature. I already pointed to Romans 1 as teaching the very opposite from the declaration of synod in the second point. Furthermore, scripture constantly declares that the natural man is wholly darkness, corrupt and evil, dead through trespasses and sins. God's evaluation of the natural man is that the imaginations of his heart are only evil continually (Gen. 6:5). The Lord looks down from heaven on the children of men to see if there are any who understand and seek God, but he finds none. They are all gone aside, they are altogether become filthy, there is none who does good, no not one (Ps. 14:2–3; 53:2–3).

Scripture teaches that even though the light shines in the darkness, the darkness does not comprehend it (John 1:5). The word of God emphatically declares concerning all men without distinction that their throats are open sepulchers; with their tongues they use deceit; the poison of asps is under their lips; their mouths are full of cursing and bitterness; and their feet are swift to shed blood (Rom. 3:9–18). It teaches that the natural mind is enmity against God; it is not subject to the law of God, neither indeed can be (Rom. 8:5–8).

Scripture judges that we are by nature dead through trespasses and sins, that we also walk in these, according to the course of this world, according to the prince of the power of the air, the spirit that now works in the children of disobedience (Eph. 2:1–2). It condemns us as being by nature children of wrath as others, having our conversations in the lusts of our flesh, fulfilling the desires of the flesh and of the mind (v. 3). It emphasizes that by nature our understandings are darkened, we are alienated from the life of God through the ignorance in us because of the blindness of our hearts, and we are given over unto lasciviousness and work all uncleanness with greediness (Eph. 4:18–19). It declares that by nature we are darkness and it is a shame even to mention the things we do in secret (Eph. 5:8, 12).

Scripture teaches that we are foolish, disobedient, deceived, serving divers lusts and pleasures, living in malice and envy, hateful and hating one another (Titus 3:3). It speaks not of a general operation of the Holy Spirit whereby sin is checked in its progress of corruption, but of an operation of wrath from heaven whereby sin is developed (Rom. 1:18–32). It finally calls out loudly, "He that is unjust, let him be unjust still; and he which is filthy, let him be filthy still," for the righteousness of God must be manifest over all ungodliness and unrighteousness of men, and sin must become fully revealed as sin, that God may be just and every mouth be stopped (Rev. 22:11).

Why quote more? Scripture always bears the same testimony. Who does not know it? Who does not feel that it is the testimony not of the word of God but of mere human philosophy that speaks of a certain goodness of the natural man through the general operations of the Holy Spirit?

And do the confessions ever speak a different language? The contrary is true. They emphasize that in paradise our nature became so corrupt that we are all conceived and born in sin; this corruption is so great that we are incapable of doing any good and are inclined to all evil.[34] They describe this corruption of our nature as "blindness of mind, horrible darkness, vanity, and perverseness of judgment," and picture fallen man as "wicked, rebellious, and obdurate in heart and will, and impure in [all] his affections."[35] Of the race the confessions say it is "a corrupt stock" producing a "corrupt offspring." Of this corrupt offspring they further say that "all men are conceived in sin, and are by nature children of wrath, incapable of any saving good, prone

34 Heidelberg Catechism Q&A 7–8, in Schaff, *Creeds of Christendom*, 3:309–10.—Ed.
35 Canons of Dordt 3–4.1, in ibid., 3:587–88.—Ed.

to evil, dead in sin, and in bondage thereto; and, without the regenerating grace of the Holy Spirit, they are neither able nor willing to return to God, to reform the depravity of their nature, nor to dispose themselves to reformation."[36]

True, there remain in man the glimmerings of natural light, but even natural light is so corrupted by sin that man wholly pollutes it and holds it under in unrighteousness, even in things natural and civil.[37] He retained a few remains of his natural gifts, but still all light in him is darkness.[38] But why multiply these quotations? It is a generally acknowledged fact that the Reformed confessions emphasize the total depravity of the human nature. Nowhere do they even suggest any improvement or reformation of this nature by a general operation of the Spirit.

Over against the second point I maintain, on the basis of the word of God and the Reformed confessions, that in paradise man's nature became wholly corrupt and depraved, so that there is no remnant of his original goodness, or righteousness, internal or external. I understand that his nature was not destroyed, that he remained a rational, moral creature, and that he retained a remnant of his original gifts from a natural viewpoint. He was not changed into another creature. He is still a being with mind and will. But in the nature—the mind and will of the natural, fallen man—all is perverse from an ethical, spiritual viewpoint. His knowledge is changed into darkness, so that he believes the lie; his righteousness is changed into unrighteousness, and his holiness is changed into corruption. His whole nature is subject to the rule and power of sin, which is enmity against God. There was no check on this corruption. His nature is exactly as corrupt as it could become.

I also maintain that the corruption and sinfulness of fallen nature come to manifestation in all their horror of darkness in the actual sins of every man, but only in keeping with the organic development of the human race. According as the race develops and life becomes more complex and gives rise to more and various relationships, sin

---

36 Canons of Dordt 3–4.2–3, in ibid., 3:588.—Ed.
37 Canons of Dordt 3–4.4, in ibid.—Ed.
38 Belgic Confession 14, in ibid., 3:398–99.—Ed.

also reveals itself as corrupting the whole of life in all its phases and relations, and the depravity of human nature comes to fuller manifestation. The root sin of Adam bears fruit in all the actual sins of the whole race until the measure of iniquity will be filled. There is no check on the corruption of the human nature, nor is the organic development of sin restrained in history.

Do not overlook that the organic development of sin is limited by various factors and influences. It is subject to the all-dominating rule of God, who gives man over in unrighteousness and punishes sin with sin in his righteous judgment, but who so directs the development of the sinful world that his counsel is fulfilled. This development is limited and determined by various gifts and talents, by disposition and character, and by times and circumstances. All men do not commit the same sins; everyone sins according to his place in the organism of the race and in history. The sin of apostate Jerusalem is greater than that of Sodom and Gomorrah. Sin is determined by various, often contradictory, motives in the deceitful heart of the sinner, such as fear of punishment, shame, ambition, vainglory, natural love, carnal lust, love of money, jealousy, envy, malice, and vengeance. These various motives often conflict with one another, but they remain sinful, although one sinful desire or motive will often prevent the sinner from satisfying another. Sin is directed in certain channels by the different forms of life and social institutions, the home and the family, the economic system, the state, and even the church.

But in all these channels and under all these determining and directing influences and factors, the current of sin moves irresistibly and uninterrupted onward, never stemmed or restrained, constantly emptying itself into the measure of iniquity determined by the Most High, until that measure will be filled. Then the judgment will come, and the lovers of iniquity will be eternally condemned to perish under God's righteous wrath.

Only when we are regenerated by the Spirit of God are we delivered from this awful power of sin and restored to God's favor, that we might be holy and without blemish before him.

CHAPTER 4

PERVERSE IN
ALL HIS WAYS

The appendage of the third point of 1924 to the confessions can be briefly expressed as follows: *the natural man is able to do good in civil things by virtue of an influence of God upon him that is not regenerative.*

There is a close relation between this point and the first two points. The first point lays the foundation of all three declarations. It postulates a general operation of grace in the hearts of all men, a gracious attitude of God toward elect and reprobate alike, which becomes manifest especially in the promiscuous preaching of the gospel. Point two further develops and applies this general, or common, grace. It consists of an operation of the Holy Spirit whereby man's nature is guarded against total corruption; remnants of good in man from paradise; and a seed of outward righteousness preserved in man's fallen nature, which seed germinates and bears fruit. It was to be expected that those two declarations would be followed by a third that definitely expresses that the natural man, under the influence of the Holy Spirit, actually performs good works in this world in natural and civil things.

Because of this intimate relation among the three points, and considering the conclusions reached with respect to the first two, an investigation of the doctrinal content of the third point is not likely to lead to the conclusion that it is Reformed. If the first two points cannot be regarded as in harmony with scripture and the confessions, it follows from the inseparable connection between these two and the third point that the latter cannot be in accord with Reformed truth. Nevertheless, we will separately test the truth of the last appendage. It will bring out more clearly how untenable is the position of those who would maintain the Reformed doctrine of total depravity as taught in the confessions and at the same time hold that natural man is able to do good.

I inquire of the leaders of the Christian Reformed Church, what according to their own interpretation is the implication of the third point? Especially with respect to this point, it is extremely difficult to obtain a definite answer regarding the correct interpretation of this synodical declaration. Again you meet Janus, the Roman two-faced idol. But especially this time, if you inquire of this strange oracle what good natural man does, he begins to spin around so swiftly that you get the impression he must be ashamed of both of his faces, the Reformed and the Pelagian.

The Reformed confessions teach in very clear and concise language that the natural man *is wholly incapable of* doing any good. They even declare that he entirely corrupts and pollutes his natural light and holds it in unrighteousness, *even in natural and civil things*. But the third point declares the very opposite, namely, that through an influence of God on him the natural man *is* able to do civil good. No wonder Janus blushes and is wholly embarrassed and begins to revolve so swiftly that you cannot distinguish either face clearly.

Let me give you a few illustrations of this. I quote from the court record of Kent County Circuit Court. Dr. Beets is in the witness chair and is answering in direct examination.

> Q. It is the claim of Herman Hoeksema, and he so states on the stand, that he does not agree with these three points, and as to the third point he says: "The question is simply whether natural man also in performing that civic righteousness is performing good before God, or whether he sins. That is the question. And then I maintain, whatever the natural man may do, no matter what he may do, as long as he assumes the attitude of hatred over against his God and does not love his God with all his heart and mind and soul and strength, as long as that love of God is not the deepest motive of all

he does, that is sin before God, no matter what he does, absolutely." Would you say that that is Reformed doctrine?

A. We distinguish between different kinds of good, sir.

Q. Well, I ask you whether or not you would say that is Reformed doctrine?

A. I would not assent to all his qualifications, no, sir.

Q. Why is it not Reformed doctrine, that which I have read?

A. Because he goes too far in some of the statements, not sufficiently differentiating.

Q. Is it the Reformed doctrine that the unregenerate, no matter what he does, that is sin before God?

A. I was going to...

Q. No, just follow that question.

A. Why will you not allow me to state?...

Q. Well, I will later on, but can that be answered? Maybe I did not make myself sufficiently clear.

A. Well, not all questions can be answered by just yes or no, sir. I should like to qualify.[39]

From this part of the examination it is perfectly clear that Dr. Beets refused to give an unqualified answer to the question, do the unregenerate always sin? The question was a very definite one. There is nothing in the question to indicate why it should not be answered by either yes or no. In fact, there is no conceivable third way of answering it. Not to answer the question by yes or no is evading the issue. This is exactly what Dr. Beets did.

Dr. Beets having explained to the court that we distinguish between four kinds of good—natural, civil, moral, and spiritual—the examination continued.

Q. But on the first three points, if an unregenerate man does do those first three points that you have mentioned, whether or not that is sin?

---

39 Record of "State of Michigan...No. 26695," 217–18.

A. I have told you that the doctrine of the Reformed churches is that we can do natural good, civic good or civil good, and moral or ecclesiastical.[40]

The reader will notice that Dr. Beets still tries to avoid the question whether the unregenerate man always sins. But the attorney persists. He was surely convinced that such a medieval doctrine of total depravity as would hold that the man of the world cannot do anything but sin was not the doctrine of the Reformed churches. Hence he pursues the subject.

Q. Well, who can do that?
A. Through common grace we all can do these things.

Q. Whether they are saved or unsaved?
A. Yes, sir.

Q. That means that the unregenerate can do these things and not be guilty of sin?
A. Of course, all our good, even our natural and civic and moral and ecclesiastical good, is all tainted with sin before a holy God.

Q. But can the unregenerate do good?
A. That is what our church declares, sir, civic good.

Q. Civic good?
A. Yes, sir.[41]

Still the lawyer is unsatisfied, and no wonder. He wanted an answer to the question, do the unregenerate always sin? He feels that he did not receive it, no matter how he urged his witness. Hence he presses on.

Q. And would you say that the claim of Herman Hoeksema, as I have read it here, is in conflict with that which synod laid down?
A. I said a while ago that I would not accept all of his qualifications. His statement has been rather sweeping.

40 Ibid., 218–19.
41 Ibid., 219.

Q. That is, he maintains that whatever the natural man may do, no matter what he may do, as long as he assumes an attitude of hatred over against God, as long as he does not love his God with all his heart and mind and soul and strength, as long as that love of God is not the deepest motive of all he does, that is sin before God, no matter what he does, absolutely. Would you say that that is...that you would agree with that?
A. What does absolutely mean, sir?

Q. Well, I don't know; I am using his language.
A. I thought I had been plain enough in stating that I do not accept all his qualifications.[42]

Obviously Dr. Beets still had not answered the question whether everything the unregenerate does is sin before God. I will trouble Dr. Beets no more for an answer to this question regarding the real and exact meaning of the third point. However, the above bit of conversation is too interesting to allow it to be relegated to oblivion.

Let us interrogate Berkhof and try to obtain an answer to this question from his booklet on the three points.

Question 1: According to your conception, professor, is the natural man wholly incapable of doing any good and inclined to all evil?

Answer: Indeed he is. "The natural man is wholly incapable of doing what is truly good. For this always proceeds from the root of faith and love to God, is not merely external, but in its deepest motives in accord with the law of God finds its ultimate aim in the glory of God. It is good in the full sense of the word. And because man by nature is dead in sin and trespasses he is unable to perform it."[43]

This is not bad. One may feel somewhat suspicious because the professor speaks of "what is truly good," as if one could also speak of what is falsely good, and because he modifies the idea of "the good" by the phrase "in the full sense of the word," as if good in the half sense of the word were conceivable too. Therefore, we remain on our

42 Ibid.
43 Berkhof, *Three Points*, 50.

guard. However, the professor here certainly maintains the truth that the natural man is of himself and by nature incapable of doing good.

Question 2: But is natural man, who is dead in sins and trespasses and incapable of doing true good, able to do what is good before God in the sphere of civil things, in the different spheres of natural life?

Answer: Indeed he is, for "in a positive sense synod declared that the unregenerated is capable of performing civil righteousness or civil good."[44]

Question 3: Can you define this good that a totally depraved man is able to do?

Answer: "It is not easy to define the good the unregenerate man can do. His works may be called good (a) in a subjective sense, insofar as they are the fruit of inclinations and affections touching the mutual relations of men, which are themselves relatively good, and by virtue of the remnants of the image of God that are still operating in man; and (b) in an objective sense, if in regard to the matter as such they are works prescribed by the law and in the sphere of social life correspond to the purpose that is well-pleasing to God."[45]

Question 4: But if you attribute to the natural man works that have their source in good inclinations and affections in harmony with the law of God and for a purpose that is acceptable to God, do you then not deny the total depravity of the human nature?

Answer: By no means. "While we acknowledge civil good, it is not denied that this relative good is at the same time sinful, if we consider it from another viewpoint. It is not good in the full sense of the word, but is only relative good. It resembles somewhat the withered fruit one may find sometimes on a tree or shrub that is cut off from its root... Even the best works of the ungodly are from a formal viewpoint and with respect to the manner in which they are performed, entirely sinful...At the same time it is good in a relative sense. The mere assertion that all the works of the unregenerate are sinful, without any qualification, fails to distinguish properly, contains only a partial truth, and is characterized by an absolutism that is condemned by the analogy of

---

44 Ibid.
45 Ibid., 50–51.

scripture, by our confessions and by Reformed theology."[46]

Question 5: Professor, do you want to teach that sin can be relatively good and that good can be relatively sinful? Are you in this way not undermining the very foundations of all ethics and morality?

Answer: "We remember that synod did not give any definition of civil good, and therefore it cannot be held responsible for any definition or qualification. It only declared that the unregenerate is capable of performing civil righteousness."[47]

Question 6: Very well, professor, but *you* certainly do interpret the third point. According to *you* civil good is a sinful good or a good sin. Can you explain how the natural man performs this sinful good?

Answer: "It appears from the declaration of synod that "it explains this civil good from an influence God exerts on man without renewing the heart. If man were left to himself, he could not perform civil good. It must be attributed to the bridle by which God governs man and to the general operations of the Holy Spirit upon intellect, will, and conscience. For this reason natural good does not entitle man to any claim of reward."[48]

Question 7: Professor, would you ascribe the withered fruit of a sinful good or a good sin to an operation of the Holy Spirit that improves man?

Answer: "I insist that "civil righteousness cannot be denied, unless one closes his eyes to the reality of life. Reformed people find the explanation of this in a working of God's common grace."[49]

Clearly we gain nothing if we allow Janus to keep on spinning around. If you say the unregenerate do nothing but sin, the reply is, "You are altogether too absolute, for the natural man does perform good in civil things." If you conclude that man is then not wholly depraved, the answer comes, "He is, for also this good is sin." Do we not become hopelessly entangled in a network of contradictions? We will do well to force Janus to come to a dead stop and to show us only

46 Ibid., 53.
47 Ibid., 52.
48 Ibid.
49 Ibid., 53.

the face portrayed in the third point, in order to determine whether its features are in harmony with Reformed lines as drawn in scripture and the confessions.

What does the third point imply? It has the following tenets.

First, the natural man is incapable of performing saving good. He can do no spiritual good; that is, he cannot attain to those works that the regenerate perform through the Spirit of Christ. Of himself he cannot come to conversion, cannot love God, and cannot in all things aim at the glory of God. He is incapable of performing saving good. God does not renew his heart.

Second, however, this natural man performs many good works in the domain of this life. Many things he does in the domain of family, social, and political life that are really good before God—morally if not spiritually good. In fact, by the good he does the child of God is often put to shame.

Third, this good does not properly proceed from the depraved man as such. Were he left to himself he could not perform civil righteousness. It does not proceed from the heart as its deepest source. The good works of the ungodly are not fruits of his corrupt nature. Therefore, the natural man who does good really has no part with his own works; he has no right to any reward.

Fourth, this good is properly the work of the Holy Spirit, the fruit of an influence of God on the natural man. He so influences the corrupt nature that in the case of the natural, unregenerated man, the evil tree brings forth good fruit. The Spirit does not penetrate to the heart of the natural man who brings forth fruits of good works in civil things. Yet he improves the nature, mind, will, conscience and directs the thoughts, desires, affections and inclinations of the ungodly so that with a heart opposed to God and filled with enmity against him, the ungodly nevertheless lives according to the law of God and pursues after purposes that please him. The Spirit forces, or compels, the operations of his wicked nature in the right direction as a helmsman forces a vessel against the wind.

Thus the natural man, in whom by the restraining power of the Holy Spirit much good remains from paradise, and who constantly is preserved by the Spirit's morally and ethically compelling influence, finally comes to the performance of actual good works, although only in natural and civil things. He lives a good world-life before God. He does not necessarily sin in his walk of life; he performs much good that is real good before God. Like the good works of the elect, his deeds are tainted with sin, but they are good nevertheless. Through the magic influence of common grace the corrupt tree brings forth good fruit. Regeneration is a wonder, common grace is magical. The same fountain brings forth sweet and bitter water!

Thus the world of darkness is changed into light. It is full of men who are totally depraved by nature, but who are actually good. In actual, practical life you find no totally corrupt men. In this life the difference between the righteous and the ungodly is completely obliterated.

How emphatically our opponents intend to maintain that the natural man is really able to do good before God by virtue of the compulsory influence of the Holy Spirit is more evident from a comparison between the doctrine of the synod of 1924 and the views Danhof and I expressed on this subject before synod held its sessions.

What then is civil righteousness? In our opinion the sinner notes the God-instituted relations, the given laws, means of fellowship, and the like. He notes the propriety and usefulness of them. He makes use of them for his own sake. If he succeeds fairly well in this, an action will result that formally appears to be in harmony with the laws of God. Then you have civil righteousness, regard for virtue, and an orderly external deportment. If this attempt fails, as is often the case, then also civil righteousness falls away; then the opposite is true. His fundamental error is, however, that also in striving for external deportment he does not seek or purpose God. To the contrary he seeks himself also in fellowship with other sinners and tries to maintain himself in his sin against God, with the entire world in whatever he does. And that is sin. This also actually has evil results for him and his fellow-creatures. His action with respect to his neighbor and fellow creatures takes place according to the same rule and with the same results. It therefore happens that sin always develops and that corruption continues, and yet there remains relatively a formally just behavior according to the laws laid down and instituted by God. Yet the natural man never performs ethical good. This is our view.[50]

We wrote that before the synod of 1924. Synod was acquainted with this fact. It condemned our view and substituted its own as expressed in the third point. Because of our view of the so-called civil righteousness it expelled us from the Christian Reformed Church (in 1926 the synod approved of the action of Classis Grand Rapids East). This proves how strongly the Christian Reformed Church intends to emphasize that the natural man does not always sin in all his ways but is really able to do what is good before God in the sphere of this present life by virtue of God's common grace.

Against this view I have many objections of a general, doctrinal nature.

First, this view certainly lowers the moral, ethical standard of life, of what is good and evil. The attempt to maintain that man is wholly depraved and yet able to perform good works leads to the view that good can be evil and evil can be good at the same time. It leads to the conception of the relativity of good and evil. Berkhof speaks of a good that is at the same time sinful and of sin that is relatively good. He speaks of good "in the full sense of the word" and of "what is truly good," implying that an ethical act can also be half good and half evil. He even considers the view that the natural man can only sin to be an "absolutism" that is to be condemned.

I consider the introduction of relativity into the sphere of ethics and morality positively pernicious, and the evil effects of this view are plainly observed in the actual lives of the people of God. All lines of distinction are being obliterated on the basis of this philosophy. It creates a sphere of transition, a common sphere of life, a domain

---

50 Danhof and Hoeksema, *Along Pure Paths*, 72–73.

where the righteous and the ungodly have fellowship with one another and live the same life. This philosophy of relative good and evil forms a very superficial conception of what is good before God. True consciousness of sin is well-nigh impossible in the light of this conception, and the true fear of the Lord is rooted out. When one considers this view in its real and fundamental tendencies, one cannot help but shudder with horror and fear for the future of a church that follows in its direction.

It is exactly the view that Berkhof condemns as "absolutism" that scripture everywhere upholds as the truth. Something is good or evil not relatively but absolutely. Sin is unrighteousness. Good is what proceeds from faith, is performed according to the law of God, and aims at the glorification of his name. All the rest is sin. Light and darkness are not relative conceptions. God is the only criterion for what is good, and he is the absolute. Only what is in harmony with his will is good, not relatively but absolutely. Such is the testimony of scripture.

The third point lowers the ethical standard of life, amalgamates light and darkness, and causes the church to be swallowed up by the world. It is detrimental to the fear of God in life. The effects of this common grace theory are already plainly visible in the life of the church.

Second, insofar as this good performed by the ungodly is ascribed to an operation of the Holy Spirit on the natural man, it is deterministic and an attack on the holiness of God.

What else is it than an attack on the holiness of God when the sinful good of the natural man, the withered fruit of the uprooted tree, is presented as the effect of an operation of the Holy Spirit? Yet it is emphatically declared that the good works of the natural man are not his own but are the fruits of the Spirit's operation. Man of himself is dead in trespasses and sins; he is like a tree cut off from its root; he is certainly incapable of bearing good fruit. Therefore, the good he does proceeds not from his heart but from the Holy Spirit, who brings forth good fruit from an evil tree. However, these fruits, which are the direct result of the operation of the Spirit of God, are rooted not in the love of God but in the love of self; they aim not at God's glory but at the

maintenance of sinful man over against God. Berkhof admits this. Yet
the Holy Spirit produces these fruits; he is their real and sole author.
From this viewpoint the third point is a denial of and an attack on the
holiness of God.

The third point is also strictly deterministic. The operation of the
Spirit that compels the natural man to do good literally destroys his
moral nature and makes him a mere tool in the power of the Spirit.
Remember that by the operation of the Holy Spirit the natural man
is not renewed. His heart is not changed. He is supposed to remain
wholly incapable of doing any good and inclined to all evil. Even his
supposedly good works are not from his heart. He does not purpose to
do good. He does not love the good but hates it. He really does not do
the good; the Holy Spirit does it. His acts are not his own.

Berkhof does not bring out this aspect of the theory, as Abraham
Kuyper did in his *Common Grace*. Kuyper literally and emphatically expressed that the ego of the natural man is not involved in his
good works at all. In his view the natural man is exactly like the ship
directed by the will of the helmsman: he is ethically dead, and he is not
a moral agent at all. That this is also Berkhof's view is clear when he
writes, "[The good of the natural man] must be attributed to the bridle
by which God governs man and to the general operations of the Holy
Spirit upon intellect, will, and conscience. For this reason natural good
does not entitle man to any claim of reward."[51] He is not rewarded for
his good works. This conception is possible only if one proceeds from
the assumption that the natural man is really not the ethical subject of
his good works. The Holy Spirit compels him, determines him and his
works. Hence man has no reward but with all his good works is cast
into eternal perdition.

Third, the third point is positively immoral and an attack on the
righteousness and justice of God, a perversion of the moral order, when
it teaches that the natural man performs good works that are never
rewarded. God is just, and the justice of God implies and demands
that he punishes the evil and rewards the good. He who denies this or
tampers with it subverts the moral order. Yet to defend the third point

51 Berkhof, *Three Points*, 52.

and the theory of common grace this becomes necessary.

Emphasized in the third point is that the natural man performs much good. He often surpasses the child of God in good works and puts him to shame. Judged by the standard of the third point and the theory of common grace, it should not be difficult to discover men in this world who do nothing but good all their lives. They commit no gross sins; they live temperately and chastely; they even sacrifice themselves for the well-being of the world and humanity. Their walk in the world is good before God. The Lord stamps their works as good. They are even fruits of the Holy Spirit.

Yet these men do not receive any reward for all their good works. When they have spent their lives doing good, they are cast into eternal perdition. Where then is the justice of God? Is God changeable? Does he approve the works of the ungodly in this life and condemn them as corrupt in the judgment day? In this way the righteousness of God is attacked and denied, and the moral order of the world is subverted. What is good before God is good forever and must surely be rewarded with good.

My chief objection against this entire theory is that it is fundamentally Pelagian. It is a denial of the total depravity of man. Setting aside all sophistical reasoning and hopeless attempts to show how a totally depraved man can do good works and a wholly corrupt tree can bring forth good fruit, the bare fact remains that according to this theory man as he actually reveals himself in this world is not totally depraved and wholly corrupt. The real view of the third point, in connection with the second, can be briefly and correctly expressed by saying that man *would have been* wholly depraved and incapable of doing any good *if there were no influence of common grace*. However, he is not wholly corrupt.

One may maintain that this view is not Pelagian because it clearly teaches that the natural man is incapable of doing any *spiritual* good; but the fact remains that according to this theory he lives a good life before God, just as good a life as the regenerate, if not better. The antithesis is obliterated, the chasm between church and world is removed, and the church is justified in making common cause with the world in the things of this life. Even as in principle the first point denies the truth that grace is particular, so the second and third points deny the Reformed truth that man by nature is wholly depraved, incapable of doing any good, and inclined to all evil. Only by a good deal of sophistry can this real implication of the third point be denied.

There is no basis for this view in the confessions of the Reformed churches, not even in the few citations made by synod, as I clearly showed in the first chapter of this booklet. The confessions mention remnants of natural good, but never do they speak of an influence of God on the natural man whereby he is improved or reformed. The confessions teach that by natural light men retained some knowledge of God and of natural things, of the difference between good and evil, but never do the confessions state or even imply that the natural man actually performs the good. The confessions declare that by natural light fallen man shows some regard for virtue and an orderly external deportment, but nowhere do the confessions express or imply that he can do good works.

The term *civil righteousness* is not only absent in the Reformed confessions, but also they deny the very idea. This is evident when Canons 3–4.4, which synod partially quoted, is read in its entirety, for it declares that the natural man is incapable of using natural light aright even in natural and civil things. Further, in various ways man renders this light, such as it is, wholly polluted and holds it in unrighteousness. The confessions do not teach an influence of God on man whereby an orderly deportment is maintained in public life, but they teach that the magistrates and the power of the police are necessary for this purpose.[52]

The confessions plainly declare that all the light within us, even natural light, is ethical and spiritual darkness.[53] The confessions declare without qualification that the unregenerated man is wholly incapable of doing any good and inclined to all evil.[54] Not a single passage of the forms of unity can be cited as proof of an influence of God, an operation of the Holy Spirit outside of the work of regeneration that

---

52 Belgic Confession 36, in Schaff, *Creeds of Christendom*, 3:432–33.—Ed.
53 Belgic Confession 14, in ibid, 3:398–99.—Ed.
54 Heidelberg Catechism Q&A 8, in ibid., 3:310.—Ed.

improves the sinner. I openly challenge Berkhof or anyone to point out where the confessions do speak of such operations.

Much less does scripture support such a theory. Synod placed itself in a pitiable position by its alleged proofs from scripture to support its third point. First, synod discovered in scripture three examples of men who were unregenerated and of whom scripture declares that they did what was right in the sight of the Lord. The three examples are Jehu, the general who became king of Israel, and Jehoash and Amaziah, kings of Judah.

The good Jehu did was to exterminate the entire house of Ahab, as God had commanded him. Scripture says that he did well in executing that commandment. At the same time we read that Jehu did not depart from the sins of Jeroboam and did not walk and took no heed to walk in the law of the Lord with all his heart (2 Kings 10:29–30). His extermination of the house of Ahab is later reckoned as blood guiltiness that will be avenged on the house of Jehu (Hosea 1:4).

Did Jehu perform any moral or ethical good before the Lord by exterminating Ahab's house? Did he perform moral or ethical good under an influence of the Holy Spirit? Was his sinful nature somewhat reformed or improved before he could begin exterminating Ahab's house? The contrary is true. Jehu did not care about Jehovah and his service. That he did not depart from the ways and sins of Jeroboam makes this clear.

His motive for executing God's command to exterminate Ahab's house was radically different. Jehu was ambitious. Love of power and glory and a desire for distinction and superiority controlled him. The command of Jehovah to destroy the house of Ahab was the way to realize his ambition. The hope of the royal crown inspired him, and Jehu's natural ability matched his ambition. Hence we need not be surprised that he did well in thoroughly and quickly executing the command of the Lord. But there was no positive ethical value in his work. No matter how well he executed Jehovah's word, his work was ethically sinful; it was rooted in self-love and aimed at his own glory and the realization of his ambitions. A special operation of the Holy Spirit in Jehu's heart to restrain sin certainly was wholly unnecessary for that purpose, and scripture does not speak of it with even a word.

Nor do we read of such an operation of common grace in Jehoash and Amaziah. In both cases the kings outwardly adapted to the law of the Lord in their reigns. They showed regard for orderly external deportment in ruling their people. Regarding Jehoash scripture distinctly says that he did right in the sight of the Lord as long as he was under the influence of the powerful priest, Jehoiada. Scripture does not imply or suggest that there was an operation of the Spirit upon these kings, an influence of God that improved their sinful natures and caused the evil trees to bring forth good fruit.

The fact that synod referred to these examples shows how hopeless the case of the third point is. Does it not teach that there an influence of God on all men whereby they can do civil good? Granted for the sake of argument that the illustrations of Jehoash and Amaziah suggest an operation of common grace, where is proof for a similar working of the Spirit on all the other wicked kings of Israel and Judah? The operation of the Spirit of the third point does not appear to be very common or general. All these and similar illustrations show that fallen man by natural light—without any operation of common grace and while remaining wholly sinful in all his deeds and perverse in all his ways—may show for various reasons and from different motives that are always sinful some regard for orderly external deportment and may adapt himself in his outward life to the law of God.

Synod also referred to some direct scriptural expressions that are supposed to teach that the natural man can do good.

First, synod referred to Luke 6:33: "And if ye do good to them which do good to you, what thank have ye? for sinners also do even the same." The citation of this passage again reveals how weak the case of the third point is, because the Lord in these words does not speak of any ethical or moral good that sinners do before God, but only of the general practice of sinners to favor one another. They do good to one another, that is, they favor those who do good to them. Further, it is Jesus' purpose to point out to his disciples that there is no ethical or moral value in this practice of sinners, for they do good only to those who favor them, which is pure selfishness and therefore ethically wrong. This morally and ethically wrong practice certainly cannot be ascribed to an influence of God on these sinners, nor is there in the text the faintest suggestion of such an influence. The text therefore offers no support of the third point.

The second passage to which synod referred appears to be more weighty. It is Romans 2:14: "For when the Gentiles, which have not the law, do by nature the things contained in the law, these, having not the law, are a law unto themselves." Berkhof offers a brief interpretation of this text: "The things contained in the law" ("the things that are of the law" according to the Greek) are things demanded by the law. Berkhof appeals to Romans 10:5 and Galatians 3:12 to support his interpretation: "Moses describeth the righteousness which is of the law, That the man which doeth those things shall live by them" (Rom. 10:5). "The law is not of faith: but, The man that doeth them shall live in them" (Gal. 3:12). According to Berkhof, both passages clearly teach that the man who does the things demanded by the law is righteous and shall live. He acquires the righteousness that is of the law.

If Berkhof's contention is correct—that the phrase "the things contained in the law" in Romans 2:14 signifies things that the law demands, as in Romans 10:5 and Galatians 3:12—it follows by rigorous logic that Paul teaches in the first passage that the Gentiles are righteous and live by the works of the law, for he declares that the Gentiles do by nature the things of the law. But this interpretation refutes itself, for it is evident from the context in Romans 2 that the apostle purposes to prove the very opposite, namely, that no man is justified by the works of the law. All have sinned and are condemned. All perish, whether they have sinned with or without the law. The Gentiles do not have the external proclamation of the law, yet they sin and are accountable.

In Romans 2:14–15 the apostle does not contradict this statement by saying that the Gentiles keep the law and do good, but he explains how it is possible that those who have not the law can nevertheless sin, be held responsible, and be judged. They show in their lives and walk that they have the work of the law written in their hearts (v. 15). What is the work of the law? To declare what is good and what is evil, to draw the lines of demarcation between light and darkness, and to proclaim the will of God concerning our lives. The Gentiles have in their hearts the work of the law, natural light by which they can discern between good and evil. They are a law unto themselves (v. 14). Thus they do by nature the things of the law, that is, they do things that the external law does among Israel: they draw the lines of demarcation between good and evil.

Although they show the work of the law written in their hearts and clearly reveal that they discern between righteousness and unrighteousness, between light and darkness, yet they follow after darkness and wallow in the most terrible iniquity, as the apostle sets forth in Romans 1:18–32. Therefore, they are responsible, for they sin consciously as moral beings, and they will perish without the law. Berkhof's interpretation must be rejected as wholly contrary to the meaning of the apostle, and synod erred seriously when it offered Romans 2:14 as proof of the contention that there is a general operation of the Holy Spirit on men whereby they are enabled to do good.

Besides, what weight of argument is there in these few passages of synod when viewed in the light of the overwhelming testimony of the word of God, which declares that the natural man never does any good? Scripture never speaks of relative good or relative evil; scripture is absolute. Scripture never teaches that the natural man is incapable of doing saving good but is capable of doing moral, natural, or civil good. It always declares the very opposite: all men, Jew and Gentile, are under sin and at all times perverse in all their ways. If any man will believe and accept this truth, he does not have to search scripture for a few isolated passages to support this faith. Nor is there any need to distort the meaning of texts to elicit from them a meaning they do not convey. On the contrary, he will discover that all of the word of God supports him in this belief, and it does so by a clear testimony that leaves no doubt as to its meaning. I refer the reader to only a few passages, selected at random, in support of the truth.

1.   They are corrupt, they have done abominable works, there is none that doeth good.

2. The LORD looked down from heaven upon the children of men, to see if there were any that did understand, and seek God.

3. They are all gone aside, they are all together become filthy: there is none that doeth good, no, not one. (Ps. 14:1–3)

Notice that especially the following passage speaks of the influence of God on the wicked, whereby they are given over to a reprobate mind—the very opposite of the influence of which the third point speaks.

28. And even as they did not like to retain God in their knowledge, God gave them over to a reprobate mind, to do those things which are not convenient;

29. Being filled with all unrighteousness, fornication, wickedness, covetousness, maliciousness; full of envy, murder, debate, deceit, malignity; whisperers,

30. Backbiters, haters of God, despiteful, proud, boasters, inventors of evil things, disobedient to parents,

31. Without understanding, covenant-breakers, without natural affection, implacable, unmerciful:

32. Who knowing the judgment of God, that they which commit such things are worthy of death, not only do the same, but have pleasure in them that do them. (Rom. 1:28–32)

9. What then? are we better than they? No, in no wise: for we have before proved both Jews and Gentiles, that they are all under sin;

10. As it is written, There is none righteous, no, not one:

11. There is none that understandeth, there is none that seeketh after God.

12. They are all gone out of the way, they are together become unprofitable; there is none that doeth good, no, not one.

13. Their throat is an open sepulchre; with their tongues they have used deceit; the poison of asps is under their lips:

14. Whose mouth is full of cursing and bitterness:

15. Their feet are swift to shed blood:

16.   Destruction and misery are in their ways:

17.   And the way of peace have they not known:

18.   There is no fear of God before their eyes. (Rom. 3:9–18)

Why quote more texts? These passages have no uncertain sound; they bear a clear testimony concerning the ways of natural man; they are in no need of interpretation unless you would distort them to harmonize with a man-made theory of the good that sinners do. The reader can find additional proof in Romans 8:5–8, Romans 14:23, Ephesians 2:2–3, Ephesians 4:17–19, Titus 3:3, James 3:11, 1 Peter 4:3, and many other passages. The synod of 1924 in its third declaration contradicted and condemned not only myself and Danhof, but also the holy scriptures. The constant testimony of scripture is that the natural man is perverse in all his ways.

Finally, I most emphatically deny an influence of God outside of regeneration on the natural man whereby he is enabled to do ethical and moral good before God. I deny that the natural man ever does good before the Most High. By this I do not deny that man, by nature and by the light in him as a moral and rational creature, tries to adapt himself in his life and walk externally to the law of God. He is able in a general way to discern the law of God and to acknowledge that the way of this law is good for him and for the community in which he lives.

In the state of righteousness man stood in the world as God's viceroy, as king-servant over the earthly creation, in order that all creatures might serve man and that with them he might serve his God. But man's relation to God was subverted through sin into its very opposite. From being a friend of God man changed into God's enemy. Man's knowledge became darkness; his righteousness became unrighteousness; his holiness became corruption and hatred of God. But man's relation to the creature, although marred and disturbed, was not destroyed. Hence the sinner constantly attempts to maintain himself in the midst of and in connection with the earthly creation, as a servant of Satan and an enemy of God. Man wills the creature to serve him, and with that creature he wants to serve sin.

The creation is also subject to the ordinances of the Lord. Insofar as man by natural light can discover these ordinances of God in creation and insofar as he discerns and acknowledges that it is expedient for him to regulate his life externally according to these ordinances, there is in him outward regard for virtue and an orderly deportment. In this attempt to adapt himself outwardly to the laws of God, man sometimes succeeds in part and for a certain length of time. Ultimately, however, his sinful heart and darkened mind deceive him and lead him astray, so that he tramples underfoot even the ordinances of God that are for the benefit of his life.

As long as man succeeds, he lives temperately and chastely, maintains peace and order in the home and in his social and political life, and prospers in the world. When he fails and the lust of the flesh deceives his wistful heart, his life is characterized by intemperance, gluttony, adultery, dissipation, and drunkenness. He destroys the home, works for the downfall of social life, and causes wars and revolutions. But whether he succeeds or fails, always he lives and works from the principle of enmity against God, and he never attains to what is good before God.

Only when man is converted, changed in the depth of his heart by the divine wonder of grace called regeneration, does he know and in principle perform what is acceptable to God, for then all his delight is in the law of the Lord.

The Three Points of Common Grace Adopted by the Synod of the Christian Reformed Church in 1924 and Herman Hoeksema's Formulations of the New Doctrines Taught Therein

Concerning the first point, with regard to the favorable disposition of God toward mankind in general, and not only to the elect, synod declares that according to the Scripture and the confessions it is determined that besides the saving grace of God, shown only to the elect unto eternal life, there is a certain kind of favor or grace of God which He shows to His creatures in general. This is evidenced by the quoted Scripture passages and from the Canons of Dort 2.5 and 3–4.8–9, which deals with the general offer of the Gospel; whereas the quoted declarations of Reformed writers from the golden age of Reformed theology also give evidence that our Reformed fathers from of old have advocated these opinions.[55]

God manifests a certain grace in the preaching of the gospel not only to the elect unto eternal life, but to all without distinction who hear the preaching of the gospel.

With respect to the second point concerning the restraint of sin in the life of individuals and in society, Synod declares that according to Scripture and the Confessions there is such a restraint of sin. This is evident from the quoted Scripture passages and from the Belgic Confession Art. 13 and 36, where we are taught that God through the general operation of His

---

55 *1924 Acts of Synod*, 145–46.

Spirit, without renewing the heart, restrains sin in its unbridled expression through which remains possible a societal relationship, while from the quoted declarations of Reformed writers from the golden age of Reformed theology it is evident that our Reformed fathers from of old have advocated these opinions.[56]

There is a general operation of grace of an ethical nature by the Holy Spirit, by which all men, apart from regeneration, are improved and reformed to such an extent that they do not break out in all manner of sins.

Concerning the third point, in regard to the doing of so-called civil good by the unregenerate, Synod declares that according to Scripture and the confessions, the unregenerate, though unable to do any saving good (Canons of Dort 3–4.3) are able to do civil good. This is evident from the quoted Scriptures, and from the Canons of Dort 3–4.4 and the Belgic Confession Art. 36, where we are taught that God, without renewing the heart, exercises such influence on mankind that it is able to carry out civil good; while from the declarations of Reformed writers from the golden age of Reformed theology it is evident that our fathers from of old advocated this [same] opinion.[57]

The natural man is able to do good in civil things by virtue of an influence of God upon him that is not regenerative.

---

56 Ibid., 146.
57 Ibid., 146–47.

THE REUNION OF THE CHRISTIAN REFORMED AND PROTESTANT REFORMED CHURCHES

Is It Demanded, Possible, Desirable?

———◆———

HERMAN HOEKSEMA

TRANSLATED BY HERMAN VELDMAN

Introduction to *The Reunion of the Christian Reformed and Protestant Reformed Churches*

T
he Reunion of the Christian Reformed and Protestant Reformed Churches is the text of a speech given by Herman Hoeksema at a conference of Christian Reformed and Protestant Reformed ministers held in March 1939. The Reformed Free Publishing Association published the speech in the Dutch language soon after the conference. Later the association published an English translation by Rev. Herman Veldman.

Among the sixteen Christian Reformed ministers in attendance at the conference were some of the leading churchmen of that time. The chairman of the conference was Dr. Henry Beets of the Christian Reformed Church. Also prominently in attendance was the Dutch theologian Dr. Klaas Schilder. He had traveled to the United States with the purpose of bringing about the reunion of the two American denominations.

Significantly for Protestant Reformed readers in the twenty-first century, this brochure shows that Hoeksema and the Protestant Reformed Churches were open to the effort to reunite the two denominations, in spite of the gross injustices perpetrated on the founding fathers of the Protestant Reformed Churches by the Christian Reformed Church. The motive for this openness was manifesting the unity of the church. But reunion had to occur on the solid basis of oneness in doctrine. This meant oneness with regard to the issues raised by the Christian Reformed Church's adoption of the three points of common grace in 1924.

Hoeksema therefore was willing, indeed eager, to discuss the doctrinal issues, as he had always been. To facilitate the discussion that might lead to reunion, he prepared a speech opening up the subject. He also formulated twenty propositions for discussion. These propositions conclude this brochure.

The Christian Reformed ministers at the conference, however, refused to discuss common grace and its implications. None of them came to the conference with a speech addressing the obstacles to reunion or setting forth the Christian Reformed view of common grace. Why they came to the conference is a mystery.

As the Christian Reformed Church was responsible for the division in the church of Jesus Christ in 1924, by adopting the theory of common grace as dogma and forcing this theory on the consciences of ministers about whom its own synod declared that they were Reformed in the fundamentals, so was the Christian Reformed Church responsible in 1939 for obstructing the attempt to heal the breach. If schism is a grievous evil and if denominational oneness is a manifestation of the unity of the church—and both are true—these iniquities of the Christian Reformed Church are not minor matters.

Hoeksema's treatment of reunion in the brochure is also worthwhile for its statement of the comprehensive nature of the Christian Reformed doctrine of common grace. The error is not isolated and minor. In addition, Hoeksema's critique of each of the three points exposes each as corruption of fundamental Reformed truth. In his criticism of the first point, the most offensive of the three, as it is also the most serious corruption of the Reformed faith, Hoeksema notes that the Christian Reformed synod of 1926, defending the three points of common grace, explicitly affirmed a "well-meant offer of salvation to all to whom the preaching of the gospel comes," in the grace of God to all. A well-meant offer is the doctrine of the first point of common grace. But the first point does not employ the terminology. The synod of 1926 used the terminology in defending the first point.

Hoeksema was also positive. The brochure contains a profound, valuable sketch of the Protestant Reformed conception of the grace of

God in connection with the development of the kingdom of Christ in history. The development of the kingdom of Christ takes place in close natural connection with, but in spiritual separation from, the kingdom of the ungodly.

This foundational document has both historical and theological significance.

—David J. Engelsma

Introduction

The immediate occasion of this meeting of certain leaders of the Christian Reformed Church and Protestant Reformed Churches is, no doubt, the visit of Dr. Klaas Schilder among us. Now and then, also before the coming of the professor at Kampen, the sentiment had been expressed that the difference between both churches was not sufficiently important or fundamental to justify their separate existences. Never, however, has this led to any definite action.

In his lectures among us Schilder not only expressed the idea, but also urged both groups to seek one another anew and try to arrange a conference at which the points that caused division would be discussed, and if possible to live together again under one ecclesiastical roof. At the conference that the Protestant Reformed ministers held with the professor, one of the first questions he laid before us was whether we would be willing and prepared to attend such a colloquy. As I wrote in the *Standard Bearer*, the hope was expressed in more than one quarter in the Netherlands that one of the fruits of Schilder's trip might be such a reunion. Therefore, I think the conclusion wholly justifiable that it was especially at his urging that certain Christian Reformed brethren ventured to call a meeting like this together. Personally I express my appreciation and gratitude for the invitation we received to attend this gathering.

I deem it of the greatest importance for the success of such an attempt that we understand one another correctly, and some preparation for our discussion of the various questions to be deliberated now or later is desirable. Even in general this is true. I am an enemy of all compromise. No blessing can be expected from a superficial discussion of the issues and a subsequent reconciliation and reunion. A thorough discussion of the differences is therefore imperative. But I believe that especially the circumstances under which this meeting was called together prompt us to be careful.

First, I believe that Schilder's coming and association with him here and there revealed an enthusiasm that beclouded the judgment of some. When presently the esteemed professor will have returned to the

Netherlands, both he and we will reflect more calmly and soberly on these matters, which is an indispensable requisite for a clear and sound understanding of them. It is not impossible that there is at present strange fire on the altar. Especially now matters must not be hastened.

Second, it is possible that our esteemed guest from the Netherlands views the matters that separate us in a different light than we do. If I am not mistaken, his judgment is that in 1924 we fought too severe a battle regarding common grace and that our differences are not sufficiently serious to warrant separate existences. With such a judgment I can agree only if it is based on a thorough discussion. In this view I do not stand alone. In one of the last numbers [issues] of *De Wachter* one can read that according to the judgment of the writer, we are walking a deeply sinful way, and while we are not to be viewed as heathens and publicans, we must nevertheless be treated as objects of admonition so that we can repent of our evil way. My presence here must not be viewed as proof of my readiness to submit to a brotherly admonition.

I do not say this because of a lack of a brotherly spirit. On the contrary, I declare myself ready, for the success of this meeting, to lay aside for the present the grievances I have and to forget them insofar as possible and to adopt an attitude of friendship. However, by way of expressing my opinion at the outset, I maintain that a meeting of this nature is justifiable and can be a blessing only when it purposes to discuss thoroughly the issues separating us. This essay may be viewed as an introduction to such a discussion and as an explanation of my viewpoint.

Is Reunion Demanded?

I begin with subjects about which we all agree. First, the church of Christ is one, one body in its head Christ Jesus the Lord, one in the Spirit, united in the body of peace through the one faith, even as there is one God and Father who is above all and in all. This unity must be realized and manifested as much as possible in the church on earth. Therefore, it is the sacred and solemn calling of all believers to seek that true unity with all that is in them.

What as church of Christ belongs together must not be separated, much less live in a relation of enmity. All schism must be avoided. Whoever causes what is truly one and belongs together to be torn asunder will bear the judgment. We agree with Calvin, who teaches that "the church is called 'catholic,' or 'universal,' because there could not be two or three churches unless Christ be torn asunder...which cannot happen!"[1] We subscribe also to the word of Bavinck: "As Christians we cannot humble ourselves enough because of the schism and discord which have existed in the church of Christ through the ages; it is a sin against God, in conflict with the prayer of Christ, and caused by the darkness of our mind and the uncharitableness of our heart."[2]

Yet it will not do to urge a union of whatever on earth calls itself church. Although it is understandable that men—prompted by a fervent desire for an erroneously conceived unity of the church—often permitted themselves to be misled to seek unity by power, artificial means, or syncretism and denial of principles. Yet we may not cooperate with such movements. The division within the church on earth is simply a fact.

That on earth which calls itself church can be distinguished as true and false church. We must certainly number with the false church those so-called churches that no longer reckon with the word of God but proclaim human wisdom instead of the gospel of Christ and have broken with the broad fundamentals of Christianity, such as the Godhead of Christ, atonement through his blood, the resurrection, and the return of the Savior. That which broadly is considered as belonging to the true church, because the word of God is known and proclaimed there in a greater or lesser degree, is characterized by various degrees of purity. There is difference in purity of confession, in the administration of the sacraments, in church government, and in the form of divine worship.

Leaving aside the false church, it will not do to bring under one ecclesiastical roof whatever may have any claim to the name of

---

1   Calvin, *Institutes*, 4.1.2, 21:1014.
2   Herman Bavinck, *Gereformeerde Dogmatiek* [Reformed dogmatics] 2nd ed. (Kampen: J. H. Kok, 1911), 4:344. See also Herman Bavinck, *Reformed Dogmatics*, ed. John Bolt, trans. John Vriend, vol. 4, *Holy Spirit, Church, and New Creation* (Grand Rapids: Baker Academic, 2008), 316.—Ed.

church. This is impossible because of practical considerations. But of far weightier importance is the chief calling of the church on earth to preserve and proclaim the word purely, and by an attempt toward fusion, the truth would not only be beclouded and increasingly adulterated, but also soon wholly lost. Especially for this reason the church is called to progressive reformation, so that it can continue to keep and maintain the truth over against evil influences from within and without, as well as to seek its further development. Because of this a church can have the calling, under specific circumstances, when it has become impossible within a certain church fellowship to maintain the truth purely, to return and separate. For this reason it is the calling of every believer to affiliate himself with the church that according to the conviction of his heart is the purest revelation of the body of Christ. Bavinck writes:

> There is great difference in the purity of the confessions and the churches. And we must abide by and strive for the purest. Whoever, therefore, becomes convinced that the Protestant Church is better than the Roman Catholic, and the Reformed is purer than the Lutheran or Remonstrant or the Baptist, must, without necessarily condemning his church as false, leave the one and affiliate himself with the other. And to remain in one's own church, notwithstanding much impurity in doctrine and life, is obligatory as long as we are not hindered in being faithful to our own confession, and, be it indirectly, are not forced to obey man rather than God.[3]

To this I add that whoever does otherwise aids the false church. This also means that when one is hindered within his church in confessing and in walking according to the purity of the truth, and there is no other church in the vicinity with which he can affiliate, he is called to strive for a new and purer revelation of the church on earth.

Therefore, the Reformed have always emphasized the knowledge of the earmarks of the true church, which are generally three, but at times

---

3 Bavinck, *Gereformeerde Dogmatiek,* 4:347. See also Bavinck, *Reformed Dogmatics,* 4:319.

two characteristics are mentioned.[4] They are the pure preaching of the word of God, the proper administration of the sacraments, and the exercise of church discipline. These three do not exist independently of each other, and in the final analysis they can all be reduced to the first: the pure preaching of the word of God. Where the purity of God's word is maintained, there the sacraments will also be administered according to that word, and church discipline will also be enforced. Moreover, it is the chief calling of the church to preserve and proclaim the word of God and to confess it in the midst of the world. Where God's word is, there is the church; where the church is, there God's word is kept, believed, confessed, proclaimed, and practiced.

Where God's word is preserved, believed, confessed, and proclaimed most purely, there is the purest revelation of the body of Christ. With that church we must affiliate. On behalf of the purity of that church we must watch. The unity of that church we must preserve. That church must be kept pure from whatever reveals itself as not belonging to it.

For us the purest revelation of the church on earth is beyond any doubt the Reformed. This we must express without any hesitation. The maintenance of the pure word of God signifies, according to our sincere conviction, the maintenance of the Reformed truth as expressed by the three forms of unity. According as a church more purely maintains the Reformed truth, it is more pure; according as it departs from that confession, it is in that measure less pure. Whoever is not willing to maintain this has not considered his confession seriously. Whoever does not dare to express this publicly, especially in our day, is unfaithful to the truth of God.

With respect therefore to this meeting and colloquy the situation is this: Whatever stands on the basis of that Reformed confession, maintains and practices that confession, belongs together. Those who embrace that confession should either live under one ecclesiastical roof

---

4 Article 29 of the Belgic Confession lists three marks of a true church. Calvin mentions two marks of a true church: the pure preaching of the word of God and the right administration of the sacraments (Calvin, *Institutes*, 4.1.9–10, 21:1023–25).—Ed.

or, when language and distance render this impossible, enter into correspondence with each other as sister churches. It is equally true that whatever departs from this confession, be it in doctrine or life or both, must remain separate or be compelled to separate from the Reformed churches. With this, I believe, we all agree.

Since 1924 two church groups exist among us, and their possible reunion is the subject of our discussion. Before 1924 these church groups were one. Both profess to stand on the basis of the Reformed confession as expressed in the three forms of unity. However, they accuse one another of departing from that confession. I will attempt to describe as objectively as possible the cause of this separate existence.

About 1920 a difference of opinion arose regarding common grace. Two brethren [Danhof and Hoeksema] noticed an ever-increasing spirit of worldly-mindedness that in many ways was revealed in the churches, as well as the clamor of some within the churches for a broader interpretation of the Reformed truth, which then was known as a "new mentality." Although the new mentality rejected the Abraham Kuyper of the antithesis, it was very enthusiastic, even fanatic, about Kuyper's common grace. These brethren examined this doctrine and compared it with scripture and the confessions. They concluded that even the *name* common grace, or general grace, was improper, we were not in need of a better presentation or further development of that doctrine, and the doctrine itself was in principle in conflict with the Reformed world and life view and therefore must be rejected. Already in 1919 the undersigned, as coeditor of the *Banner*, in connection with his description and evaluation of the covenant with Noah, revealed in unmistakable terms his sentiments with respect to this doctrine. At that time nobody opposed his presentation.

In connection with the Janssen case, however, in which the undersigned took an active part, the opposition broke loose. A controversy ensued. From both sides brochures were written. Protests were lodged at the respective consistories. Shortly before the synod of Kalamazoo in 1924, the matter came before the classes. From the classes the case went to synod. The synod of Kalamazoo settled the issue of common grace in the well-known three points.

The first point teaches that besides the saving grace of God, which concerns only the elect, there is also a general, nonsaving grace, a gracious disposition in God in which the reprobate and elect share, which also appears from the preaching of the gospel to all men. The second point teaches that there is an operation of the Holy Spirit besides regeneration, whereby sin in the natural man and in the community is restrained. The third point teaches that by an influence of God upon him, the natural man is enabled to perform civil good.

Subsequently the synod declared that the accused brethren are Reformed with respect to the fundamental truths as formulated in the confessions, but that various expressions in the writings of the accused brethren could not be harmonized with the three points. It also decided to admonish the brethren, as well as the churches in general, to guard themselves against one-sidedness, and it noted that there was cause for warning against world conformity and the misuse of the doctrine of common grace. The synod took no further action. It did not admonish the brethren personally at the meeting, it did not demand them to declare or promise agreement with the adopted points, and it did not make the case pending at the respective consistories, which did take place in the Bultema case in 1918.[5]

Synod neglected to do this, although the advisory committee *ad hoc* had advised such an admonition and the demand of a promise by the brethren at the meeting of synod, and although the accused brethren had unequivocally declared by word and in writing at the meeting of synod that they could not submit to the decisions of synod. The conclusion of Danhof's protest presented at the same synod is as follows:

> Even though I readily agree that several of the expressions in the writings of the Brothers Danhof and Hoeksema do not rhyme very well with what is presented by Synod in points A, B, and C, I am thoroughly convinced that their expressions, if left in the proper context, are not in conflict with the

---

5   The synod did not demand that the consistories of Danhof and Hoeksema examine or discipline them regarding their denial of common grace. In the case of Bultema in 1918, the synod did require his consistory to work with him regarding his doctrine of dispensationalism.—Ed.

Confessions and the Scriptures. Thus, quite apart from the fact that each particular [discussion] dealing with a specific point, exactly because it is specific and touches on a well-defined point, will lead toward a certain limited conclusion, I maintain that the Brothers were earnestly striving for a rich and many-faceted presentation of God's revealed truth, and that is also evident from their writings. Even though they differ with the three points under discussion, I believe that I must emphatically state before Synod that their sentiments are in harmony with the Confessions and the Scriptures.

In as much as this is my deepest held conviction, Synod will surely understand me when I declare at this time that I believe it is my calling before God and the churches not only to protest formally against these synodical decisions, but I also hope to take practical measures against them, both as a delegate from Classis Grand Rapids West and as one of the two brothers who are condemned in relation to the above-mentioned three points. Honesty demands it is my duty to say so.[6]

Although synod took no further action, both classes where the accused brethren belonged did so, especially when a beginning was made in the *Standard Bearer* to fulfill the promise both brethren had expressed at the meeting of synod, and they began to submit the synodical declarations to a thorough criticism. The classes demanded of the consistories that they place their pastors before the question whether they would agree with the adopted three points and promise, with the right of appeal, never to teach anything, privately or publicly, that conflicted with those points. The consistories refused to heed this demand of the classes and appealed to the synod of 1926. The pastors were in agreement with the consistories. Thereupon the ministers were suspended from office because of insubordination to the "proper ecclesiastical authorities." On the same ground the consistories were deposed.

True, there was formally a slight difference between the action of Classis Grand Rapids East and that of Classis Grand Rapids West. The

---

6   *1924 Acts of Synod*, 199.—Ed.

first declared the consistory of Eastern Avenue Christian Reformed Church outside of the church fellowship; the latter simply deposed the consistory of First Kalamazoo Christian Reformed Church. But essentially there was no difference also in this respect, since also Classis Grand Rapids East advanced as the ground for its action that the consistory of Eastern Avenue was guilty of insubordination to the "proper ecclesiastical authorities." The ministers were deposed from office by a later meeting of classis.

However, the consistories and ministers continued to function in their offices and paid no attention to the decisions of the classes. The overwhelming majority of their congregations, moreover, supported the consistories. They also united provisionally at the outset with the consistory of Hope Christian Reformed Church, who with its pastor, Rev. George Ophoff, had meanwhile become involved in the issue and also had been deposed by Classis Grand Rapids West. Later also Rev. D. Jonker, after he had presented his objections against the three points, was deposed by Classis Zeeland.

Until 1926 these churches called themselves the Protesting Christian Reformed Churches. When their appeal to the synod of 1926 had been disallowed, dismissed by that gathering because they stood outside of the church fellowship,[7] they organized into a church organization and adopted the name Protestant Reformed Churches.[8] To the present day these churches have stood and increased in membership. I believe I may say that we all can agree on this representation of the origin of the Protestant Reformed Churches and the historical occasion and cause of a separate existence.

---

7   Danhof and Hoeksema and their consistories appealed to the Christian Reformed synod of 1926. See *Acts of Synod of the Christian Reformed Church* in Session June 9 to June 28, 1926 at Englewood, Chicago, Illinois. In article 89 of the minutes of this synod the synod refused to receive protests against the three points of common grace that the Christian Reformed synod of 1924 had adopted, including a protest from the Eastern Avenue Protesting Christian Reformed Church, of which Herman Hoeksema was the pastor, "because the protestants are outside the church federation" (113).—Ed.

8   For the history of the organization of the Protestant Reformed Churches, first under the name Protesting Christian Reformed Church, see Hoeksema, *Protestant Reformed Churches in America*, 248–282.—Ed.

Now I come to the questions facing this gathering: Is it required that the breach be healed? Is it possible? Is it desirable?

The first question is the most important, and in a certain sense decisive. It may and must be worded thus: is it the will of God that the above-named church groups unite? If it is God's will, it must be done. Then we certainly face the calling to exert ourselves through faith to the utmost to realize this union. More than once Schilder has emphasized this calling in the Netherlands and during his stay among us. We agree with him that what according to God's will belongs together may not be separated by us or remain separated. I have sufficient confidence of faith to declare that what according to God's will is our calling can also be carried out. If it becomes clear to me that it is truly the will of God that the Protestant Reformed Churches and Christian Reformed Church heal the breach that has been made and live together as brethren under one ecclesiastical roof, I declare myself prepared with all that is in me to settle accidental and personal matters and grievances in the proper way. The important question before which we stand is, does God will it?

The answer to this question depends entirely on the answer to another: do we really stand together on the basis of the Reformed confessions? The question of the truth must govern and dominate this discussion. This implies that we must discuss thoroughly the issue of common grace, which also includes the three points adopted in 1924. To unite first in the hope that we will be able to solve the differences would now be impossible. This could have been done before 1924. Since then the Protestant Reformed Churches have made history, and it is impossible to ignore that history. The Christian Reformed Church has adopted the three points and later defended them; the Protestant Reformed Churches have rejected and in every way opposed them and in detail have presented the grounds on which the churches deem them un-Reformed. If the churches ever are to unite, discussions of the truth, of common grace, and of the three points are first demanded.

We can mutually agree on only two options as possibilities. On the one hand, the possibility is conceivable that the Christian Reformed brethren convince the Protestant Reformed Churches that we erred in 1924 when we refused to subscribe to the three points. To do this we offer them ample opportunity by means of this discussion. On the other hand, the possibility exists that we convince them that the three points are un-Reformed, the synod of 1924 never should have adopted them, and they therefore must be retracted unconditionally. To that end the Christian Reformed brethren should give us equally full opportunity.

If they succeed in convincing us, we will acknowledge that we erred and that we must unite with them on the basis of the three points. If we succeed in convincing them, they must acknowledge that they erred in 1924. Then they will retract the three points, and they will stand with us on the same confessional basis. Only in this manner may we proceed. Any other way is the way of compromise, which I will continue to refuse.

If we agree in this way, certainly the most important purpose of this colloquy has been realized. Yet difficulties will remain. We may not deceive ourselves into believing that they do not exist. We may not ignore the attitudes of our people, especially our Protestant Reformed people. Most of the present generation lived through the history of 1924 and still feel deeply grieved. Synodical reunion side-by-side with local division, as in the Netherlands with the A and B churches, I do not deem desirable.[9] Also our people must be convinced that reunion is our calling. They must be kept fully informed concerning the course and the results of our discussions. Moreover, there are grievances that certainly must be adjusted according to the word of God.

Besides, the Protestant Reformed Churches have made history in the last fourteen years. The denomination has its own organization and twenty-one churches. Each church has acquired property with a total value of hundreds of thousands of dollars, mostly debt free. For years the churches have met as a classis and are now ready to organize into a synod. The denomination has formed ministers in its own theological school, to which a preparatory course is about to be added.

---

9 "A and B churches" is a reference to two Reformed denominations in the Netherlands that united in 1892 as the Reformed Churches in the Netherlands but tended to retain their separate identities and to perpetuate their historical differences.—Ed.

These churches have developed in fourteen years, and this development has been of such a nature that the Protestant Reformed Churches and the Christian Reformed Church have separated from one another farther since the breach of 1924.

Not only has the Christian Reformed Church developed in the line of the three points, whereas the Protestant Reformed Churches have moved on in the opposite direction, but since 1924 declarations have been made that make the breach between the churches more pronounced. There is the matter of the relation of broader gatherings to the consistory. We have maintained the autonomy of the local church; you have declared that classis and synod actually have power above the consistory. Moreover, we differ in regard to unions, to divorce, to the baptism of adopted children. All these differences exist, and they do not render reunion any easier.

Nevertheless, I will take the stand that if we actually come to an agreement on the issue of common grace, especially the three points, we have in the main achieved the purpose of this colloquy and may cherish the hope that the reunion will be effected. Therefore, all emphasis must be laid on this point. How long these discussions continue is insignificant. No matter how often we must confer, we will maintain our purpose to discuss these issues thoroughly. If we desire to hold conferences under the leadership of Schilder, we can arrange for his coming again. If we would also invite one or more of the other Dutch professors to confer with us, there is no objection whatsoever. The world today is small, and the finances are assured. If the Christian Reformed brethren prefer that Dr. Hepp be present at our gatherings, I have no objection. But I will insist on one point: thorough discussion of common grace and of the three points in particular is the absolute requirement. These conferences may not have or conceive of any other purpose.

The Divisive Issue of the
Christian Reformed Dogma of Common Grace

Regarding what I have said thus far there can be but little, if any, difference of opinion. In the rest of this essay I offer an introduction from the Protestant Reformed viewpoint to the discussion of our doctrinal differences, submitting this introduction to your free discussion and criticism. I consider it advisable that one of the Christian Reformed brethren would present such an introduction. This makes the discussion definite. Besides, then we also have something black on white, so that later no misunderstanding can arise concerning what we are discussing here. Thereby it will be easier for our people to remain informed concerning the course and the results of our discussion.

In this introduction I will first speak about common grace in general, then about the three points, and conclude by submitting twenty propositions for discussion.

Common grace concerns God's attitude toward and influence on the whole of created things in their mutual connection and development in time, in connection and harmony with God's counsel in general, including predestination with election and reprobation, the realization of God's eternal covenant, grace and sin, favor and wrath, nature and grace, creation and re-creation, Adam and Christ. Common grace inquires into the place and calling of God's people in and over against the present world. Viewed thus, it is a matter of great importance with respect to both doctrine and life.

I proceed from the scriptural idea that all creatures are one. God did not create in the beginning an aggregate of creatures, separate and independent of one another. He created a world, a cosmos, a harmonious, organic whole. God is one. The world is also one. In the midst of the earthly creation stood man, whom God formed after his own image, in true knowledge, righteousness, and holiness, so that in a creaturely sense he resembled God. This man stood at the head of creation as king over the earthly world.

Man stood in God's covenant of friendship from the beginning. In that covenantal relation God would be his sovereign friend and cause him to taste the blessedness of the communion of his friendship, in which is life. In that covenantal relation man stood as friend-servant of the Most High, to represent him in the earthly creation, to take up in his heart the praise and honor of all creatures, to interpret and express that praise and honor before the face of God, to love the Lord his God with all his heart, and in the name of and according to the will of God to rule over all creatures. Man was officebearer—prophet, priest, and king—with the commission, the command and the right, the power as well as the authority to subject creation unto himself and to cultivate it. In his heart lay the spiritual, ethical center of God's creation.

Through that central point the entire creation was united in love with God. The creatures, each according to its nature, were taken up into God's covenant of friendship and shared in the good favor of the Lord. Those creatures—sustained by God's omnipresent power, through man and each in its own place and according to its own nature—stood in the service of God. Also now the Lord God sustains and governs all creatures so that they may serve man, in order that man may serve his God.[10]

In this harmonious relation of all things to God sin struck a breach. This breach was struck in the spiritual, ethical center of the earthly cosmos—in the heart of man. Man violated God's covenant. The break is therefore spiritual and ethical. An *essential* change in the relation of things was not brought about by sin. Sin cannot have as its result the annihilation of creation or an essential change in the mutual relation between the creatures and the relation of the creatures to man, so that the creation would have been turned into a chaos if common grace had not intervened. To be sure, the creature bears the curse temporally in connection with man and is subject to vanity, but the unity of creation was not broken. The natural, organic affinity continued undisturbed.

Fallen man became very limited in his gifts, powers, and natural light, so that he has retained only remnants of natural light. But even in his fallen state he retained his position at the head of creation. Although it cannot be said that man is still officebearer of God and therefore has the right to serve in God's house, in his position in creation and with all his gifts and means he certainly continues to stand before the demand to serve his God in love. However, he cannot, will not, and cannot will to serve his God in love, for a spiritual, ethical breach was made in man's relation to God. The life of man's heart was subverted into its opposite. The working of the image of God, whereby

---

10 Belgic Confession 12, in Schaff, *Creeds of Christendom*, 3:395–96.—Ed.

man with mind, will, and all his strength went out to God in the state of rectitude, was turned about into its opposite.

Upon this, all emphasis must be laid. It is not sufficient to say that man through the fall lost the image of God; far less correct is it to say that he lost that image only in part. If this last thought is the result of the distinction of the image of God into the narrower and the broader senses, it is better to abandon this distinction.

The image of God turned about into its opposite. Man's light became darkness, his knowledge changed into the lie, his righteousness became unrighteousness, and his holiness became impurity and rebellion in all his willing and inclinations. His love changed into enmity against God. Sin is not merely a defect or lack but a *privatio actuosa* [active privation]. The servant and covenantal friend of the Lord became a friend and covenantal ally of the devil. However, the Lord continued to sustain and govern creation by his providential power, and the entire organic existence of things remained essentially unaffected. If now in this state of things no further change is wrought, the final result of history will be that the completed spiritual, ethical fruit of the life of creation is the opposite of what it should be according to God's creation ordinance.

All this, although effected through the willful disobedience of the first man, took place according to the counsel and will of God. Accidents, from the viewpoint of God, never occur. God is God. He is in heaven, and he does all his good pleasure not merely in spite of the attempts of Satan and sin, but also through those attempts. At all times God proceeds directly to his goal. Never is he hindered by the creature. There is with him no change or shadow of turning.

Also the fall is wholly according to the counsel of God's will, and it serves him in the realization of his purpose. He has provided something better for us. His objective was not attained with the rest of the seventh day. That rest was only a figure of the eternal rest in the eternal and heavenly tabernacle, in the eternal kingdom, in which all things will be united in Christ as their head, when all things in heaven and on earth will eternally be concentrated in the heart of Christ.

Christ is the image of the invisible God, the firstborn of all creatures.

As the firstborn from the dead, he is the head of the body, the beginning, in order that he should be the first in all things. Through him all things in heaven and on earth, visible and invisible, were created, whether they be thrones, or dominions, or principalities, or powers; all things were created by him and for him, for it pleased the Father that in him all fullness should dwell (Col. 1:15–19). Thus it is according to God's eternal decree. The eternal covenant of friendship of God must be established in Christ and be realized by him unto its final eternal and heavenly destiny, when the tabernacle of God shall be with man. Therefore, God, immediately at the fall of man, maintains his covenant in spite of Satan and sin. Now that covenant is eternally and firmly established in Christ. Through the realization of that covenant immediately at the fall, the friendship with Satan in the heart of man was brought to naught, and through the operation of grace, enmity was wrought in the heart of man against Satan.

Here we face the decree of predestination, for not all the children of Adam have been predestined to enter into the eternal covenant of God's friendship. Grace follows the line of election. Only the kernel is affected by grace; the shell is rejected. Exactly through this the antithesis is realized in the world.

Also now the creatures in the natural sense continue to exist in organic connection. Even as sin, grace does not bring an essential change in the temporal existence of things. Out of one blood God created the entire human race; naturally all men are one, and man continues to stand in organic connection with the cosmos, in the midst of which he moves and develops. There is therefore no dualism. Nature and grace are not opposites. Grace cannot become the cause for a man who becomes partaker of it to go out of the world.

The antithesis of sin and grace is called into being by the breach of sin and the entrance of grace, with grace developing along the line of election. All things continue to exist and develop according to their own natures, sustained by God's almighty power, in natural affinity. But amid this temporal existence of things there arises and develops the spiritual, ethical antithesis of sin and grace, of light and darkness, of the love of God and enmity against him, of life and death, of heaven and hell. Through all this God does all his good pleasure, and he leads all things to their eternal destiny—the eternal separation of chaff and wheat, the eternal realization of the covenant of his friendship.

Grace, therefore, is never common.

The word *grace* has a variety of meanings in Holy Writ. We lack time to enter into these details, but allow me to present the line that I believe is found in scripture regarding this concept. The Hebrew word *chen* (grace) in scripture has the meaning of "bending, inclining, attraction, beauty, charm, favor." The derivation of the Greek word *charis* (grace) is less certain, although it is plain that also in the New Testament the word has a great variety of meanings. It signifies "pleasantness, favor, forfeited favor, operation of grace and benefits of grace, thankfulness." In Paul's epistles the word is often used in contrast with merit and work.

A comparison of many scriptural passages where "grace" appears teaches that God is in the absolute sense the gracious one. He is gracious irrespective of any relation to the creature. Grace is a virtue of God. He is gracious in himself. He is the absolutely and infinitely good and glorious God, the implication of all perfection. Therefore, he is also the charming, the attractive, the gracious God. At his right hand are pleasures for evermore. As the triune God he beholds and knows himself perfectly; he is attracted to himself, loves himself, and has pleasure in himself.

God also has pleasure in the creature. The creature, especially man, who was formed after God's image and in the highest sense is his church in Christ, God has willed as beautiful. Therefore, for his name's sake God also has pleasure in the creature, and it finds grace in God's eyes. He lavishes on that creature the evidence of his favor and draws it unto himself with cords of love into his eternal covenant of friendship. When that creature lies in guilt and sin—so that in itself it cannot be an object of God's pleasure and favor but of his wrath and aversion; and if that creature in Christ is from eternity beheld, elected, foreordained by God's sovereign grace to become conformed to the image of the Son, justified and glorified, found precious in his eyes and engraved in the palms of God's hands; and when that eternal grace goes out to the creature—that grace is forfeited favor, and it stands wholly in contrast with work and merit. That grace blots out all our transgressions, justifies us in the blood of the cross, and grants us the adoption unto children and the right to eternal life.

That grace is also a power and an operation within us whereby we are redeemed from the repulsiveness and domination of sin, become conformed to the image of the Son, and become pleasing to God, formed according to the image he has engraved of us in the palms of his hands. For that sinner redeemed by grace, in his consciousness and experience, God becomes the only good, the attractive and charming God, whose loving-kindness is better than life and who is alone worthy to receive all praise and adoration and thanksgiving. In adoration he falls down before God and gives him *charis*.

I am convinced that there is no essential distinction between such concepts as grace, love, goodness, mercy, and whatever related concepts may appear in scripture. Some have thought that they came closer to the truth when the last word in the expression *common grace* was replaced by *favorable inclination, goodness,* or *mercy,* but essentially this makes no difference. Fundamentally all these concepts have the same meaning and are one.

One can readily understand in light of the above definition that we cannot speak of common grace. The sinful and corrupt creature cannot be pleasing to God but is the object of his dislike, wrath and indignation, hatred and curse. Only as that creature has been incorporated into and is eternally beheld in Christ can it be pleasing to God and an object of his sovereign favor. Only from the eternal counsel of election can the grace of God in Christ go out to him. There proceeds out of the eternal good pleasure of God in Christ an operation of grace on the elect kernel of our race in connection with the organic whole of all creatures. By that wonder of grace that elect kernel in Christ, always in connection with the whole of things, is redeemed, saved, liberated, glorified, and lifted out of darkness, guilt, sin, death, curse, and vanity into the heavenly glory of God's covenant of friendship. Likewise the wrath of God abides on the reprobate shell outside of Christ, and an operation proceeds from God's aversion and wrath, indignation and repulsion and hardening, whereby this reprobate shell becomes ripe for destruction.

God proceeds directly to his goal. He never takes a detour. He never retraces his steps. His work is never frustrated. His purpose is never thwarted at any moment in history. The development and operation of God's grace and aversion, drawing and casting off, blessing and cursing, and softening and hardening continue constantly according to his eternal good pleasure and in connection with the operation of his providence and the organic development of the human race.

Therefore, one cannot speak of a checking of this process. To be sure, the end does not appear immediately at the beginning. The development of grace and sin is according to God's good pleasure and connected by his providential management with the organic existence of all things. But that process is not restrained. It proceeds as rapidly as it possibly can, for Christ comes quickly, and his reward is with him to give to every man according as his work shall be.

This is the Protestant Reformed conception of the attitude and operation of God with respect to the organic whole of temporal things, in connection with the counsel and the good pleasure of God, the covenant of his friendship, sin and grace, creation and redemption, Adam and Christ, and the natural and the spiritual. We have therefore no individualistic, particularistic conception of the tremendous work of redemption by the grace of God. Neither do we involve merely the church as the body of Christ as the new mankind in the organic conception.

This Kuyper does. He indeed has an eye for the fact that God did not elect a number of individuals to redeem them as the severed branches of the tree of the human race, but that the organism as the body of Christ, as the actual mankind, is saved and glorified by God. But he does not apply this thought to the organic whole of all creatures. Therefore, he speaks of an original creation idea. Because of this he always presents the matter as if Satan made an essential breach in the work of God, and sin and death would actually hinder God in the realization of his original creation idea, were it not that at that juncture common grace restrainingly intervened. To this end he presents

God as concluding a covenant of friendship with the godless world outside of Christ in order that sinful man could choose God's side against Satan. Thus he has man living a relatively good life from the principle of a certain righteousness left him by common grace, and he has made possible a conception of sinful man who by the grace of God practices culture. All of history thereby becomes an interim. God carries out the covenant of his election and saves the new mankind, but common grace actually runs a parallel line, along which God realizes his original creation idea.

We, however, include all creatures in mutual connection within the circle of the organic conception and distinguish between the elect kernel and the reprobate shell. We maintain that upon the whole of created things, in organic connection with each other, there proceeds not only an operation of God's grace but also of his aversion, not only his favor but also his wrath, not only election but also reprobation, according to the counsel of his will and the nature of the creature, each in its place in the whole.

In this sense we understand that God loves the world, in its elect kernel, so that whoever believes shall be saved, but the wrath of God abides on whoever believes not. Thus we understand that Christ is not only the head of the church, but also the beginning of the creation of God and therefore also the end, the firstborn of all creatures and the firstborn from the dead, in whom all the fullness should dwell, and by whom and for whom all things were created. In this sense we understand that God purposed by himself to gather together in one in Christ all things in heaven and on earth.

Then we can also understand the covenant with Noah, which certainly is not a separate covenant with the world outside of Christ, but is God's eternal covenant of friendship with the elect kernel in Christ in connection with the whole of created things, revealed to the church as recently delivered by the flood. Noah becomes heir of the world by the grace of God. The sign thereof we have in the all-embracing rainbow, painted by the sunlight on the dark clouds. Thus we also understand that an operation of God's grace issued through the preaching of Jonah to Nineveh, figure of the world, in which the resurrected Christ will presently celebrate his triumphs, and that Nineveh repented upon the preaching of Jonah. There were also thousands of children who could not discern between their right and left hands, as well as much cattle.

In light of the preceding it will be understood that the Protestant Reformed Churches have nothing in common with the Anabaptists who would avoid the world. To be sure, we would not be of the world. We know of no synthesis. We do not join Athens in wedlock with Jerusalem. We do not cultivate culture in the name of common grace in cooperation with the godless world. We recognize the antithesis.

We do acknowledge the natural affinity of the entire race in connection with all things. We would not go out of the world. We have all things in common. We work with the same means, gifts, talents, and powers as the world. We must deal with and make use of the same institutions of the home, society, church, and state.

It cannot be the calling of the Christian to improve the world, which is impossible. But it surely is his calling to live throughout his life, in connection with all things and with all possible means, out of the new life principle of regeneration and over against the life that arises out of the principle of sin. It is surely also his calling to represent in the midst of the world the cause of Christ, the cause of the Son of God, in word and walk. To that purpose he subjects as much as possible all things, and unto the realization of that purpose he uses all means and institutions that may be in his service.

We would be in the world but not of the world. We desire the Christian home, the Christian society, the Christian government and state, the Christian school, Christian science, and Christian culture in general. In the nature of the case the concrete realization of these things does not always and everywhere succeed. The world is powerful and often deprives us of our means and position. It may be possible to a certain extent in a small country as the Netherlands, with a relatively strong Christian population, to maintain Christian politics and to speak of a Christian government, but in the United States this is well-nigh impossible. Some periods in history are thereunto more conductive and favorable than others. God at times gives to his people the power and the means to assume control in various phases of life; at others almost everything is denied them.

Nevertheless, whether we have power or not, never may we become of the world and affiliate with that world. If we adopt this procedure to exercise power, we are lost. At all times we must represent the cause of Christ, even if we do so only by witnessing of the word of God. If then we must suffer, we will remember the word of scripture that it is given us of grace, in the behalf of Christ, not only to believe in him, but also with him to suffer. The victory is always ours. We have therefore good courage, knowing that Christ has overcome the world.

Critique of the Christian Reformed Dogma of Common Grace

It will now not be difficult for the brethren to understand that it was impossible for me to subscribe to the three points or to promise that privately or publicly I would never teach anything in conflict with those points. Such a promise would forever silence my mouth and cause my pen to become dry. Although it is my conviction that the synod of 1924 saw the trees of the three points but not the forest of common grace, yet it is beyond all doubt that in those points it really adopted the entire common grace view of Kuyper. Nevertheless, I desire to express my objections against the three points in particular.

The first point speaks of a favorable inclination in God toward all creatures. I have declared more than once that if it were possible to take this expression by itself, I would have no objection against the implied proposition. I have always emphasized that God's grace is not directed individually to a few elect, but to all creatures in organic connection. This, however, is not the case here. This explanation of the first point may never be given. The contrast in the first point is not elect only or all creatures but elect only or also reprobate. The first point teaches that in God there is a gracious attitude toward all men, among whom reprobates are included. Apart from the saving grace of God shown only to the elect, there is also a nonsaving grace of God, both as an inclination in God and as an operation proceeding on the creature, in which reprobates share.

That this is the implication of the first point appears clearly from the discussion that preceded its adoption at synod. That was the issue. This is plain from the texts synod quoted to substantiate the teaching of the first point. This is especially clear from the proof synod quoted from the confessions regarding the preaching of the gospel. Moreover, this also appears from the later discussions about the three points. Concerning this there is no difference among us.

We cannot accept this gracious inclination of God and operation of grace toward the reprobate wicked. Over against this we maintain that the grace of God goes out to the organic whole of the creatures in mutual affinity and in connection with the elect in Christ, as the elect kernel. We declare that at the same time an operation of God's wrath and indignation proceeds upon the reprobate shell.

However, the first point expresses more. The synod of Kalamazoo included the preaching of the gospel in the gracious inclination in God and the operation of his grace. Synod, in my modest opinion, did this willy-nilly. It sought proof for common grace in the Reformed confessions, especially in the Canons. These confessions do not speak of common grace in the Kuyperian sense. The synod of Dordrecht busied itself with the matter of salvation. A grace that did not save lay beyond the pale of its views and deliberations. The Canons only use the term *common grace* in the sense of natural light and therefore in a nonsaving sense, and they lay the term on the lips of the Remonstrants.

Therefore, synod, seeking proof for common grace in the confessions, was compelled to arrive at the general preaching of the gospel, whereof the confessions speak, but the grace whereof they always conceive is particular. Thus synod adopted in the first point the proposition that God is gracious in the preaching of the gospel, that is, he is prompted by a gracious inclination not only toward the elect, but also toward all men. This was expressed by the synod of 1926 at Englewood still more clearly than by the synod of 1924. In Englewood's answer to the consistory of Middleburg, Iowa, which had protested against the declaration of 1924, it speaks of a "goodness of God evident in well-meant character of the invitation of the gospel for everyone to whom the call of the gospel comes," as well as of "a certain grace, goodness, or favorable attitude of God revealed toward a group of people which is broader than the group of the elect, and that this among other things clearly appears from the fact that God well-meaningly calls everyone to whom the loving invitation of the gospel comes."[11]

This presentation does not harmonize with Holy Writ and the Reformed confessions. Over against it we maintain that the preaching of the gospel is grace only for the elect and at the same time is a savor of death unto death for the reprobate. That the preaching of the gospel is general we understand very well. But we believe that the content of the preaching is always particular, that it promises salvation only to those who believe, that is, to the elect, and that it cannot be said that it is an evidence of grace to all who hear the gospel. According to our earnest conviction synod with that declaration switched to the camp of the Remonstrants.

The second point speaks of a general operation of the Holy Spirit outside of regeneration, whereby sin is restrained in the individual man and in the community. If this means anything at all, it implies that outside of regeneration, a spiritual, ethical operation of the Holy Spirit proceeds on sinful man for his good, with the result that in reality he is not as sinful and corrupt as he would be without that working of the Spirit. Kuyper differentiates here between mind, will, and inclinations on the one hand and the ego on the other hand. In the ego he distinguishes further between the kernel of the ego and the different functions and movements of the ego. According to him, common grace can influence the entire man, except the kernel of the ego.

Having correctly understood this, one will perceive immediately how only the ego, as the innermost kernel, remains what it is, but how on the other hand those inclinations, that thinking and willing activity, by reaction, undergo a certain influence of common grace. Test this yourself by taking three or four thin brass wires and fasten them together at a certain point, spreading them out in various directions. Underneath where the wires join, with your left hand bend them toward

11 *Acts of Synod...1926*, 116.

the left, at the same time with your right hand bend the upper half of the wires to the right. Then you will feel how the pressure exercised by your right hand not only bends the ends of the wires to the right, but will also exercise a certain pressure on the lower half of the wires, which sensation you clearly feel in the fingers of your left hand. The same is true of common grace. At whatever point of the line it takes hold of that line and bends it to the right, this will produce a tension, a pressure downwards, which will never affect the *center* of the ego, but will have its effect on the inclination, on the consciousness and the will. This explains how the unconverted undergoes the influence of common grace in his inclinations, in his consciousness, and in his will. [12]

Whatever one may think of the psychological distinction between the ego and the center of the ego, one thing is certain: if words have any significance, and we replace the copper wires with reality, Kuyper teaches a spiritual, ethical improvement effected by the influence of divine grace on natural man, his understanding and will, even changing the deepest inclinations and motives of the heart in the proper ethical direction, changing him wholly for the good, except for the kernel of his ego. Kuyper also makes the Heidelberg Catechism give the following answer to the well-known eighth question: "that there is in the ego inability to do any good and a continuous inclination to all evil. Whatever of this ego is improved or does not reveal itself is not of the ego, but of common grace." He writes literally that the Catechism expresses it in that manner.[13] This spiritual, ethical operation of grace for good is even similar to regeneration, differing from it merely in that it does not affect the center of the ego. If the same operation were to penetrate to that center, it would regenerate the man.

That doctrine of Kuyper the synod of Kalamazoo sought to express and exalt to an ecclesiastical dogma in the second point. This surely appears from the declaration "that God through the general operation

---

12 Kuyper, *Common Grace*, 2:306.
13 Ibid., 2:307.

of His Spirit, without renewing the heart, restrains sin in its unbridled expression."[14] What Kuyper understands to be the center of the ego the synod of Kalamazoo understood to be the heart. The synod somewhat improved on Kuyper's conception by adding the phrase "through the general operation of His Spirit." In any case I do not say too much when I assert that the second point teaches that by a general operation of grace the natural man is wholly improved, except for his heart. His mind and will and all his inclinations can be changed or inclined for the good.

We have various objections against this presentation. We do understand, as article 13 of the Belgic Confession teaches, that God restrains all evil men, yea, even the devil. But of a general operation of the Spirit whereby God improves the mind, will, and inclinations of the natural man the confession surely does not speak. The English translation might allow the presentation of synod, inasmuch as it reads "that he so restrains the devil and all our enemies."[15] But the Dutch translation, "*hij de duivelen en al onze vijanden in den toom houdt,*" is undoubtedly more correct. We read in the French: "*En quoi nous nous reposons, sachant qu'il tient les diables en bride, et tous nos enemis, qui ne nous peuvent nuire sana sa permission et bonne volente.*"[16]

In answer to a protest against that declaration by the synod of Kalamazoo, the synod of Engelwood of 1926 observed that this expression ["God through the general operation of His Spirit, without renewing the heart, restrains sin in its unbridled expression"] indeed does not appear in the confessions, but that it is not less correct, because

---

14 *1924 Acts of Synod*, 146.
15 Belgic Confession 13, in Schaff, *Creeds of Christendom*, 3:397.—Ed.
16 The Dutch translation of the phrase at issue is, in English: "He [God our Father] keeps in check the devils and all our enemies." "Keeps in check" is literally "holds in, or, by the bridle." The Dutch is a faithful translation of the French original *en bride* (a bridle). The important doctrinal point is that article 13 of the Belgic Confession does not teach a restraint of sin in the ungodly by a work of God's (common) grace within them, as the Christian Reformed Church explains. Rather, God governs the ungodly by his almighty power of providence. Between a controlling power—a "bridle"—and an operation of grace upon and within the unregenerated sinner that negates his total depravity is a fundamental difference—the difference between Reformed orthodoxy and semi-Pelagian heresy.—Ed.

as it is certain that "as God in creation worked through his Spirit, so he still works through that same Spirit in the work of providence. And since, after man's fall, that work of the Spirit has not ceased but continues, so also the checking of sin is to be attributed to the general operations of God's Spirit."[17] As if the truth that in the works of God *ad extra* all three persons of the divine Trinity operate according to their own places in the divine household would necessitate the conclusion that a spiritual, ethical operation of grace proceeds from God on the natural man, improving him in his mind and will and inclinations. The keeping of devils and evil men under bridle (*in den toom houden*) is something altogether different from the restraining of the process of sin in the individual man and in mankind. Duly understanding that God bridles and governs all the actions of devils and men, unto the realization of his counsel and the salvation of his own in Christ, we deny that outside of regeneration there is such an operation of grace by the Spirit, whereby the natural man is improved to any degree.

As stated above, we have many objections to this view. Viewed psychologically it is absurd. It does not even hold with respect to the copper wires, much less with respect to man. I reject with all that is in me the determinist view that the natural man could perform deeds in which his ego or the kernel of his ego, his heart, would not be involved. Scripture teaches that from the heart are all the issues of life.

My weightiest objection is that according to this view, the Reformed teaching that the natural man is so corrupt that he is wholly incapable of doing any good and inclined to all evil has become a mere abstraction. He may be ever so corrupt in the kernel of his ego; that center is shut off from the actual world by common grace. What the natural man actually does in this life does not come forth out of his ego, or heart, but out of his mind, will, and inclinations, and these have been greatly improved by the general operation of grace by the Spirit. As the natural man appears, he is not wholly corrupt, but he certainly exceeds one's expectations.

This view conflicts not only with the Reformed confessions, but also with Holy Writ. Scripture knows of no such wholesome operation of

17 *Acts of Synod...1926*, 118.

the Holy Spirit but teaches the very opposite. It teaches that an operation of God's wrath is revealed from heaven, whereby he operates upon
the godless deserter of the way of the Lord, upon his lusts and desires,
so that he is given up in an evil sense to do things unseemly, to proceed
from bad to worse. While we readily admit that the sinner is restrained
in various ways by the all-controlling providence of God according to
the counsel of his will, and at the same time duly understand that the
process of sin is bound to the organic development of the human race,
and finally also clearly perceive that every man does not commit all the
actual sins but that each, according to his own place and time, his own
adaptability and character, gifts and means, develops the one root sin of
Adam unto the completed fruit, we will continue to maintain that the
second point conflicts with scripture and the confessions.

With respect to the third point I can be brief, as it stands or falls
with the second. In the third point synod declared that God, without renewing the heart, so influences man that, although incapable of
performing any saving good, he can perform civil good. It is evident
from the content of the expression, as well as in light of the discussion
that preceded that declaration, that civil good means doing good in
civil life. Here we meet the doctrine of spheres (*terreinen leer*). In the
sphere of the first table of the law man is unable to do any good. This
is spiritual good. But in the sphere of the second table of the law he
can perform good. The "influence of God" in the third point means
the same as the "general operation of His Spirit" in the second point.

Before the synod of 1924, Danhof and I had written concerning
so-called civil good. Therefore, synod consciously condemned our
view in this matter. In *Along Pure Paths* we wrote:

> What then is civil righteousness? In our opinion the sinner
> notes the God-instituted relations, the given laws, means of
> fellowship, and the like. He notes the propriety and useful-
> ness of them. He makes use of them for his own sake. If he
> succeeds fairly well in this, an action will result that formally
> appears to be in harmony with the laws of God. Then you
> have civil righteousness, regard for virtue, and an orderly
> external deportment. If this attempt fails, as is often the case,

then also civil righteousness falls away; then the opposite is true. His fundamental error is, however, that also in striving for external deportment he does not seek or purpose God. To the contrary he seeks himself also in fellowship with other sinners and tries to maintain himself in his sin against God, with the entire world in whatever he does. And that is sin. This also actually has evil results for him and his fellow-creatures. His action with respect to his neighbor and fellow creatures takes place according to the same rule and with the same results. It therefore happens that sin always develops and that corruption continues, and yet there remains relatively a formally just behavior according to the laws laid down and instituted by God. Yet the natural man never performs ethical good. This is our view. Who now will venture another explanation?[18]

Synod did not want this view, which completely explains the so-called civil righteousness out of the totally corrupt man without any influence of common grace upon him, who nevertheless has natural light. Synod wanted to put something else in its place. That something else was the wholesome influence of God, those general influences of the Spirit, those general operations of grace by God upon the nature of sinners, whereby these are enabled to perform civil good. This view we deem to be in conflict with scripture and the confessions.

It is unnecessary to quote scripture. However, Canons 3–4.4 teaches that man has retained glimmerings of natural light and that he thereby has some knowledge of God and of natural things as well as of the difference between good and evil. It adds the part that the synod of 1924 forgot to quote: he does not use that light rightly even in natural and civil things; yea, he renders it wholly polluted and holds it in unrighteousness. We will stand by this last.

I conclude by placing before you certain propositions for discussion:

1. God is God, and he always performs all his good pleasure. Therefore, he also always proceeds directly to his goal, according to his eternal counsel; while all things, Satan and

---

18 Danhof and Hoeksema, *Along Pure Paths*, 72–73.

sin and the godless world included, serve him thereunto. At no moment in history, from creation to the parousia, can we speak of a frustration of an original plan.

2. God's grace is not directed individually and particularly to the elect, but it is directed to the organic whole of the church in Christ as its head and in connection with the organic whole of all creatures of the entire cosmos. However, the godless reprobate is never the object of this grace, viewed either as an inclination in God or as an operation of grace.

3. Besides the operation of God's drawing and saving and exalting and glorifying grace, acting only on the elect kernel of the created things, there is also an operation of God's rejecting, repulsing wrath, acting on the reprobate shell.

4. The covenant with Noah is no friendship covenant of common grace established with the sinful world as such and outside of Christ, but is a revelation of the one covenant of God's friendship in Christ, as it embraces and takes up into itself the entire cosmos. Temporally creation bears the curse, but presently the dumb creature will also share in the liberty of the glory of the children of God.

5. All things of this present life—rain and sunshine, good and gladness, gifts and talents, houses and goods, name and position and might—are means that God uses and that man uses as a rational, moral creature. Inasmuch as God uses them, they serve him in the fulfillment of his counsel. Inasmuch as man uses them, they are so many obligations whereby he is placed before the demand to thank and serve God.

6. The preaching of the gospel is as such neither a blessing nor a curse. It addresses man as a rational, moral being who is therefore responsible before God. God uses preaching to realize his counsel of predestination, both election and reprobation, so that he, without nullifying the ethical nature and responsibility of man, calls the one unto salvation and hardens the other. The preaching of the gospel is

therefore never grace for the reprobate, neither does God intend it to be such.

7. Bound to the organic development of our race and bridled by God's all-controlling providence, sin develops as rapidly as possible, also through an operation of God's wrath on the lusts of the flesh. There is no operation of the Holy Spirit whereby the natural man without regeneration is improved to any extent. Every man bears the fruit of the root sin of Adam according to his time, place, circumstances, means, adaptability, and character.

8. Man has some remnants of natural light, but not of his original knowledge, righteousness, and holiness. These latter not only were wholly lost, but they have turned into their opposites. Consequently, the natural man can do nothing else than wholly pollute his natural light and hold it under in unrighteousness.

9. Civil righteousness is an attempt of the sinful man for his own benefit—inasmuch as he perceives by natural light the God-instituted relations and laws in the cosmos and recognizes their usefulness—to adapt his external life to God's laws in connection with the lives of his fellow creatures. If he succeeds, God, who holds himself to his own ordinances, grants him success. But success is not blessing. In the way of success he becomes ever greater, becomes ever more responsible, and under the wrath of God increases his own judgment.

10. There is in Holy Writ no essential distinction in meaning among such terms as *grace, favor, love, friendship, goodness,* and *mercy.* They all concern the relation and operation of God's covenant of friendship toward the elect kernel.

11. The idea of a common grace begins in the dogmatic-historical sense not with Calvin, neither can it be traced to Augustine, but its beginning must be sought in the age of the Scholastics, particularly with Thomas Aquinas. It cannot be said that this doctrine is preeminently Calvinistic.

12. The three forms of unity know of no common grace. The only place where the term *common grace* appears, the Canons of Dordt place it on the lips of the Remonstrants. The three points are not explanations but additions to the confession of the Reformed churches.

13. The synod of Kalamazoo in the three points essentially exalted Kuyper's *gemeene gratie* (common grace) to a dogma and thereby rendered all further study of this question impossible.

14. The Christian does not separate himself from the world in an Anabaptist sense; neither is it his calling to better the world, but to live throughout his life in the world from the principle of regeneration and according to the word of God and to represent the cause of the Son of God as of the party of the living God.

15. Inasmuch as the distinction between the image of God in a broader and in a narrower sense can easily occasion misunderstanding, as if a remnant of the positive operation of the original righteousness remained in fallen man, it is better to speak of the image of God in the formal and the material sense, and to say that the latter was changed into its opposite through sin.

16. The so-called covenant of works was not a covenant of works but the first and earthly manifestation of God's covenant of friendship. In this covenant man could not merit eternal life nor ever attain unto it, but merely in the way of obedience he would retain the earthly life he possessed.

17. Government as such, irrespective of the sword power, was not instituted because of sin but arose out of the family. Its authority can therefore be defended by appealing to the fifth commandment.

18. A godless magistrate stands in the place of authority wherewith he is clothed by God but does not rule by the grace of God.

19. Synod and classes are not assemblies clothed with a power higher than that of the consistory but are merely larger or broader assemblies. They therefore cannot have the authority to depose officebearers.

20. History abundantly proves that the Protestant Reformed Churches did not secede from the Christian Reformed Church but were expelled from its fellowship because they[19] felt obliged to resist the declarations of the synod of Kalamazoo.

---

19 "They" refers to the members of the Christian Reformed Church who cooperated to form the Protestant Reformed Churches, because these members opposed the doctrine of common grace, especially Hoeksema and Danhof.—Ed.

THE PLACE OF REPROBATION IN THE PREACHING OF THE GOSPEL

HERMAN HOEKSEMA

TRANSLATED BY CORNELIUS HANKO

Introduction to *The Place of Reprobation in the Preaching of the Gospel*

This pamphlet by Herman Hoeksema goes back to the very beginnings of the Protestant Reformed Churches. Hoeksema gave the lecture, of which this pamphlet is the printed form, in 1927—a mere three years after the Christian Reformed Church adopted the theory of common grace as official church dogma, thus occasioning the separate existence of the Protestant Reformed Churches.

Already in May 1927 the lecture was published as a pamphlet, in the Dutch language. The pamphlet was made available to the public in an English translation, by Rev. Cornelius Hanko, for the first time in 1993. This is the version of Hoeksema's lecture that is published here.

As the pamphlet originates in and helps to explain the early history of the Protestant Reformed Churches, so is its subject fundamental, not only regarding their theology, but also regarding the Reformed faith. The subject is the decree of reprobation and therefore the decree of predestination. The concern of the pamphlet is the *preaching* of reprobation, specifically, *how* reprobation is to be preached in relation not only to the decree of election, but also to the entire message of the gospel of Jesus Christ.

The instruction of the pamphlet proceeds on the basis of two convictions. First, the Bible teaches reprobation. Second, reprobation therefore *must* and *can* be preached. Hoeksema does not argue these convictions. He presupposes them, and he trusts that his Reformed audience and readership will presuppose them with him.

Both convictions are widely controverted today by nominally Reformed ministers and in nominally Reformed churches. Even ministers who profess to believe reprobation fail to preach it. Preaching reprobation consists of far more than mentioning it on the rare occasion. Thus is evident the apostasy of the Reformed churches and the necessity of the wide distribution of this pamphlet.

Hoeksema declares that reprobation must be preached and is only rightly preached in relation to election, which aspect of predestination reprobation serves. In its inseparable relation to election, reprobation must be preached and is only rightly preached in connection with the gospel message of the great love of God in Jesus Christ for his elect people. Reprobation accentuates the love of God for the elect human race.

In his explanation of the preaching of reprobation, Hoeksema gives the lie to common accusations against his theology and that of the Protestant Reformed Churches. One is that Hoeksema taught the "equal ultimacy" of election and reprobation. On the contrary, the Protestant Reformed theologian taught that reprobation, though equally eternal and sovereign with election, is subordinate and subservient to election.

A second false charge is that Hoeksema delighted in preaching reprobation, constantly and as a separate decree. On the contrary, "reprobation should not be preached with a certain delight in the doctrine. He who is forever preaching reprobation shows not only that he is harsh and cruel, but also that he has not understood the work of the Lord God. God's love remains the central thought. He has chosen in his eternal love, and for the sake of this love, he has also reprobated."

The reader will perceive that Hoeksema has penetrated into the mysteries of predestination, as revealed in the Bible, more deeply than many orthodox theologians before him (or after him). It is not enough to view reprobation as making known the justice of God in the eternal punishment of reprobate, impenitent sinners. Reprobation is "necessary" for the salvation of the elect. Thus reprobation "serves election."

Although Hoeksema never refers to it, the Christian Reformed doctrine of common grace was in the background of the lecture in 1927. With its well-meant offer, this doctrine denies reprobation and makes the preaching of reprobation an absolute impossibility. The teaching that God loves and is graciously inclined toward all humans, sincerely desiring their salvation, *is* the denial of the decree of reprobation. Reprobation is the doctrine that God has determined not to save some humans and, in his eternal hatred of them, has appointed them to damnation, so that in the preaching of the gospel he does not save them or desire to save them, but he hardens them in their unbelief.

No preacher who proclaims a well-meant offer to all hearers can or will preach reprobation. He certainly cannot preach reprobation in the same sermon in which he proclaims the well-meant offer. Even the most paradoxical preacher will find it difficult to declare, "God is gracious to all hearers of the gospel and desires to save all of you," and in the next breath, "God hates some humans and is pleased to damn them." Inevitably, over time he will cease preaching reprobation in all his sermons. If for a short season there is, by some in a denomination, the contradictory preaching of reprobation one Sunday and of the well-meant offer the next Sunday, the preaching of a well-meant offer in a denomination of churches will soon result in the silencing of reprobation altogether. The disciples of a Louis Berkhof and of an H. J. Kuiper will be the Harold Dekkers, the Harry Boers, the James Daanes, and the multitudes of present-day Christian Reformed ministers who preach only the love of God for all and the sincere desire of God to save all and who never preach reprobation, because they do not believe it.

The well-meant offer drives reprobation out of the preaching. Because of the inseparable relation of reprobation and election, with reprobation is driven out election. And because election is the source of the gospel and its salvation, with the driving out of election goes out the entire gospel of salvation in Jesus Christ by grace alone.

Not only the Protestant Reformed Churches, but also all Reformed churches need to read, and to heed, *The Place of Reprobation in the Preaching of the Gospel.*

—David J. Engelsma

The following lecture was given at the request of the Men's Society of the First Protestant Reformed Church in Grand Rapids, Michigan.

It was not originally intended for publication, but at the request of the Men's Society and at the insistence of many others, I gladly acquiesce regarding this purpose. I would have preferred first to revise and expand the lecture, but lack of time prevented this. It follows here, in printed form, unchanged from the spoken lecture.

May the Lord be pleased to use the printed form of the lecture to lead our people more deeply into the mysteries of salvation concerning God's sovereign good pleasure, unto edification in the knowledge of our Lord Jesus Christ and unto the glory of his glorious name.

—The author
Grand Rapids, Michigan
May 1927

Introduction

The subject of this pamphlet is not an easy one, but it is of great importance for those who love the Reformed truth. A Reformed person thinks and lives theologically. For him it is of greatest importance to know his God as he has revealed himself in his works and word. The Reformed man understands perfectly that he cannot comprehend God, because God is infinite, his being is unfathomable, and his works always fill us with adoring wonder. But still a Reformed man desires to know more and more about his God and to comprehend what God has revealed of himself.

God is one. There must be unity in his revelation, unity of thought and purpose in all his works. Therefore, a child of God, especially a Reformed child of God, cannot rest until he has learned to see and understand this unity of thought and purpose. It is from this viewpoint that we consider the place of reprobation in the preaching of the gospel.

I proceed in the discussion of this subject from the assumption that I am speaking to Reformed people. I will not therefore speak about election or reprobation as such. In fact, I will not even attempt to defend the contention that reprobation should have a place in the preaching of the gospel. I assume this. Rather, I will attempt to trace the unity of God's works and then place before us this question: what is the place of reprobation in that unity?

I have said that we will consider the place of reprobation in the preaching of the gospel. If reprobation must be preached, what is its place? How must it be presented? What is its relation to election and to the whole of truth? With what emphasis must it be presented?

It is obvious that in the preaching or instruction of the truth the various aspects must be placed in their proper light and in their relation to one another. If I would describe a masterpiece of an artist, and if I would attempt to describe the individual parts on the canvas without relating them to the whole, that masterpiece would be ruined by my description. Or if I would attempt to portray my impression of the whole and lay so much stress on the background that it becomes the foreground, I do not do justice to the work of the artist. So it is with respect to the work of salvation. One can very well preach on election and later on reprobation without setting forth these truths correctly, because he has not preached them in their mutual relation and in connection with the entire truth of scripture.

The question of the place of reprobation in the preaching of the gospel is inseparably connected with another: what is the proper place of reprobation in the entire body of truth? Both election and reprobation are parts of predestination, and predestination is part of the counsel of God in the full sense as it pertains to all things. To determine the place of reprobation in the works of God and in the preaching of the gospel, we must review the whole plan of God concerning all things, answer the question how predestination appears in the full counsel, and determine the relation in which reprobation stands to election, insofar as this is possible in the light of scripture.

God's Decree and Election

What is the relation of election to God's decree concerning all things? What is the place of election in the entirety of the counsel of God? To ascertain this, we must consider the counsel of God in general. God's counsel in a broad sense is the eternal thought and will of God concerning all things, man and angels, moon and stars, the animate and the inanimate creation.

This decree, or counsel, of God is eternal, since there was never a beginning of the thoughts of God regarding creation. Those thoughts are as eternal as God. The counsel of God is all-inclusive. From before the foundation of the world, all things were with him in his divine thoughts, not only as he made them in the beginning, but also as they would develop throughout history. God has from before the foundation of the world decreed in his eternal counsel how things will be eternally. He determined the end of all things from the beginning. God determined how he would create all things in the beginning with a view to the consummation of all things. Creation is planned with a view to re-creation, generation with a view to regeneration, the beginning with a view to the end. Moreover, with a view to that end God the Lord planned the course of events so that everything in its mutual working and development must work together to attain his eternal purpose.

Let us never forget that God's works are a unity and that every creature is organically related to every other creature. Everything is planned with a view to everything else. God has so determined everything in his counsel that the end of all things must be the realization of what he has purposed in himself.

Therefore, nothing can be excluded from God's counsel. Rain and drought, fruitful and unfruitful years, health and sickness, war and peace, yea, the animals of the field and the sparrows of the housetops must serve the purpose and end God has determined in himself. Notice too that this includes the evil things: sin, pain, death, and all that is related to them. Never may we conceive of God's counsel as if it allows for adjustments or for events not included in it. On the contrary, God decided the end, and he sovereignly determined the way and the means that would lead to that end, sin and death included.

Already at this point we can establish that God's goal, which he determined in himself, is that all the works of his hands must show forth his praise to the fullest extent and must witness of the magnificence of his name. The Lord has made all things for his own sake, even the wicked unto the day of evil (Prov. 16:4), for he is God and he alone, and he does all his good pleasure.

How did God conceive of this end of all things to which everything in his counsel is directed? What will that unity of all things be, that consummation of all things, through which God's name will be most fully glorified and his virtues most gloriously revealed? Note that the question should be put this way. The question is frequently asked, in what manner is God glorified in the individual works of his hands? But not enough attention is given to the relation of these works to one another.

Take again the example of a work of art. I can stand in front of a beautiful building and focus my attention on the individual parts of the building. I can note the beautiful stones, the colored windows, the lofty vaults, the pointed arches, and whatever else. If one architect has planned it all, then I can, in pointing out the separate parts, praise the ability of the architect. This also can be done with the works of God. This is the method usually employed.

God is glorified in the wonderful, omnipotent works he has established in the beginning. The heavens declare the glory of God, and the firmament shows forth his handiwork, and the entire creation speaks of his eternal power and Godhead. With wisdom the Lord has made it all. So I can speak of the work of salvation and, as subdivisions, speak separately of his gracious election and just reprobation. Thus I can praise God for the revelation of his sovereign love in election and say that in reprobation he reveals his justice and wrath as well as his great power.

Yet you immediately feel that we may not leave it at that. If the architect really was capable, there was in that building one principal idea, and with a view to that all the other parts were determined. If I attend only to the parts, the result is twofold. First, I have not grasped the principal idea of the whole, in which the marvelous realization of the idea is brought out. Second, I have not done justice to the parts, because I have not shown their place and purpose in relation to the whole. Thus it is with God's works. God is one. His work is one. One magnificent idea governs all. If I wish to glorify God in his work, I must attend not only to the parts but first to the whole, and then show how each part is related to that whole.

Regarding reprobation I can say that God sovereignly predestined some to destruction in order to glorify himself; but if I say no more, I have presented God as a tyrant who destroys creatures for the sole purpose of glorifying himself. Then one will say to himself, "This is a hard saying; who can hear it?" Surely God is sovereign: he does with his own what he wills, and no one can say, "What doest thou?" But that does not take away the thought that repeatedly arises in our hearts: why has the all-wise God done this? Therefore, we must place ourselves before the question, what is the goal, the consummation? What is the outcome? What has God determined in himself? What is the end of all the works of his hands?

We must take as our starting point in Ephesians 1:9–10: "Having made known unto us the mystery of his will, according to his good pleasure which he hath purposed in himself: that in the dispensation of the fulness of times he might gather together in one all things in Christ, both which are in heaven, and which are on earth; even in him."

I cannot now give a complete explanation of this beautiful and comprehensive passage. Let it suffice to point out the chief teachings of the text insofar as this is necessary for the treatment of the present subject. Clearly the apostle reveals that God the Lord has purposed in himself in his counsel regarding the eternal purpose of all his works. There can be no doubt that the text deals with the eternal good pleasure of God. He has purposed in himself from before the foundation of the world how things should be in their consummation. One can hardly deny that the apostle speaks of all things, the whole creation, the fullness of all God has made. He says emphatically "all things" both in heaven and on earth. This has been explained as if it refers to the militant and triumphant church. Yet this conflicts with the plain meaning of the word. The discussion is in regard to all things. We may take this to mean: What has God, from before the foundation of the world, determined in himself with respect to this present creation? What shall its consummation be?

First, according to the text, the entire creation will be an intimately related and harmonious unity. All the creatures in heaven and on the earth will be brought together under one head so that all creation will form a perfect unity. This was not the case in the beginning. There was then not one head of the entire creation. There was an earthly and a heavenly creation. The earthly creation was united under its earthly head, Adam, who was king and head, but his kingship did not include the things in heaven, for Adam as he stood in the first paradise was made a little lower than the angels.

Even his kingship, however, was devastated by sin. Adam fell. He broke the covenant, separating himself along with the earthly creation from the God of the covenant. The creatures now are mutually parted and separated. It is now man against man, people against people, plant against plant, and animal against animal. The animal world is mutually divided and separated from man. The harmony in the earthly creation is broken. Some such division also took place in heaven among the angels of God. But Ephesians 1 teaches that it was God's purpose from before the foundation of the world to unite all things again into a higher and all-inclusive unity, both the things in heaven and the things on earth.

Second, in light of the text, God had determined in himself so to unite all things that they are governed by Christ as king. Christ must become the head of the new creation. Adam may not be the head. The ruling principle of the new creation will be that Christ is Lord over all. All creation has its harmonious unity in him. As far as Christ is exalted above Adam, so far the future creation will shine in blazing glory above the present creation.

This means not only that all creatures will be gathered together in perfect unity under the one head, Christ, but also that creation will then be most intimately united with God, for Christ is Immanuel, God with us, the Word who became flesh. In him are the divine and human natures, Creator and creature in closest union one with the other. In Christ God joins himself most intimately with us through the bond of the covenant. In Christ God's tabernacle will be spread over us, and through us all things will be included in this tabernacle of God. The glorified creation will eternally lie close to God's heart in Christ Jesus.

Thus considered, the counsel of predestination (more specifically election, with its necessary complement, reprobation) is the heart of God's decree. This counsel of predestination determines the place that God's rational creatures, both angels and men, will have in the eternal unity of all things. Man, who was made in the image of God and whose nature Christ assumed, occupies the chief place among the rational creatures. When all the works of God will have reached their consummation, man in Christ Jesus will be in closest communion and live in most intimate fellowship with God.

For this reason it is impossible to place the decree of predestination on the same line with the decree of providence. Both form a unity, but in such a way that predestination has the pivotal place around which all the rest revolves and in which all finds its unity, according to the all-wise counsel of God. This unity is formed in such a way that the decree of election has the chief place in predestination, not only in the sense that election is the positive side and reprobation the negative side, but also in the sense that reprobation serves election.

I will enlarge on this presently. However, already now it can be said that since it was God's determination in the fullness of time to unite and to gather all things in Christ Jesus, God's main concern is not with what falls eternally outside of that glorified creation. When one constructs a building, his chief concern is not the stones that never find a place in the completed structure, even though they were formed as stones. Thus it is in God's counsel. Election is and remains the main purpose to which reprobation is subordinate, whatever purpose it may serve.

So conceived, election is that part of God's counsel in which he, from before the foundation of the world, has determined which individuals will have a glorious place in the final unity of all things. Election is God's appointment of individuals to the glory of the new and everlasting creation. Election is indeed discriminating. It implies that God has chosen some in distinction from others. Nevertheless it is chiefly predestination. Therefore, election in this connection is the decree of God by which he sovereignly and freely, out of pure grace, without respect to merits, chose to give some a place with Christ in eternal glory. The primary purpose is the glorification of God. The motive is deepest love. He desired to glorify his children with a glory to which they could never have attained in the first Adam.

Moreover, election is personal. God has known his own people by name from eternity. But election is to be thought of organically. Although election deals with individuals and is personal, it is also true that the elect form a unity in Christ, a glorious inheritance of God in which each has his own place. The elect constitute the body of Christ in which each member is chosen to a certain personal destination, to his own place in the body.

Election and Reprobation

Now we are prepared to give an answer to the question, what is the place of reprobation in that scheme? God has reprobated as well as chosen. Taken by itself, reprobation is the decree of God in which he has determined, as sovereignly as in election, that some individuals should not enter eternal glory but are destined for destruction. Thus it should be expressed.

I realize it seems milder to say that God decided to leave others in their sins and ruin. This is the way it is formulated in the Canons, in which the Synod of Dordt adopted the infralapsarian standpoint, contrary to the wishes and protestations of Gomarus. Yet this is not a milder way of expressing it. We may close our eyes to the problem and refuse to seek an answer, but the problem remains. The question inevitably arises, how did these people fall into the sin in which God permitted them to lie? Another question also arises: why did God leave them in this sin and misery when he could have saved them? I fully realize that all questions cannot be answered. But by closing our eyes to the problems that arise we fail to find a solution.

Besides, scripture certainly teaches more. The potter does with the clay as he pleases, and no one can deny him the right to form of one lump of clay a vessel unto honor and from another form a vessel unto dishonor. Surely, here we are taught more than that God permits something to lie where it has fallen. The vessels unto dishonor are also made by him in accordance with his appointment. Therefore, I would rather say that reprobation is the decree of God by which he sovereignly destined some to destruction. Certainly the condemnation will be on the basis of the sin and guilt of the reprobate, but never as if reprobation rests on foreseen sin. Reprobation, even as election, is entirely, sovereignly free.

At present, however, we are not so much concerned about reprobation as such, but about its relation to election. The question is, what is the relation of reprobation to election? Or the weightier question, why did God reprobate? You say, to the glorification of his name. Correct. We agree. God the Lord has wrought all things for his own sake, even the wicked for the day of evil. I grant that. But the question arises, is God the Lord glorified to a greater extent by having reprobated some, rather than if he had saved all? Granted that the damnation of the reprobate glorifies him eternally, would his honor not have been greater if

he had saved all? Again you say, no, because then his righteous indignation would never have been revealed. But is that true? We agree that
in the destruction of the reprobate God reveals his righteous anger
and is thereby glorified. Was that anger not sufficiently revealed in the
suffering of Christ?

Every time the same question confronts us: why has God reprobated some? To find an answer to this we must place ourselves before
the question, what is the relation of election to reprobation? Do these
form a dualism? Then there would be dualism in God also; then God
would be a God of highest love and at the same time of deepest hatred.
This surely is impossible. God does not desire the destruction of the
reprobate in the same way in which he delights in the salvation and
glory of his chosen people. Therefore, I maintain that scripture gives
the following answer to this very important question: reprobation
exists in order that election may be realized; reprobation is necessary to bring the chosen to the glory that God in his infinite love has
appointed for them.

God loved his people with an infinite love. In his great love he
determined to lead them to the glory he had appointed for them in
Christ. If he determined to attain this greatest glory and lead the elect
into it, it was necessary for him, reverently speaking, to reprobate some.
This was not because all could not find a place in glory, for then the
question would arise, why did God decree to create more people than
could have a place in the organism of the body of Christ? But those
who will be damned must for a time serve the salvation of the elect, be
it antithetically. In this sense, reprobation is a divine necessity, and the
reprobate exist for the sake of the elect. They are in a certain sense the
price, the ransom that God pays for the higher glory of his children.

You will ask if I can prove this. I think I can. This idea is not
strange to God's general revelation in nature and in history. You find it
proven in the life of the nations and of people in particular. On many
monuments erected in honor of soldiers who lost their lives on the
battlefield, you can read the inscription, "They gave their lives so that
we might live." Here is a figure of election and reprobation as we are
now considering it. How often it occurs that thousands lose their lives

on the battlefield so that others may live. They do not merely give their lives, but their lives are required of them. They were reprobated that the nation might live.

It is no different in the lives of individual persons and animals. The mother gives life to her child, not infrequently at the expense of her own life. It is virtually always true that one generation lives and dies to make room for the next. There are species of animals in which the male dies after mating. The male is cast off (reprobated) to give life to the young.

According to the scriptures, the plant kingdom is no different. When a farmer sows seed in the field, he sows much more than he needs. When the seed sprouts, he removes the super-abundant plants so that the chosen ones can ripen. This is an example of election and reprobation. Again, when the seed falls into the earth and dies, there appear not only the kernels of wheat for which the seed was planted, but also the stem, the straw, and even the chaff. Without the stem and the chaff the grain could never have germinated and ripened. The stem and the chaff serve the grain, the seed. Yet both will presently be burned by fire so that the grain can be gathered into the barn. Here also we find election and reprobation in such a way that the latter serves the former and is necessary to it.

Not only do you find a figure of this truth in the general revelation of God, but it is also literally proven in scripture in various texts and the historical accounts. The Lord declares to Israel in Isaiah 43:4, "Since thou wast precious in my sight, thou hast been honourable, and I have loved thee: therefore will I give men for thee, and people for thy life." Although this passage refers to what the Lord did for Israel in the past, it also refers to the eternal counsel of God's good pleasure, for God has loved his people from eternity. In his counsel they are precious in his eyes. Thus the text refers to the eternal love of God. In that eternal love he has desired to glorify and magnify his people and to lead them to the highest possible glory in his eternal inheritance. The text says that to accomplish this God has given other people in the place of his chosen people. Because he loved his people, those others had to pay for Israel's salvation with their lives.

Israel's history proves this time and time again. Pharaoh and his host perish. They must serve Israel temporarily, but God does not hesitate to give people for the life of his people. When Israel enters Canaan, people are again given in the place of Israel. This is effectuated by the sins of these people. They have filled the measure of iniquity when Israel enters into the rest, and they are destroyed to make room for Israel. So it is throughout the history of Israel. Babylon serves the purpose of chastising Jerusalem, thereby making itself ripe for judgment. When it has served to realize God's counsel, Babylon is destroyed.

Thus it is literally presented in Proverbs 11:8: "The righteous is delivered out of trouble, and the wicked cometh in his stead." The idea here is that the ungodly serve to deliver the righteous out of trouble, to glorify them. Having done so, they perish for their sins. Still stronger is the language of Proverbs 21:18: "The wicked shall be a ransom for the righteous, and the transgressor for the upright." Here again is the idea that God gives the wicked as ransom, which he pays to glorify the righteous.

This does not detract from the other truth that in reprobation God also reveals his righteousness and is glorified in revealing his holy name. The reprobate do not serve the salvation of the elect willingly but as godless and in spite of themselves. For this reason they become guilty in serving this purpose and are worthy of condemnation. In serving God's purpose they become ripe for destruction. Just as chaff ripens for destruction while it serves the grain, so the godless become ripe for perdition while they serve the elect.

More evident this is in the case of our Savior. Surely, for the glorification of the elect, the blood of the Savior must flow. But if this blood is to flow, there must be a wicked and reprobate world to shed it. There must be a Judas who betrays him; there must be a Sanhedrin that condemns him; there must be a mighty and godless Roman power that finally brings him to the cross. In all this, the reprobate serve the glorification of the elect. Without that ungodly world, the cross cannot be imagined. It is also true that the world becomes ripe for destruction in crucifying the Savior, through which it serves the glorification of the elect.

As it was then, so it is now. So it will be to the end of the world.

When the end comes the ungodly will be righteously condemned and damned, in sin having served God's counsel. The elect will be eternally glorified with the Savior in the inheritance of the saints. Thus in the unity of God's plan, reprobation necessarily serves election. God's love toward his people reigns supreme in his counsel. To reveal and to realize this love fully he brings into existence people who must finally be damned. Reprobation is the necessary, antithetical counterpart of election.

Reprobation in the Preaching

On this basis we can determine the place of reprobation in the preaching of the gospel and its place in every presentation of the truth. Surely reprobation must be preached. This follows from God's revelation of it; the complete counsel of God certainly must be preached. We can understand this necessity. Without the preaching of reprobation, election, its counterpart, cannot be preached and justice to God's electing love cannot be given. God's great love must always be our chief concern. That love is manifested in that he has given his only begotten Son, that whosoever believes in him shall not perish but have everlasting life. This becomes still more glorious if we understand that to realize this love God has given people in the stead of his people and given the wicked as a ransom for the righteous.

Moreover, it must become evident in the preaching that God is sovereign, also when a part of what he first formed falls away. When we see a farmer pull out the little plants he had previously planted, it seems sad and foolish, until we understand that this has its purpose. So too with the work of God. Unless we consider the matter from God's viewpoint and are enlightened by his wise counsel, the world's history seems a great pity, a great misery. Although God is the ultimate victor and will finally glorify his people, many creatures he had formed are eternally lost though the wiles of the devil and the powers of death and sin. Not so, if we present reprobation in the proper light. Then God remains sovereign. There is no accident. Whatever God does is well done, for he does all things in wisdom.

We must not surrender an inch of ground to the idea that God wills to save all, some of whom are nevertheless lost. God's counsel will stand, and he will remain sovereign—sovereign regarding eternal life, and at the same time sovereign regarding eternal perdition. Therefore, reprobation must be preached, for God must remain sovereign even over the kingdom of darkness. Reprobation must be preached to the congregation from the viewpoint of election. Believers must understand that salvation is not of him who wills, nor of him who runs, but of God who shows mercy. According to God's good pleasure they have received a place in the consummation of all things. This means so much more to us when we understand that God could also sovereignly have reprobated us. There can be no question that reprobation should be preached if one wishes to divide the word of truth properly.

Thus it has become evident how reprobation should be preached and what place it should be given in the preaching of the gospel. We must not have sermonettes devoted to reprobation. This is also true of election. This is true of every aspect of the truth. He who occasionally preaches only on election, without relating it whatsoever to reprobation, is not preaching election. This is still truer of reprobation, the antithetical counterpart of election. It belongs with election. It can be understood only in the light of election. It must accordingly be presented in its relation to election.

When preaching on election and reprobation, we must not place them dualistically over against each other. They are not on the same level. They are not corresponding halves of the same thing, but together they form a unity. Reprobation should always be presented as subordinate to election, as serving it according to God's counsel. From this it follows that reprobation should not be preached with a certain delight in the doctrine. He who is forever preaching reprobation shows not only that he is harsh and cruel, but also that he has not understood the work of the Lord God. God's love remains the central thought. He has chosen in his eternal love, and for the sake of this love, he has also reprobated. Thus all God's work becomes a beautiful organic unity. In this way he is and remains God and he alone. At the conclusion, we exclaim in adoration with the apostle, "O the depth of the riches both of the wisdom and knowledge of God!...for of him, and through him, and to him are all things: to whom be glory forever" (Rom. 11:33, 36).

God will presently make all things new. Then he will fully reveal his everlasting and glorious kingdom to all his children. The kingdom of Christ, including his chosen church, will be inseparably united with God. It will appear that this divine and beautiful work is so marvelous and so glorious that not only was it doubly worth all the suffering of this present time, but also it is costly enough to give people as a ransom for it. The glory of the Lord will through Jesus Christ shine forth with heavenly radiance over all the works of his hands forever!

AFTERWORD

A t the request of the publisher, I conclude this book with an afterword.

I summarize and clarify what the reader has finished reading.

The Rock is the authoritative account of the doctrinal and church historical origin of the Protestant Reformed Churches in America. It is this account, not in the form of a dispassionate, scholarly analysis some years after these churches came into existence. But the account consists of the doctrinal debate, the controversial writings, and the reflections on church political actions that were actually in the process of causing division in the Christian Reformed Church and forming the Protestant Reformed Churches. The book puts the reader into the Christian Reformed Church and, more particularly, into the circumstances of the controversy over common grace in that church, in the early twentieth century.

The content of the book is the primary documents of that reformation of the church.

Nor may one object that the book presents the controversy and the resulting separation from the viewpoint of the Protestant Reformed Churches, for the content lays out the Christian Reformed theology, and arguments on behalf, of common grace fully and fairly. In addition, the advocates of common grace are quoted at length. As for the historical details, no one has ever challenged their accuracy.

In this compelling way, the book does not so much explain as vividly demonstrate what the Protestant Reformed Churches are, and why, in the ecclesiastical purpose of God, they continue to exist still in 2015 as a truly orthodox denomination of Reformed churches, unchallengeably and determinedly faithful to the Reformed confessions; vigorously contending on behalf of the Reformed faith and life against all assaults on this faith; and exerting themselves, by sanctifying grace, to keep themselves from the filth and folly of the ungodly world, that is now alluring, corrupting, and, thus, destroying entire Reformed denominations all over the world.

The book makes crystal-clear that the origin of the Protestant Reformed Churches, which describes and identifies them to this day, was the gospel of particular, sovereign grace, rooted in the eternal decree of election, accompanied by an eternal decree of reprobation, which gospel has both the power and the imperative of the antithesis—to the glory of the gracious and holy God.

For confessing this gospel, the Protestant Reformed Churches were cast out of the Christian Reformed Church!

For confessing this gospel, the Protestant Reformed Churches are commonly slandered by the community of Reformed and Presbyterian churches!

"Hyper-Calvinists!" "Anabaptists!" "Radicals!"

Let the reader judge.

God has already judged, in the subsequent, contrasting histories of the Christian Reformed Church and the Protestant Reformed Churches. And the entire Reformed community of churches is, or can be, well aware of the divine judgment.

The Rock makes plain also why the Protestant Reformed Churches are polemical. The churches were conceived and born in intense struggle, which is not unusual either in physical or in spiritual and ecclesiastical conception and birth. The controversy of contending for the faith once delivered is part of their spiritual DNA. This has been a blessing, indeed their salvation. By willingness and readiness to contend for the truth of the gospel, the Protestant Reformed Churches have survived as soundly Reformed churches for almost one hundred years. In addition, they have developed and flourished.

These basic truths about these churches *The Rock* reveals to every reader.

Other aspects of the earliest days, and of the founding fathers, of the Protestant Reformed Churches can be overlooked. They make a deep impression on this spiritual son of these churches, and physical grandson of founding members of these churches. I mention some of these aspects, briefly.

Danhof and Hoeksema did not want to break with the Christian Reformed Church. Again and again, they pleaded with the leaders of that church not to make the theory of common grace binding doctrine in the church, but to allow ministers and theologians to examine, discuss *amiably*, and debate the issue.

The Christian Reformed Church acted with precipitous, inexcusable, and suspicious haste in adopting the theory of common grace as binding church doctrine. That church's decision, which assured the ouster of Danhof, Hoeksema, and other sound, faithful members of the Christian Reformed Church, as well as schism in the church, offered not a shred of solid evidence from the creeds that common grace is, in fact, a fundamental element of Reformed doctrine.

The "affair Janssen" played a powerful role in the Christian Reformed Church's adoption of common grace as official church doctrine in 1924, and in more ways than the one that is obvious. The obvious influence of the Janssen case upon the common grace decision was that the many, influential supporters of Professor Janssen were determined to get revenge upon Danhof and Herman Hoeksema for the ouster of their champion from Calvin seminary and from the Christian Reformed Church. In this respect, the Christian Reformed synod of 1924 and the Christian Reformed classes that soon followed were the arena of despicable, bloody "church politics"—the Christian Reformed equivalent of the Roman Catholic stakes at which popes had their personal enemies executed, painfully.

But, as Hoeksema came belatedly to see, more than personal vengeance moved the synod of 1924, and the vehement attacks on Danhof and Hoeksema that preceded the synod. As Janssen himself vigorously contended after his deposition in 1922, the fundamental issue in his case—higher critical denial of the inspiration of the Old Testament—was the question whether the Christian Reformed Church would be the compromising, common grace church of the well-meant offer and of conformity to the prevailing culture, and thus acceptable to and influential with the broader church world in North America, or the uncompromising, particular grace church of the Canons of Dordt and of separation from and enmity against the world of the ungodly. At this point, men like Louis Berkhof, Y. P. de Jong, H. J. Kuiper, and others who had opposed Janssen and his higher critical views of the Old Testament caved, and not only caved, but also allied themselves with their former foes in the Christian Reformed Church to destroy their former friends and allies.

Admittedly, here Abraham Kuyper cast his long shadow. The influential Dutch Reformed theologian had proposed a cultural common grace of God that was supposed to allow the church to cooperate with the world in the world's academic, scientific, and broadly cultural endeavors, in order to create an earthly kingdom of God (although Kuyper himself admitted that this common grace kingdom of God would end in the kingdom of antichrist). So highly did many Reformed theologians and ministers in the Reformed churches of Dutch ancestry regard the learned, able Kuyper that his theological word was virtually law.

With regard to the influence of Kuyper on the Christian Reformed Church in the early 1920s, the history of the common grace controversy is a reminder to the true church and to the true believer that the call of God in any doctrinal conflict is "to the law and to the testimony" (Isa. 8:20). In article 7, the Belgic Confession declares that only the "divine Scriptures" are the "infallible rule" that establishes what the church believes and teaches. Abraham Kuyper's theological speculation is not "divine Scriptures." Kuyper's three volumes on common grace are not the "infallible rule" for Reformed churches.

In 1924 the Christian Reformed Church committed herself to the theory of common grace. She became, by her own official decision, essentially, a common grace church, even though for some years she tried to balance her common grace identity with feeble protestations also of the particular grace of the Reformed confessions, thus deceiving the unwary and salving her conscience.

How today common grace dominates every aspect of the

Christian Reformed Church is abundantly evident to everyone. Her theology is the universalism of Harold Dekker, Harry Boer, and James Daane, as the inevitable development of the "well-meant offer" of the Christian Reformed Church's doctrine of common grace. Her compromise with and conformity to the world of unbelief and ungodliness (at the heart of her three points of common grace) extend to the denial of the inspiration of Genesis 1 in its teaching of creation in six days, under the influence in the Christian Reformed Church and her schools of the theory of evolution, now widely accepted; to the implementation of worldly feminism by the approval and practice of women in church office; to the surrender of the fundamental ordinance of God in civil society and the church, namely, marriage, in the permission of the adultery of divorce and remarriage for any reason; and to the yielding to the deepest depths of degradation in the world of the ungodly by the unashamed plea for recognition of sodomite "marriage" by leading theologians (Lewis Smedes, among others) and by the editor of her church paper, the *Banner*, on the pages of the magazine. The Christian Reformed Church's repudiation of the antithesis in her doctrine of common grace now takes form in ecumenical fellowship with thoroughly apostate church bodies.

Having sown the wind, the Christian Reformed Church now reaps the whirlwind. *The Rock* shows her sowing the wind.

The documents that make up *The Rock* indicate that God warned the Christian Reformed Church. He warned that church clearly and sharply. He sent her prophets. Their names were especially Henry Danhof and Herman Hoeksema. But as an apostate Israel has always done, the Christian Reformed Church slew her prophets. Christian Reformed classes deposed and excommunicated Danhof and Hoeksema. This is the modern form of stoning.

Finally, *The Rock* bespeaks heroism—the most courageous doctrinal and churchly bravery. To be willing to give up everything that is dear to a minister of the gospel—name, position, and office—and to be willing to suffer reproach, shame, and even church discipline for the sake of the purity of the gospel and the glory of the name of God, this is heroism at the highest level. And this leaves out of sight, as Danhof and Hoeksema did, financial support for one's family. This is heroism in the cause of God in the world. This is heroism in the most important and hottest warfare, the warfare of Jesus Christ on earth.

And then to be willing to spend the many, long years of the rest of one's ministry as it were in a corner, unrecognized, despised, isolated, spoken of only in derogatory terms!

Enemies charge that we Protestant Reformed people worship Herman Hoeksema. The charge is false. It is more slander, intended to detract from the real issue—the necessity of confessing the truth.

But we loved him.

We honor his memory.

And we thank God for the gift of him—for ourselves, for our children and grandchildren, for the true, faithful bride of Jesus Christ in the world, and, above all, for the sake of the truth of the gospel of grace with its accompanying life of holiness.

—David J. Engelsma

APPENDIX OF NAMES

BIOGRAPHICAL SKETCHES OF THE MAIN COMBATANTS IN THE COMMON GRACE CONTROVERSY

DAVID J. ENGELSMA

Bavinck, Herman (1854–1921). Bavinck was a learned, influential Dutch Reformed theologian in the late 1800s and early 1900s. Bavinck succeeded Abraham Kuyper as professor of theology at the Free University of Amsterdam in 1902 and continued there until his death in 1921.

Author of a magisterial four-volume set of Reformed dogmatics, Bavinck also wrote *De Algemeene Genade* (Common grace), defending and promoting a common grace of God that supposedly accomplishes a Christianizing of worldly culture. Bavinck therefore was one with his colleague Kuyper in the advocacy of a cultural common grace and its program of making non-Christian and anti-Christian societies "Christian" in some sense. To the authoritative Bavinck and Kuyper, their Christian Reformed disciples appealed in their successful effort to make the theory of common grace binding dogma in their church in 1924.

In opposing the theory of common grace, Danhof and Hoeksema were combatting the Reformed heavyweights of their day. Without denying or even disparaging the theological abilities of Bavinck and his soundness in many other aspects of Reformed theology, Danhof and Hoeksema insisted that the common grace theology of Bavinck must be put to the test of scripture and the Reformed creeds and that when this is done the theory of common grace fails the test. Bavinck was a great man. But, as the proverb puts it, "great men err greatly."

Beets, Henry. He was a prominent Christian Reformed minister during the common grace conflict. Beets was also editor of the Christian Reformed church magazine the *Banner* from 1903 to 1928. Beets used his powerful position in the Christian Reformed Church to defend the doctrine of common grace and to condemn Danhof, Hoeksema, and eventually the Protestant Reformed Churches for their rejection of the theory of common grace.

Such was the prominence of Beets that he was honored with chairing the strange conference of Protestant Reformed and Christian Reformed ministers in the Pantlind Hotel in Grand Rapids, Michigan, in March 1939. Mainly at the urging of Dr. Klaas Schilder, Dutch Reformed theologian, who was present at the conference and hoped that it would serve to heal the breach between the two Reformed denominations in the United States, a number of Christian Reformed and Protestant Reformed ministers gathered to discuss the possibility of the reunion of their churches. At this meeting, Hoeksema delivered his thorough speech "The Reunion of the Christian Reformed and Protestant Reformed Churches," which is part of the content of this book. The Christian Reformed men who were present displayed their complete indifference to the purpose of the meeting and to any debate of the issue of common grace.

Berkhof, Louis. This longtime professor of theology at Calvin Theological Seminary is widely and rightly regarded as the "father" of the three points of common grace adopted by the synod of the Christian Reformed Church in 1924. Berkhof was an advisory member of the synodical committee of pre-advice that guided the synod in its treatment of the protests against Danhof and Hoeksema for their rejection of the theory of common grace and that drew up the three points of common grace that synod adopted as official, binding church dogma.

In 1925 Berkhof wrote *De Drie Punten in Alle Deelen Gereformeerd*

(The three points, Reformed in all parts), which defended the three points of common grace that the Christian Reformed Church adopted in 1924. In this booklet, regarding the affirmation of the preaching of the gospel as a gracious, well-meant offer of salvation to all hearers, Berkhof declared that the meaning of this affirmation is indeed that the preaching of the gospel is "a sign of God's grace to [all] sinners [who hear the preaching], is for them a blessing on the part of the Lord...The offer of salvation [is] a temporal blessing...also for them who do not accept the invitation." Berkhof condemned the doctrine that God "does not bless [the reprobate unbeliever] by it [the preaching of the gospel], but curses them by it" (21; the translation of the Dutch is mine; the booklet has not been translated into English).

Berkhof was one of the four professors whose objections to the higher critical views of the Old Testament on the part of their colleague, Dr. Ralph Janssen, were rejected by the governing body of the Christian Reformed seminary and by the synod of the Christian Reformed Church until Hoeksema intervened (fatally for him regarding his office and position in the Christian Reformed Church) with substantial proof of Janssen's heretical views. When Janssen responded to his adversaries, including Berkhof, by charging them with denying common grace (thus indicating at the very least that common grace is the handmaiden of theological modernism), Berkhof turned against Hoeksema, attacking his denial of common grace as un-Reformed, indeed heretical, in that the denial warranted deposition from office and expulsion from the Christian Reformed Church.

Bouma, Clarence. This professor of theology at Calvin Theological Seminary played a strategic role in the adoption of the three points of common grace by the Christian Reformed synod of 1924. Bouma was part of the committee of pre-advice that formulated the three points of common grace and that advised the synod to adopt the theory of common grace as church dogma, thus upholding the protests against Danhof and Hoeksema and condemning Danhof's and Hoeksema's rejection of common grace.

Breen, Quirinus. In 1924 Breen was a young pastor in the Christian Reformed Church, an ardent supporter of Janssen, and a vigorous advocate of common grace. Upon the condemnation of Janssen's teachings and the discipline of Janssen in 1922, Breen became a determined foe of Danhof and Hoeksema. Such was Breen's support for Janssen and his higher critical teaching that within a short time after the condemnation of Janssen in 1922 Breen left the Christian Reformed Church.

Bultema, Harry. This Christian Reformed minister was deposed by the Christian Reformed Church in 1918 for his heretical doctrine of premillennial dispensationalism. Hoeksema took a leading role in the discipline of Bultema, calling the church's attention to the truth that in article 27 the Belgic Confession calls Christ "an eternal King" of *the church*.

Like Janssen and his supporters, Bultema argued that the opposition to his teaching was due to his adversaries' rejection of common grace. In a little-known booklet, *Wat Zegt de Schrift van de Algemeene Genade?* (What does the scripture say about common grace?), written in 1925 but the text of a speech that Bultema had been giving earlier, that is, during the height of the common grace controversy in the Christian Reformed Church, Bultema contended that common grace is necessary for "a biblical eschatology." What Bultema had in mind was the coming glory of the entire creation during the earthly millennium of the reign of Jesus from Jerusalem. Bultema's appeal to and defense of the theory of common grace on behalf of his dispensational premillennialism demonstrate, at the very least, that the theory of common grace has strange bedfellows.

Hoeksema's role in the condemnation of Bultema's dispensationalism aroused also the antipathy of Bultema's supporters in the Christian Reformed Church. By his uncompromising stand for Reformed orthodoxy, Hoeksema was acquiring determined foes in the Christian Reformed Church who were eager for the opportunity to destroy him when the occasion presented itself and to drive him, his theology, and his uncompromising insistence on Reformed orthodoxy out of the Christian Reformed Church. In the common grace controversy, they had their occasion. They used it effectively.

Cocceius, Johannes (1603–69). He was a German theologian who emphasized the centrality of the biblical revelation of the covenant. Cocceius taught the development in scripture of the reality of the covenant by means of a series of covenants that differed significantly from each other. Because of his stress on the differences among the covenants revealed in the Bible, Cocceius was charged by some Reformed theologians with teaching dispensationalism.

The theology of Cocceius entered into the controversy over common grace in the Christian Reformed Church because of Danhof's and Hoeksema's affirmation of the centrality in Reformed theology of the covenant of grace and their insistence that the covenant is established with the elect children of believers only.

Danhof, Henry. In 1924 Danhof was a Christian Reformed pastor in Kalamazoo, Michigan, who worked closely with Herman Hoeksema in the early twentieth century to resist the theory of common grace with its "Americanization" (as its proponents deceptively described the purpose and power of common grace) of the members of the Christian Reformed Church.

As still a minister in the Christian Reformed Church in good standing, in 1919 Danhof delivered the important address, which he later published as a booklet, *De Idee van het Genadeverbond* (The idea of the covenant of grace). The English translation of this ground-breaking address is included in this book.

For refusing to subscribe to the Christian Reformed dogma of common grace, as adopted at the synod of 1924, Danhof was deposed from the ministry in the Christian Reformed Church. Although he cooperated with Hoeksema briefly in the forming of the new denomination that would become the Protestant Reformed Churches, Danhof soon abandoned the new federation of churches and spent the rest of his ministry as the pastor of an independent Reformed church in Kalamazoo. Toward the end of his ministerial career, he and his congregation returned to the Christian Reformed denomination. Nevertheless, in his own, strange, disappointing way, Danhof became one of the founding fathers of the Protestant Reformed Churches.

De Jong, Ymen Peter. De Jong was a prominent Christian Reformed minister during the common grace controversy in the 1920s and 1930s. In the time between the Christian Reformed synod of 1920, which found no cause to condemn Janssen's teaching, and the synod of 1922, which would condemn Janssen's teaching, with Danhof, Hoeksema, H. J. Kuiper, and four professors of theology at Calvin Theological Seminary, De Jong published *Waar het in de Zaak Janssen om Gaat* (What the issue in the case of Janssen really is), which exposed and condemned the higher critical teachings of Janssen. The booklet has not been translated into English.

Prior to the outbreak of the common grace controversy, De Jong shared with Danhof and Hoeksema deep concerns over the increasing worldliness of the Christian Reformed Church and her members. When the controversy broke upon the church, De Jong cut his ties with his former friends and colaborers, Danhof and Hoeksema, vigorously defended the theory of common grace, and joined in the severe condemnation of his former allies. In fact, De Jong was a member of the committee of pre-advice that composed and proposed the three points of common grace at the Christian Reformed synod of 1924.

Doekes, G. Doekes was a Dutch theologian at the time of the common grace controversy in the Christian Reformed Church. Doekes condemned the use of the theory of common grace to defend Janssen's modernism in the Dutch Christian Reformed periodical *De Wachter.* Doekes also condemned the booklet by B. K. Kuiper defending Janssen, *De Janssen Kwestie en Nog Iets* [The Janssen question and still more] (Grand Rapids: Eerdmans-Sevensma, June 1922). The booklet has not been translated into English. Doekes made plain that there was unease in the Netherlands as well as in North America over the use that was being made of Kuyper's theory of common grace.

Fortuin, Karel Wilhelm. In 1922 he was the minister of the Borculo, Michigan, Christian Reformed Church. In the Christian Reformed Dutch periodical *De Wachter,* Fortuin praised Van Baalen's booklet defending Janssen's teaching, which had just been condemned by the

Christian Reformed synod. Fortuin called for immediate action by the Christian Reformed Church, evidently against Danhof and Hoeksema, who had been instrumental in the condemnation of Janssen's modernist teaching regarding the Old Testament.

In the Christian Reformed Church at that time, there was widespread unhappiness over the discipline of Janssen and noisy opposition to Hoeksema for his part in the condemnation of Janssen's teaching.

Groen, Johannes. Groen was a Christian Reformed minister who was pastor of Eastern Avenue Christian Reformed Church in Grand Rapids, Michigan, from 1900 to 1919. Groen was Hoeksema's predecessor in Eastern Avenue. Groen was a leading advocate in the Christian Reformed Church at that time of conformity to the world according to the principles of a common grace of God under the guise of "Americanization."

It is a testimony to the power both of Hoeksema's preaching and of the gospel of particular grace and the antithesis that after only a few years of Hoeksema's ministry among them the vast majority of the members of Eastern Avenue rejected the theology of Groen, embraced the theology of particular grace, and willingly suffered the persecution of being expelled from the Christian Reformed denomination.

Grosheide, F. W. Grosheide was a prominent Dutch theologian who found a cause of the alarming "worldliness" of Reformed youth in the Netherlands in the earliest twentieth century in a false conception of common grace. With the caution that was prudent in the circles of Kuyper and Bavinck at that time, Grosheide did not attribute the worldliness to the theory of common grace itself but to a "false conception" of common grace. Evident in Grosheide's flaccid warning, at the very least, was the readiness of the theory of common grace to serve the powerful temptation of worldliness especially among the Reformed youth. Evident also was the determination of Reformed theologians and pastors to maintain the doctrine of common grace regardless of the spiritually destructive effects of the doctrine on the life of the church and her members.

Hepp, Valentijn. Hepp was a distinguished Dutch Reformed theologian who succeeded Bavinck as professor of theology at the Free University of Amsterdam, the Netherlands.

Although Hepp was not convinced of the truth of Kuyper's theology of common grace, Hepp injected himself into the controversy over common grace in the Christian Reformed Church in America. Hepp came down on the side of the Christian Reformed Church and its dogma of common grace. In 1923 he contributed to the abundant literature of the controversy with a pamphlet entitled *Het Misverstand in zake de Leer der Algemeene Genade.* (The misunderstanding in the matter of the doctrine of common grace).

With insufferable condescension, Hepp proposed that the misunderstanding at the bottom of the common grace controversy in the Christian Reformed Church in the United States was the failure of Danhof and Hoeksema rightly and thoroughly to grasp "the concept 'grace.'" With complete disregard of the abundant work Danhof and Hoeksema had done exposing the theory of a common grace of God as unbiblical and without support in the Reformed creeds, Hepp casually suggested that the misunderstanding of Danhof and Hoeksema was that they failed to recognize another, common grace of God in addition to particular, saving grace. Hepp exhorted Hoeksema to submit to the Christian Reformed Church and its theology of common grace.

Hoeksema responded by inviting Hepp to mind his own business in the Netherlands.

Heyns, William. Heyns was a longtime professor of theology at Calvin Theological Seminary and one of the instructors of seminarian Herman Hoeksema. Heyns was a proponent of Kuyperian common grace, but his most notable teaching was his theology of the covenant of God, particularly regarding the children of godly parents. Heyns taught that at their baptism God established his covenant with all the baptized infants of believers alike both by promise and by a work of "subjective," saving grace within them all. Whether this beginning of the gracious work of God would actually and finally save the children was conditioned on their subsequent faith and obedience. Heyns taught a gracious, conditional covenant with all the baptized children of believers alike. This is essentially the doctrine of the covenant of Klaas Schilder and the liberated Reformed and the theology of the covenant popularized in recent times as the federal vision. The theology of Heyns indicates the close relation always between the theory of a common grace of God and the theology of a saving grace of God that is common in the sense that it is wider than election.

The history of the Reformed churches demonstrates that it is impossible to teach a common grace of God and to retain the particularity of grace in the realm of salvation. The truths of grace and of the covenant are interdependent. The doctrinal origins of the Protestant Reformed Churches are particular (saving) grace and the unconditional covenant of grace with (elect) believers and their elect offspring.

Of vital importance to the founding and subsequent history of the Protestant Reformed Churches (the rock whence they were hewn) is not only the gospel of particular, sovereign grace but also the gospel of the unconditional covenant of grace with the elect children of believing parents.

Although a historical reality, the account of a meeting soon after his ordination into the Christian Reformed ministry of the young Herman Hoeksema and his former professor, William Heyns, is the stuff of legend. Having met on public transportation, Heyns casually asked Hoeksema, "Herman, what do you think of my doctrine of the covenant?" Hoeksema replied, "Professor Heyns, I do not yet know what the truth of the covenant is, but I do know that it is not what you teach. And I intend to find out what the truth of the covenant is."

Hodge, Charles (1797–1878). Hodge was an illustrious, influential Presbyterian theologian.

Christian Reformed theologians appealed to Hodge on behalf of their doctrine of common grace and with some right. But this merely illustrates the truth that there is development of doctrinal understanding in the history of the church of Jesus Christ.

The development of the understanding of the truth of grace that exposed the prevalent theory of a common grace and that established that the grace of God is one, saving, and particular took place by means of the controversy in the Christian Reformed Church in the 1920s. The doctrine of the covenant of grace developed in and confessed by the Protestant Reformed Churches in America represents important development of the understanding of a vital doctrine of scripture on behalf of the entire community of Reformed and Presbyterian churches worldwide.

Hoeksema, Gerrit. Having the same surname as Herman did not hinder this Christian Reformed minister from becoming one of the fiercest foes of Herman Hoeksema in the controversy over common grace. Gerrit Hoeksema was a member of that part of a divided investigatory committee that defended Janssen in 1921–22, whereas Herman Hoeksema was a member of that part of the committee that condemned the teachings of Janssen.

Later Gerrit Hoeksema secretly wrote, or helped to write, the protests against Herman Hoeksema issued by several members of Herman Hoeksema's congregation, one of whom was the brother of Gerrit Hoeksema.

Hoeksema, Herman. Already as a seminarian in the Christian Reformed Church's Calvin Theological Seminary, Hoeksema rejected the doctrine of the covenant of his professor William Heyns. As a young Christian Reformed pastor, Hoeksema questioned and then condemned Kuyper's theory of a cultural common grace of God, mainly because of the spiritually detrimental effect this theory was having on the lives of the members of the Christian Reformed Church. It made their lives worldly.

His decisive exposure of theological modernism, especially regarding the content of Old Testament scripture, of Janssen, then professor of theology at Calvin Theological Seminary, achieved the discipline of Janssen by the synod of the Christian Reformed Church in 1922. It also brought upon Hoeksema the unholy wrath of Janssen's numerous and powerful supporters, which mightily contributed to the condemnation and expulsion of Hoeksema by the Christian Reformed Church in 1924–25.

While still a young minister in the Christian Reformed Church,

Hoeksema also played a leading role in the condemnation of the premillennial dispensationalism of Bultema.

Through all this history of spiritual and theological warfare, as well as by indefatigable theological labor, Hoeksema became not only the founder of the Protestant Reformed Churches in America, but also the exponent of the pure gospel of salvation by particular, sovereign grace, the developer of a rich understanding of the covenant of grace as an unconditional bond of friendship between God in Christ and his elect people, and generally the able witness to and defender of sound Reformed orthodoxy according to the creeds.

For many years Hoeksema edited and was the voice of the widely read Reformed periodical the *Standard Bearer*; taught at the Theological School of the Protestant Reformed Churches; preached regularly in First Protestant Reformed Church in Grand Rapids, Michigan, of which he remained a pastor; and wrote many books.

Largely because of the unsparing and unrelenting criticism of him by the influential Christian Reformed Church, Hoeksema has not received the recognition of which he is worthy. But his day is coming. In certain fundamental respects, his day has already come. The gross worldliness and grave apostasy of the Christian Reformed Church in North America and of the Reformed Churches in the Netherlands are the demonstration in history of the truth of Hoeksema's polemic against the theory of a cultural common grace. The bold universalism—universal election, universal atonement, and even forms of universal salvation—now rearing its head in Reformed churches that have accepted the well-meant offer, to which this universalism appeals in defense of itself, confirms Hoeksema's exposure of the well-meant offer as Arminianism. The increasingly popular covenantal theology that calls itself the federal vision, openly denying justification by faith alone, substantiates Hoeksema's criticism of the doctrine of the covenant that severs the covenant and its salvation from election and that makes the covenant and its salvation conditional.

The Rock Whence We Were Hewn shows the young Hoeksema's spiritual concerns, his theological depth, breadth, and soundness, his godly courage, and his writing ability.

Janssen, Ralph. Janssen was a learned and popular professor of theology at Calvin Theological Seminary of the Christian Reformed Church in the early years of the twentieth century. Janssen was publicly criticized by four of his fellow professors, including Berkhof, Heyns, Ten Hoor, and Volbeda, and then disciplined by the Christian Reformed synod of 1922 on the ground of his higher critical, modernist views of the Old Testament Bible.

Because Hoeksema was instrumental in Janssen's discipline, Janssen and his many influential supporters launched a campaign against Hoeksema that resulted in his ouster from the Christian Reformed ministry and from the Christian Reformed Church in 1924–25. The doctrinal tenet that accomplished Hoeksema's destruction in the Christian Reformed Church was the theory of a common grace of God, which tenet Hoeksema denied and refused to subscribe.

The theory of common grace was not merely an instrument to accomplish Hoeksema's discipline and expulsion from the Christian Reformed Church. But the theory was, in fact, as Janssen and his supporters argued, the basis of Janssen's higher critical view of Old Testament scripture, that is, theological modernism. There was truth to the charge of Janssen and his supporters that the underlying reason for Hoeksema's principled opposition to Janssen's teaching was Hoeksema's denial of common grace.

By adopting the dogma of common grace, therefore, the synod of the Christian Reformed Church actually reversed the stand it had taken earlier in its discipline of Janssen and opened up the Christian Reformed Church to theological modernism, including the very teachings about the Old Testament on account of which Janssen was condemned.

Ralph Janssen would not, *could* not, be disciplined by the Christian Reformed Church in 2015. Nor would his teachings about events recorded as historical in the Old Testament—including the creation of the world in six days of one evening and one morning each, that these events are not historical and miraculous—be condemned by a synod of the Christian Reformed Church today.

The dogma of common grace that branded and banished Hoeksema resuscitated and restored Janssen. 1924 undid 1922.

Jonker, Dirk. In 1924 Jonker was a Christian Reformed minister in Holland, Michigan (Rusk). In the years of the common grace controversy in the Christian Reformed Church, Jonker gave up his pastorate in the Christian Reformed Church, leaving that church and casting in his lot with the fledgling Protestant Reformed Churches. For many years Jonker was a prominent member of First Protestant Reformed Church in Grand Rapids, Michigan, and the stated clerk of Classis East of the Protestant Reformed Churches.

Keegstra, Henry. In 1924 this Christian Reformed preacher was pastor of a Christian Reformed Church in Holland, Michigan. As editor of the Christian Reformed publication *De Wachter*, Keegstra weighed in on the debate over common grace, defending the theory and criticizing Danhof's and Hoeksema's rejection of common grace to the readers of the Dutch publication.

Danhof and Hoeksema had all the Christian Reformed publications against them. Access to these publications was denied them, so that although they were severely criticized in all the publications and their doctrine of particular grace condemned, they could not respond to the accusations or explain their doctrinal position. These hard, unjust realities were the reason for the creation of the *Standard Bearer* as a means by which they might defend themselves against false charges against them and explain and promote their theology of particular grace.

Kuiper, B. K. Kuiper was yet another prominent defender of Janssen, proponent of common grace, and adversary of Danhof and Hoeksema in the Christian Reformed Church in the early 1920s. Kuiper was professor of theology in Calvin Theological Seminary.

In a sixty-odd page booklet published shortly before the 1922 synod of the Christian Reformed Church, Kuiper vigorously defended Janssen and vehemently attacked Janssen's adversaries, especially H. Hoeksema. The booklet is *De Janssen Kwestie en Nog Iets* (The Janssen question and still more).

In the booklet Kuiper expresses agreement with Janssen's argument that "Hoeksema could have objection against his [Janssen's] instruction only because he himself [Hoeksema] is not Reformed; and indeed more specifically because he errs in the matter of common grace." Kuiper called attention to the "relation between the denial of the doctrine of common grace and having objection against the fundamental thoughts of Dr. Janssen." Kuiper focused on the "one great argument" of Janssen in defense of his modernist teaching about the Old Testament: "That the brothers [Danhof and Hoeksema] suppose that I [Janssen] err originates only from this: they themselves err... If the brothers themselves did not err, they would not suppose that I err." And the error of Danhof and Hoeksema, according to Janssen and Kuiper, "concerned the matter of common grace." According to B. K. Kuiper, there was a "disturbingly great element of truth...in the contention of Dr. Janssen that his opponents supposed that he errs, because they themselves err in the matter of common grace" (31–32). To the doctrine of common grace, Kuiper attributed "very great weight and very broad application." "Acceptance or rejection of the doctrine of common grace determines one's view concerning the relation of nature and grace, of Christ and humanity, of Christianity and culture, of Christianity and the world, of Israel and the nations, of faith and reason, or science." Accordingly, "acceptance or rejection of common grace must have influence on the viewing of almost all points that are at issue in the Janssen question." One who rejects common grace must conclude that Janssen errs in his higher critical views of the Old Testament. One who accepts common grace, by the same token, must approve Janssen's higher critical view of holy scripture (33; all translations are mine; the booklet has not been translated into English).

Although Kuiper's astute and vigorous defense of Janssen on the basis of common grace did not save Janssen and his theological modernism at the Christian Reformed synod of 1922, it prevailed in the adoption of the theory of common grace at the synod of 1924 and the subsequent excommunication of Hoeksema and his rejection of common grace from the Christian Reformed Church.

The further history of the Christian Reformed Church, to the present day, tells the tale of the consequences.

Kuiper, Henry J. In the early 1920s this Christian Reformed minister cooperated with three fellow pastors in the Christian Reformed Church, Danhof, De Jong, and Hoeksema, and with four professors at Calvin seminary publicly to oppose the teachings of Janssen in the booklet *Waar het in de Zaak Janssen om Gaat* (What the issue in the Janssen case really is).

As soon as Janssen responded to his critics by grounding his teachings in the theory of common grace and by charging his critics with denying common grace, Kuiper left off his controversy with Janssen and took up the cudgels against Danhof and Hoeksema for their rejection of common grace.

Already early in 1925, Kuiper published *The Three Points of Common Grace*, a booklet consisting of sermons he had recently preached defending the three points of common grace that the 1924 synod of the Christian Reformed Church had adopted. In the booklet Kuiper proclaims a saving grace of God toward all who hear the gospel, sincerely desiring their salvation, those who perish in unbelief as well as those who are saved by this grace—the well-meant offer; a grace of God working in the unregenerated wicked that "restrains the worldly man from much sin," so that the godly may have "fellowship" with him; and a grace of God that works in reprobate, unregenerated sinners so that they perform works that are truly good, including "*religious* impulses, convictions, feelings and desires in the hearts of the unregenerate." The booklet concludes with a paean of praise to common grace: "The doctrine of common grace is of...[great] value for [elect] saint and [reprobate] sinner—For one thing, it should convince the sinner that God loves him, has gracious dealings with him, and sincerely offers him salvation in Christ." In addition, common grace keeps the unconverted sinner from the condition of "total depravity" inasmuch as by the working of common grace such a sinner "is able to perform civic righteousness." "Civic righteousness," for Kuiper and his likeminded Christian Reformed colleagues, is a genuine, though inferior, good in the judgment of God himself.

In 1944 Kuiper became editor of the Christian Reformed periodical the *Banner* until his retirement in 1956. During his editorship Kuiper devoted a great deal of his energy and editorial space to opposing the effects of the theory of common grace in the Christian Reformed Church. He and his "conservative" Christian Reformed colleagues were men who seriously damaged the dike of the gospel of particular, sovereign grace and of the antithesis between the ungodly world and the holy church by their doctrine of the three points of common grace in 1924. They then spent the next twenty-five or thirty years of their ministries fearfully sticking their fingers into the holes in the dike they themselves had made, in order, futilely, to keep back the waters of universalism and of worldliness.

In the 1960s the dike itself collapsed, because of the impact on it of the theory of common grace, and a tidal wave of universalism and of worldliness engulfed the Christian Reformed Church.

Kuyper, Abraham. Kuyper was a highly influential Dutch Reformed theologian in the late nineteenth and early twentieth centuries. With his almost equally influential colleague, Bavinck, Kuyper was responsible for injecting the theory of a cultural common grace into the bloodstream not only of Reformed churches worldwide, but also of many Presbyterian and evangelical churches. By "cultural" common grace is meant a nonsaving favor of God and operation of the Holy Spirit that the godless share with the godly, so that the wicked world and the holy church are able to cooperate in order to produce a Christian culture in the nation and eventually in the whole world. Kuyper proposed and extensively developed this theory in three volumes on the subject, published in Dutch at the turn of the twentieth century.

In 1924 the Christian Reformed Church intended to make Kuyper's theory official, binding church doctrine by the adoption of its three points of common grace. In fact, the Christian Reformed Church added an element of common grace that Kuyper repudiated, namely, the doctrine that the preaching of the gospel is a well-meant offer of salvation to all hearers—the doctrine of a universal, ineffectual, *saving* grace of God, dependent for its efficacy on the will of the sinner. This aspect of the Christian Reformed Church's doctrine of common grace was most offensive to Hoeksema, as it is to the Protestant Reformed

Churches to the present day. Kuyper's advocacy of common grace was much of the power of the Christian Reformed Church's adopting its doctrine of common grace in 1924.

For refusing to subscribe to Kuyper's doctrine of common grace and the Christian Reformed Church's addition of the well-meant offer, Danhof and Hoeksema were disciplined by and expelled from the Christian Reformed Church in 1924–25. This was the origin of the Protestant Reformed Churches.

Neither Hoeksema nor the Protestant Reformed Churches repudiate Kuyper, his theology, and his church reforming work entirely. Hoeksema always claimed that there were "two Kuypers": the Kuyper of particular grace and the antithesis, on the one hand; and the Kuyper of common grace and world conformity, on the other hand. The latter Kuyper, the Protestant Reformed Churches reject; the former, they claim, honor, and benefit from.

Which of the two Kuypers prevails in the Reformed churches generally in the twenty-first century is evident to all. Of the Kuyper of particular grace and of the antithesis, almost nothing at all is heard in the Reformed churches at the beginning of the twenty-first century.

Maccovius, Johannes (1588–1644). He was a Polish Reformed theologian who became professor of theology at the Reformed university in Franeker, the Netherlands. Maccovius was a very strong proponent of the truth of salvation by sovereign grace. As an ardent supralapsarian regarding the order of the divine decrees, Maccovius troubled even his orthodox colleagues by his strong statements on salvation by the sovereign grace of God.

Because of informal charges against him of deviating into heresy by his strong statements on the sovereignty of God in salvation, Maccovius subjected himself to an examination regarding his orthodoxy at the Synod of Dordt in 1618–19. The synod exonerated him of heresy, although the admonition in the Conclusion of the Canons of Dordt likely was directed at Maccovius: "Finally, this Synod exhorts all their brethren in the gospel of Christ to conduct themselves piously and religiously in handling this doctrine [the sovereignty of God in salvation, rooted in predestination]...and to abstain from all those phrases which exceed the limits necessary to be observed in ascertaining the genuine sense of the Holy Scriptures, and may furnish insolent sophists with a just pretext for violently assailing, or even vilifying, the doctrine of the Reformed Churches" (Schaff, *Creeds of Christendom*, 3:597).

The treatment of Maccovius by the Synod of Dordt, refusing to discipline him and approving his strong supralapsarian formulation of predestination, even though the synod adopted the infralapsarian presentation of the order of the decrees, exposes the unjust and traditionally un-Reformed condemnation of Hoeksema by the Christian Reformed Church for what was, essentially, Hoeksema's strong, indeed supralapsarian, confession of predestination. The Christian Reformed synod of 1924 would have ridden Maccovius out of the church on a rail.

Manni, Jacob. In 1924 Manni was the pastor of a Christian Reformed congregation in Sheboygan, Wisconsin. He was a delegate to the synod of 1924. Manni distinguished himself at the synod by proposing that, rather than adopting a binding doctrine of common grace, synod appoint a large study committee, including as members Danhof and Hoeksema, that would present its findings to the following synod. Manni grounded his motion in the fact that the time was not ripe for a binding decision on common grace. Manni's substitute motion pointed the synod in the right direction. However, the synod rejected Manni's motion and proceeded to adopt the three points of common grace.

Two years earlier, at the Christian Reformed synod of 1922, Manni was one of the four members of a majority of a committee that had been appointed to study the teachings of Janssen. The majority advised the synod to condemn the teachings of Janssen, which the synod did. The other members of the majority of the committee were Danhof, Hoeksema, and H. J. Kuiper.

Ophoff, George M. As a newly ordained, young minister in the Christian Reformed Church in the early 1920s, Ophoff found himself in agreement with Danhof and Hoeksema regarding the controversial issue of common grace. Because of his refusal to express agreement with the dogma of common grace adopted by the Christian Reformed Church in 1924, Ophoff too was disciplined by the Christian Reformed Church. He was then instrumental in having his congregation, now the Hope Protestant Reformed Church in Walker, Michigan, unite with Danhof's congregation in Kalamazoo and with Hoeksema's congregation in Grand Rapids in forming the Protestant Reformed denomination of Reformed churches. Ophoff therefore was one of the three founding ministers of the Protestant Reformed Churches.

Ophoff later became professor of theology at the Theological School of the Protestant Reformed Churches, mainly teaching Old Testament subjects. He was a fiery preacher, as well as personality. During the controversy over common grace in the Christian Reformed Church, the Grand Rapids *Press* featured a picture of Ophoff, with the headings "Ophoff Prefers Death [rather than signing the three points of common grace.]" and "Local Pastor Tells Christian Reformed Body He Will Not Subscribe."

Schans, Martin. In 1924 Schans was pastor of the Kelloggsville, Michigan, Christian Reformed Church. Schans showed himself a strong defender of common grace and a determined foe of Hoeksema and Danhof. Schans overtured Classis Grand Rapids East in May 1924 to request the 1924 synod to examine Danhof and Hoeksema regarding their stand on the content of the theory of common grace, including a well-meant offer of salvation. This examination was to include an inquiry whether Danhof and Hoeksema over-emphasized predestination. This overture by Schans, which he had never shown to Hoeksema, became one of the main means by which the Christian Reformed synod of 1924 took up the issue of the theory of common grace, the result of which was the adoption of the doctrine of common grace as official church dogma.

Schilder, Klaas. Schilder was a notable Reformed theologian in the Netherlands in the first half of the twentieth century. Disciplined by the Reformed Churches in the Netherlands for his covenant doctrine in the early 1940s, Schilder became the founder of the Reformed Churches in the Netherlands (liberated).

Despite their sharply differing conceptions of the covenant, Schilder and Hoeksema developed a close, friendly relationship, based largely on their commitment to the creedal Reformed faith (always with the exception of Schilder's un-Reformed doctrine of the covenant); their mutual rejection of a common grace of God; and their sharing the conviction that they had been abused by hierarchical church bodies.

Schilder was the driving force behind the conference in the Pantlind Hotel in Grand Rapids, Michigan, which was to explore and further the reunion of the Christian Reformed Church and the Protestant Reformed Churches, to no avail.

The close contact of Schilder with the Protestant Reformed Churches, which Hoeksema encouraged, ended badly for the Protestant Reformed Churches. Many Protestant Reformed ministers embraced Schilder's doctrine of the covenant—a conditional covenant with all the baptized infants of believers alike—essentially the covenant doctrine of Heyns of the Christian Reformed Church, which Hoeksema had repudiated early in his ministry, indeed in his seminary days, as a form of universal, saving grace, conditioned on the faith and obedience of the sinner. The result of the contact with Schilder for the Protestant Reformed Churches was a grievous schism in 1953. The lasting result for the Protestant Reformed Churches was clearer understanding, and a binding ecclesiastical decision that the covenant of grace is an unconditional bond of gracious fellowship governed by God's gracious, sovereign election.

Tanis, Edward James. In 1924 Tanis was the minister of the First Christian Reformed Church in Grand Rapids, Michigan. Tanis was yet another Christian Reformed minister who vigorously defended and promoted the theory of common grace and therefore opposed Danhof and Hoeksema.

Tanis was incensed that the two as-yet Christian Reformed ministers should begin a magazine, the *Standard Bearer*, to explain their doctrinal views on the grace and covenant of God.

Ten Hoor, Foppe M. This Christian Reformed theologian with the engaging first name was professor of theology at Calvin Theological Seminary in 1924. Ten Hoor was one of the four professors, with Berkhof, Heyns, and Volbeda, who brought the unsound teachings of their colleague Janssen to the attention of the theological school committee, to the synod of 1920, and then, with the aid of four ministers, to the attention of the general Reformed public by the publication of the booklet *Waar het in de Zaak Janssen om Gaat* (What the issue in the Janssen case really is).

Ten Hoor's support for Kuyper's theory of common grace was weak at best, as Janssen charged. Ten Hoor was reported to have expressed himself concerning his belief of common grace in these words: "I believe the doctrine, but I do not know what it is." For his opposition to Janssen and for his lack of enthusiasm for the theory of common grace, Ten Hoor drew upon himself the literary wrath of Janssen and his supporters. They charged Ten Hoor with opposing Janssen because of Ten Hoor's lack of enthusiasm for common grace.

In Janssen's defense of himself in 1922 against the accusations of his colleagues, including Ten Hoor, Janssen charged that the explanation of their opposition to him was their denial of the theory of common grace. With specific reference to Ten Hoor, Janssen alleged that "it is commonly known how Professor Ten Hoor continuously, both in the Netherlands and in America, has opposed Doctor Kuyper, one of our greatest authorities in the area of the doctrine of common grace. Opposed [Kuyper]...on the matter of the doctrine of common grace" (*De Crisis in De Christelijke Gereformeerde Kerk in Amerika* [The Crisis in the Christian Reformed Church in America], 6; my translation of the Dutch; the booklet has not been translated into English. Janssen went on to demonstrate at length Ten Hoor's rejection of common grace (*De Crisis*, 6–7).

Although he was not part of the posse hunting down Danhof and Hoeksema for their rejection of common grace, neither did Ten Hoor rise to the aid of the two preachers in their ecclesiastical distress. He retired peacefully in the Christian Reformed Church.

Van Baalen, Jan Karel. In 1924 Van Baalen was a minister of the First Christian Reformed Church in Munster, Indiana. He was perhaps the leading defender of Janssen in the early 1920s, when Janssen's higher critical teachings were under attack not only by Danhof and Hoeksema, but also by four colleagues of Janssen in the Christian Reformed seminary and by several other ministers.

After Janssen's discipline Van Baalen became the most determined foe of Danhof and especially Hoeksema, whom he regarded, with right, as the one most responsible for Janssen's condemnation. In an influential booklet of some ninety pages (*De Loochening der Gemeene Gratie: Gereformeerd of Doopersch?* [The denial of common grace: Reformed or Anabaptist?]), Van Baalen charged that the reason for Hoeksema's opposition to Janssen's teachings was Hoeksema's denial of Kuyper's theory of common grace. Van Baalen quoted with approval the judgment of Prof. H. van Andel that the doctrines of "the absolute antithesis between good and evil and...of God's common grace are nothing less than the Jachin and the Boaz of the Reformed conception of life" (10; my translation of the Dutch). Van Baalen alluded to the two great pillars in the temple of Solomon (1 Kings 7:21). By this description of the theory of common grace, Van Baalen was asserting that the doctrine of a common grace of God was both outstandingly prominent in Reformed theology and a fundamental support of the whole of Reformed theology. The denial of common grace would mean both the loss of the majesty of the Reformed body of truth and the collapse of Reformed theology. Such was the fervor, if not frenzy, on behalf of the theory of common grace in the Christian Reformed Church in the early 1920s—a theory that is neither taught nor even named positively in the Reformed confessions.

Van Baalen was particularly exercised by Danhof's judgment of the love of the pagan Hector for his wife, Andromache, as "devilish or bestial [*duivelsch of bestiaals*]." The very first of the "questions to Reverends Hoeksema and Danhof" in the last chapter of Van Baalen's booklet is, "May we beseech Rev. Danhof whether he will be so good as to make plain to us what appears as devilish or bestial in the love between Hector and his spouse, as sung by Homer?" (87).

To this booklet by Van Baalen, Danhof and Hoeksema responded with a booklet of their own, entitled, in English translation, "Not Ana-baptist but Reformed: Provisional Response to Rev. Jan Karel van Baalen concerning the Denial of Common Grace." That booklet is part of the content of this book.

Van Baalen was a delegate at the synod of 1924 that adopted the three points of common grace as official church dogma. In fact, Van Baalen had a protest against Danhof and Hoeksema regarding their denial of a common grace of God at the 1924 synod of the Christian Reformed Church, occasioning the adoption of the doctrine of common grace by the Christian Reformed Church. In his protest Van Baalen charged sin against the two pastors and demanded retraction of their doctrinal error or, in case of the refusal of the two ministers to retract their confession of particular grace, discipline.

Van Lonkhuyzen, John. In 1924 he was the minister of the Christian Reformed Church in Berwyn, Illinois. Van Lonkhuyzen distinguished himself in the common grace controversy as a strong advocate on behalf of the theory of common grace and as a committed adversary of Danhof and Hoeksema.

As was typical of their adversaries, Van Lonkhuyzen first crossed swords with Danhof and Hoeksema in the conflict regarding the teaching of Janssen. Van Lonkhuyzen was a member of the minority of the study committee that advised the Christian Reformed synod of 1920 to approve the higher critical teachings of Janssen and to exonerate him. Danhof and Hoeksema were members of the majority of the committee recommending condemnation of the teachings of Janssen.

After the Christian Reformed synod of 1924, which adopted the three points of common grace but declined to instigate disciplinary action against Danhof and Hoeksema for their avowed rejection of the doctrine, Van Lonkhuyzen wrote in a Dutch periodical that circulated widely in the Christian Reformed Church, criticizing the synod for its failure to advise and otherwise begin proceedings for the discipline of the two ministers. Quite correctly, he noted that the synod had left

Danhof and Hoeksema at liberty to preach and teach their rejection of common grace.

Volbeda, Samuel. In 1924 Volbeda was professor of theology at Calvin Theological Seminary. Volbeda was one of the four professors at the seminary who accused their colleague, Janssen, of teaching higher critical false doctrine, but who did not prevail until Hoeksema involved himself in the matter. With three colleagues at the seminary and four ministers in the Christian Reformed Church at the time, Volbeda wrote the booklet *Waar het in de Zaak Janssen om Gaat* (What the issue in the Janssen case really is). This booklet was published after the 1920 synod of the Christian Reformed Church that refused to condemn the teachings of Janssen and before the 1922 synod that would condemn his teachings and discipline Janssen.

With his three seminary colleagues, Volbeda also wrote the eighty-odd page booklet *Nadere Toelichting omtrent de Zaak Janssen* (A closer analysis concerning the Janssen case). The booklet has not been translated into English. In this booklet the four professors indicate more fully the higher critical views of Janssen concerning Old Testament scripture and subject them to a more thorough criticism.

After the 1922 synod of the Christian Reformed Church that condemned Janssen's teachings, Volbeda coauthored the sixty-page booklet *Verdediging van het Besluit der Synode van 1922 ter Afzetting van Dr. Janssen* (Defense of the decision of the synod of 1922 deposing Dr. Janssen). The booklet has not been translated into English. The other authors of the booklet were professors Berkhof, Heyns, and Ten Hoor. The sole minister who cooperated in this defense of the synodical decision was H. J. Kuiper. Noticeably missing were Danhof and Hoeksema, who had been influential in the condemnation of Janssen's teachings and who had helped to write an earlier booklet exposing Janssen's errors. No doubt, the campaign against them by this time concerning their rejection of common grace rendered them *persona non grata* to their former allies. In any case, Volbeda's criticism of Dr. Janssen and effort to have Janssen's teachings condemned by the authorities in the Christian Reformed Church were attributed by Janssen to Volbeda's denial of the theory of common grace.

Defending himself against the charge by Volbeda and the others that his teaching was unsound, Janssen charged in response that Volbeda denied the doctrine of common grace and that this denial was the reason for his condemnation of Janssen's teachings. Volbeda, declared Janssen, has shown himself "as a virtual opponent of the Reformed doctrine of common grace." "In his teaching," Janssen continued, "according to the testimony of students, Volbeda virtually denies the doctrine of common grace and natural revelation." Janssen concluded that he himself "knows from his own experience that Professor Volbeda virtually denies the doctrine of common grace" (*De Crisis in de Christelijke Gereformeerde Kerk in Amerika*, 5–6; my translation of the Dutch).

There may have been something to Janssen's accusation of Volbeda that he denied common grace. In his account of the history of the controversy over common grace, Hoeksema judges that the charge by Janssen that the four professors and four ministers who opposed him in print denied the theory of common grace was false in the case of the four professors "except, perhaps, in the case of Doctor Volbeda" (*The Protestant Reformed Churches in America*, 24).

If he did, in fact, deny common grace, Volbeda remained conspicuously silent in the controversy over common grace that immediately followed the Janssen case. Hoeksema found no support from leading men in the Christian Reformed Church, not even from those who like him saw the dangers in the church and whom he had helped successfully to fight one of those threats.

In this connection I remember well the anecdote related to me years ago by Richard Newhouse, one of the founding members of what was originally the Hope Christian Reformed Church and is now the Hope Protestant Reformed Church in Walker, Michigan. Newhouse was an elder in the congregation from its very beginning until almost the end of his long life. When the congregation was still a Christian Reformed church and the controversy over common grace was raging, Volbeda was often a guest minister at Hope. After one of Volbeda's sermons,

Newhouse, who had little formal education but was Reformed to the marrow of his bones, possessing what the Dutch call *Gereformeerde gevoelhoren* (Reformed antennae), accosted Volbeda in the church yard: "Why is it, Professor Volbeda, that whenever you preach for us you preach strong sermons on the sovereignty of God, but you will not speak out in defense of Reverend Hoeksema?" There was no answer.

Vos, Geerhardus. In 1924 Vos was professor of theology at Princeton Theological Seminary. To this noted Presbyterian theologian and author, Van Baalen appealed in support of his forceful defense of common grace and vehement attack on Danhof and Hoeksema for their denial of common grace (*De Loochening der Gemeene Gratie: Gereformeerd of Doopersch? 59–60*). Janssen appealed to Vos in support of certain of his views of the Old Testament that his critics found objectionable (R. Janssen, *Voortzetting van den Strijd* [Continuation of the conflict], Grand Rapids, MI: n. p., 1922). The booklet has not been translated into English.

Vos was originally Christian Reformed and was strongly influenced by Kuyper's theory of common grace.

Wielenga, B. In 1906 this well-respected Dutch theologian in the Reformed Churches in the Netherlands published a commentary on the Reformed baptism form, *Ons Doopsformulier* (Our form of baptism; a second revised edition appeared in 1920, published by J. H. Kok of Kampen). An excellent commentary on the authoritative Reformed baptism form, the book was in the time of the common grace controversy and remains today especially significant for its demonstration that according to the Reformed baptism form election governs God's covenant with the children of believers. The (saving) grace of God in the covenant is not universal, or general, in the sphere of the word and sacraments as the doctrine of a well-meant offer teaches, but it is particular, toward and in the elect children of believing parents.

One important aspect of the theory of common grace that dominated the Christian Reformed Church in 1924, it will be remembered, was the teaching of Heyns that at baptism God graciously establishes his covenant with all the infants alike, not only expressing toward all a gracious attitude of the sincere desire to save them all, but also working in them all the power to accept God's "offer" of salvation when they would come to years of maturity, dependent on their own will. Apart from the blatantly heretical notion of an internal, "subjective" grace in all the children alike, enabling all to accept God's well-meant offer of salvation, this universalizing of the "saving" grace of God toward all the baptized infants of believers prevails in Reformed and Presbyterian churches today.

The Reformed Free Publishing Association will be publishing Wielenga's significant commentary on the baptism form in English translation, for the first time, in the near future.

BIBLIOGRAPHY

1924 Acts of Synod of the Christian Reformed Church Held from 8 June to 15 July, 1924, in Kalamazoo, MI. Translated by Henry De Mots. Grand Rapids, MI: Archives of the Christian Reformed Church.

Acts of Synod 1946 of the Christian Reformed Church, art. 88. Grand Rapids, MI: Christian Reformed Publishing House.

Acts of Synod 1948 of the Christian Reformed Church, art. 114. Grand Rapids, MI: Christian Reformed Publishing House.

Acts of Synod of the Christian Reformed Church in Session June 9 to June 28, 1926, at Englewood, Chicago, Illinois.

Bavinck, Herman. "Common Grace." Translated by R. C. Van Leeuwen. *Calvin Theological Journal* 24, no. 1 (April 1989): 38–65.

———. *De Algemeene Genade* [Common grace]. Grand Rapids, MI: Eerdmans-Sevensma, n.d.

———. *Gereformeerde Dogmatiek* [Reformed dogmatics]. 2nd ed. 4 vols. Kampen: J. H. Kok, 1911.

———. *Reformed Dogmatics*. Edited by John Bolt. Translated by John Vriend. Vol. 4, *Holy Spirit, Church, and New Creation*. Grand Rapids: Baker Academic, 2008.

Berkhof, Louis. *Banner*, July 26, 1929.

———. *De Drie Punten in Alle Deelen Gereformeerd* [The three points, Reformed in all parts]. Grand Rapids, MI: Wm. B. Eerdmans Publishing Co., 1925.

———. "The Spectre of Anabaptism." *Witness.*

Bos, T. *Genadeverbond en Bondzegelen* [The covenant of grace and the seals of the covenant]. Kampen: J. H. Kok, 1904.

Bosma, M. J. *Onderwijzing in De Gereformeerde Geloofsleer* [Exposition of Reformed doctrine]. Grand Rapids, MI: B. Sevensma, 1910.

Bratt, James D. *Dutch Calvinism in Modern America: A History of a Conservative Subculture*. Grand Rapids, MI: Eerdmans, 1984.

Calvin, John. *Calvin's Calvinism: The Eternal Predestination of God [and] The Secret Providence of God.* Translated by Henry Cole. London: Sovereign Grace Union, 1927.

———. *Calvin's Calvinism: God's Eternal Predestination and Secret Providence together with* A Brief Reply *and* Reply to the Slanderous Reports. Edited by Russell J. Dykstra. 2nd ed. Jenison, MI: Reformed Free Publishing Association, 2009.

———. *Institutes of the Christian Religion.* Edited by John T. McNeill. Translated by Ford Lewis Battles. The Library of Christian Classics, vol. 20 and 21. Philadelphia: Westminster Press, 1960.

The Confessions and the Church Order of the Protestant Reformed Churches. Grandville, MI: Protestant Reformed Churches in America, 2005.

Danhof, Henry. *De Idee van het Genadeverbond* [The idea of the covenant of grace]. Grand Rapids, MI: Van Noord Book and Publishing Company, 1920.

Danhof, Henry, and Herman Hoeksema. *Langs Zuivere Banen: een Wederwoord aan Bezwaarde Broederen* [Along pure paths: a reply to aggrieved brothers]. Kalamazoo, MI: Dalm Printing Co., n.d.

———. *Niet Doopersch maar Gereformeerd: Voorloopig Bescheid aan Ds. Jan Karel van Baalen betreffende de Loochening der Gemeene Gratie* [Not Anabaptist but Reformed: provisional response to Rev. J. K. van Baalen concerning the denial of common grace]. Grand Rapids, MI: Grand Rapids Printing Co., n.d.

———. *Om Recht en Waarheid: Een Woord van Toelichting en Leiding* [For the sake of justice and truth: a word of clarification and direction]. Kalamazoo, MI: Dalm Printing Co., n.d.

———. *Van Zonde en Genade* [Of sin and grace]. Kalamazoo, MI: Dalm Printing Co., n.d.

De Jong, Y. P. *Christian Journal,* Thursday, March 6, 1924.

———. *Witness,* December 1923.

Hanko, Herman. *For Thy Truth's Sake.* Grandville, MI: Reformed Free Publishing Association, 2000.

———. "A Study of the Relation between the Views of Prof. R. Janssen and Common Grace." Master's thesis, Calvin Theological Seminary, 1988.

Hellenbroek, Abraham. *Voorbeeld der Goddelyke Waarheden Voor Eenvoudigen* [Model of the divine truth for simple folk]. Nijkerk: G. F. Callenbach, 1907.

Hepp, Valentijn. *De Reformatie,* February 29, 1924.

———. *De Reformatie*, April 25, 1924.

———. *Het Misverstand in zake de Leer der Algemeene Genade* [The misunderstanding in the matter of the doctrine of common grace]. 2nd ed. Grand Rapids, MI: Eerdmans–Sevensma, 1923.

Hoeksema, Herman. *Banner*, April 10, 1919.

———. *Banner*, April 17, 1919.

———. *Banner*, June 12, 1919.

———. *Banner*, April 8, 1920.

———. *Banner*, June 17, 1920.

———. *Believers and Their Seed: Children in the Covenant*. Rev. ed. Grandville, MI: Reformed Free Publishing Association, 1997.

———. *The Protestant Reformed Churches in America: Their Origin, Early History and Doctrine*. Grand Rapids, MI: n.p., 1936.

———. *Reformed Dogmatics*. Grand Rapids, MI: Reformed Free Publishing Association, 1966.

Homer. *The Iliad*. Translated by W. H. D. Rouse. New York: The New American Library, 1950.

Janssen, Ralph. *De Crisis in de Christelijke Gereformeerde Kerk in Amerika* [The crisis in the Christian Reformed Church in America]. Grand Rapids, MI: Grand Rapids Printing Co., 1922.

———. *De Synodale Conclusies* [The synodical conclusions]. Grand Rapids, MI, 1923.

———. *Het Synodale Vonnis en zijne Voorgeschiedenis Kerkrechtelijk Beoordeeld* [The synodical judgment and its prehistory, criticized in light of the Church Order]. Grand Rapid, MI: M. Hoffius, 1922.

Kline, Meredith G. *By Oath Consigned: A Reinterpretation of the Covenant Signs of Circumcision and Baptism*. Grand Rapids, MI: Eerdmans, 1968.

———. *Treaty of the Great King: The Covenant Structure of Deuteronomy, Studies and Commentary*, with its discussion of "suzerainty treatises." Grand Rapids, MI: Eerdmans, 1963.

Kuiper, H. J. *The Three Points of Common Grace: Three Sermons at Broadway Avenue Christian Reformed Church*. Grand Rapids, MI: Wm. B. Eerdmans, 1925.

Kuyper, Abraham. *De Gemeene Gratie* [Common grace]. 3 vols. Amsterdam: Höveker & Wormser, 1902–4.

———. *Dictaten Dogmatiek* [Dictated dogmatics]. Vol. 3, *Locus de Providentia, Peccato, Foedere, Christo* [*Locus* concerning providence, sin, covenant, Christ]. Grand Rapids, MI: B. Sevensma, 1910.

———. *Encyclopaedie der Heilije Godgeleerdheid* [Encyclopedia of holy theology]. 2nd ed. Kampen: Kok, 1909.

Maccovius, Johannes. *Godgeleerde onderscheidingen en wijsgeerige regelingen* [Theological distinctions and philosophical regulations]. Translated by Dirk van der Meer. Leeuwarden: H. Bokma, 1658.

McCosh, James. *The Method of Divine Government, Physical and Moral.* Edinburgh, 1850.

Orr, James. *The Progress of Dogma: The Elliot Lectures Delivered at the Western Theological Seminary, Allegheny, Pennsylvania, 1897.* London: Hodder and Stoughton, 1901.

The Psalter with Doctrinal Standards, Liturgy, Church Order, and added Chorale Section. Reprinted and revised edition of the 1912 United Presbyterian *Psalter.* Grand Rapids, MI: Eerdmans, 1927; rev. ed. 1995.

Schaff, Philip, ed. *The Creeds of Christendom with a History and Critical Notes.* 6th ed. 3 vols. New York: Harper and Row, 1931; repr., Grand Rapids, MI: Baker Books, 2007.

State of Michigan, in the Circuit Court for the County of Kent, in Chancery. December Term, 1924. Before Hon. Major L. Dunham, Circuit Judge. William Holwerda, Et Al Plaintiffs, Vs. Herman Hoeksema, Et Al Defendants, No. 26695. Grand Rapids, MI. Monday A.M., February 9, 1925.

Ten Hoor, Foppe M. *Korte Schets der Gereformeerde Dogmatiek* [Brief outline of Reformed dogmatics].

Van Andel, Henry J. "The Foe Within the Gates." *Religion and Culture,* 1922

Van Baalen, Jan Karel. *De Loochening der Gemeene Gratie: Gereformeerd of Doopersch?* [The denial of common grace: Reformed or Anabaptist?]. Grand Rapids, MI: Eerdmans-Sevensma Co., 1922.

———. *Nieuwigheid en Dwaling: De Loochening der Gemeene Gratie* [Novelty and error: the denial of common grace]. Grand Rapids, MI: Eerdmans-Sevensma Co., 1923.

Vos, Geerhardus. *De Verbondsleer in de Gereformeerde Theologie* [The doctrine of the covenant in Reformed theology].

Wielenga, B. *Ons Doopsformulier* [Our Reformed baptism form]. Kampen: J. H. Kok, 1906.

Zwier, Daniel. "*Niet te heet van stal loopen*" [Don't walk off like a hothead]. *Witness,* May 1924.